# 7th Workshop on Computational Approaches to Subjectivity, Sentiment and Social Media Analysis (WASSA 2016)

Held at the 2016 Conference of the North American Chapter of the Association for Computational Linguistics: Human Language Technologies (NAACL HLT 2016)

San Diego, California, USA
16 June 2016

ISBN: 978-1-5108-2526-0

Printed by Curran Associates, Inc. (2016)

For permission requests, please contact the Association for Computational Linguistics
at the address below.

Association for Computational Linguistics
209 N. Eighth Street
Stroudsburg, Pennsylvania 18360

Phone:   1-570-476-8006
Fax:      1-570-476-0860

acl@aclweb.org

**Additional copies of this publication are available from:**

Curran Associates, Inc.
57 Morehouse Lane
Red Hook, NY 12571 USA
Phone: 845-758-0400
Fax:     845-758-2634
Email:   curran@proceedings.com
Web:    www.proceedings.com

NAACL HLT 2016

# 7th Workshop on Computational Approaches to Subjectivity, Sentiment and Social Media Analysis
## WASSA 2016

## Proceedings of the Workshop

June 16, 2016
San Diego, California, USA

WASSA 2016 is endorsed by SIGNLL, the ACL's Special Interest Group on Natural Language Learning.

# Introduction (TODO)

Emotions are an important part of our everyday lives. However, until quite recently, human affect was regarded in a dual manner - positively, for its regulatory power and negatively, as a sort of a "weakness" of the human spirit, that should ideally be rational, logical, *thinking* in a very matter of fact and consequence-based fashion.

Recent discoveries in Neuropsychology and the possibilities opened by the functional Magnetic Resonance Imaging have made it clear that emotions play a very important role for the well-functioning of the human body, both psychologically, as well as physically.

Apart from the importance emotions have for each human being individually, research in Social Psychology and disciplines such as Marketing, Mass-media Communication or Political Science, has shown time and time again that the emotional discourse, its content - in words with affective connotation and the combination thereof - is of paramount difference between the success and failure of social actions, consumer products or political candidates.

Given that nowadays messages with (sometimes) high emotional connotations are so easily shared using Social Media platforms and that their high volume makes manual sifting mostly impossible, the automatic processing of Subjectivity, Sentiment and Emotions in texts, especially in Social Media contexts is highly relevant.

Bearing these observations in mind, the aim of the 7th Workshop on Computational Approaches to Subjectivity, Sentiment and Social Media Analysis (WASSA 2016) was to continue the line of the previous editions, bringing together researchers in Computational Linguistics working on Subjectivity and Sentiment Analysis and researchers working on interdisciplinary aspects of affect computation from text. Starting with 2013, WASSA has extended its scope and focus to Social Media phenomena and the impact of affect-related phenomena in this context. The past two editions have shown important breakthroughs in dealing with the challenges of these types of texts, in monolingual, multilingual and cross-domain contexts.

WASSA 2016 was organized in conjunction to the 15th Annual Conference of the North American Chapter of the Association for Computational Linguistics: Human Language Technologies in San Diego, California, on June 16, 2016.

For this year's edition of WASSA, we received a total of 32 submissions, from universities and research centers all over the world, out of which 8 were accepted as long and another 13 as short papers. Each paper has been thoroughly reviewed by at least 2 members of the Program Committee. The accepted papers were all highly assessed by the reviewers, bringing novelty in the technical and knowledge employed and creativity into the research area.

The main topics of the accepted papers are related to challenges in dealing with language and phenomena in Social Media - Twitter and Facebook mining, but also the use of the particular structure of Social Media texts to improve the sentiment and subjectivity classification. The abundance of applications stemming from Sentiment Analysis shows more and more the importance of work in this field and the high number of scenarios where tools performing Sentiment Analysis are becoming of high importance.

Additionally, articles presenting valuable work concentrating on building lexica for this field demonstrate that there is still a high requirement to develop such resources. Finally, some articles deal with the issue of sentiment visualization and the use of such tools to improve the performance of automatic systems for emotion detection and classification.

This year's edition has again shown that the topics put forward to discussion by WASSA are of high interest to the research community and that the papers chosen to be debated in this forum bring an important development to the SSA research area.

We would like to thank the NAACL HLT 2016 Organizers and Workshop Chairs for the help and support at the different stages of the workshop organization process. We are also especially grateful to the Program Committee members and the external reviewers for the time and effort spent assessing the papers. We would like to extend our thanks to our invited speakers – Dr. Seth Grimes, Dr. Morteza Dehghani and Dr. Richard Socher - for accepting to deliver the keynote talks, opening new horizons for research and applications of Sentiment Analysis.

Secondly, we would like to express our gratitude for the official endorsement we received from SIGNLL - ACL's Special Interest Group on Natural Language Learning.

We would like to express our gratitude to Yaniv Steiner, who created the WASSA logo and to the entire Europe Media Monitor team at the European Commission Joint Research Centre, for the technical support they provided.


**Alexandra Balahur, Erik van der Goot, Piek Vossen and Andrés Montoyo**

**WASSA 2016 Chairs**

**Organizers:**

**Alexandra Balahur**
European Commission Joint Research Centre
Institute for the Protection and Security of the Citizen


**Erik van der Goot**
European Commission Joint Research Centre
Institute for the Protection and Security of the Citizen


**Piek Vossen**
University of Amsterdam
Department of Language, Literature and Communication


**Andrés Montoyo**
University of Alicante
Department of Software and Computing Systems


**Program Committee:**

Nicoletta Calzolari, CNR Pisa (Italy)
Erik Cambria, University of Stirling (U.K.)
Veronique Hoste, University of Ghent (Belgium)
Dirk Hovy, University of Copenhagen (Denmark)
Ruben Izquierdo Bevia - Vrije Universiteit Amsterdam (The Netherlands)
Manfred Klenner, University of Zuerich (Switzerland)
Roman Klinger, University of Bielefeld (Germany)
Gerard Lynch, University College Dublin (Ireland)
Isa Maks - Vrije Universiteit Amsterdam (The Netherlands)
Diana Maynard - University of Sheffield (U.K.)
Saif Mohammad, National Research Council (Canada)
Karo Moilanen, University of Oxford (U.K.)
Günter Neumann, DFKI (Germany)
Constantin Orasan, University of Wolverhampton (U.K.)
Viktor Pekar, University of Wolverhampton (U.K.)
Jose-Manuel Perea-Ortega, University of Extremadura (Spain)
Paolo Rosso, Technical University of Valencia (Spain)
Josef Steinberger, Charles University Prague (The Czech Republic)

Mike Thelwall, University of Wolverhampton (U.K.)
Dan Tufis, RACAI (Romania)
Alfonso Ureña, University of Jaén (Spain)
Janyce Wiebe - University of Pittsburgh (U.S.A.)
Michael Wiegand, Saarland University (Germany)
Taras Zagibalov, Brantwatch (U.K.)


**Invited Speakers:**

Dr. Morteza Dehghani - University of Southern California
Dr. Seth Grimes - Alta Plana Corporation
Dr. Richard Socher - MetaMind


**Invited Papers from:**

Manfred Klenner - University of Zuerich
Saif Mohammad - National Research Council Canada
Preslav Nakov - Qatar Computing Research Institute (QCRI)
Fabrizio Sebastiani - Qatar Computing Research Institute (QCRI)
Carlo Strapparava - Fondazione Bruno Kessler

# Table of Contents

# Conference Program

**Thursday, June 16, 2016**

**08:40–09:00    Opening Remarks and Intro Talk**

08:45–09:00    *Sentiment Analysis - What are we talking about?*
Alexandra Balahur

**09:00–10:30    Session 1: Sentiment Analysis Perspectives in Social Media**

09:00–09:40    *Sentiment, Subjectivity, and Social Analysis Go ToWork: An Industry View - Invited Talk*
Seth Grimes

09:40–10:05    *Rumor Identification and Belief Investigation on Twitter*
Sardar Hamidian and Mona Diab

10:05–10:30    *Modelling Valence and Arousal in Facebook posts*
Daniel Preoţiuc-Pietro, H. Andrew Schwartz, Gregory Park, Johannes Eichstaedt, Margaret Kern, Lyle Ungar and Elisabeth Shulman

**10:30–11:00    *Coffee Break***

**11:00–12:30    Session 2: Sentiment Detection for Social Media Applications**

11:00–11:40    *Purity Homophily in Social Networks - Invited Talk*
Morteza Dehghani

11:40–12:05    *Hit Songs' Sentiments Harness Public Mood & Predict Stock Market*
Rachel Harsley, Bhavesh Gupta, Barbara Di Eugenio and Huayi Li

12:05–12:30    *Fashioning Data - A Social Media Perspective on Fast Fashion Brands*
Rupak Chakraborty, Senjuti Kundu and Prakul Agarwal

**12:30–14:00    *Lunch Break***

# Thursday, June 16, 2016 (continued)

**14:00–15:30**  **Session 3: New Approaches in Sentiment Analysis**

14:00–14:40  *Deep Learning for Sentiment Analysis - Invited Talk*
Richard Socher

14:40–15:05  *Sentiment Lexicon Creation using Continuous Latent Space and Neural Networks*
Pedro Dias Cardoso and Anindya Roy

15:05–15:30  *The Effect of Negators, Modals, and Degree Adverbs on Sentiment Composition*
Svetlana Kiritchenko and Saif Mohammad

**15:30–16:00**  *Coffee Break*

**16:00–17:40**  **Session 4: Overview and Applications of Sentiment Analysis**

16:00–16:25  *How can NLP Tasks Mutually Benefit Sentiment Analysis? A Holistic Approach to Sentiment Analysis*
Lingjia Deng and Janyce Wiebe

16:25–16:50  *An Unsupervised System for Visual Exploration of Twitter Conversations*
Derrick Higgins, Michael Heilman, Adrianna Jelesnianska and Keith Ingersoll

16:50–17:10  *Threat detection in online discussions*
Aksel Wester, Lilja Øvrelid, Erik Velldal and Hugo Lewi Hammer

17:10–17:30  *Classification of comment helpfulness to improve knowledge sharing among medical practitioners.*
Pierre André Ménard and Caroline Barrière

**17:20–17:30**  *Break*

**18:00–19:30     Session 5: Posters**

*Political Issue Extraction Model: A Novel Hierarchical Topic Model That Uses Tweets By Political And Non-Political Authors*
Aditya Joshi, Pushpak Bhattacharyya and Mark Carman

*Early text classification: a Naïve solution*
Hugo Jair Escalante, Manuel Montes y Gomez, Luis Villasenor and Marcelo Luis Errecalde

*Semi-supervised and unsupervised categorization of posts in Web discussion forums using part-of-speech information and minimal features*
Krish Perumal and Graeme Hirst

*Linguistic Understanding of Complaints and Praises in User Reviews*
Guangyu Zhou and Kavita Ganesan

*Reputation System: Evaluating Reputation among All Good Sellers*
Vandana Jha, Savitha R, P Deepa Shenoy and Venugopal K R

*Improve Sentiment Analysis of Citations with Author Modelling*
Zheng Ma, Jinseok Nam and Karsten Weihe

*Implicit Aspect Detection in Restaurant Reviews using Cooccurence of Words*
Rrubaa Panchendrarajan, Nazick Ahamed, Brunthavan Murugaiah, Prakhash Sivakumar, Surangika Ranathunga and Akila Pemasiri

*Domain Adaptation of Polarity Lexicon combining Term Frequency and Bootstrapping*
Salud María Jiménez-Zafra, Maite Martin, M. Dolores Molina González and L. Alfonso Urena Lopez

*Do Enterprises Have Emotions?*
Sven Buechel, Udo Hahn, Jan Goldenstein, Sebastian G. M. Händschke and Peter Walgenbach

*A semantic-affective compositional approach for the affective labelling of adjective-noun and noun-noun pairs*
Elisavet Palogiannidi, Elias Iosif, Polychronis Koutsakis and Alexandros Potamianos

*Fracking Sarcasm using Neural Network*
Aniruddha Ghosh and Dr. Tony Veale

**19:30–20:00**   **Closing discussion - "Where do we go from here?"**

*An Hymn of an even Deeper Sentiment Analysis*
Manfred Klenner

*Sentiment Analysis in Twitter: A SemEval Perspective*
Preslav Nakov

*The Challenge of Sentiment Quantification*
Fabrizio Sebastiani

*A Practical Guide to Sentiment Annotation: Challenges and Solutions*
Saif Mohammad

*Emotions and NLP: Future Directions*
Carlo Strapparava

# Sentiment Analysis – What Are We Talking about?
## - Intro Talk -


**Alexandra Balahur**
European Commission Joint Research Centre
Institute for the Protection and Security of the Citizen
Via E. Fermi 2749, Ispra (VA), Italy
alexandra.balahur@jrc.ec.europa.eu


Automatic affect detection and classification from text is a complex task in Natural Language Processing, whose tackling requires not only the use of established methods in the field, but also the use of knowledge extracted from theories in Psychology, Cognitive Science, Social Psychology or Neuropsychology.

For the past decade, there has been a large amount of research done in the field. Nevertheless, many issues remain to be tackled, starting from a common understanding of what we mean by the concepts involved and integrating the research in the appropriate context.

In this intro talk, my aim is to give a broad overview of the issues involved in tackling the task, from the definition of the terms, to some of the tasks that have been defined and some of the methods employed.

1. Introduction – terms definition: opinion, sentiment, belief, emotion, feeling, attitude, subjectivity versus objectivity. Affect theories in Psychology (main theories on emotion, main models of emotion), Social Psychology (role of affect as social regulator), Cognitive Science (conceptual models of affect) and recent findings in Neuropsychology (What happens in our brain when we feel emotion? Why do we feel certain emotions?).
2. The three levels of affect analysis: text, author, reader

3. Analysis of directly expressed affect and sentiment in different types of text (reviews, blogs, newspaper articles, microblogs, social network posts) – resources (dictionaries, annotated corpora), tasks and approaches
4. Analysis of indirectly expressed affect and sentiment in text (what is the author trying to convey affect-wise? How can we detect bias or subjective opinions of the author?)– resources, tasks and approaches.
5. Analysis of implicit expressions of affect in text. Reader interpretations. The use of common-sense knowledge to detect the affective reaction of readers to texts.




*Proceedings of NAACL-HLT 2016*, page 1,
San Diego, California, June 12-17, 2016. ©2016 Association for Computational Linguistics

# Sentiment, Subjectivity, and Social Analysis Go To Work: An Industry View - Invited Talk

**Seth Grimes**
Alta Plana Corporation
`grimes@altaplana.com`

Affective computing has a commercial side. Numerous products and projects provide sentiment, emotion, and intent extraction capabilities, applied in consumer and financial markets, for healthcare and customer care, and for media, policy, and politics. Academic and industry researchers are naturally interested how sentiment and social technologies are being applied and in commercial market opportunities and trends, in what's being funded, what's falling flat, and what's on business's roadmap. Analyst Seth Grimes will provide an industry overview, surveying companies and applications in the sentiment and social analytics spaces as well as work at the tech giants. He will discuss commercialization strategy and the affective market outlook.

Dr. Seth Grimes is the leading industry analyst covering NLP, text analytics, sentiment analysis, and analysis on the confluence of structured and unstructured data sources. Seth founded Washington DC based Alta Plana Corporation, an information technology strategy consultancy, in 1997. He consults on product design, commercialization strategy, and the competitive market to established technology and solutions companies and startups. Seth created and organizes the industry-focused Sentiment Analysis Symposium and Language Technology-Accelerate conferences and was founding chair of the Text Analytics Summit (2005-13). He writes frequently for trade-press outlets including VentureBeat, KDNuggets, and InformationWeek and for his own Breakthrough Analysis blog. He is on Twitter at @SethGrimes



*Proceedings of NAACL-HLT 2016*, page 2,
San Diego, California, June 12-17, 2016. ©2016 Association for Computational Linguistics

# Rumor Identification and Belief Investigation on Twitter

**Sardar Hamidian and Mona T Diab**
Department of Computer Science
The George Washington University
`sardar,mtdiab@gwu.edu`

## Abstract

Social media users spend several hours a day to read, post and search for news on microblogging platforms. Social media is becoming a key means for discovering news. However, verifying the trustworthiness of this information is becoming even more challenging. In this study, we attempt to address the problem of rumor detection and belief investigation on Twitter. Our definition of rumor is an unverifiable statement, which spreads misinformation or disinformation. We adopt a supervised rumors classification task using the standard dataset. By employing the Tweet Latent Vector (TLV) feature, which creates a 100-d vector representative of each tweet, we increased the rumor retrieval task precision up to 0.972. We also introduce the belief score and study the belief change among the rumor posters between 2010 and 2016.

## 1 Introduction

Traditionally television, radio channels, and newspapers were the only news sources available. They are still the top trusted news sources but there is a large new trend toward digital sources. A considerable ratio of newspaper readers now read them digitally and the number of people relying on social media as a news source doubled since 2010. Social media helps you post your news online by a single click, this feasibility leads novel breaking news to show up first on micro blogs. Twitter is one of the most popular microblogging platforms with more than 250 million users. Accessibility, speed and ease-of-use have made Twitter a valuable platform to read and share information. However, the same features which make Twitter or any microblogging platform a great resource, but combined with lack of supervision make them fertile grounds for malicious or accidental misinformation in social media. Accordingly, this can lead to harmful incidences especially in sensitive circumstances, which then could cause damaging effects on individuals and society. There are many information seekers who do not rely on a single source to get information, but this is not always a good solution since even other news outlets sometime rely on social media when it comes to novel breaking news. Smart phones enable everyone to capture and tweet every single moment hours before TV cameras arrive. Considering that, social media is an appealing option for those who crave novel tempting news but on the other hand, could deceive anyone by well-structured and formatted rumors. In this study we work on a standard dataset of rumors collected by Qazvinian et al. (Qazvinian et al., 2011). In their work, the definition of rumor is defined as a statement whose truth value is unverifiable or deliberately false. We are using the same definition and not investigating the stimulus behind rumors creation.

We investigate the problem of detecting rumors in Twitter data. We start with the motivation behind this research, and then the history of similar studies about rumors is overviewed. Then the overall pipeline is exposed, in which we adopt a supervised machine learning framework, and then we investigate the belief change for president Obama rumors in three years, and finally, we compare our results to the current state of the art performance on the task.



*Proceedings of NAACL-HLT 2016*, pages 3–8,
San Diego, California, June 12-17, 2016. ©2016 Association for Computational Linguistics

We prove that our approach yields superior results in comparison to other works to date.

## 2 Related Work

There is an extension body of related works on trustworthiness and misinformation detection. In this section we only focus on closely related works on the Natural Language Processing field that concentrate on information propagation and trustworthiness on social media, and specially on Twitter.

### 2.1 Social media and Trustworthiness

After the earthquake and tsunami occurred in Japan on March 11th 2012, Takahashi and Igata, (Takahashi and Igata, 2012) targeted two sets of related rumor tweets about the earthquake. They create the model to detect other candidate rumor tweets relying on a sequence of processes. Takahashi and Igata detect the target rumor list using the entities and then the re-tweet ratio for target rumors is calculated, and finally the clue keywords get extracted by analyzing the scoring of each content word $w$, using the ratio of word occurrence in correction tweets *(num in correction(w))* over rumor tweets *(num in rumor(w))*. In a similar study, Soroush, (Vosoughi, 2015) proposes his two step rumor detection and verification model on the Boston Marathon bombing tweets. The Hierarchical-clustering model is applied for rumor detection, and after the feature engineering process, which contains linguistic, user identity, and pragmatic features, he adopts the Hidden Markov model to find the veracity of each rumor. Soroush also analyses the sentiment classification of tweets using the contextual Information, which shows how tweets in different spatial, temporal, and authorial contexts have, on average, different sentiments.

Sina is the popular Chinese microbloging platform like Twitter. Yang et al. (Yang et al., 2012) studied the rumors classification problem on both Twitter and Sina. He extended his primary features including content, client, account, location, and propagation by adding client-based features, which refers to a program that is being used to post on a microblog and also the location-based feature, which is a binary feature, that indicates being inside or outside of China. Yang et al. cover a significant range of meta-data features and fewer sentiment and con-

**Table 1:** List of Annotated Rumors (Qazvinian et al, 2011)

| Rumor | Rumor Reference | # of tweets |
|---|---|---|
| Obama | Is Barack Obama muslim? | 4975 |
| Michele | Michelle Obama hired many staff members? | 299 |
| Cellphone | Cell phone numbers going public? | 215 |
| Palin | Sarah Palin getting divorced? | 4423 |
| AirFrance | Air France mid-air crash photos? | 505 |

textual features in the aforementioned work. The most relevant related works to ours are Qazvinian et al. (Qazvinian et al., 2011)(V11) which use three sets of features, including content-based, network-based, and Twitter specific meme features. For content-based features, they extract lexical and part-of-speech patterns. For network-based features, they build two features to capture four types of network-based properties utilizing the log likelihood of re-tweet and reply properties in Tweets, and finally, the Twitter specific meme features include hashtags and URLs. In our previous work (Hamidiain and Diab, 2015)(S15) we used the V11 data set with a new set of features, more labels, different machine learning, and an experimental approach. We proposed Rumor Detection and Classification (RDC) within the context of microblogging social media and suggested Single-step and Two-step models (SRDC and TRDC) in a supervised manner and investigate the effectiveness of the proposed list of features and various preprocessing tasks.

## 3 Problem Definition and Approach

S15 and V11 results indicate that content features outperform other features in the Rumor Retrieval (RR) task. In this study we perform the rumor retrieval task with a new set of features. We employ content unigram feature, which lead to the highest results in among the content features. We employ the Tweet Latent Vector (TLV) to overcome the missing word and short length tweet issue. We extend the V11 data set to investigate the belief change for the specific rumor in different years.

### 3.1 Data

V11 published an annotated Twitter data set for the five different established rumors as listed in Table 1. The general annotation guidelines are presented in

**Table 2:** Rumor Detection Annotation Guidelines

| | |
|---|---|
| 0 | If the tweet is not about the rumor |
| 11 | If the tweet endorses the rumor |
| 12 | If the tweet denies the rumor |
| 13 | If the tweet questions the rumor |
| 14 | If the tweet is neutral |
| 2 | If the annotator is undetermined |

Table 2. The original data set as obtained from V11 did not contain the actual tweets for both the Obama and Cellphone rumors, but they only contained the tweet IDs. Hence, we used the Twitter search API for downloading the specific tweets using the tweet ID. Accordingly, the size of our data set is different from that of V11 amounting to 9000 tweets in total for our experimentation as it is shown in Table 3. The following examples are a sample of each of the annotation labels 0 (If the tweet is not about the rumor,) 11(If the tweet endorses the rumor,) and 12 (if the tweet denies the rumor) from the Obama rumor collection.

- **0**: 2010-09-24 15:12:32 , nina1236 , Obama:Muslimš2019 Right To Build A Manhattan Mosque: While celebrating Ramadan with Muslims at the White House, Presi... http://bit.ly/c0J2aI

- **11**: 2010-09-28 18:36:47 , Phanti , RT @IPlantSeeds: Obama Admits He Is A Muslim http://post.ly/10Sf7 - I thought he did that before he was elected.

- **12**: 2010-10-01 05:00:28 , secksaddict , barack obama was raised a christian he attended a church with jeremiah wright yet people still beleive hes a muslim

### 3.2 Silver Data

V11 uses Twitter search API with regular expression queries, and collects data from the period of 2009 to 2010. We also run the same queries with the same keywords for the Obama rumor and collected more than 7000 tweets from 2014 and 2016. Collected tweets are labeled by applying the Rumor Retrieval (RR) pipeline. We named the new data as silver-data and use them to investigate how belief has changed toward the "Is Barak Obama Muslim?"

rumor from 2010 to 2016. Table 3 shows statistics for the extracted tweets and silver-data. We labeled the silver-data as 0(Non-Rumor), 11(Believe), and merged 12(Deny-12, Doubtful-13, and Neutral-14). For tagging the silver data we used the original Obama data set as the train data set. Table 5 shows what labels are being used for the rumors retrieval and silver-data creation experiment.

**Table 3:** List Of Annotated Tweets Per Label Per Rumor

| Rumor | 0 | 11 | 12 | 13 | 14 | 2 | Total |
|---|---|---|---|---|---|---|---|
| Obama | 945 | 689 | 410 | 160 | 224 | 1232 | 3666 |
| Michelle | 83 | 191 | 24 | 1 | 0 | 0 | 299 |
| Palin | 86 | 1709 | 1895 | 639 | 94 | 0 | 4423 |
| Cellphone | 92 | 65 | 3 | 3 | 3 | 0 | 166 |
| Air France | 306 | 71 | 114 | 14 | 0 | 0 | 505 |
| Mix | 1512 | 2725 | 2452 | 817 | 321 | 1232 | 9059 |

**Table 4:** List of Tweets in Silver Data

| | 0 non-rumor | 11 Believe | 12 (Deny/ Doubtful/ Neutral) | Total |
|---|---|---|---|---|
| Obama2014 | 2940 | 3055 | 678 | 3738 |
| Obama2016 | 1250 | 856 | 379 | 2485 |

### 3.3 Features

In designing the new set of features for the Rumor Retrieval (RR) task we considered two key points. First, addressing the missing words and length issue in Twitter (TLV) and second, extracting a feature that implies the user's belief about each rumor. We also present and conduct RR experiment applying S15 features as one of our baselines. We designed and employed a new set of features in S15 which are tagged by "*" in Table 6. Untagged features represent the features that are used in V11.

### 3.3.1 Tweet Latent Vector (TLV)

The main intuition behind TLV is to create the latent vector representative of each tweet, since in most of the tweets, there are too few observed words

**Table 5:** Labels Used in Rumor Retrieval and Rumor Type Classification for Silver Data

| 1st Step | | 2nd Step |
|---|---|---|
| Method | Labels | Labels |
| (2-way, 2 step) | (0,2)(11-14) | (11)(12,13,14) |

| | ID | Value |
|---|---|---|
| | * Time | Binary |
| Twitter and | * Hashtag | Binary |
| Network | Hashtag Content | String |
| Specific | URL | Binary |
| | Re-Tweet | Binary |
| | *Reply | Binary |
| | User ID | Binary |
| | Content Unigram | String |
| Content | Content Bigram | String |
| | Pos Unigram | String |
| | Pos Bigram | String |
| | *NER | String |
| Pragmatic | *Event | String |
| | *Sentiment | String |
| | *Emoticon | Binary |

**Table 6:** List of S15 features used for RR Experiment .

to tell us what the sentence is about. We assume that the semantic space of both the observed and missing words make up the complete semantic profile of a sentence. We propose the Tweet Latent Vector (TLV) feature by applying the Semantic Textual Similarity (STS) model proposed by (Guo and Diab, 2012) (Guo et al., 2014), which built on the Word-Net+Wiktionary+Brown+training data set. STS pre-process each short text by tokenization and stemming, then changes the preprocessed data by removing infrequent words and TF-IDF weighting, and finally uses the model to extract the latent semantics, which is represented as a 100-dimension vector.

### 3.3.2 Committed Belief

For the belief feature we investigate the level of committed belief for each tweet, which is a modality in natural language, and indicates the author's belief in a proposition. We relied on the Werner et al. (Werner et al., 2015) belief tagger to tag the Committed Belief as(CB) where someone(SW) strongly believes in the proposition, Non-committed belief (NCB) where SW reflects a weak belief in the proposition, and Non Attributable Belief (NA) where SW is not (or could not be) expressing a belief in the proposition (e.g., desires, questions etc.) There is also the ROB tag where SW's intention is to report on SW else's stated belief, whether or not they themselves believe it. The feature values are set to a binary 0 or 1 for each CB, NCB, NA, and ROB corresponding to unseen or observed. The following example illustrates how the belief feature

values are created.

*Did yall <NA>know</NA> 1 in 5 people <CB>thought</CB> obama is a Muslim*

Feature Values : CB:1 NCB:0 NA:1 ROB:0

### 3.3.3 Content Unigram

Similar to the content lexical features proposed in S15 and V11 we use the bag of word (BOW) feature set comprised of word unigrams. The feature values are set to a binary 0 or 1 for the word unigram vector representative of each tweet.

## 4 Experimental Design

All the experiments are conducted and evaluated based on various experimental settings. We utilized different data sets, features, and machine learning approaches, which are elaborated in this section.

### 4.1 Data

We conduct our experiments with two data sets: for the RR experiment we use the mixed data set (MIX) which comprises all the data from the five rumors. We split each of the three data sets into 80% train, 10% development, and 10% test. For the belief investigation experiment we only rely on the Obama dataset. After tagging the silver data by applying the RR model, we randomly select 400 rumors (200 believer-11 and 200 denier-12) from 2010(Gold Data), 2014, and 2016(Silver-data), and investigate how tweet writer's beliefs about the Obama rumors have changed in recent years.

### 4.2 Baseline

For the RR experiment we adopt three baselines: Majority, S15 features, and the V11 model. The Majority baseline assigns the majority label from the training data set to all the test data. In the S15 baseline we perform the RR experiment by relying on the features that are proposed in S15 and shown in Table 6. We performed the RR experiment with different models in Weka platform and chose the SMO, which yield to the highest result in this experiment. We also compared our results with V11, which reported the results as Mean Average Precision.

### 4.3 Machine Learning Tools

For the experiments we employ SVM Tree Kernel model, which was proposed by Alessandro Moschitti (Moschitti, 2004). In another experiment, we perform the RR task by applying S15 features, which are illustrated at Table 6 by hiring the SMO classifier on Weka (Hall et al., 2009).

### 4.4 Experiments and Evaluations

We implement two main experimental pipelines: Rumor Retrieval (RR) and Belief investigation. Content and TLV features are employed for the RR task and then we conduct our experiment in two different phases. In the development phase we utilized development data for tuning. Then the model, which could reach the highest performance, is used on the test data set. Evaluating the performance of the proposed technique in rumor detection should rely on both the number of relevant rumors that are selected (recall) and the number of selected rumors that are relevant (precision), since both of them are presented in this work. In another experiment we investigate the belief change in the Obama rumors. We define two scores for analyzing the belief for the rumor poster/ writer. $T_{iCB}$ and $T_{iNCB}$ are defined for each rumor in the Obama data set. Each of $T_{iBeliefTag}$ corresponds to a number of seen tag in each tweet. We calculate the belief scores for each Obama rumor dataset separately. We apply formula 1 on believer (11) and denier (12) rumor in the Obama data sets.

$$\frac{\#R_{11}BeliefTag}{\#R_{12}BeliefTag} \tag{1}$$

## 5 Results

In this section the impact of different experimental setups are discussed. We first elaborate on each experiments and then compare our methodology with the baselines.

### 5.1 Rumors Retrieval

We perform the RR task by applying two sets of features and compare the results with the three baselines. We perform the RR experiment by employing the gold data set to detect Not-Rumor(0 and 2) and Rumor(11, 12, 13, and 14) in one-step two-way classification experiment. For the S15 baseline we applied all the 15 features listed in Table 6. We investigated the performance of different classifiers including J48( Decision Tree), Naive Base( NB,) and SMO and picked SMO which has outperformed the others. In similar experiment for the TLV task we employe TLV and Content features by applying the SVM Tree Kernel model, which lead to 0.972, 0.99 for the MIX and 0.971, 1.0 (precision and Recall) for the Obama gold data set. Table 7 shows how we outperform the other baselines (Majority, S15, and V11) by employing the proposed features.

**Table 7:** Precision and Recall Of RR task by Employing TLV+Content Unigram, S15, and V11 is reported as Mean Average Precision (MAP)

| Data | Method | S15(pr,rec) | V11 | TLV |
|---|---|---|---|---|
| | Majority | 0.51,0.71 | — | — |
| MIX | RR | 0.94,0.94 | **0.965** | **0.972,0.99** |
| | Majority | 0.27,0.52 | — | — |
| Obama | RR | **0.91,0.91** | —— | **0.971,1.0** |

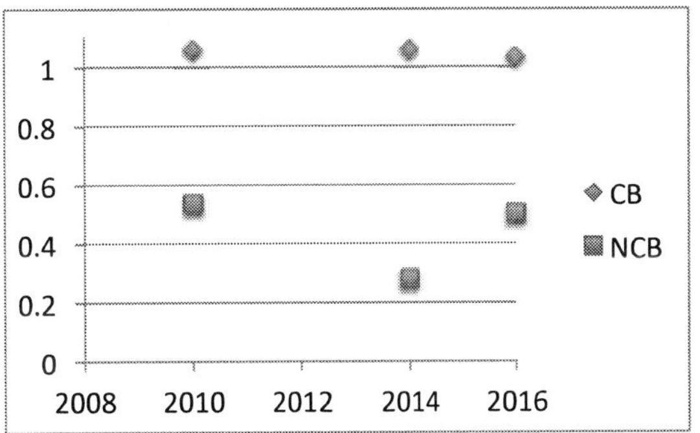


**Figure 1:** The CB and NCB score for the Obama Data set in 2010, 2014, and 2016

### 5.2 Belief Analysis

We propose formula 1 to measure the belief score for the Obama data set in different years. Then we investigate how the Committed Belief (CB) and Non Committed Belief (NCB) have changed among rumor believers as well as deniers from 2010 to 2016. Figure-1 shows the Committed Belief and Non-Committed Belief scores among the three data sets. Scores above one mean that the number of the committed belief words in rumor believers is more than in rumor deniers. It is interesting to see that the belief score for the all three years are higher than one. A simple interpretation of that would be, in all 2010, 2014, and 2016, people who were rumor believers in "Obama Being Muslim" show more belief than those who deny Obama being Muslim. On the other hand we see the NCB ratio, which is less than one for the same years. NCB means when SW presents a weak belief towards something. Having below one for NCB could be interpreted as deniers showing weak belief toward the fact that Obama is not a Muslim in 2010, 2014, and 2016. It is important to state that by receiving more data, we can attain more accurate behavior belief.

## 6 Conclusion and Future Work

In this paper, we proposed and studied the impact of Tweet Latent Vector and Belief on the problem of Rumor Detection in the context of twitter data. A new set of features are employed in our experiments to boost the overall performance of rumor retrieval and give better results in comparison to the other similar body work. We also proposed and analyzed the belief change model among rumor believers and deniers by defining the belief score. We are planning to expand the proposed methodology and investigate the trustworthiness problem from the belief and sentiment points of view and apply the model for streaming data on social media.

## Acknowledgement

This paper is based upon work supported by the DARPA DEFT Program.

## References

Weiwei Guo and Mona Diab. 2012. Modeling sentences in the latent space. In *Proceedings of the 50th Annual Meeting of the Association for Computational Linguistics: Long Papers-Volume 1*, pages 864–872. Association for Computational Linguistics.

Weiwei Guo, Wei Liu, and Mona T Diab. 2014. Fast tweet retrieval with compact binary codes. In *COLING*, pages 486–496. Citeseer.

Mark Hall, Eibe Frank, Geoffrey Holmes, Bernhard Pfahringer, Peter Reutemann, and Ian H Witten. 2009. The weka data mining software: an update. *ACM SIGKDD explorations newsletter*, 11(1):10–18.

Sardar Hamidiain and Mona Diab. 2015. Rumor detection and classification for twitter data. *The Fifth International Conference on Social Media Technologies, Communication, and Informatics, SOTICS, IARIA*, pages 71–77.

Alessandro Moschitti. 2004. A study on convolution kernels for shallow semantic parsing. In *Proceedings of the 42nd Annual Meeting on Association for Computational Linguistics*, page 335. Association for Computational Linguistics.

Vahed Qazvinian, Emily Rosengren, Dragomir R Radev, and Qiaozhu Mei. 2011. Rumor has it: Identifying misinformation in microblogs. In *Proceedings of the Conference on Empirical Methods in Natural Language Processing*, pages 1589–1599. Association for Computational Linguistics.

Tatsuro Takahashi and Nobuyuki Igata. 2012. Rumor detection on twitter. In *Soft Computing and Intelligent Systems (SCIS) and 13th International Symposium on Advanced Intelligent Systems (ISIS), 2012 Joint 6th International Conference on*, pages 452–457. IEEE.

Soroush Vosoughi. 2015. *Automatic detection and verification of rumors on Twitter*. Ph.D. thesis, Massachusetts Institute of Technology.

Gregory J Werner, Vinodkumar Prabhakaran, Mona Diab, and Owen Rambow. 2015. Committed belief tagging on the factbank and lu corpora: A comparative study. *ExProM 2015*, page 32.

Fan Yang, Yang Liu, Xiaohui Yu, and Min Yang. 2012. Automatic detection of rumor on sina weibo. In *Proceedings of the ACM SIGKDD Workshop on Mining Data Semantics*, page 13. ACM.

# Modelling Valence and Arousal in Facebook posts


**Daniel Preoțiuc-Pietro**
Positive Psychology Center
University of Pennsylvania
danielpr@sas.upenn.edu

**H. Andrew Schwartz**
Department of Computer Science
Stony Brook University
has@cs.stonybrook.edu

**Gregory Park** and **Johannes C. Eichstaedt**
Positive Psychology Center
University of Pennsylvania

**Margaret Kern**
Centre for Positive Psychology
University of Melbourne

**Lyle Ungar**
Computer & Information Science
University of Pennsylvania
ungar@cis.upenn.edu

**Elizabeth P. Shulman**
Department of Psychology
Brock University
eshulman@brocku.ca



## Abstract

Access to expressions of subjective personal posts increased with the popularity of Social Media. However, most of the work in sentiment analysis focuses on predicting only valence from text and usually targeted at a product, rather than affective states. In this paper, we introduce a new data set of 2895 Social Media posts rated by two psychologically-trained annotators on two separate ordinal nine-point scales. These scales represent valence (or sentiment) and arousal (or intensity), which defines each post's position on the circumplex model of affect, a well-established system for describing emotional states (Russell, 1980; Posner et al., 2005). The data set is used to train prediction models for each of the two dimensions from text which achieve high predictive accuracy – correlated at $r = .65$ with valence and $r = .85$ with arousal annotations. Our data set offers a building block to a deeper study of personal affect as expressed in social media. This can be used in applications such as mental illness detection or in automated large-scale psychological studies.


## 1 Introduction

Sentiment analysis is a very active research area that aims to identify, extract and analyze subjective information from text (Pang and Lee, 2008). This generally includes identifying if a piece of text is subjective or objective, what sentiment it expresses (positive or negative; often referred to as valence),

what emotion it conveys (Strapparava and Mihalcea, 2007) and towards which entity or aspect of the text i.e., aspect based sentiment analysis (Brody and Elhadad, 2010). Downstream applications are mostly interested in automatically inferring public opinion about products or actions. Besides expressing attitudes towards other objects, texts can also express the emotions of the ones writing them, most common recently with the rise of Social Media usage (Rosenthal et al., 2015). This study focuses on presenting a gold standard data set as well as a model trained on this data in order to drive research in learning about the affective norms of people posting subjective messages. This is of great interest to applications in social science which study text at a large scale and with orders of magnitude more users than traditional studies.

Emotion classification is a widely debated topic in psychology (Gendron and Barrett, 2009). Two main theories about emotions exist: the first posits a discrete and finite set of emotions, while the second suggests that emotions are a combination of different scales. Research in Natural Language Processing (NLP) has been focused mostly on Ekman's model of emotion (Ekman, 1992) which posits the existence of six basic emotions: anger, disgust, fear, joy, sadness and surprise (Strapparava and Valitutti, 2004; Strapparava and Mihalcea, 2008; Calvo and D'Mello, 2010). In this study, we focus on the most popular dimensional model of emotion: the circumplex model introduced in (Russell, 1980). This model suggests that all affective

9


*Proceedings of NAACL-HLT 2016*, pages 9–15,
San Diego, California, June 12-17, 2016. ©2016 Association for Computational Linguistics

states are represented in a two-dimensional space with two independent neurophysiological systems: valence (or sentiment) and arousal. Any affective experience is a linear combination of these two independent systems, which is then interpreted as representing a particular emotion. For example, fear is a state involving the combination of negative valence and high arousal (Posner et al., 2005). Previous research in NLP focused mostly on valence or sentiment, either binary or having a strength component coupled with sentiment (Wilson et al., 2005; Thelwall et al., 2010; Thelwall et al., 2012).

In this paper we build a new data set consisting of 2895 anonymized Facebook posts labeled with both valence and arousal by two annotators with psychology training. The ratings are made on two independent nine point scales, reaching a high agreement correlations of .768 for valence and .827 for arousal. Data set statistics suggest that while the dimensions of valence and arousal are associated, they present distinct information, especially in posts with a clear positive or negative valence.

Further, we train a bag-of-words linear regression model to predict ratings of new messages. This model achieves high correlation with actual mean ratings, reaching Pearson $r = .85$ correlation on the arousal dimension and $r = .65$ on the valence dimension without using any other sentiment analysis resources. Comparing our method to other established lexicons for valence and arousal and methods from sentiment analysis, we demonstrate that these methods are not able to handle well the type of posts present in our data set. We further illustrate the most correlated words with both dimensions and identify opportunities for improvement. The data set and annotations are freely available online.[1]

## 2 Data set

We create a new data set with annotations on two independent scales:

- **Valence (or sentiment)** represents the polarity of the affective content t in a post, rated on a nine point scale from 1 (very negative) to 5 (neutral/objective) to 9 (very positive);

[1] http://mypersonality.org/wiki/doku.php?id=download_databases

- **Arousal (or intensity)** represents the intensity of the affective content, rated on a nine point scale from 1 (neutral/objective post) to 9 (very high).

Our corpus is comprised of Facebook status updates shared by participants as part of the MyPersonality Facebook application (Kosinski et al., 2013), in which they also took a variety of questionnaires. All authors have explicitly given permission to include their information in a corpus for research purposes. We have manually anonymized the entire corpus by removing any references to other names of persons, addresses, telephone numbers, e-mails and URLs, and replaced them with placeholders.

In order to reduce biases due our participant demographics, the data set sample was stratified by gender and age and we have not rated more than two messages written by the same person. Research is inconclusive about whether females express more emotions in general (Wester et al., 2002). With regards to age, an age positivity bias has been found, where positive emotion expression increases with age (Mather and Carstensen, 2005; Kern et al., 2014).

The data originally consisted of 3120 posts. All of these posts were annotated by the same two independent raters with a training in psychology. The raters performed the coding in a similar environment without any distractions (e.g., no listening to music, no watching TV/videos) as these could have influenced the emotions of raters, and therefore the coding.

The annotators were instructed to sparingly rate messages as *un-ratable* when they were written in other languages than English or that offered no cues for a accurate rating (only characters with no meaning). The annotators were instructed to rate a message if they could judge at least a part of the message. Then, the raters were asked to rate the two dimensions, valence and arousal, after they have explicitly been briefed that these should be independent of each other. The raters were provided with anchors with specified valence and arousal and were instructed to rate neutral messages at the middle of the scale in terms of valence and 1 if they lacked arousal.

| Dimension | R1 $\mu \pm \sigma$ | R2 $\mu \pm \sigma$ | IA Corr. |
|---|---|---|---|
| Valence | $5.274 \pm 1.041$ | $5.250 \pm 1.485$ | .768 |
| Arousal | $3.363 \pm 1.958$ | $3.342 \pm 2.183$ | .827 |

Table 2: Individual rater mean and standard deviation and inter-annotator correlation (IA Corr).

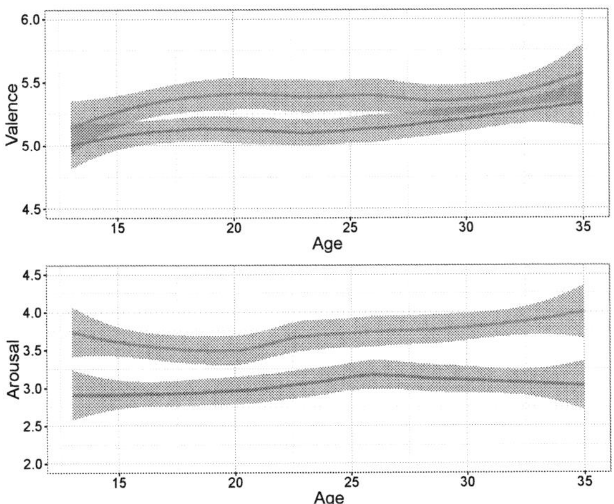

Figure 2: Variation in valence and arousal with age in our data set using a LOESS fit. Data is split by gender: Male (coral orange) and Female (mint green).

In total, 2895 messages were rated by both users in both dimensions. Table 1 shows examples of posts rated in all quadrants of the circumplex model.

The correlation between the raters and the mean and standard deviation for each rater are presented in Table 2. The inter-annotator agreement on deciding un-ratable posts is measured by Cohen's Kappa of $\kappa = .93$. The histograms of ratings are presented in Figure 1. The data set is released with the scores of both individual raters.

We study the correlation between the valence and arousal scores for posts in Table 3. We chose to split values based on different valence thresholds in order to remove posts rated as neutral in valence (5) from the analysis, as they are expected to be low in intensity (1). We observed an overall correlation between the valence and arousal ratings, which holds for both positive and negative valence tweets when the neutral posts are removed (.222, .226 correlation). However, when the posts are both more positive and negative in valence, arousal is only mildly correlated (.047 and .085). This highlights that the

| Valence of posts | 1–9 | 1–3.5 | 1–4 | 6–9 | 6.5–9 |
|---|---|---|---|---|---|
| Correlation to arousal | .222 | -.047 | -.201 | .226 | .085 |
| Mean arousal | 3.35 | 3.85 | 3.47 | 4.31 | 4.68 |

Table 3: Correlation with arousal and mean arousal values for different posts grouped by valence.

presence of either positive and negative valence is correlated with a arousal score different than 1, but this correlation is weaker when the positive or negative valence passes a certain threshold (i.e. 3.5 and 6.5 respectively). We also note that the high overall correlation is also due to higher mean arousal for positive valence posts compared to negative posts (4.68 cf. 3.85)

Figure 2 displays the relationship between the age of the user at posting time and the valence and arousal of their posts in our data set, and further divided by gender. We notice some patterns emerge in our data. Valence increases with age for both genders, especially at the start and end of our age intervals (13–16 and 30–35), confirming the aging positivity bias (Mather and Carstensen, 2005). Valence is higher for females across almost the entire age range. Posts written by females are also significantly higher in arousal for all age groups. Age does not play a significant effect in post arousal, although there is a slight increase with age especially for females. Overall, these figures again illustrate the importance of age and gender as factors to be considered in these types of application (Volkova et al., 2013; Hovy, 2015).

## 3 Predicting Valence and Arousal

To study the linguistic differences of both dimensions, we build a bag-of-words prediction model of valence and arousal from our corpus.[2] We train two linear regression models with $\ell_2$ regularisation on the posts and test their predictive power in a 10-fold cross-validation setup. Results for predicting the two scores are presented in Table 4.

We compare to a number of different existing general purpose lexicons. First, we use the ANEW (Bradley and Lang, 1999) weighted dictionary to compute a valence and arousal score as the weighted sum of individual word valence and arousal scores. Similarly, we use the affective norms

---

[2]Available at `http://wwbp.org/data.html`

11

| Message | V | A |
|---|---|---|
| Is the one whoz GOing to Light Up your Day!!!!!!!!!!!! | 7 | 8 |
| Blessed with a baby boy today ... | 7.5 | 2 |
| the boring life is back :( ... | 3 | 2.5 |
| IS SUPER STRESSED AND ITS JUST THE SECOND MONTH OF SCHOOL ..D: | 2.5 | 7 |

Table 1: Example of posts annotated with average valence (**V**) and arousal (**A**) ratings.

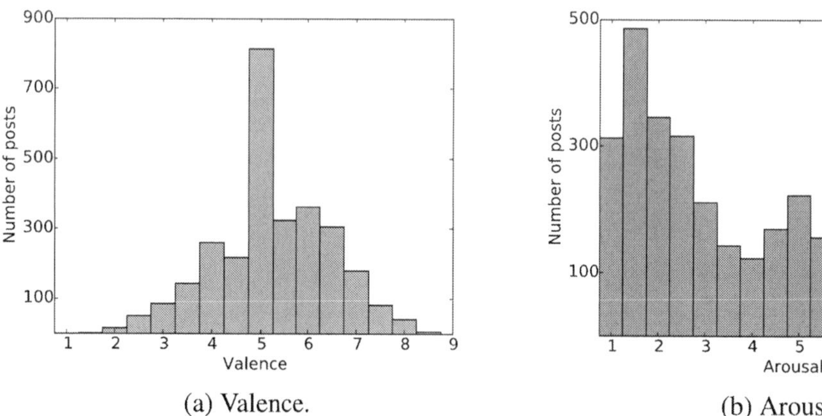

(a) Valence.

(b) Arousal.

Figure 1: Histrograms of average rating scores.

of words obtained by extending ANEW with human ratings for $\sim$14000 words (Warriner et al., 2013). We also benchmark with standard methods for estimating valence from sentiment analysis. First, we use the MPQA lexicon (Wilson et al., 2005), which contains 7629 words rated for positive or negative sentiment, to obtain a score based on the difference between positive and negative words in the post. Second, we use the NRC Hashtag Sentiment Lexicon (Mohammad et al., 2013), which obtained the best performance on the Semeval Twitter Sentiment Analysis tasks.[3]

Our method achieves very high correlations with the target score. Arousal is easier to predict, reaching $r = 0.85$ correlation between predicted and rater score. ANEW obtains significant correlations with both of our ratings, however these are significantly lower than our model. The extended list of affective norms obtains, perhaps surprisingly, lower correlation for valence, but stronger correlation with arousal than ANEW. For valence, both sentiment analysis lexicons provide better performance

| Method | Valence | Arousal |
|---|---|---|
| **ANEW** | .307 | .085 |
| **Aff Norms** | .113 | .188 |
| **MPQA** | .385 | – |
| **NRC** | .405 | – |
| **BOW Model** | .650 | .850 |

Table 4: Prediction results for valence and arousal of posts reported in Pearson correlation on 10-fold cross-validation for the BOW model.

than the affective norms lexicons, albeit lower than our model trained on parts of the same data set.

The performance improvement is most likely driven by the domain of the data set. While our method is trained on held-out data from the same domain in a cross-validation setup, the other methods suffer from lack of adaptation to this domain. The NRC lexicon, trained for predicting sentiment on Twitter, obtains the highest performance of the established models, due to the fact that is trained on a more similar domain. The lower performance of the existing models can also be explained by the fact that they predict a score used for *classification* into positive vs. negative, while our target score repre-

---

[3]https://www.cs.york.ac.uk/semeval-2013/task2/

sents the *strength* of the positive or negative expression. Moreover, the affective norms scores are hand-crafted dictionaries where the weights assigned to words are derived in isolation of context, contain no adaptations to new words, spellings and to the language use from Facebook.

## 4 Qualitative Analysis

In this section we highlight the most important unigram features for each dimension as well as the qualitative difference between the two dimensions of valence and arousal. To this end, we show the words with the highest univariate Pearson correlation with either of the two dimensions in Table 5. Each score is represented by the mean of the two ratings.

|          | **Valence** | $r$ | **Arousal** | $r$ |
|----------|-------------|------|-------------|------|
| Positive | !           | .251 | !           | .773 |
|          | :)          | .237 | Birthday    | .097 |
|          | Birthday    | .212 | Happy       | .081 |
|          | Happy       | .197 | Its         | .079 |
|          | Thank       | .196 | Wishes      | .076 |
|          | Great       | .195 | Soooo       | .074 |
|          | Love        | .195 | Thanks      | .073 |
|          | Thanks      | .179 | Christmas   | .071 |
|          | Wishes      | .170 | Sunday      | .069 |
|          | Wonderful   | .159 | Yay         | .064 |
| Negative | Hate        | -.163 | [..]*      | -.206 |
|          | :(          | -.159 | .           | -.164 |
|          | ?           | -.117 | Status      | -.064 |
|          | Sick        | -.112 | Life        | -.064 |
|          | Why         | -.102 | People      | -.060 |
|          | :'(         | -.094 | Bored       | -.059 |
|          | Not         | -.093 | :/          | -.056 |
|          | Bored       | -.092 | Of          | -.056 |
|          | Stupid      | -.089 | Deal        | -.056 |
|          | ...         | -.087 | Every       | -.054 |

Table 5: Words most correlated positively and negatively with the two dimensions.

The results show that both dimensions have similar top features as well as distinct ones. Tokens such as '!', 'Happy', 'Birthday', 'Thanks', 'Wishes' are indicative of both positive valence and arousal, while tokens like 'Bored' and '...' are indicative of both negative valence and low arousal. We notice however tokens that are only indicative of positive valence ('Wonderful', 'Love'), positive

arousal ('Sunday', 'Yay'), negative valence ('Why', 'Stupid') or negative arousal ('Life', 'Every', 'People'). The question mark is correlated to negative valence, together with the word 'Why', showing that questions on Facebook are usually negative in valence. Also in terms of punctuation, positive valence and arousal is expressed through exclamation marks, while negative valence and especially arousal is expressed through repeated periods. This behavior is specific to Social Media and which standard emotion lexicons usually does not capture.

Emoticons also exhibit an interesting pattern across the two dimensions. The smiley *:)* is the second most correlated feature with valence, but is not in the top 10 for arousal. Similarly, the frown emoticons (*:(, :'(*) are amongst the top 10 features correlated with negative valence, but have no relationship with arousal. The only emoticon correlated highly with low arousal is the undecided emoticon (*:/*).

## 5 Conclusion

In this work, we introduced a new corpus of Social Media posts mapped to the circumplex model of affect. Each post is annotated by two annotators with a background in psychology on two independent nine point scales of valence and arousal, who were calibrated before rating the statuses. We described our annotation process and reviewed the annotation guidelines. In total, we annotated 2895 Facebook posts, discarding the un-ratable ones. The corpus and our valence and arousal bag-of-words prediction models are publicly available.

The results of the annotations have very high agreement. A linear regression model using a bag of words representation trained on this data achieves high correlations with the outcome annotations, especially when predicting arousal. Standard sentiment analysis lexicons predicted both dimensions with lower accuracies.

Our system can be further improved by leveraging the vast amount of available data for Twitter sentiment analysis. We consider this model extremely useful for computational social science research that aims to measure individual user valence and arousal, its relationship to demographic traits and its changes over time or in relation to certain life events.

13

## Acknowledgements

The authors acknowledge the support of the Templeton Religion Trust, grant TRT-0048.

## References

Margaret Bradley and Peter Lang. 1999. Affective Norms for English Words (ANEW): Stimuli, Instruction Manual, and Affective Ratings. Technical report.

Samuel Brody and Noemie Elhadad. 2010. An Unsupervised Aspect-Sentiment Model for Online Reviews. In *Proceedings of the 2010 Annual Conference of the North American Chapter of the Association for Computational Linguistics*, NAACL, pages 804–812.

Rafael Calvo and Sidney D'Mello. 2010. Affect Detection: An Interdisciplinary Review of Models, Methods, and their Applications. *IEEE Transactions on Affective Computing*, 1(1):18–37.

Paul Ekman. 1992. An Argument for Basic Emotions. *Cognition & Emotion*, 6(3-4):169–200.

Maria Gendron and Lisa Feldman Barrett. 2009. Reconstructing the Past: A Century of Ideas about Emotion in Psychology. *Emotion Review*, 1(4):316–339.

Dirk Hovy. 2015. Demographic Factors Improve Classification Performance. In *Proceedings of the 53rd Annual Meeting of the Association for Computational Linguistics*, ACL, pages 752–762.

Margaret L Kern, Johannes C Eichstaedt, H Andrew Schwartz, Greg Park, Lyle H Ungar, David J Stillwell, Michal Kosinski, Lukasz Dziurzynski, and Martin EP Seligman. 2014. From "sooo excited!!!" to "so proud": Using language to study development. *Developmental Psychology*, 50:178–188.

Michal Kosinski, David Stillwell, and Thore Graepel. 2013. Private Traits and Attributes are Predictable from Digital Records of Human Behavior. *Proceedings of the National Academy of Sciences of the United States of America (PNAS)*, 110(15):5802–5805.

Mara Mather and Laura L Carstensen. 2005. Aging and Motivated Cognition: The Positivity Effect in Attention and Memory. *Trends in Cognitive Sciences*, 9(10):496–502.

Saif M. Mohammad, Svetlana Kiritchenko, and Xiaodan Zhu. 2013. NRC-Canada: Building the State-of-the-Art in Sentiment Analysis of Tweets. In *Proceedings of the 7th International Workshop on Semantic Evaluation*, SemEval, pages 321–327.

Bo Pang and Lillian Lee. 2008. Opinion Mining and Sentiment Analysis. *Foundations and Trends in Information Retrieval*, 2(1-2):1–135.

Jonathan Posner, James A Russell, and Bradley S Peterson. 2005. The Circumplex Model of Affect: An Integrative Approach to Affective Neuroscience, Cognitive Development, and Psychopathology. *Development and Psychopathology*, 17(3):715–734.

Sara Rosenthal, Preslav Nakov, Svetlana Kiritchenko, Saif M Mohammad, Alan Ritter, and Veselin Stoyanov. 2015. Semeval-2015 Task 10: Sentiment Analysis in Twitter. In *Proceedings of the 9th International Workshop on Semantic Evaluation*, SemEval, pages 451–463.

James A. Russell. 1980. A Circumplex Model of Affect. *Journal of Personality and Social Psychology*, 39(6):1161–1178.

Carlo Strapparava and Rada Mihalcea. 2007. SemEval-2007 Task 14: Affective Text. In *Proceedings of the 4th International Workshop on Semantic Evaluations*, SemEval, pages 70–74.

Carlo Strapparava and Rada Mihalcea. 2008. Learning to Identify Emotions in Text. In *Proceedings of the 2008 ACM Symposium on Applied Computing*, SAC, pages 1556–1560.

Carlo Strapparava and Alessandro Valitutti. 2004. Wordnet affect: an affective extension of wordnet. In *Proceedings of the Fourth International Conference on Language Resources and Evaluation*, volume 4 of *LREC*, pages 1083–1086.

Mike Thelwall, Kevan Buckley, Georgios Paltoglou, Di Cai, and Arvid Kappas. 2010. Sentiment strength detection in short informal text. *Journal of the American Society for Information Science and Technology*, 61(12):2544–2558.

Mike Thelwall, Kevan Buckley, and Georgios Paltoglou. 2012. Sentiment Strength Detection for the Social Web. *Journal of the American Society for Information Science and Technology*, 63(1):163–173.

Svitlana Volkova, Theresa Wilson, and David Yarowsky. 2013. Exploring Demographic Language Variations to Improve Multilingual Sentiment Analysis in Social Media. In *Proceedings of the 2013 Conference on Empirical Methods in Natural Language Processing*, EMNLP, pages 1815–1827.

Amy Beth Warriner, Victor Kuperman, and Marc Brysbaert. 2013. Norms of Valence, Arousal, and Dominance for 13,915 English Lemmas. *Behavior Research Methods*, 45(4):1191–1207.

Stephen R Wester, David L Vogel, Page K Pressly, and Martin Heesacker. 2002. Sex Differences in Emotion a Critical Review of the Literature and Implications for Counseling Psychology. *The Counseling Psychologist*, 30(4):630–652.

Theresa Wilson, Janyce Wiebe, and Paul Hoffmann. 2005. Recognizing Contextual Polarity in Phrase-level Sentiment Analysis. In *Proceedings of the Conference on Empirical Methods in Natural Language Processing*, EMNLP, pages 347–354.

# Purity Homophily in Social Networks - Invited Talk

**Morteza Dehghani**
University of Southern California
mdehghan@usc.edu

Does sharing moral values encourage people to connect and form communities? The importance of moral homophily (love of same) has been recognized by social scientists, but the types of moral similarities that drive this phenomenon are still unknown. In this talk, I will present a series of experiments (both large-scale, observational social-media analyses and behavioral lab experiments) that investigate which types of moral similarities influence tie formations. Our results indicate that social network processes reflect moral selection, and both online and offline differences in moral purity concerns are particularly predictive of social distance.

Dr. Morteza Dehghani is an Assistant Professor of psychology, computer science and the Brain and Creativity Institute at University of Southern California. His research spans the boundary between psychology and artificial intelligence, as does his education. His work investigates properties of cognition by using documents of the social discourse, such as narratives, social media, transcriptions of speeches and news articles, in conjunction to behavioral studies.



*Proceedings of NAACL-HLT 2016*, page 16,
San Diego, California, June 12-17, 2016. ©2016 Association for Computational Linguistics

# Hit Songs' Sentiments Harness Public Mood & Predict Stock Market

**Rachel Harsley[1], Bhavesh Gupta[2], Barbara Di Eugenio[1], and Huayi Li[1]**
[1]University of Illinois at Chicago, Chicago, IL, USA
[2]Cerner Corporation, Kansas City, MO, USA
`{rharsl2, bdieugen, hli47}@uic.edu`
`bhavesh.gupta@cerner.com`

## Abstract

This work explores the relationship between the sentiment of lyrics in Billboard Top 100 songs, stocks, and a consumer confidence index. We hypothesized that sentiment of Top 100 songs could be representative of public mood and correlate to stock market changes as well. We analyzed the sentiment for polarity and mood in terms of seven dimensions. We gathered data from 2008 to 2013 and found statistically significant correlations between lyrical sentiment polarity and DJIA closing values and between anxiety in lyrics and consumer confidence. We also found strong Granger-causal relationships involving anxiety, hope, anger, and both societal indicators. Finally, we introduced a vector autoregression model with time lag which is able to capture stock and consumer confidence indices ($R^2$=.97, p<.001 and $R^2$=0.72, p<.01 respectively).

## 1 Introduction

Many would agree that the success of top songs is due to a complicated mix of marketing, popularity, and blockbuster theory in which companies invest big money into few products. Yet, we also hypothesized that the lyrical sentiment of top songs can be viewed as transient, but genuine snapshot of public mood. There is a plethora of research which unequivocally confirms both the influence of mood on music choice and the influence of music on mood and even buying behavior (Areni and Kim, 1993; Bruner, 1990; Chen et al., 2007; R McCraty, 1998)

While researchers have attempted to model public opinion indices and the stock market via sentiment analysis of news articles, microblogging and social media sites, no research has taken this correlation-seeking approach using popular song lyrics. We hypothesized that song lyrics from the Billboard Hot 100, a weekly listing of the top 100 songs, is representative of public mood. Moreover, we aimed to explore correlating, causal, and even predictive relationships between song lyrics, public opinion, and the stock market.

Thus, we aimed to explore the sentiment of top song lyrics in a manner similar to researchers who used Twitter to ascertain public mood and correlated this sentiment to public opinion polls (Bollen et al., 2011; O'Connor et al., 2010). While Twitter offers a fine-grained time-based approach to harnessing public expressions, other mediums, such as popular song lyrics, may offer the same insight while being less costly to obtain and less susceptible to the "burstiness" of Twitter. In other words, use of popular song lyrics would automatically filter out the noise of ephemeral, popular happenings which pervade Twitter.

The Hot 100 listing is calculated based on a single's selling performance, radio airplay audience impression, and online streaming activity (Trust, Gary, 2013). We explored if correlation would reflect in the Thomson Reuters/University of Michigan Consumer Confidence Index (ICC) and the Dow Jones Industrial Average (DJIA), a major U.S. stock market index.

For our work, we gathered the entire set of weekly Hot 100 songs between 2008 and 2013. We used OpinionFinder to analyze the positive and negative polarity of lyrics (Wilson et al., 2005). We then used a second tool, WordNet Affect, to perform sentiment analysis along nine-dimensions (Strapparava and Valitutti, 2004). We assessed the strength of sentiment correlation to the DJIA and ICC. We then explored poignant Granger-causal relations and created a predictive model for both societal indicators. In this work, we discover, there are indeed correlating and causal relationships between the song sentiments and these societal indicators.

17

*Proceedings of NAACL-HLT 2016*, pages 17–25,
San Diego, California, June 12-17, 2016. ©2016 Association for Computational Linguistics

## 2  Related Work

Bollen et al. (2011) explored the notion that public mood can be correlated to and even predictive of economic indicators. They used sentiment analysis of large scale twitter feeds and compare it with the Dow Jones Industrial Average over time. High correlation results led them to create a neural network to predict the DJIA given their Twitter sentiment insights. They reached 87% accuracy in predicting the daily up and down changes of the DJIA. Similarly, O' Connor et al. (2010) connected measures of public opinion measured from polls with the results of sentiment analysis over text on twitter feeds. They analyzed several surveys on consumer confidence and political opinion between 2008 and 2009 and found correlation between sentiment word frequencies in twitter messages.

Acerbi et al. (2013) examined the usage of "mood" in the context of 20th century books written in English. They used WordNet Affect to perform sentiment analysis on the literature and found evidence for distinct historical periods of positive and negative moods in American Literature. Further, these periods often correlated to historical happenings.

Daas and Puts (2014) explored changes in the sentiment in Dutch public blogs and social media messages i.e. Twitter, Facebook and LinkedIn over a 3.5-year period. They performed sentiment analysis on the text and compared results with changes in Netherlands monthly consumer confidence. They discovered a high correlation (up to r=0.9) and that changes in social media sentiment precede the consumer confidence changes.

While there has been much interest in automatically determining the sentiment of songs from both acoustic and natural language processing communities, there has been far less success in performing the task. Xia et al (2008) proposed using a sentiment vector space model in conjunction with a support vector machine to overcome the hurdle of lyrical data sparseness. Other research has focused on combining audio and lyrical data for ascertaining the mood of a given song (Hu and Downie, 2010; Zhong et al., 2012).

While past work has looked at correlations between Twitter, literature, and other social media in regards to stocks and public opinion, our work looks at the correlation between the sentiment of popular song lyrics and these societal measures. There is an abundance of research linking the effect of music on mood and social behaviors including buying decisions and even it's inverse; the role of mood in music choice(Areni and Kim, 1993; Bruner, 1990; North and Hargreaves, 1997; R McCraty, 1998; Sloboda, 2011). Due to the strong relationship between music and mood, we considered it to be a reasonable hypothesis that top music choice of the nation, via the Hot 100, could in some ways be representative of public mood.

## 3  Dataset

### 3.1  Lyrics

The first step in preparing our analysis was to collect the song listings themselves. Our dataset spans six years, 2008 through 2013. In order to perform this, we consulted the Ultimate Music Database (http://www.umdmusic.com/) which has the full listing of Billboard Music Charts songs available. We collected a total of 36,000 song listings (with some songs being repeated). For each listing, we queried and scraped LyricsWikia (http://lyrics.wikia.com/) for actual lyrics. The lyrical data along with full chart listings are available for public use by contacting the authors.

### 3.2  Societal Indicators

For the purpose of this research, we examined two societal indicators; Dow Jones Industrial Average (DJIA) and Thomson Reuters/University of Michigan Index of Consumer Confidence (ICC). The two were chosen due to their role in previously researched correlations as described in the Related Work section.

The DJIA shows how 30 large publicly owned companies based in the United States have traded during a standard trading session in the stock market. It is the second oldest U.S. market index and is influenced by many factors. The ICC aims to measure consumers' level of optimism towards their own financial situation, short term general economy and long term general economy, according to their share of spending and savings (Curtin, 2004).

## 4  Methods

In this section, we describe our approach to find correlations between the lyrical sentiment of top songs and societal indicators.

### 4.1 Sentiment Analysis

We chose to utilize two simplistic approaches to sentiment mining given the insight of past work showing the uniqueness of song sentiment classification. Positive results using the simplest of sentiment analysis techniques would be indicative of opportunities for fine-tuning the sentiment analysis method for enhanced results. We performed our first analysis of the lyrics using OpinionFinder. OpinionFinder performs sentiment analysis by labeling words as either positive, negative, or neutral. It generates a text file that tags the words in the document with respect to their contextual polarity. Using OpinionFinder results, we calculated the polarity for a song using the following ratio:

$$polarity = \frac{num\_pos + num\_neut + .1}{num\_neg + num\_neut + .1} \qquad (1)$$

where *num_pos, num_neut,* and *num_*neg represent the number of words with positive, neutral, and negative sentiment valance. We used 0.1 to accommodate smoothing in the case of missing values. For example, we could not automatically retrieve lyrics for a song in year 2008 due to a mislabeling of artist in the lyrics data.

We performed a second sentiment analysis using multi-dimensional sentiment classification. We found this step to be necessary in order to capture holistic public mood, which is rich, multifaceted, and not limited to bipolarity. For this we use the text analysis tool WordNet Affect. WordNet Affect labels a given word with one of over 300 possible sentiment labels. Labels fall under distinct hierarchies. These hierarchies include: emotion, mood, trait, cognitive state, physical state, hedonic signal, emotion eliciting, situation, emotional response, behavior, attitude, and sensation. Our analysis exclusively considers labels branching under the emotion hierarchy.

We automatically labelled and aggregated the lyrical data on a weekly basis. Moreover, after retrieving labels, we narrowed our focus to the seven most frequently occurring given the sentiment analysis results. The seven labels are as follows: anxiety, anger, expectation, dislike, joy, negative fear, and sorrow. The ambiguous expectation sentiment can be seen as a measure of hope or fever in the lyrics. Further, *negative fear* is distinguished in contrast to *fear,* which may also signify reverence. Finally, we included positive emotion and negative emotion to compare to OpinionFinder's polarity results.

In order to effectively compare the range of sentiment counts and the societal indicators, each time series was normalized to their z-score using the overall mean and standard deviation. The normalization allows all time series to fluctuate around a zero mean and be expressed on the scale of a single standard deviation. The Z score of time series X is denotes $Z_X$ is defined as:

$$Z_X = \frac{X_t - \bar{X}}{\sigma} \qquad (2)$$

where $\bar{X}$ and $\sigma$ represent the mean and standard deviation of the X time series.

### 4.2 Correlation Analysis

We began by examining the Pearson Correlation Coefficient for the sentiment time series in comparison to the societal indicator data. Pearson's correlation coefficient (r) measures the strength of the association between two quantitative, continuous variables. The Pearson correlation analysis allowed us to quantitatively determine the relationship between the societal indicators and sentiments. Graphical plots of the time series for each lyrical sentiment method and each societal indicator afforded opportunity for visual correlation analysis and cross validation of our sentiment analysis findings to known socio-cultural events. Additionally,

We then measured the correlation between the trend obtained from our sentiment analysis and each societal indicator using multiple regression. The regression model is shown below:

$$Y_i = \alpha + \sum_{j=1}^{N} \beta_j X_j + \varepsilon_t \qquad (3)$$

where i=1,2 and $Y_i$ is the societal indicator trend and N=9, $X_1$, $X_2$,...$X_N$ represent the mood time series obtained from the multi-dimensional sentiment analysis. The regression model allows us to further quantify any relation between the lyrical sentiment and societal indicators.

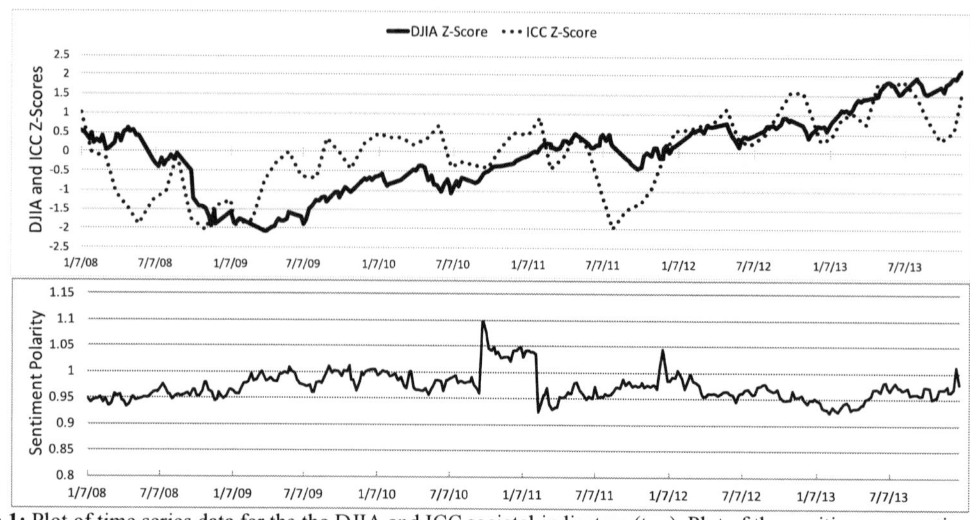


**Figure 1:** Plot of time series data for the the DJIA and ICC societal indicators (top). Plot of the positive vs. negative polarity for song lyrics (bottom). Note, the z-scores of the societal indicators are used.

## 5   Results

### 5.1   Polarity-Based Sentiment Correlations

We quantified the correlation between the song polarity and the societal indicators using the Pearson Correlation Coefficient and t-tests (used in order to establish the significance of the correlation). As a baseline, we calculated the correlation of ICC, the standard of public mood, to the DJIA (r= .6563, p<.001). We wanted to measure how top songs' lyrical sentiments compared to this baseline as another measure of public mood. The results indicated that the lyrical polarity and DJIA have a significant negative correlation (shown in Table 1). However, the absolute value of the correlation coefficient is half that of the baseline, which indicates the association is not as strong.

The plot of lyrical polarity for each week from the year 2008 to 2013 is shown in Figure 1. We compared it to the time series of societal indicators z-scores also shown in Figure 1. There were little visual similarities between the plots. However, interestingly, we noted that the polarity plot is able to capture some of the trends of typical U.S. holidays. For example, the polarity exhibits local peaks of high positivity during the Christmas holiday time from 2010 through 2013. Similarly, the polarity reaches its lowest on Valentine's Day of 2011, suggesting a time of negative feelings. In order to gain an intuition that the sentiment analysis system was performing reasonably well and the dip was not due to inaccuracy of the system, we manually examined song changes between the two weeks. As expected, the Valentine's week Hot 100 added several

songs to the list which contained hints of negative sentiments in juxtaposition to themes of love. These included, *Loveeeeeee Song* by Rihanna and *Same Love* by Macklemore, and *As Long as You Love Me* by Justin Bieber.

|  | Correlation Coefficient | t | p |
|---|---|---|---|
| DJIA | -0.3679 | -3.3108 | **0.0014*** |
| ICC | -0.0212 | -0.1777 | 0.8594 |

**Table 1:** Pearson Correlation results for song polarity in comparison to DJIA and ICC.

### 5.2   Multi-dimensional Sentiment Correlations

In addition to polarity, we also plotted the trend series for the nine sentiments of interest as shown in Figure 2. Visual inspection of the plots suggested a high correlation between anxiety and ICC. The anxiety seems to be almost a shift of the ICC with a three-month lag. Moreover, visual analysis offered another interesting insight. The anger plot exhibits a large rise during the time of the November 2012 Presidential Election. Further, the peak of the anger occurs on the day following Election Day 2012 as shown in Figure 3. We examined the reason for this through manually comparing difference in top songs from the prior week. During election week, songs by Taylor Swift and Kendrick Lamar entered into the Hot 100 listing. They introduced a variety of sentiments including anger, for example, in Swift's song *Stay Stay Stay* she repeatedly uses the word *mad* to describe her emotional state in a dating relationship.

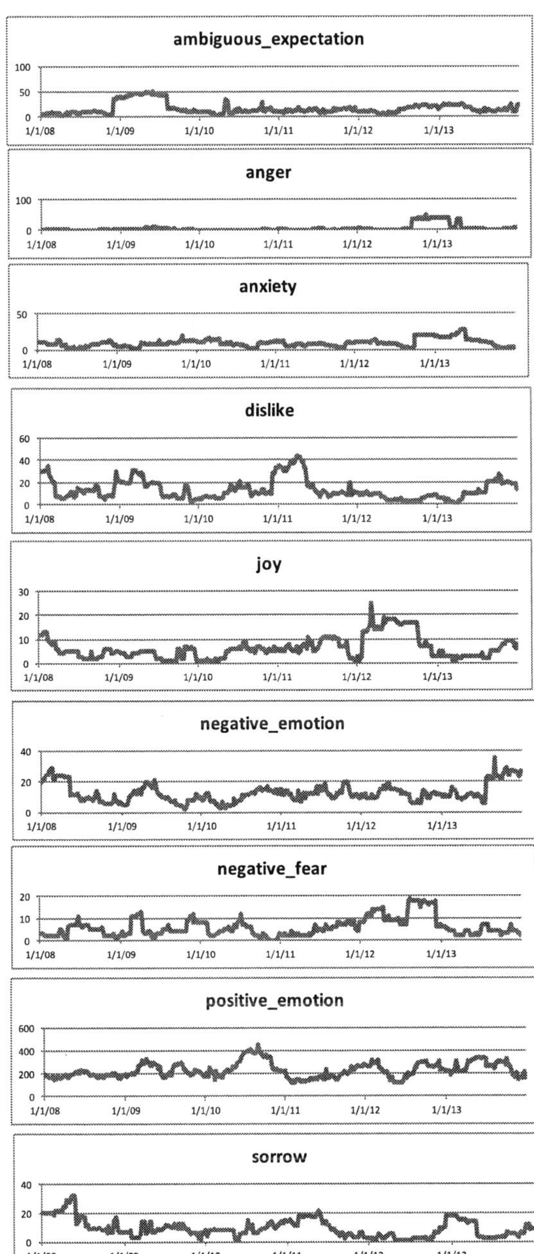

**Figure 2:** The trend series for the nine sentiments of interest. Z-score not shown.

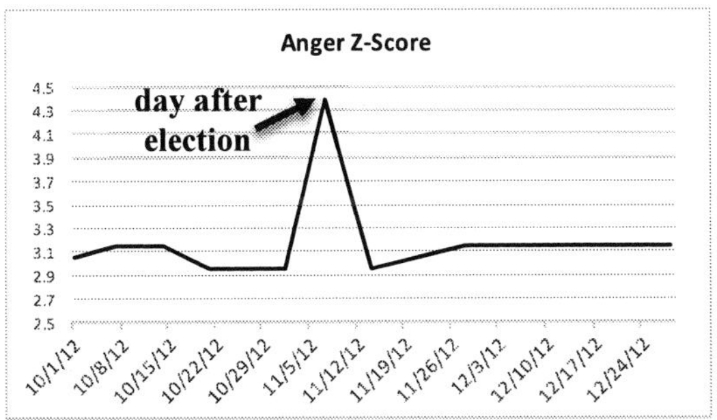


**Figure 3:** The trend series for *anger* during weeks prior to and after the November 2012 Presidential Election.

21

As in the polarity analysis, we also examined the quantitative correlation between the nine sentiments and the societal indicators using the Pearson Correlation Coefficient and with t-tests in order to establish the significance of the correlation. The results of the analysis between the sentiments and ICC are shown in Table 2. The result of the comparison between sentiments and DJIA is shown in Table 3.

The analysis results indicated that anxiety is significantly correlated to the Michigan ICC ($r=0.4761$, $p < 0.001$) and the correlation is almost as strong as that between the ICC and the DJIA. Additionally, anger exhibits a correlation which is significant ($p<.05$) though not as strong and more difficult to ascertain upon visual inspection. Surprisingly, joy, which may be seen as the opposite of anger, did not significantly correlate with the Michigan ICS.

| Sentiment | Correlation Coefficient | t | p |
|---|---|---|---|
| Anxiety | 0.4761 | 4.5 | **0.000**** |
| Anger | 0.2974 | 2.6 | **0.011*** |
| Ambiguous_ Expectation | -0.2056 | -1.7 | 0.083 |
| Dislike | -0.1043 | -0.8 | 0.383 |
| Joy | 0.1494 | 1.2 | 0.210 |
| Negative_ Emotion | 0.1582 | 1.3 | 0.184 |
| Negative_ Fear | 0.1554 | 1.3 | 0.192 |
| Positive_ Emotion | 0.1967 | 1.6 | 0.097 |
| Sorrow | -0.2233 | -1.9 | 0.059 |

*p<.05  **p<.001

**Table 2:** Pearson Correlation Results for WordNet Affect Sentiments and Michigan ICC

The correlation results for the DJIA and nine sentiments shows there is an especially strong correlation between the societal indicators and both ambiguous expectation and negative emotion ($p<.001$). As the DJIA values increases, the ambiguous expectation decreases. We suspected this trend may have been indicative of positive correlations with time lag. Further, both anxiety and joy exhibit strong correlation with the DJIA ($p<.05$). Though several correlations where significant and strong, they were not intuitive as the visual plots did not align with either of the societal indicators. Thus, we deemed it necessary to explore causal relationships and time lag as described in Section 5.3.

| Sentiment | Correlation Coefficient | t | p |
|---|---|---|---|
| Anxiety | 0.2504 | 2.1 | **0.033*** |
| Anger | 0.2248 | 1.9 | 0.057 |
| Ambiguous_Expectation | -0.4734 | -4.4 | **0.000*** |
| Dislike | -0.1312 | -1.1 | 0.271 |
| Joy | 0.2582 | 2.2 | **0.028*** |
| Negative_Emotion | 0.4328 | 4.0 | **0.000*** |
| Negative_Fear | 0.0964 | 0.8 | 0.420 |
| Positive_Emotion | 0.0024 | 0.0 | 0.983 |
| Sorrow | -0.0038 | 0.0 | 0.974 |

*p<.05   **p<.001

**Table 3:** Pearson Correlation Results for WordNet Affect Sentiments and DJIA

### 5.3 Modelling, Causality and Time-lag

In order to gain a greater understanding of the relationship between the multidimensional lyrical sentiments and the societal indicators, we performed multiple regression using the model described in Equation 3. The multiple regression models moderately captured stock and consumer confidence indices ($R^2$=.61, p<.001 and $R^2$=.52, p<.001). As expected, the sentiments with significant and strong Pearson correlations, anger, anxiety, ambiguous expectation, were all significant features for modelling each societal indicator. Additionally, sorrow was significant in modelling the ICC and DJIA while negative emotion was significant in modelling the DJIA. The results for ICC are shown in Table 4 while the results for DJIA are in Table 5.

We discovered several non-intuitive correlations, including the negative correlation between ambiguous expectation and the DJIA. However, this strange correlation could be indicative of positive correlation with a lag. Given this, we recognized that more fine-tuning of the model would better fit the societal indices. Further, due to the non-intuitive correlation between several sentiments and the societal indicators, we deemed it worthwhile to explore the role of time lag. With the addition of time based modelling, we also aimed to discover whether causal relationships existed among the sentiments and the societal indicators.

In order to accomplish this, we utilized the statistical concept of Granger causality in a similar manner as in Bollen's (2011) Twitter-based stock market predictions. The key intuition in Granger causality is as follows; if a variable X causes Y then changes in Y will be 1) be preced-

ed by changes in X and 2) be better predicted by using information from time-lagged X and Y rather than information than solely Y. In effect, Granger causality then tests whether one time series has predictive information about the other by checking for statistically significant correlations between the time lagged X and the resulting Y.

| | Coefficient | Standard Error | t Stat | P-Value |
|---|---|---|---|---|
| Sorrow | -0.315 | 0.112 | -2.8 | **0.006*** |
| Pos-Emo | 0.016 | 0.092 | 0.1 | 0.861 |
| Neg-Fear | -0.156 | 0.135 | -1.1 | 0.251 |
| Neg-Emo | 0.499 | 0.097 | 5.1 | **2.9E-06*** |
| Joy | 0.071 | 0.116 | 0.6 | 0.543 |
| Dislike | 0.070 | 0.102 | 0.6 | 0.493 |
| Anxiety | 0.114 | 0.119 | 0.9 | 0.339 |
| Anger | 0.515 | 0.141 | 3.6 | **0.0005*** |
| Ambig-Expectation | -0.623 | 0.104 | -5.9 | 1.175 |

$R^2$= 0.5234   p<.001          *p<.05   **p<.001

**Table 4:** Multiple regression results for WordNet Affect Sentiments vs ICC

| | Coefficient | Standard Error | t Stat | P-Value |
|---|---|---|---|---|
| Sorrow | -0.421 | 0.125 | -3.3 | **0.001*** |
| Pos-Emo | 0.164 | 0.104 | 1.5 | 0.119 |
| Neg-Fear | -0.107 | 0.151 | -0.7 | 0.481 |
| Neg-Emo | 0.281 | 0.108 | 2.5 | 0.012 |
| Joy | 0.150 | 0.130 | 1.1 | 0.255 |
| Dislike | 0.270 | 0.115 | 2.3 | 0.022 |
| Anxiety | 0.519 | 0.133 | 3.8 | **0.000*** |
| Anger | 0.291 | 0.158 | 1.8 | 0.071 |
| Ambig-Expectation | -0.333 | 0.116 | -2.8 | **0.006*** |

$R^2$= 0.6179 p<.001          *p<.05   **p<.001

**Table 5:** Multiple regression results for WordNet Affect Sentiments vs DJIA

We tested for Granger Causality given an X-month lag and found that there is significant Granger Causality between several of the sentiments and the DJIA along with the ICC. The Granger causality test rejects the null hypothesis that the ICC does not predict both anxiety and ambiguous expectation. In agreement with earlier findings, we confirmed that consumer confidence Granger-causes anxiety with a 5-month lag. By visualizing the time lag in more detail, the correlation between anxiety, ambiguous expectation and the ICC become quite clear. Moreover, we discovered that anger Granger-causes consumer confidence shifts.

The use of time lag and Granger causality brought clarity to the prior findings in which ambiguous expectation was negatively correlated to the DJIA and ICC. Both the DJIA and consumer confidence changes Granger-cause ambiguous expectation, or hope, in popular song lyrics. They require minimal time lag, especially for consumer confidence. In effect, consumers listen to more hopeful music when stocks and consumer confidence are high. The opposite can also be said. The full results for Granger causality are shown in Table 6 and Table 7.

We plotted several causal relationships with appropriate time lag in Figure 4. We note the visible alignment given the introduced time lag. For example, the time series of negative emotion and the DJIA frequently overlap or point in the same direction given that negative emotion Granger-causes the DJIA with a six month delay.

|  | S to I | I to S | P-Value | Months |
|---|---|---|---|---|
| Sorrow |  | X | 0.032 | 1 |
| Pos-Emo |  | X | 0.039 | 16 |
| Neg-Emo | X |  | 0.036 | 16 |
| Joy | X |  | 0.074 | 17 |
| Anxiety |  | X | 0.013 | 5 |
| Anger | X |  | 0.048 | 4 |
| Ambig-Expectation |  | X | 0.009 | 1 |

**Table 6:** Sentiment (S) and Granger Causality ICC (I) along with amount of lag. S to I denotes that S Granger-causes I. While I to S denotes I Granger-causes S.

|  | S to D | D to S | P-Value | Months |
|---|---|---|---|---|
| Sorrow | X |  | 0.013 | 5 |
| Pos-Emo | X |  | 0.049 | 1 |
| Neg-Fear |  | X | 0.036 | 1 |
| Neg-Emo | X |  | 0.035 | 6 |
| Dislike | X |  | 0.041 | 17 |
| Anger |  | X | 0.036 | 15 |
| Ambig-Expectation |  | X | 0.000 | 3 |

**Table 7:** Sentiment (S) and Granger Causality DJIA (D) along with amount of lag. S to D denotes that S Granger-causes D. While D to S denotes D Granger-causes S.

As a final measure, we added further predictability to our analysis through the use of vector autoregression. Vector autoregression is an econometric technique that allows for multiple time series to be captured for linear interdependencies. Vector autoregression is a natural extension of univariate autoregression in which more than one variable is able to lag. We obtained tighter fit models for both the DJIA and ICC ($R^2$=.97, p = 0.0 and $R^2$=0.72, p<.01). We then computed the mean square error of the predictor time-series on data from 2014 using VAR. The model predicted the Z-score of either societal indicator and achieved greater success on the DJIA. The results are shown in Table 8.

|  | MSE |
|---|---|
| DJIA | 0.109 |
| ICC | 0.748 |

**Table 8:** Mean squared error of VAR model prediction for 2014 data of societal indicators.

Sorrow, with a five-month lag, was the most significant of the time-lagged features for modelling the DJIA (p<.01). Unsurprisingly, sorrow also was shown to Granger cause the DJIA with a five-month lag. Additionally, ambiguous expectation with a three-month lag was significant (p<.05) in the DJIA model. The dual role of ambiguous expectation in both influencing and being influenced by the DJIA is unsurprising given the prior research in music and mood and it's inverse relationship. Similarly, ambiguous expectation (one-month lag), anxiety (one-month lag), and negative fear (two-months lag) were all significant features (p<.05) in modelling the ICC.

## 6 Conclusion

In this paper, we explored whether Billboard Hot 100 lyric sentiment is indicative of public mood. We measured this by comparison to correlations with the Michigan Consumer Confidence Index (ICC). Moreover, we investigated whether this type of public mood measure is causally related to both the ICC and the Dow Jones Industrial Average (DJIA). We analyzed lyrics based on positive and negative sentiment polarity. We also performed a multi-dimensional sentiment analysis that examines nine emotions. Visual analyses of trend plots showed notable correlation between song lyrics sentiment and societal indicators. Moreover, the Pearson Correlation analysis quantified the relationship between song polarity and DJIA to be statistically significant, though some correlations were non-intuitive.

We confirmed correlating relationships through use of Granger causality and the introduction of time lag. This revealed a Granger-causal relationship between ICC and between anger and ICC and anxiety. We also discovered

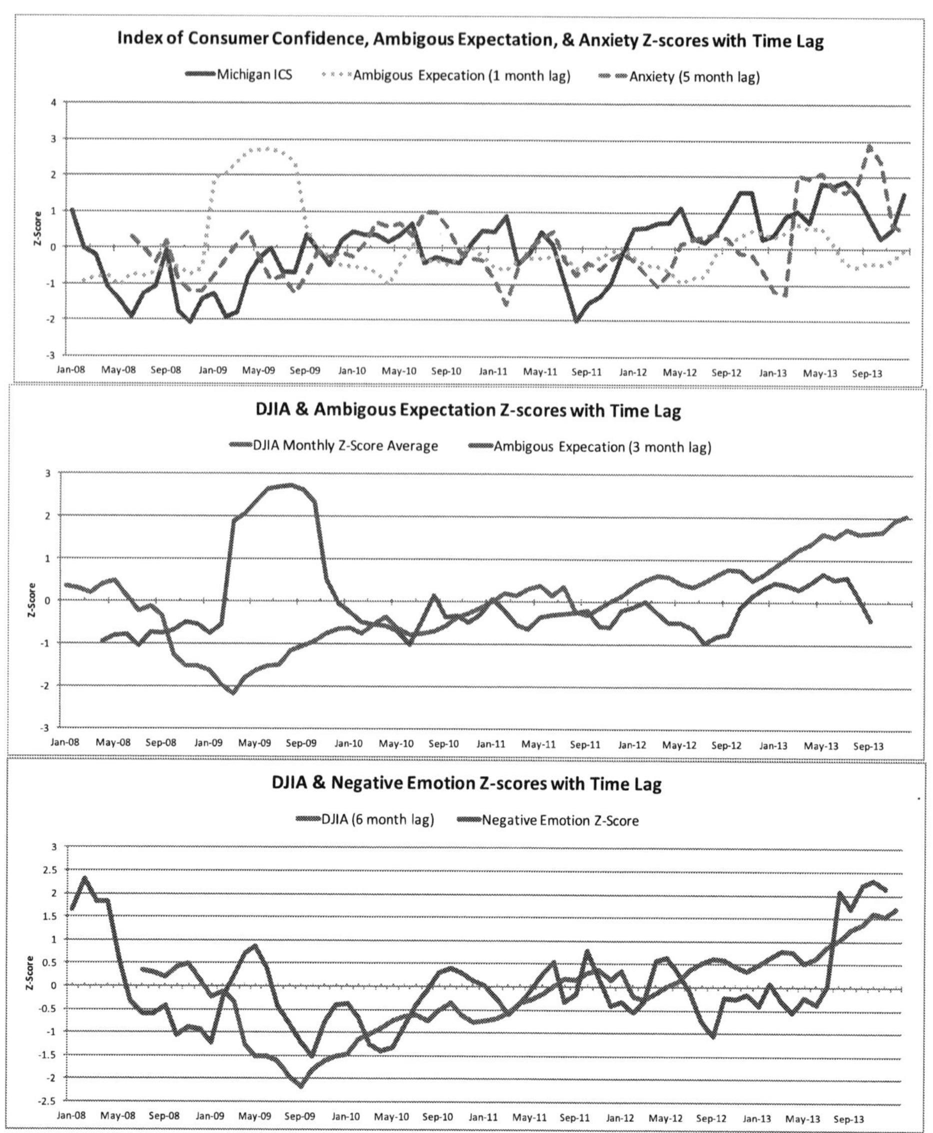



**Figure 4:** Plot of the X-month time lagged sentiments and DJIA or ICC

Granger-causal relationships between DJIA and hope. We presented both a multiple regression model and an improved VAR model that incorporate the multi-dimensional sentiment analysis components to DJIA and ICC. The model solidified our finding in regards to the role of anger in influencing the ICC and the role of sorrow in influencing the DJIA.

In future work, we plan to improve our prediction model by focusing on the features with known causal relationships. We also plan to explore other prediction models beyond VAR. We acknowledge that past work has shown that song lyrics use creative language, slang, and metaphors which typically are not accounted for by valance based sentiment analysis. We will integrate these factors in our modeling of the senti-ment of the song. All lyrics data can be retrieved by contacting the authors.

## References


Alberto Acerbi, Vasileios Lampos, Philip Garnett, and R. Alexander Bentley. 2013. The Expression of Emotions in 20th Century Books. *PLoS ONE*, 8(3):e59030, March.

Charles S. Areni and David Kim. 1993. The influence of background music on shopping behavior: classical versus top-forty music in a wine store. *Advances in consumer research*, 20(1):336–340.

Johan Bollen, Huina Mao, and Xiaojun Zeng. 2011. Twitter mood predicts the stock market. *Journal of Computational Science*, 2(1):1–8, March.

Gordon C. Bruner. 1990. Music, Mood, and Marketing. *Journal of Marketing*, 54(4):94–104.

Lei Chen, Shuhua Zhou, and Jennings Bryant. 2007. Temporal Changes in Mood Repair Through Music Consumption: Effects of Mood, Mood Salience, and Individual Differences. *Media Psychology*, 9(3):695–713, May.

Richard Curtin. 2004. Consumer Sentiment Surveys. In *articolo presentato alla 27 a conferenza del CIRET*, pages 15–18.

P. J. H. Daas and M. J. Puts. 2014. *Social Media Sentiment and Consumer Confidence. Statistics Paper Series, No. 5. European Centeral Bank.*

Xiao Hu and J. Stephen Downie. 2010. Improving Mood Classification in Music Digital Libraries by Combining Lyrics and Audio. In *Proceedings of the 10th Annual Joint Conference on Digital Libraries*, pages 159–168, New York, NY, USA. ACM.

Adrian C. North and David J. Hargreaves. 1997. Music and consumer behaviour.

Brendan O'Connor, Ramnath Balasubramanyan, Bryan R. Routledge, and Noah A. Smith. 2010. From tweets to polls: Linking text sentiment to public opinion time series. *ICWSM*, 11:122–129.

B. Barrios-Choplin R McCraty. 1998. The effects of different types of music on mood, tension, and mental clarity. *Alternative therapies in health and medicine*, 4(1):75–84.

John A. Sloboda. 2011. Music in Everyday Life: The Role of Emotions. In Patrik N. Juslin and John Sloboda, editors, *Handbook of Music and Emotion: Theory, Research, Applications*. OUP Oxford.

Carlo Strapparava and Alessandro Valitutti. 2004. WordNet Affect: an Affective Extension of WordNet. In *LREC*, volume 4, pages 1083–1086.

Trust, Gary. 2013. Ask Billboard: How Does The Hot 100 Work? September.

Theresa Wilson, Janyce Wiebe, and Paul Hoffmann. 2005. Recognizing Contextual Polarity in Phrase-Level Sentiment Analysis. In *Proceedings of HLT/EMNLP 2005*, pages 34–35. Association for Computational Linguistics.

Yunqing Xia, Linlin Wang, and Kam-Fai Wong. 2008. Sentiment Vector Space Model for Lyric-Based Song Sentiment Classification. *International Journal of Computer Processing of Languages*, 21(04):309–330, December.

Jiang Zhong, Yifeng Cheng, Siyuan Yang, and Luosheng Wen. 2012. Music sentiment classification integrating audio with lyrics. *Journal of Information and Computational Science*, 9:35–44.

# Fashioning Data – A Social Media Perspective on Fast Fashion Brands


**Rupak Chakraborty**
Adobe Systems Inc.
A5, Sector-132, Noida – 201304
rupak97.4@gmail.com

**Senjuti Kundu**
McGill University
506 Pine Avenue, Montreal, QC, H2W1S6
senjuti.kundu@mail.mcgill.ca

**Prakul Agarwal**
University of California, Irvine
Irvine, CA 92697, United States
prakula@uci.edu



## Abstract

In this paper, we study the performance of N-gram language models on classification tasks such as sentiment analysis and spam detection and evaluate the effect of prior probability estimates on the results. Our data is in the form of public online posts pertaining to fast fashion brands, from different social media channels (Twitter and Facebook). We propose a novel ensemble model based on the combination of different N-grams in order to deal with the heteroskedastic nature of data collected from these social media channels. This has been further extended to increase the efficacy of the classification results.


## 1 Introduction

In recent years, the rise of social media channels like Twitter, Facebook and Instagram have opened new avenues for people to express their opinions and generate their own content. Companies such as Simplymeasured (www.simplymeasured.com) and Gnip (www.gnip.com) aggregate data from different networks to help brands form a more complete understanding of how well they engage with users and perform online. Companies such as Metamind, Alchemy and Semantria provide online APIs for sentiment analysis and associated tasks.

Sentiment analysis is a growing area of Natural Language Processing with research ranging from document level classification (Pang and Lee [1]) to learning the polarity of words and phrases (Esuli and Sebastiani [2]). Given the character limitations on tweets, classifying the sentiment of Twitter messages is most similar to sentence-level sentiment analysis. Some researchers have explored the use of part-of-speech features [3] but results

remain mixed. Researchers in [4] and [5] have reported different ways of automatically collecting training data by relying on emoticons for defining the sentiment labels in their training data. However as per our observations the presence of an emoticon does not necessarily divulge its sentiment and hence we have taken the approach of manually labeling the training and test data. Da Silva et al. [6] have introduced an approach of using classifier ensembles to determine the sentiment of tweets. However they only consider a binary classification of tweets (i.e. positive and negative) and use a heterogeneous ensemble of classifiers like Multinomial Naïve Bayes, SVM, Logistic Regression and Random Forests.

Agarwal et al [7] propose a method of sentiment analysis using a tree kernel and a set of hand crafted POS features. Twitter hashtags have been extensively used in [8] to train a classifier using the Adaboost algorithm. In recent years several competitions like SemEval 2014 have included sentiment analysis of tweets as a major task. This has led to several state-of-the-art performances like [9] where the authors have used a Deep Learning approach using a combination of sentiment specific semantic word embeddings and hand crafted features. The authors in [10] have enhanced Twitter sentiment classification using contextual information like geolocation, timezones etc.

While a great deal of recent research has focused on sentiment analysis of Twitter data and spam detection (Wang et al [11]) less attention has been devoted to extending these classification tasks to public Facebook posts. Furthermore, while domains such as politics (Bakliwal et al. [12]; Yang et al. [13]) and sports (Hong and Skiena [14]) have received strong coverage, the genre of commercial

26


*Proceedings of NAACL-HLT 2016*, pages 26–35,
San Diego, California, June 12-17, 2016. ©2016 Association for Computational Linguistics

fashion brands has not been mined as frequently for predictive and classification tasks

The absence of literature on cross channel sentiment analysis with a special focus on the implications of prior distributions on the classification results has motivated us to undertake the following study. The niche segment of fast fashion brands was chosen because it remains largely unexplored. An attempt has been made to provide a clear comprehensive view of the performance metrics across different channels (Twitter and Facebook in our case) while noting the difference in trends among them.

The major contributions of the present work are as follows: We have collected and manually annotated a dataset[**] of posts from major social media channels (Twitter and Facebook). Our dataset was based on posts about fast fashion brands, thereby extending the application of sentiment analysis and spam detection to this infrequently-explored genre. The inclusion of more than one social channel provides a cross sectional view of the social media spectrum. It was also helpful in gauging the performance of the same algorithm on channels with disparate content (different in terms of syntactic and semantic structure).

We have extensively analyzed the effect of priors on the associated tasks and compared different N-gram models on many statistical performance metrics like Accuracy, Precision, Recall, Specificity and F1-score. Use of N-grams as features obviates the need for tedious feature engineering which often entails a classification task. The proposed generative ensemble model provides an easily implementable and lightweight framework which can be extended to any classification problem. This is because it does not make any implicit/explicit assumption about the nature or distribution of the data. Thus, we have developed a roadmap for cross channel text analysis and classification, thereby providing a unified and holistic view of any topic or subject (fashion brands in our case).

The key brands identified were fast fashion brands (Zara, Forever 21, H&M etc.) which target young customers in their late teens and early twenties and have a high turnover rate as part of their business strategy. We were particularly interested in studying this demographic since their customers frequently take to social media to express their satisfaction or dissatisfaction with products purchased. Due to the high turnover rate and short shelf-life of most of their products, opinions about their newest items are created every few months. This made data collection easier and more attuned to public opinion. We divide the paper as follows: In Section 2 we discuss the collection and distribution of data in details, we also include the steps taken for pre-processing the data, in Section 3 the algorithms used for spam detection and sentiment analysis have been detailed along with intuitive explanation of why they work, in Section 4 we present our experiments and observations which includes a detailed analysis of the proposed algorithm for each channel along with a cross channel view of different performance metrics, in Section 5 we conclude the paper.

## 2 Data Collection and Distribution

We collected data in the form of posts from Facebook and Twitter over a period of 3 months (August to November 2015). The nine selected fashion brands were Forever 21, Mango, Levis, H&M, Guess, Free People, True Religion, Rag & Bone and 7 For All Mankind.

We have used the official Twitter Search API to fetch the data. Tweets containing hashtags and names of the mentioned brands were selected. Apart from these we have sieved tweets containing the official Twitter handles of these brands. For example, searching by "@7fam" retrieves tweets containing the tag @7fam which corresponds to the official Twitter handle of 7 for all mankind.

In case of Facebook, posts were fetched from the official pages of the selected brands using the official Facebook Graph API. Since the brands advertise their latest arrivals through these pages the posts were filtered by the author names, so any self-advertising content has been excluded.

From our observations Twitter is a more fast paced channel (i.e. frequency of posts is more) in comparison to Facebook. This is reflected in the significantly lower number of Facebook posts. On the other hand Facebook posts are more informative and verbose compared to 140 character tweets.

Each post has been hand labelled. For sentiment analysis each post is assigned either of the three class labels positive, negative or neutral depending on the content. In case of spam detection it is assigned a binary label of spam and ham/not spam.

Each post has been labelled by two annotators. The average agreement between the two annotators has been observed to be 83.2%

We are not detecting spam in a traditional sense here, it is more of a word sense disambiguation. For example, we need to filter out posts pertaining to Mango the fruit from those relating to the actual denim brand. Similarly we need to distinguish between Levis stadium and Levis the company. As most of the fashion brand names we have selected are proper or common nouns the need to add this additional filter arose, which has been modelled as a spam detector. Additionally posts promoting freebies and advertising one's own fashion collection have been included in the category of spam because they do not contain useful opinion words or sentences and hence they introduce noise in the training data instead of adding value to it.

Each post is passed through a pre-processing pipeline before extracting the N-gram features. The salient steps in the pipeline are as follows – 1. Cleaning the data of URLs, HTML tags, punctuation marks, emoticons and similar noise. 2. Stopword removal (using an English stopword lexicon). 3. Stemming – Reducing each word to its root word using the Snowball Stemmer which is based on Porters Stemmer.

## 2.1 Distribution of the Training Data

**Table 1: Distribution of Train Data for Sentiment Analysis**

| Channel | Positive | Negative | Neutral | Total |
|---|---|---|---|---|
| Facebook | 165 (11%) | 46 (3%) | 1337 (86%) | 1548 |
| Twitter | 987 (27%) | 393 (11%) | 2893 (62%) | 3705 |

**Table 2: Distribution of Train Data for Spam Analysis**

| Channel | Spam | Ham | Total |
|---|---|---|---|
| Facebook | 253 (14%) | 1548 (86%) | 1801 |
| Twitter | 1220 (25%) | 3705 (75%) | 4925 |

Table 1 lists the distribution of training data (posts) for sentiment analysis as can be inferred, the class label distribution is highly skewed, majority of the posts are neutral for both the channels. The data for spam detection is equally biased (i.e. the majority of the posts are not spam) as can be seen in Table 2. This kind of a data distribution closely resembles real-life scenarios where majority of the online posts are likely to belong to a single class. Motivated by this skewed data distribution, an attempt has been made to make the classifier fairly invariant to class label distribution which led to the proposed ensemble model.

## 2.2 Distribution of the Test Data

**Table 3: Distribution of Test Data for Sentiment Analysis**

| Channel | Positive | Negative | Neutral | Total |
|---|---|---|---|---|
| Facebook | 192 (20%) | 67 (7%) | 712 (73%) | 970 |
| Twitter | 369 (23%) | 138 (8%) | 1120 (69%) | 1627 |

**Table 4: Distribution of Test Data for Spam Analysis**

| Channel | Spam | Ham | Total |
|---|---|---|---|
| Facebook | 41 (4%) | 970 (96%) | 1011 |
| Twitter | 613 (25%) | 1627 (75%) | 2440 |

The test data distribution closely tails the training data (as can be seen from tables 3 and 4). This provides a level ground for measuring model performance, though it would be interesting to see the performance on a uniformly distributed dataset. In order to get a clearer picture of classifier performance, metrics like precision and specificity have been included. This skewed distribution makes the effect of priors more prominent thereby enabling us to study them for our specific test conditions.

## 3. Algorithms

Naïve Bayes classifier with N-grams as the features has been used. Algorithm 1 (see section 3.1) is used to combine the output of different N-gram models in order to calculate a single class probability. Each classifier outputs two things: the probability of the most likely class and its corresponding class label. After experimenting with different N-gram models ($N = 1$ to $N = 7$), it can be seen that there is no significant gain in performance after $N = 5$ on the test data. So for the proposed algorithm N-gram models up to only order 5 have been used.

The use of Naïve Bayes as the classifier of choice has been motivated by the fact that our main intention is to study the effect of priors using N-gram features and Naïve Bayes has proven to be very effective for many text classification tasks, often matching state-of-the-art results obtained by using SVMs and the like. Algorithm 1 proposed aggregates the outputs of all the classifiers (each classifier is trained on a different N-gram model, with values of N ranging from 1 to 5) and predicts the final class label as the one which has highest probability among the five input class labels.

The reason why this approach increases the performance is - N-gram models match the N-grams in the test sample with the probabilities of the N-grams calculated during training, thus a larger posterior probability implies a greater degree of match of the N-grams of the test sample with the training set. Hence, intuitively a greater probability increases the likelihood that the model has seen a similar post/sample during training, so taking the class label of the maximum probable N-gram as the final prediction increases the chances of a correct classification. The algorithms have been presented in the form of a pseudocode where each step has been clearly mentioned, it has been further grouped into separate training and testing phases (with additional hyperparameter adjustment phase wherever necessary). Algorithm 2 (see section 3.2) is our proposed ensemble algorithm which is built on top of Algorithm 1.

### 3.1 Algorithm 1: Combining Different N-grams

**Training Phase:**

**Input:** Training data after being passed through the preprocessing pipeline. Each sample consists of N-gram features and its associated class label.

**Output:** Trained N-gram models (N = 1 to N =5) using the maximum likelihood probability estimate followed by add one smoothing.

**Testing Phase**:

**Input:** An unknown test sample.

**Output:** The class label (of the most likely class) to which the sample belongs.

**Step 1:** For a given test sample calculate the pair *(Pi, Ci)* where *Pi* is the probability value

output of the *ith* N-gram model (in our case *i* = 1 to 5) and *Ci* is its corresponding class label. So we will have five such pairs of *(Pi, Ci)*.

**Step 2:** Find the max value of *Pi* and take its corresponding *Ci* to be the final class label.

**Step 3:** Output the class label calculated in the Step 2

Algorithm 1 proposed cannot effectively deal with the skewness in the data. This is because it is trained on the entire dataset and hence its performance is limited by and equal to the best performing N-gram model (which is N = 5 in most cases across both classification tasks). In order to deal with the inherent single class bias of the dataset the training data has been randomly split into N mutually exclusive and exhaustive parts. N-gram models have been trained on each of these N parts using Algorithm 1 and the weighted output of these N-gram models has been used to predict the final class label. The proposed algorithm for ensemble learning includes a hyper-parameter adjustment phase where the weight of each model is calculated based on its performance on a held out set.

Randomly splitting up the training data into mutually exclusive and exhaustive parts reduces the effect of a single class bias which is prevalent in the data. By training individual models on each of these disjoint parts of the feature space, each model receives the unique ability to learn the final hypothesis differently. This prevents overfitting the data which often plagues individual N-gram models trained on the entire dataset. The weights of the models are tuned as per their performance on a held out set. Hence, the predictions of well performing models are given more weightage in comparison to those with lower performance on the held out set. Taking the final prediction (i.e. final class label) as the modal (most frequently occurring class) class label of the weighted output of the individual models ensures that the predicted class label is the one on which majority of the models agree upon. Thus, in spirit our ensemble model works in the same way as Random Forests [15] which have shown to be better at learning final hypothesis in comparison to individual decision trees.

## 3.2 Algorithm 2: Ensemble of Combined N-Grams

**Training Phase:**

**Input**: Training data after being passed through the preprocessing pipeline. Each sample consists of N-gram features and its associated class label

**Output**: A total of K N-gram models each trained using Algorithm 1.

**Step 1**: Randomly split the training dataset into N mutually exclusive and exhaustive parts.
**Step 2**: For each part $N_i$ train model $K_i$ by Algorithm 1.
**Step 3**: Save these models for testing and later use.

**Hyper parameter Adjustment Phase:**

**Input**: Trained models $K_i$ and held out dataset.

**Output**: Model Weights $W_i$ corresponding to each $K_i$

**Step 1**: For each model $K_i$ calculate the number of correct predictions ($Xi$) and the number of incorrect predictions ($Yi$).
**Step 2**: Calculate weight $W_i$ of each model as
$e^{xi/(yi+1)}$
**Step 3**: Save the model weights $W_i$


**Testing Phase:**

**Input**: An unknown test sample.

**Output**: The class label (of the most likely class) to which the sample belongs.

**Initialize**: $f = \{ \}$ (Empty List to hold the class labels)

**Step 1**: For each model $K_i$ calculate the class label $C_i$ using Algorithm 1.
**Step 2**: For each $K_i$ let $Q_i = W_i \times C_i$ (i.e. each class label $C_i$ is counted $W_i$ times)
**Step 3**: For each $K_i$ $f = f \cup Q_i$ (i.e. Add the class label computed in Step 2 to the list)
**Step 4**: Output the final predicted class label as the modal class of $f$

## 4. Experiments and Results

N-gram models have been trained for different values of N (N = 1 to N = 7). During the classification phase using the Naïve Bayes classifier, we have experimented under two conditions
1. Calculating the class label probabilities while discounting the prior probabilities learned during the training phase (i.e. assuming equal prior class distribution). 2. Taking the prior probabilities into account while calculating the class label probabilities.
In order to get a clear insight into the effects of priors on different classification tasks across different channels, we have studied each scenario independently. First we present the results of each channel separately on the twin classification tasks then we provide a cross channel view of the effect of priors.

### 4.1 Results for Facebook

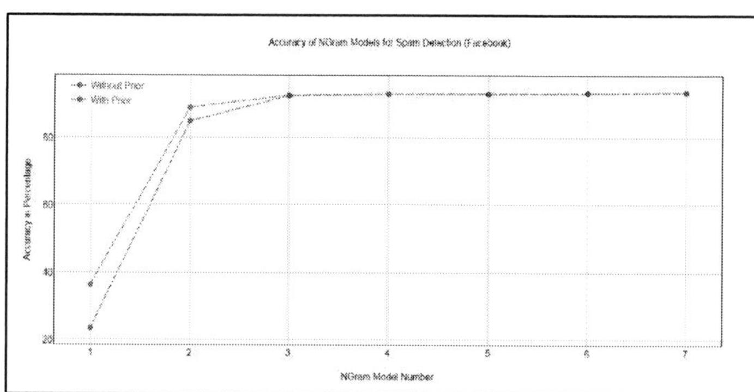

**Figure 1: Comparison of N-gram Models for Spam Detection on Facebook**

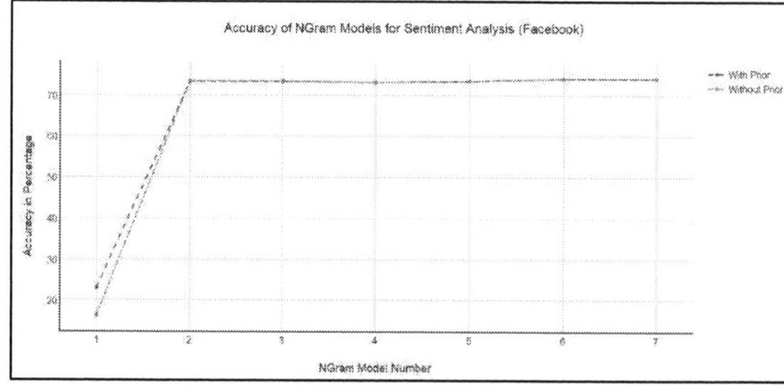

**Figure 2: Comparison of N-gram Models for Sentiment Analysis on Facebook**

Figure 1 illustrates the performance (in terms of accuracy) of different N-gram models for spam detection on Facebook, as can be seen from the figure the effect of priors is more profound on the unigrams and bigrams in comparison to the higher order N-grams. Another notable feature is how the performance almost plateaus after N=4 for both cases (i.e. taking the prior into account and discounting the prior). Figure 2 juxtaposes the performance of different N-gram models for sentiment analysis on Facebook, it follows the same trend as in figure 1 but the overall classification accuracy is less in this case, the best performing N-gram model (N = 7) has an accuracy of 74.15% for sentiment analysis while it is 93.28% (for N = 7) in case of spam detection . The obvious reason for this is that spam detection is a two class classification problem (only 2 class labels spam and ham), while sentiment analysis is a three way classification task (positive, negative and neutral class labels). Thus, priors play an important role in the prediction of classes especially if the data is highly biased (as in our case).

**Table 5. Performance Metrics for Sentiment Analysis of Facebook Posts (Without Priors)**

| N-gram Model Number | Accuracy | Precision | Recall | Specificity | F1Score |
|---|---|---|---|---|---|
| 1 | 16.27 | 37.57 | 47.37 | 26.19 | 41.91 |
| 2 | 73.53 | 64.16 | 59.74 | 65.21 | 61.87 |
| 3 | 73.53 | 64.11 | 42.94 | 60.28 | 51.44 |
| 4 | 73.22 | 62.88 | 39.64 | 59.14 | 48.62 |
| 5 | 73.53 | 63.60 | 39.65 | 59.29 | 48.85 |
| 6 | 74.15 | 65.81 | 39.93 | 59.77 | 49.70 |
| 7 | 74.15 | 66.12 | 39.68 | 59.59 | 49.59 |

**Table 6. Performance Metrics for Sentiment Analysis of Facebook Posts (With Priors)**

| N-gram Model Number | Accuracy | Precision | Recall | Specificity | F1Score |
|---|---|---|---|---|---|
| 1 | 22.96 | 42.66 | 51.99 | 32.66 | 46.87 |
| 2 | 73.32 | 65.94 | 49.63 | 62.01 | 56.64 |
| 3 | 73.42 | 64.87 | 42.20 | 59.93 | 51.13 |
| 4 | 73.22 | 62.88 | 39.64 | 59.14 | 48.62 |
| 5 | 73.53 | 63.60 | 39.65 | 59.29 | 48.85 |
| 6 | 74.15 | 65.81 | 39.93 | 59.77 | 49.70 |
| 7 | 74.15 | 66.12 | 39.68 | 59.59 | 49.59 |

Tables 5 and 6 elucidates the performance metrics of N-gram models for sentiment analysis on Facebook, in order to evaluate the effect of priors on different N-gram models, we take the results of table 5 as the baseline. There is a spike in the accuracy of unigrams (41% over the baseline) while for the rest there is marginal (in case of bigrams and trigrams) or no decrease (for N >= 4). The same trend is visible across other performance parameters like precision, recall and specificity. A possible explanation for this behavior is that Facebook posts are mostly highly structured (i.e. in proper English) in comparison to tweets and hence higher order N-grams effectively model the language structure which obviates the effects of prior probabilities as is evident from the results.

**Table 7. Performance Metrics for Spam Detection of Facebook Posts (Without Priors)**

| N-gram Model Number | Accuracy | Precision | Recall | Specificity | F1Score |
|---|---|---|---|---|---|
| 1 | 23.22 | 48.60 | 43.99 | 44.81 | 46.18 |
| 2 | 84.78 | 52.30 | 56.71 | 57.07 | 54.42 |
| 3 | 92.29 | 52.48 | 52.65 | 52.81 | 52.56 |
| 4 | 92.78 | 53.04 | 52.90 | 53.07 | 52.97 |
| 5 | 92.88 | 52.05 | 51.82 | 51.95 | 51.93 |
| 6 | 93.08 | 52.29 | 51.92 | 52.06 | 52.11 |
| 7 | 93.28 | 52.55 | 52.28 | 52.16 | 52.28 |

Tables 7 and 8 depict the performance of spam detection on Facebook they are exactly are in the same vein as the results for sentiment analysis. There is a massive increase in the accuracy for unigrams (56%) when we include priors into the equation however this has side effects of decreasing the precision and recall.

**Table 8. Performance Metrics for Spam Detection of Facebook Posts (With Priors)**

| N-gram Model Number | Accuracy | Precision | Recall | Specificity | F1Score |
|---|---|---|---|---|---|
| 1 | 36.26 | 48.57 | 41.67 | 42.27 | 44.86 |
| 2 | 88.83 | 54.16 | 58.82 | 59.18 | 56.39 |
| 3 | 92.39 | 52.58 | 52.70 | 52.86 | 52.64 |
| 4 | 92.78 | 53.04 | 52.90 | 53.07 | 52.97 |
| 5 | 92.88 | 52.05 | 51.82 | 51.95 | 51.93 |
| 6 | 93.08 | 52.29 | 51.92 | 52.06 | 52.10 |
| 7 | 93.28 | 52.02 | 52.02 | 52.16 | 52.28 |

**Table 9: Performance Metrics for Sentiment Analysis on Facebook (Proposed Method i.e. Algorithm 2)**

| Ensemble Model | Accuracy | Precision | Recall | Specificity | F1-Score |
|---|---|---|---|---|---|
| Without Prior | 66.69 | 51.94 | 60.95 | 61.65 | 56.09 |
| With Prior | 88.04 | 50.77 | 51.57 | 51.76 | 51.17 |

**Table 10: Performance Metrics for Spam Detection on Facebook (Proposed Method i.e. Algorithm 2)**

| Ensemble Model | Accuracy | Precision | Recall | Specificity | F1-Score |
|---|---|---|---|---|---|
| Without Prior | 56.95 | 49.62 | 65.78 | 58.68 | 56.57 |
| With Prior | 76.10 | 62.61 | 66.73 | 68.66 | 64.61 |

Tables 9 and 10 depict the performance of the proposed method on sentiment analysis and spam detection respectively. The improvements by including priors is measured against the baseline of discounting priors. Though there is an improvement in accuracy for both classification tasks, however the precision, recall and specificity in case of spam detection decreases marginally. There is an increase of 33.62% in accuracy for sentiment analysis whereas for spam detection there is a leap of 32.01%. Precision for sentiment analysis improves by 26.17% whereas for spam detection a decline of 2% is noted. Recall and specificity improvements for sentiment analysis is negligible hovering somewhere around 1%. However in case of spam detection both decrease by 1.5% and 1.6% respectively, this may be attributed to the overwhelming presence of ham labels in the test data (about 75%).Thus, as a general trend the effect of priors becomes more dominant with the increase in the number of classes in data especially if the distribution of class labels is skewed.

Facebook has unique challenges in comparison to Twitter. First the verbosity of the posts in comparison to 140 character tweets is something which needs to be taken into account. It takes a longer time to make predictions because of the greater number of N-grams. Second, the posts are in proper English and the use of emoticons and acronyms is less in comparison to Twitter.

## 4.2 Results for Twitter

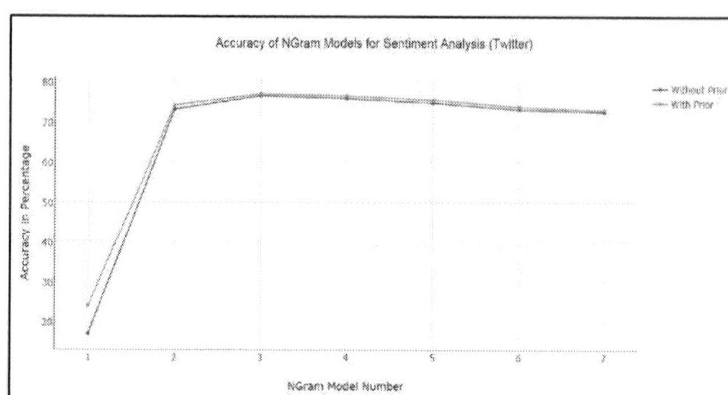

**Figure 3: Comparison of N-gram Models for Sentiment Analysis of Tweets**

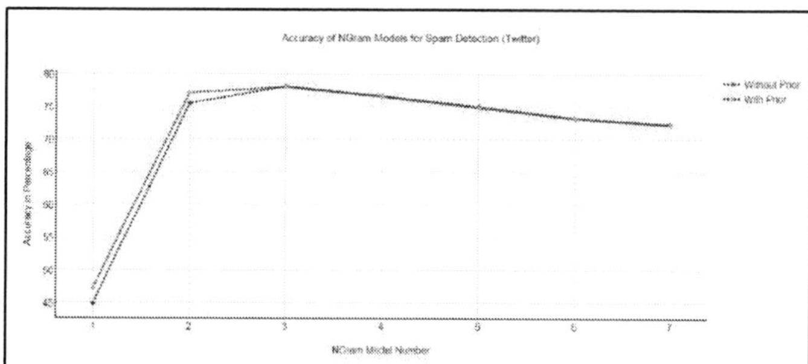

**Figure 4: Comparison of N-gram Models for Spam Detection of Tweets**

Figures 3 and 4 depict the performance of N-gram models for sentiment analysis and spam detection on Twitter data, they follow the same general trend as the N-gram models for Facebook. Similarly the exclusion of prior probabilities (i.e. considering equal prior distribution for all classes) has a deeper impact on the lower order N-grams in comparison to the higher order N-grams (N >= 3). The intuitive reason for this may be that unigrams and bigrams assume a higher degree of conditional independence of the different words in a sentence hence, cannot effectively model the syntactic and semantic level dependencies of the language. The differentiating factor of the Twitter N-gram models is that their performance decreases for higher order N-grams (N >= 3) whereas in case of Facebook it is almost constant. Also the overall accuracy of the Twitter models is less than the Facebook ones both in case of sentiment analysis and spam detection.

**Table 11: Performance Metrics for Sentiment Analysis of Tweets (Without Priors)**

| N-gram Model Number | Accuracy | Precision | Recall | Specificity | F1Score |
|---|---|---|---|---|---|
| 1 | 16.95 | 37.46 | 40.05 | 23.01 | 38.71 |
| 2 | 73.21 | 69.41 | 69.55 | 71.49 | 69.48 |
| 3 | 76.65 | 75.08 | 69.02 | 73.27 | 71.92 |
| 4 | 75.98 | 74.47 | 66.61 | 71.66 | 70.32 |
| 5 | 74.87 | 73.34 | 61.99 | 69.24 | 67.19 |
| 6 | 73.21 | 72.04 | 57.93 | 66.17 | 64.22 |
| 7 | 72.65 | 71.86 | 54.65 | 64.52 | 62.09 |

**Table 12: Performance Metrics for Sentiment Analysis of Tweets (With Priors)**

| N-gram Model Number | Accuracy | Precision | Recall | Specificity | F1Score |
|---|---|---|---|---|---|
| 1 | 23.95 | 34.65 | 40.72 | 28.96 | 37.44 |
| 2 | 74.26 | 71.81 | 67.98 | 71.44 | 69.84 |
| 3 | 77.14 | 75.67 | 68.47 | 73.34 | 71.89 |
| 4 | 76.65 | 75.33 | 66.37 | 71.92 | 70.56 |
| 5 | 75.61 | 74.42 | 61.89 | 69.62 | 67.58 |
| 6 | 73.89 | 73.19 | 57.92 | 66.59 | 64.67 |
| 7 | 73.09 | 72.94 | 54.17 | 64.70 | 62.17 |

**Table 13: Performance Metrics for Spam Detection of Twitter Posts (Without Priors)**

| N-gram Model Number | Accuracy | Precision | Recall | Specificity | F1Score |
|---|---|---|---|---|---|
| 1 | 44.89 | 51.99 | 51.87 | 51.92 | 51.93 |
| 2 | 75.46 | 73.51 | 68.02 | 68.08 | 70.66 |
| 3 | 78.08 | 82.32 | 68.36 | 68.42 | 74.69 |
| 4 | 76.60 | 81.45 | 66.03 | 66.08 | 72.93 |
| 5 | 75.01 | 80.43 | 63.51 | 63.56 | 70.98 |
| 6 | 73.24 | 79.29 | 60.71 | 60.76 | 68.77 |
| 7 | 72.34 | 79.09 | 59.21 | 59.25 | 67.72 |

**Table 14: Performance Metrics for Spam Detection of Twitter Posts (With Priors)**

| N-gram Model Number | Accuracy | Precision | Recall | Specificity | F1Score |
|---|---|---|---|---|---|
| 1 | 47.23 | 50.77 | 50.82 | 50.87 | 50.87 |
| 2 | 77.08 | 77.14 | 68.67 | 68.72 | 72.66 |
| 3 | 77.95 | 82.31 | 68.15 | 68.20 | 74.56 |
| 4 | 76.52 | 81.82 | 65.78 | 65.83 | 72.93 |
| 5 | 74.80 | 80.36 | 63.17 | 63.22 | 70.74 |
| 6 | 73.16 | 79.36 | 60.56 | 60.60 | 68.70 |
| 7 | 72.22 | 78.94 | 59.02 | 59.07 | 67.54 |

For sentiment analysis the best performing Facebook model (N = 7) achieves an accuracy of 74.15% whereas the Twitter N-gram has an accuracy of 76.65%, in case of spam detection the accuracy is 93.28% and 77.95% for Facebook and Twitter respectively. Tables 11 and 12 illustrate the performance of different N-gram models for sentiment analysis, as can be seen the effect of priors is deeper on unigrams and bigrams in comparison to the higher order N-grams. By taking the performance of the N-grams without prior (table 11) as the baseline we notice the following improvements – for unigrams there is a massive improvement in accuracy (41.30%) but at the cost of a decrease in precision of 7.47%. For rest of the N-grams (N >= 2) a marginal increase in accuracy (1.42% to 0.64%) entails an increase in precision and specificity, with an expected dip in recall (2.25% to 0.05%).

Tables 13 and 14 describe the performance of the N-gram models for spam detection, the performance gain for unigrams and bigrams is marginal while it decreases for rest of the higher order N-grams when taking the priors into account. This is consistent with the general trend for Twitter as shown in [16]. The decrease in accuracy (for N >= 3) is in tandem with the dip in the precision, recall, specificity and f1-score.Unigrams perform uniquely while including the priors, there is an increase in accuracy of 5.1% while the precision decreases by 2.36% at the same time.

**Table 15: Performance Metrics for Sentiment Analysis of Tweets (Proposed Method i.e. Algorithm 2)**

| Ensemble Model | Accuracy | Precision | Recall | Specificity | F1-Score |
|---|---|---|---|---|---|
| Without Prior | 47.42 | 47.16 | 56.65 | 51.44 | 51.44 |
| With Prior | 62.03 | 52.22 | 54.50 | 59.96 | 53.33 |

**Table 16: Performance Metrics for Spam Detection of Tweets (Proposed Method i.e. Algorithm 2)**

| Ensemble Model | Accuracy | Precision | Recall | Specificity | F1-Score |
|---|---|---|---|---|---|
| Without Prior | 69.76 | 68.61 | 70.82 | 70.88 | 69.69 |
| With Prior | 75.01 | 72.58 | 67.93 | 67.99 | 70.18 |

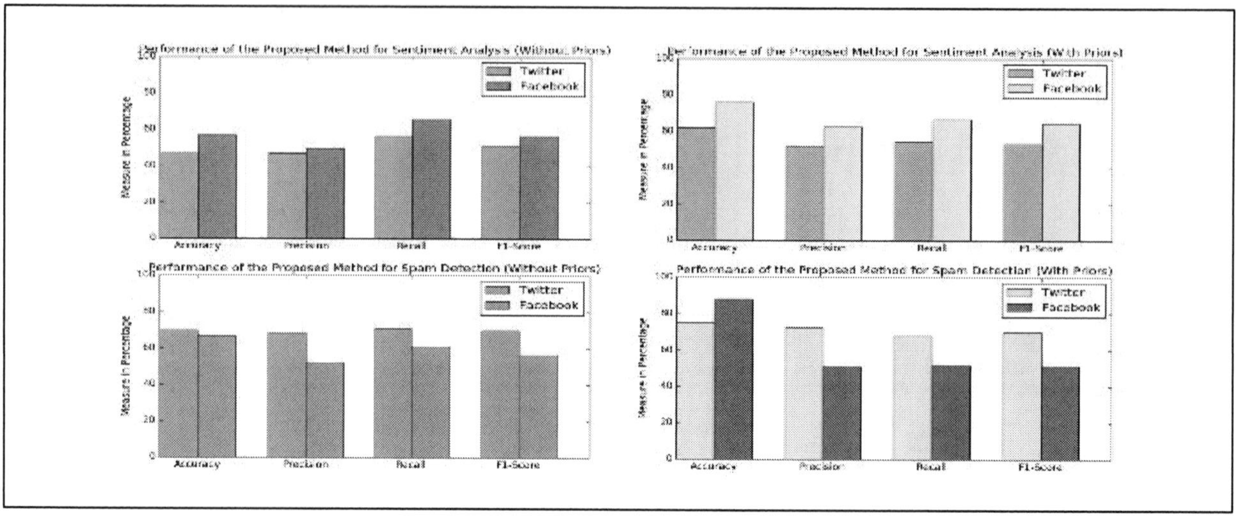

**Figure 5. Compares the relative performance of the proposed method across the channels (Twitter and Facebook) for the twin tasks of sentiment analysis and spam detection. The first row contains results of sentiment analysis under two conditions considering the prior probability and discounting it. The second row juxtaposes the results for spam detection for the same channels under the same conditions. They have been compared across four performance metrics like Accuracy, Precision, Recall and F1-measure.**

Tables 15 and 16 depict the performance of the proposed algorithm for sentiment analysis and spam detection respectively. As stated before, they are compared under two given conditions including the priors and excluding them. In order to compare the effect of priors on the proposed model, the performance of the proposed ensemble algorithm while discounting priors is set as the baseline. Inclusion of prior probabilities in the proposed model has a marked improvement in accuracy and precision, while there is a marginal improvement in the f1 measure. For sentiment analysis there is a leap of 30.80% in the accuracy while for spam detection an improvement of only 7.5% has been observed. Precision for sentiment analysis increases by 10.72% while for spam detection an increase of 5.78% in seen. Recall decreases as the precision improves since they are inversely proportional to each other, the decrease in recall for spam detection is 4.08% while for sentiment analysis it is 3.79%. Another notable thing in case of spam detection is the decrease in specificity by 4.07% which means it classifies some spam tweets as ham, although it is acceptable in our use case since we are not doing spam detection in a traditional sense.F1 measure for sentiment analysis increases by 3.67% while for spam detection is it a meagre 0.7%.

An important thing to note about Twitter is that the proposed algorithm does not perform as well as the naïve N-grams (in terms of accuracy and precision) for both the tasks of spam detection and sentiment analysis.

For sentiment analysis the proposed method with priors has an accuracy of 62% while for N-gram it has an accuracy of 76.60% (for N = 3).in case of spam detection the difference is marginal in terms of accuracy but more profound for precision, 72% versus 83.31% (for trigrams).

### 4.3 Cross Channel View of Results

Figure 5 illustrates a cross channel view of the proposed method under two experimental conditions (with and without considering the prior probability distributions) and across a set of four performance metrics - accuracy, precision, recall and f1-measure. As is evident from the figure, for sentiment analysis the Facebook models outperform the Twitter models by a sizable margin however the tables are turned in case of spam detection where the Twitter models are the clear winner across the different metrics. The only metric where they lag behind Facebook is in the case of accuracy (while taking priors into account).

An important conclusion to draw from the given results is that priors affect not only accuracy but also precision and recall – which are perhaps more important metrics for a classifier. Priors also affect different channels differently: the effects are more significant for Facebook than Twitter (in terms of increase of accuracy precision and specificity. For small datasets the priors have been found to be more effective than large uniform datasets.)

In the proposed algorithm since we are training each model on a random subset of the dataset the prior probability distribution is different for each model hence their impact is much more significant in comparison to vanilla N-grams which are trained on the entire dataset.

## 5   Conclusion and Future Work

In the future we plan to extend our work to include other social media channels like Instagram and Reddit in order to study the effect of the proposed algorithm on other datasets, thereby providing a more comprehensive view of the performance of our classification strategy across the social media spectrum. It will be interesting to see the performance of the proposed algorithm on a larger dataset and validate if the results reported here are consistent with the increase in data size.
The data preprocessing pipeline can be enhanced by the addition of emoticon detectors, acronym lexicons and spell checkers. In place of the currently used naïve Add One smoothing, other sophisticated smoothing techniques such as Good-Turing, Witten-Bell and modified Keysner smoothing could be used.

The accuracy rate can also be improved by augmenting the feature set using POS tags, word polarity and punctuation marks. The effect of including hashtags, in case of Twitter, could also be studied. The proposed ensemble model can be further improved by adjusting the hyper-parameters of each individual model to reflect the accuracy on a per class basis (not using average accuracy as is presently done), thereby enabling each model to respond to different class labels differently. Additionally we would also like to explore a smarter way of combining the output of the ensemble by using a neural gating network as is often done.

## Acknowledgments

The authors would like to thank their family, friends and colleagues for their constant help and support.

## References

[1] Pang, B., and Lee, L. 2008. Opinion mining and sentiment analysis. *Foundations and Trends in Information Retrieval* 2(1-2):1–135.

[2] Esuli, A., and Sebastiani, F. 2006. SentiWordNet: A publicly available lexical resource for opinion mining. In *Proceedings* of LREC.

[3] Barbosa, L., and Feng, J. 2010. Robust sentiment detection on Twitter from biased and noisy data. In *Proc. of Coling*.

[4] Bifet, A., and Frank, E. 2010. Sentiment knowledge discovery in Twitter streaming data. In *Proc. of 13th International Conference on Discovery Science*.

[5] Pak, A., and Paroubek, P. 2010. Twitter as a corpus for sentiment analysis and opinion mining. *In Proc. of LREC*

[6] Da Silva, Nadia FF, Eduardo R. Hruschka, and Estevam R. Hruschka. "Tweet sentiment analysis with classifier ensembles." *Decision Support Systems* 66 (2014): 170-179.

[7] Agarwal, A., Xie, B., Vovsha, I., Rambow, O., and Passonneau, R. 2011. Sentiment analysis of Twitter data. Proceedings of the Workshop on Languages in Social Media (LSM '11). *Association for Computational Linguistics*, Stroudsburg, PA, USA, 30-38.

[8] Kouloumpis, Efthymios, Theresa Wilson, and Johanna Moore. "Twitter sentiment analysis: The good the bad and the omg!." *Icwsm 11* (2011): 538-541.

[9] Tang, Duyu, et al. "Coooolll: A deep learning system for Twitter sentiment classification." *Proceedings of the 8th International Workshop on Semantic Evaluation (SemEval 2014)*. 2014.

[10] Vosoughi, Soroush, Helen Zhou, and Deb Roy. "Enhanced Twitter sentiment classification using contextual information." *Association for Computational Linguistics*, 2015.

[11] Wang, Alex Hai. "Don't follow me: Spam detection in Twitter." Security and Cryptography (SECRYPT), Proceedings of the 2010 *International Conference on. IEEE*, 2010.

[12] Bakliwal, Akshat, et al. "Sentiment analysis of political tweets: Towards an accurate classifier." *Association for Computational Linguistics*, 2013.

[13] Yu, Yang, and Xiao Wang. "World Cup 2014 in the Twitter World: A big data analysis of sentiments in US sports fans' tweets." *Computers in Human Behavior* 48 (2015): 392-400.

[14] Hong, Yancheng, and Steven Skiena. "The wisdom of bookies? sentiment analysis vs. the NFL point spread." *Proceedings of the international conference on Weblogs and Social media (icWSm-2010)*. 2010.

[15] Breiman, Leo. "Random forests." *Machine learning* 45.1 (2001): 5-32

[16] Martínez-Cámara, Eugenio, et al. "Sentiment analysis in Twitter." *Natural Language Engineering* 20.01 (2014): 1-28.

# Deep Learning for Sentiment Analysis - Invited Talk

**Richard Socher**
MetaMind
richard@socher.org

Richard Socher is the CEO and founder of Meta-Mind, a startup that seeks to improve artificial intelligence and make it widely accessible. He obtained his PhD from Stanford working on deep learning with Chris Manning and Andrew Ng and won the best Stanford CS PhD thesis award. He is interested in developing new AI models that perform well across multiple different tasks in natural language processing and computer vision.

He was awarded the Distinguished Application Paper Award at the International Conference on Machine Learning (ICML) 2011, the 2011 Yahoo! Key Scientific Challenges Award, a Microsoft Research PhD Fellowship in 2012 and a 2013 "Magic Grant" from the Brown Institute for Media Innovation and the 2014 GigaOM Structure Award.



*Proceedings of NAACL-HLT 2016*, page 36,
San Diego, California, June 12-17, 2016. ©2016 Association for Computational Linguistics

# Sentiment Lexicon Creation using Continuous Latent Space and Neural Networks

**Pedro Miguel Dias Cardoso**
Synthesio / 8 rue Villedo, Paris
pedro@synthesio.com

**Anindya Roy**
Synthesio / 8 rue Villedo, Paris
aroy@synthesio.com

## Abstract

This work presents a novel approach for automatic creation of sentiment word lists. In this approach, words are first mapped into a continuous latent space, which serves as input to a multilayer perceptron (MLP) trained using sentiment-annotated words. When evaluated using manually annotated EmoLex corpus, our approach compares favourably with SentiWordNet 3.0, another automatically generated word list.

## 1 Introduction

Many of the state of the art sentiment analysis systems uses input features based on sentiment word lists (Mohammad et al., 2013). While such lists may be manually curated, automatic approaches are privileged if large lists need to be generated. SentiWordNet 3.0 (Baccianella et al., 2010) is an example of such an automatically generated sentiment word list.

In this work, we present a novel approach for automatic generation of sentiment word lists. In this approach, words are mapped into a continuous latent space using two embedding methods Word2Vec (Mikolov et al., 2013a)(Mikolov et al., 2013b) and GloVe (Pennington et al., 2014). The mappings are given as input to a MLP trained using sentiment annotated words, which outputs a sentiment class or score for each word. Results show that our method can create large sentiment lexicons with higher accuracy.

The method is based on a small annotated lexicon and large un-labeled corpora. Hence, it could be easily applied to domain-specific contexts or under-resourced languages.

## 2 Related Work

### 2.1 Word embeddings

In classical vector space representation of text, individual words directly correspond to dimensions in the feature vector. This approach does not take into account the *semantic* proximity between words. Recent advances have tried to overcome this limitation by representing words as points in continuous latent space, where proximity between points in space indicates *semantic* proximity e.g. Word2Vec. However, these systems based on word context do not necessarily encode word *sentiment* information. For example, based on word distances in a 300-dimensional latent space, the word "good" is closest to "bad" because "good" and "bad" are often found in similar contexts. In this work, we leverage the advantage of continuous latent spaces but add a MLP to infuse sentiment information.

### 2.2 Sentiment classification and word lists

Initially, sentiment classification was approached as a *document* classification problem. An early study of sentiment classification (Pang et al., 2002) compared Naive Bayes, Logistic Regression and Support Vector Machine (SVM) classifiers. An early example of sentiment analysis using *microblogs* is presented in (Pandey and Iyer, 2009). A comprehensive review of recent developments is presented in (Vinodhini and Chandrasekaran, 2012).

Recently, sentiment classification has seen increased use of word lists with associated sentiment

37

*Proceedings of NAACL-HLT 2016*, pages 37–42,
San Diego, California, June 12-17, 2016. ©2016 Association for Computational Linguistics

values, set either manually or automatically. Among automatic methods, (Turney and Littman, 2003) and (Esuli and Sebastiani, 2006) compute word sentiment based on context of known sentiment words using Pointwise Mutual Information. In (Mohammad et al., 2013), specific Twitter hashtags with positive or negative sentiment were exploited. In our experiments, we use SentiWordNet 3.0 (Baccianella et al., 2010). SentiWordNet was built in two steps, a first semi-supervised step and a second random walk step. Sentiment values of a set of seed words (Turney and Littman, 2003) were propagated using WordNet's binary relations.[1] Propagated labels were used to train a classifier which was applied on all words. The second step is a random walk on WordNet, where sentiment is propagated if most of the terms used to define a given term and the term itself are of a specific sentiment value. SentiWordNet is publicly available.

## 2.3 Word embeddings for sentiment

Works which use word embeddings for sentiment classification include (Amir et al., 2014) where the Word2Vec vector of all words present in the document are summed and used to detect sentiment. In (Irsoy and Cardie, 2014) Recursive Neural Networks are used with Word2Vec as input. In (Tang et al., 2014b) and (Tang et al., 2014a), tweets are represented using *sentiment-specific* word embeddings. Note that these approaches deal with sentiment classification of *documents*. In contrast, our work uses word embeddings with MLP for sentiment classification of *words*. Furthermore, (Tang et al., 2014b) requires *sentiment-annotated* corpora to learn latent space embeddings, while our approach uses unsupervised methods which may be trained using any suitable unannotated corpora.

## 3 Methodology

We created two MLP-based systems to estimate sentiment value of words. The first is a classifier system that predicts sentiment class (positive, negative, neutral). The second is a regressor system predicting a sentiment value for each word in a continuous range. The classifier and regressor systems use as inputs two different word representations in em-

| Lexicon | Training Data | | | Evaluation Data | | |
|---|---|---|---|---|---|---|
| | Neg | Neu | Pos | Neg | Neu | Pos |
| SynthesioLex | 3544 | 2204 | 1500 | 880 | 552 | 375 |
| EmoLex | 2591 | 6146 | 1845 | 648 | 1537 | 462 |
| MxDiff | 260 | | 431 | 62 | | 109 |

**Table 1:** Classification lexicon size

bedded continuous space: Word2Vec[2] model trained with 100 billion tokens and GloVe[3] trained with two corpora, one containing 42 billion tokens and second containing 840 billion tokens. The two represent each word in a 300-dimensional space.

### 3.1 Lexicons

For classification experiments, we use two lexicons. First one is curated by us over time and denoted in this work by SynthesioLex. It contains positive, negative or neutral sentiment class for each word. The second, EmoLex (Mohammad and Turney, 2013), is a publicly available lexicon[4]. For each word it contains a combination of sentiment tonality (positive, negative) and one of eight possible emotion classes (anger, anticipation, disgust, fear, joy, sadness, surprise, trust) for each word. In case of neutral words, all labels for tonality and emotion are 0. We keep only words that have sentiment tonality value and neutral ones. For regression, we use publicly available MaxDiff lexicon (Kiritchenko et al., 2014)[5]. It contains words with sentiment value in a continuous range from -1 to 1 and from 0 to 1 obtained manually by crowdsourcing (Orme, 2009). Table 1 gives more details about each lexicon. Note that EmoLex is bigger, and biased towards neutral class. SynthesioLex is slightly biased towards negative class. For each lexicon, we used 80% of the data for training and 20% for evaluation, uniformly sampled.

### 3.2 Test Setup

At its core, the system has a MLP with 3 layers: (1) input layer with linear activation function and 300 units, the same as the word representation space. (2) hidden layer with a tanh activation function and number of units varying from 20 to 500. (3) output layer with softmax activation function with

---

[1] http://wordnet.princeton.edu

[2] https://code.google.com/p/Word2Vec

[3] http://nlp.stanford.edu/projects/glove/

[4] http://saifmohammad.com/Lexicons/NRC-Emotion-Lexicon-v0.92.zip

[5] http://saifmohammad.com/WebDocs/MaxDiff-Twitter-Lexicon.zip

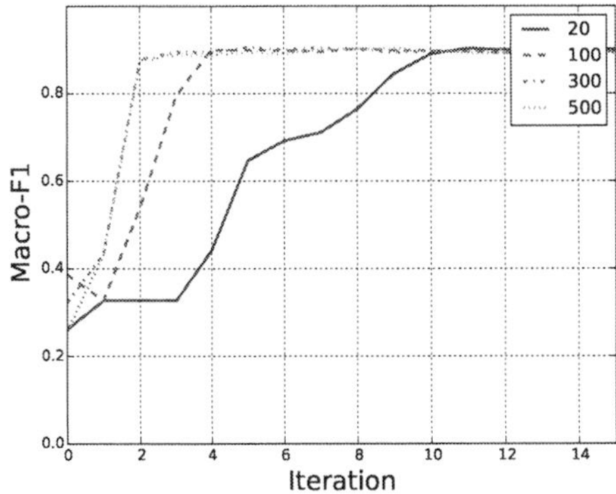

(a) Effect of varying hidden unit size

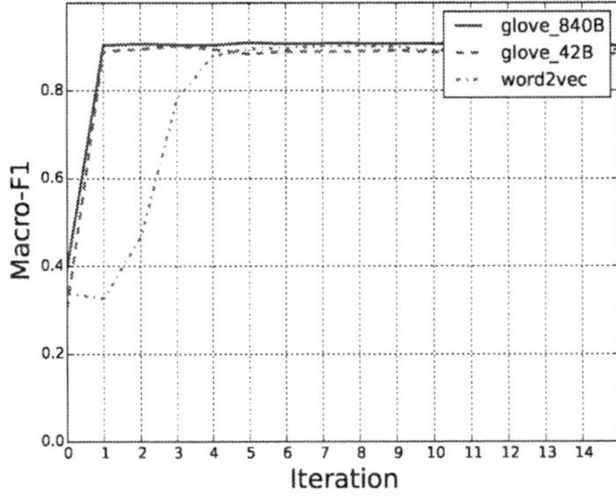

(b) Effect of different word embeddings

Figure 1: Results on SynthesioLex

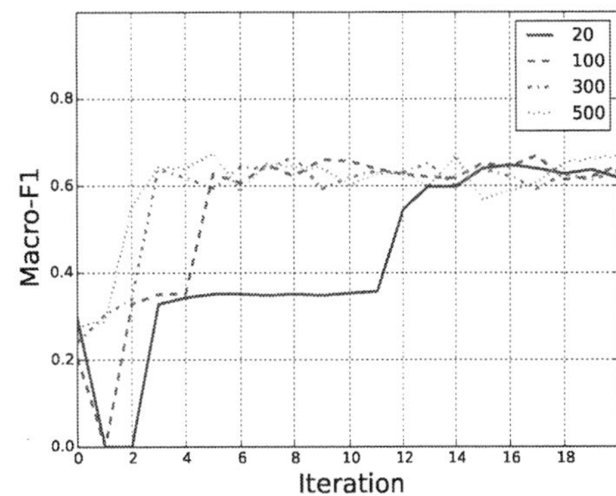

(a) Effect of varying hidden unit size

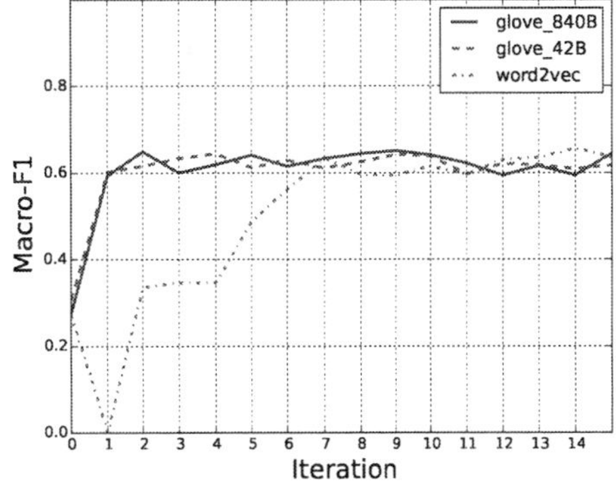

(b) Effect of different word embeddings

Figure 2: Results on EmoLex

2 or 3 units for classification, and linear function with single unit for regression. MLP training is done with mean square error as cost function using Keras library,[6] a Python package built on top of Theano[7] (Bergstra et al., 2010).

## 4 Results

Evaluation metric for classification is Macro-F1 between negative and positive classes. F1 measure of Neutral class is not considered, following the SemEval evaluations on twitter sentiment classification (Rosenthal et al., 2014). For regression, we use mean square error as evaluation metric.

### 4.1 Classification

In figure 1 and 2, we present Macro-F1 on evaluation data for each training epoch. All models con-

verged quickly, and towards similar results. In sub-figures 1(a) and 2(a) we see that convergence results are similar, independent of number of hidden units. With 20 units, model took longer to converge but it is evident that the model was able to train even with small number of units. Based on this, we used 100 hidden units for subsequent evaluations. In figures 1(b) and 2(b) we compare results for different word embedding spaces and again all converge to similar values, with Word2Vec taking longer time to stabilise. Classification results for the two lexicons are shown in Table 2. The *binary* cases represent binary classification where only positive and negative data were retained and all neutral data removed. The system performs better on SynthesioLex than on EmoLex, possibly due to higher number of neutral words in EmoLex. Results for the two lexicons are similar if we only use positive and negative sentiment classes (binary case, last two rows). This can be seen also in the confusion matrices in Tables 3

---

[6]http://keras.io/

[7]http://deeplearning.net/software/theano/

and 4 for SynthesioLex and EmoLex lexicons. For EmoLex, many sentiment words were classified as neutral, reducing recall. Also, when compared with SynthesioLex results, many neutral words are seen as having a sentiment, reducing precision.

| Lexicon | Word rep | Macro-f1 | Best iter |
|---|---|---|---|
| SynthesioLex | Word2Vec | 90.23 | 6 |
| | glove_42B | 89.05 | 4 |
| | glove_840B | 90.96 | 7 |
| EmoLex | Word2Vec | 75.85 | 18 |
| | glove_42B | 74.33 | 2 |
| | glove_840B | 74.78 | 6 |
| SynthesioLex Binary | Word2Vec | 93.91 | 2 |
| | glove_42B | 93.42 | 2 |
| | glove_840B | 94.76 | 6 |
| EmoLex Binary | Word2Vec | 91.16 | 5 |
| | glove_42B | 90.31 | 4 |
| | glove_840B | 92.02 | 5 |

**Table 2:** Results for classification problem.

| | Neg | Neu | Pos |
|---|---|---|---|
| Neg | 835 | 29 | 16 |
| Neu | 29 | 510 | 13 |
| Pos | 32 | 23 | 320 |

**Table 3:** SynthesioLex confusion matrix, row: groundtruth, column: predicted.

| | Neg | Neu | Pos |
|---|---|---|---|
| Neg | 431 | 211 | 6 |
| Neu | 91 | 1317 | 129 |
| Pos | 14 | 203 | 245 |

**Table 4:** EmoLex confusion matrix, row: groundtruth, column: predicted

In Section 1, we mentioned that the current method can be used for automatic generation of sentiment word list. To test this proposition, we trained the MLP using SynthesioLex and compared it with another semi-supervised method, SentiWordNet 3.0. We used EmoLex lexicon for evaluation. For SentiWordNet, the sentiment value for each word was computed as average sentiment value over all possible synsets. Confusion matrix for the two methods can be seen in 5 and 6. SentiWordNet achieves very low recall for positive and negative emotion classes, predicting most words as neutral. Macro-F1 results are 44.85% for our method and 6.31% for SentiWordNet.

| | Neg | Neu | Pos |
|---|---|---|---|
| Neg | 94 | 1392 | 13 |
| Neu | 71 | 6392 | 28 |
| Pos | 15 | 1369 | 40 |

**Table 5:** Confusion matrix between EmoLex (row) and SentiWordNet (column)

| | Neg | Neu | Pos |
|---|---|---|---|
| Neg | 1120 | 311 | 68 |
| Neu | 1826 | 3445 | 1220 |
| Pos | 186 | 558 | 680 |

**Table 6:** Confusion matrix between EmoLex (row) and current method (column)

## 4.2 Regression

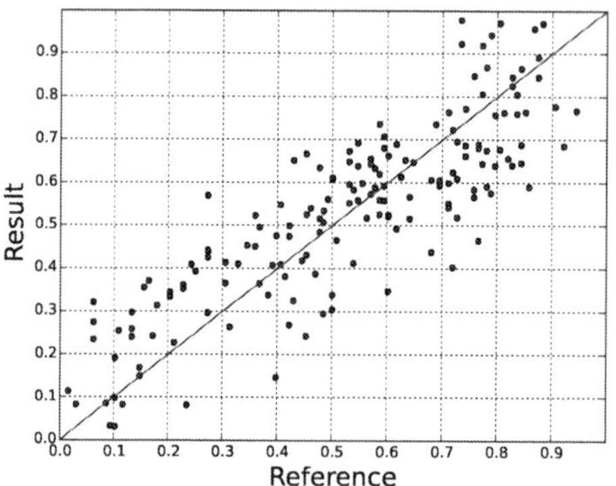

**Figure 3:** Regression results

For regression, we used same method for training as for classification. Optimal results were obtained with 100 hidden units. Best word representation is GloVe trained with 840 billion tokens. Lowest mean square error is 0.014. Regression results are shown in Figure 3. There is strong correlation of sentiment value between reference and result (correlation coefficient 0.85). One way to test this is to transform regressor to classifier by setting all words with sentiment value below 0.5 as negative and all with value above 0.5 as positive, keeping same training and evaluation splits. Figure 4 shows performance of such a classifier. Errors are associated with words close to decision boundary. For those whose sentiment is strongly positive or negative, there are few mistakes. This suggests setting to neutral all words whose regression values are close to decision boundary.

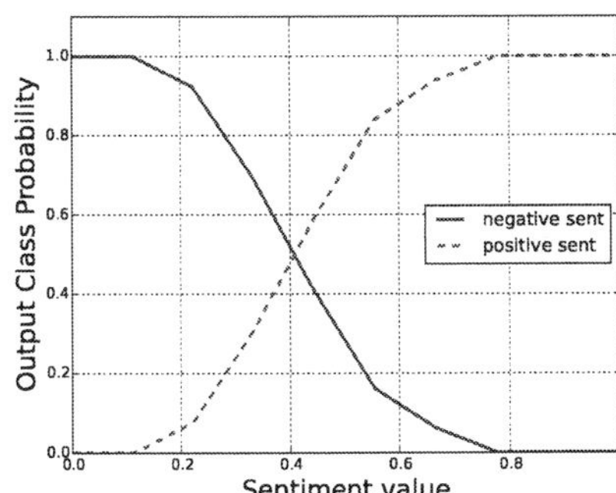

Figure 4: Performance of regressor as classifier

## 4.3 Discussion

Word embeddings like Word2Vec and GLoVE map "good" as closest to "bad" in latent space (ref. Section 1). MLP succeeds in mapping such opposite sentiment words far from each other at the hidden layer output space (ref. Section 3.2). In terms of cosine distance using the hidden layer of our MLP output, "good" was closest to "dignified", "compassionate", while "bad" was closest to "embarrassment", "contemptuous". "good" and "bad" were not part of the training data for this study.

## 5 Conclusion

Although the presented mappings do not consider sentiment information in word context, good results were obtained for word sentiment classification using these mappings as input to a MLP classifier trained and tested on two lexicons, SynthesioLex and EmoLex. When trained on SynthesioLex and tested on EmoLex, proposed approach performed better than SentiWordNet 3.0. We also studied a regression system which can be used to create features in a continuous sentiment space. This is a work in progress focusing on sentiment word list creation. In future, it is planned to integrated this approach in a complete document sentiment classification system.

## References


Silvio Amir, Miguel Almeida, Bruno Martins, Joao Filgueiras, and Mário J Silva. 2014. Tugas: Exploiting unlabelled data for twitter sentiment analysis. *SemEval 2014*, page 673.

Stefano Baccianella, Andrea Esuli, and Fabrizio Sebastiani. 2010. Sentiwordnet 3.0: An enhanced lexical resource for sentiment analysis and opinion mining. In *LREC*, volume 10, pages 2200–2204.

James Bergstra, Olivier Breuleux, Frédéric Bastien, Pascal Lamblin, Razvan Pascanu, Guillaume Desjardins, Joseph Turian, David Warde-Farley, and Yoshua Bengio. 2010. Theano: a CPU and GPU math expression compiler. In *Proceedings of the Python for Scientific Computing Conference (SciPy)*, June. Oral Presentation.

Andrea Esuli and Fabrizio Sebastiani. 2006. Sentiwordnet: A publicly available lexical resource for opinion mining. In *Proceedings of LREC*, volume 6, pages 417–422.

Ozan Irsoy and Claire Cardie. 2014. Opinion mining with deep recurrent neural networks. In *Proceedings of the 2014 Conference on Empirical Methods in Natural Language Processing (EMNLP)*, pages 720–728.

Svetlana Kiritchenko, Xiaodan Zhu, and Saif M. Mohammad. 2014. Sentiment analysis of short informal texts. *Journal of Artificial Intelligence Research (JAIR)*, 50:723–762.

Tomas Mikolov, Kai Chen, Greg Corrado, and Jeffrey Dean. 2013a. Efficient estimation of word representations in vector space. *arXiv preprint arXiv:1301.3781*.

Tomas Mikolov, Wen-tau Yih, and Geoffrey Zweig. 2013b. Linguistic regularities in continuous space word representations. In *HLT-NAACL*, pages 746–751.

Saif M. Mohammad and Peter D. Turney. 2013. Crowdsourcing a word-emotion association lexicon. 29(3):436–465.

Saif M Mohammad, Svetlana Kiritchenko, and Xiaodan Zhu. 2013. Nrc-canada: Building the state-of-the-art in sentiment analysis of tweets. In *Proceedings of the Second Joint Conference on Lexical and Computational Semantics (SEMSTAR13)*.

Bryan Orme. 2009. Maxdiff analysis: Simple counting, individual-level logit, and hb. *Sawtooth Software*.

Vipul Pandey and C Iyer. 2009. Sentiment analysis of microblogs. *CS 229: Machine learning final projects*.

Bo Pang, Lillian Lee, and Shivakumar Vaithyanathan. 2002. Thumbs up?: sentiment classification using machine learning techniques. In *Proceedings of the ACL-02 conference on Empirical methods in natural language processing-Volume 10*, pages 79–86. Association for Computational Linguistics.

Jeffrey Pennington, Richard Socher, and Christopher D Manning. 2014. Glove: Global vectors for word representation. *Proceedings of the Empiricial Methods in Natural Language Processing (EMNLP 2014)*, 12.

Sara Rosenthal, Alan Ritter, Preslav Nakov, and Veselin Stoyanov. 2014. Semeval-2014 task 9: Sentiment analysis in twitter. In *Proceedings of the 8th International Workshop on Semantic Evaluation (SemEval 2014)*, pages 73–80.

Duyu Tang, Furu Wei, Bing Qin, Ting Liu, and Ming Zhou. 2014a. Coooolll: A deep learning system for twitter sentiment classification. In *Proceedings of the 8th International Workshop on Semantic Evaluation (SemEval 2014)*, pages 208–212.

Duyu Tang, Furu Wei, Nan Yang, Ming Zhou, Ting Liu, and Bing Qin. 2014b. Learning sentiment-specific word embedding for twitter sentiment classification. In *Proceedings of the 52nd Annual Meeting of the Association for Computational Linguistics*, volume 1, pages 1555–1565.

Peter D Turney and Michael L Littman. 2003. Measuring praise and criticism: Inference of semantic orientation from association. *ACM Transactions on Information Systems (TOIS)*, 21(4):315–346.

G Vinodhini and RM Chandrasekaran. 2012. Sentiment analysis and opinion mining: a survey. *International Journal*, 2(6).

# The Effect of Negators, Modals, and Degree Adverbs on Sentiment Composition

**Svetlana Kiritchenko** and **Saif M. Mohammad**
National Research Council Canada
{svetlana.kiritchenko,saif.mohammad}@nrc-cnrc.gc.ca

## Abstract

Negators, modals, and degree adverbs can significantly affect the sentiment of the words they modify. Often, their impact is modeled with simple heuristics; although, recent work has shown that such heuristics do not capture the true sentiment of multi-word phrases. We created a dataset of phrases that include various negators, modals, and degree adverbs, as well as their combinations. Both the phrases and their constituent content words were annotated with real-valued scores of sentiment association. Using phrasal terms in the created dataset, we analyze the impact of individual modifiers and the average effect of the groups of modifiers on overall sentiment. We find that the effect of modifiers varies substantially among the members of the same group. Furthermore, each individual modifier can affect sentiment words in different ways. Therefore, solutions based on statistical learning seem more promising than fixed hand-crafted rules on the task of automatic sentiment prediction.

## 1  Introduction

Sentiment associations are commonly captured in sentiment lexicons—lists of associated word–sentiment pairs (optionally with a score indicating the degree of association). They are mostly used in sentiment analysis (Pontiki et al., 2014; Rosenthal et al., 2015), but are also beneficial in stance detection (Mohammad et al., 2016a; Mohammad et al., 2016b), literary analysis (Hartner, 2013; Kleres, 2011; Mohammad, 2012), detecting personality traits (Grijalva et al., 2015; Mohammad and Kiritchenko, 2015), and other applications.

Manually created sentiment lexicons are especially useful because they tend to be more accurate than automatically generated ones; they can be used to automatically generate large high-coverage lexicons (Tang et al., 2014; Esuli and Sebastiani, 2006); they can be used to evaluate different methods of automatically creating sentiment lexicons; and they can be used for linguistic analysis such as examining how modifiers (negators, modals, degree adverbs, etc.) impact overall sentiment. However, most existing manually created sentiment lexicons tend to provide only lists of positive and negative words with very coarse levels of sentiment (Stone et al., 1966; Wilson et al., 2005; Mohammad and Turney, 2013). The coarse-grained distinctions may be less useful in downstream applications than having access to fine-grained (real-valued) sentiment association scores.

Manually created sentiment lexicons usually include only single words. Yet, the sentiment of a phrase can differ markedly from the sentiment of its constituent words. Sentiment composition is the determining of sentiment of a multi-word linguistic unit, such as a phrase or a sentence, from its constituents. Lexicons that include sentiment associations for phrases as well as for their constituents are useful in studying sentiment composition. We refer to them as *sentiment composition lexicons (SCLs)*.

We created a sentiment composition lexicon for phrases formed with negators (such as *no* and *cannot*), modals (such as *would have been* and *could*), degree adverbs (such as *quite* and *less*), and their combinations. Both the phrases and their constituent content words were manually annotated with real-valued scores of sentiment association using a tech-

43

*Proceedings of NAACL-HLT 2016*, pages 43–52,
San Diego, California, June 12-17, 2016. ©2016 Association for Computational Linguistics

nique known as Best–Worst Scaling, which provides reliable annotations. We refer to the resulting lexicon as *Sentiment Composition Lexicon for Negators, Modals, and Degree Adverbs (SCL-NMA)*. The lexicon is also known as *SemEval-2016 General English Sentiment Modifiers Lexicon.*[1]

We calculate the minimum difference in sentiment scores of two terms that is perceptible to native speakers of a language. For sentiment scores between -1 and 1, we show that the perceptible difference is about 0.07 for English speakers. Knowing the least perceptible difference helps interpret the impact of sentiment composition. For example, we can determine whether a modifier significantly impacts the sentiment of the word it composes with by calculating the difference in sentiment scores between the combined phrase and the constituent, and checking whether this difference is greater than the least perceptible difference.

We use the phrasal terms in the created lexicon to analyze the impact of common modifiers on the sentiment of the terms they modify. We measure the effect of individual modifiers as well as the average effect of the groups of modifiers on overall sentiment. We show that the sentiment of a negated expression (such as *not w*) on the [-1,1] scale is on average 0.926 points less than the sentiment of the modified term *w*, if the *w* is positive. However, the sentiment of the negated expression is on average 0.791 points higher than *w*, if the *w* is negative. Similar analysis for modals and degree adverbs shows that they impact sentiment less dramatically than negators. Furthermore, the impact of modifiers substantially varies even within a group, e.g., the average change in sentiment score brought by the negator '*will not be*' is 0.41 larger than the change introduced by the negator '*never*'. Likewise, each individual modifier can affect sentiment words in different ways. As a result, in automatic sentiment prediction solutions based on statistical learning seem more promising than fixed hand-crafted rules.

In related work (not described here), we also created a sentiment composition lexicon for another challenging category of phrases—phrases that include at least one positive word and at least one negative word (Kiritchenko and Mohammad, 2016b). We call such phrases opposing polarity phrases. Both lexicons have been used as official test sets in SemEval-2016 Task 7 'Determining Sentiment Intensity of English and Arabic Phrases' (Kiritchenko et al., 2016).[2] The lexicons are made freely available to the research community.[3]

## 2 Related Work

**Sentiment Lexicons:** There exist a number of manually created lexicons that provide lists of positive and negative words, for example, General Inquirer (Stone et al., 1966), Hu and Liu Lexicon (Hu and Liu, 2004), and NRC Emotion Lexicon (Mohammad and Turney, 2013). Only a few manually created lexicons provide real-valued scores of sentiment association (Bradley and Lang, 1999; Warriner et al., 2013; Dodds et al., 2011). None of these lexicons, however, contain multi-word phrases. Manually created sentiment lexicons can be used to automatically generate larger sentiment lexicons using semi-supervised techniques (Esuli and Sebastiani, 2006; Turney and Littman, 2003; Mohammad et al., 2013; De Melo and Bansal, 2013; Tang et al., 2014). (See Mohammad (2016) for a survey on manually created and automatically generated affect resources.)

Automatically generated lexicons often have real-valued sentiment association scores, are larger in scale, and can easily be collected for a specific domain; therefore, they were found to be more beneficial in downstream applications, such as sentence-level sentiment prediction (Kiritchenko et al., 2014). However, any analysis of the relationship between the sentiment of a phrase and its constituents is less reliable when made from an automatically generated resource as opposed to when made from a manually created resource (as automatically generated resources are less accurate). In this work, we provide an extensive analysis of the impact of different modifiers on sentiment based on reliable fine-grained manual annotations.

---

[1]This lexicon was first introduced in (Kiritchenko and Mohammad, 2016a) where we investigated the applicability and reliability of the Best–Worst Scaling annotation technique in capturing word–sentiment associations. In this paper, we provide further details on the creation of the lexicon and present analysis of how negators, modals, and degree adverbs impact the sentiment of the words they modify.

---

[2]http://alt.qcri.org/semeval2016/task7/
[3]http://www.saifmohammad.com/WebPages/SCL.html

**Contextual Valence Shifters:** Negators, modals, and degree adverbs impact the sentiment of the word or phrase they modify and are commonly referred to as contextual valence shifters (Polanyi and Zaenen, 2004; Kennedy and Inkpen, 2005; Jia et al., 2009; Wiegand et al., 2010; Lapponi et al., 2012). Conventionally, the impact of contextual valence shifters is captured by simple heuristics. For example, negation is often handled by reversing the polarities of the sentiment words in the scope of negation (Polanyi and Zaenen, 2004; Kennedy and Inkpen, 2005; Choi and Cardie, 2008) or by shifting the sentiment score of a term in a negated context towards the opposite polarity by a fixed amount (Taboada et al., 2011). However, such heuristics do not adequately capture the true sentiment of multi-word expressions (Zhu et al., 2014). Liu and Seneff (2009) relax the assumption of a fixed shifting margin and estimate these margins for each modifier separately from data. Kiritchenko et al. (2014), on the other hand, estimate the impact of negation on each individual sentiment word through a corpus-based statistical method. Ruppenhofer et al. (2015) automatically rank English adverbs by their intensifying or diminishing effect on adjectives using ratings metadata from product reviews.

**Annotation techniques:** A widely used method of annotation for obtaining numerical scores is the *rating scale* method—where one is asked to rate an item on a five-, ten-, or hundred-point scale. While easy to understand, rating items on a scale is not natural for people. It is hard for annotators to remain consistent when annotating a large number of items. Also, respondents often use just a limited part of the scale reducing the discrimination among items (Cohen, 2003). To obtain reliable annotations, the rating scale methods require a high number of responses, typically 15 to 20 (Warriner et al., 2013; Graham et al., 2015). A more natural annotation task for humans is to compare items (e.g., whether one word is more positive than the other). Most commonly, the items are compared in pairs (Thurstone, 1927; David, 1963). In this work, we use *Best–Worst Scaling*—a technique that exploits the comparative approach to annotation while keeping the number of required annotations small (Section 3.2). It has been shown to produce reliable annotations of terms by sentiment (Kiritchenko and Mohammad, 2016a).

| Term | Sentiment score |
|---|---|
| favor | 0.653 |
| would be very easy | 0.431 |
| did not harm | 0.194 |
| increasingly difficult | -0.583 |
| severe | -0.833 |

**Table 1:** Example entries with real-valued sentiment scores from SCL-NMA.

## 3 Creating SCL-NMA

We now describe the term selection process and the Best–Worst Scaling annotation technique used to create the Sentiment Composition Lexicon for Negators, Modals, and Degree Adverbs. Table 1 shows a few example entries from the lexicon. We also describe how we calculated the minimum difference in sentiment scores of two terms that is perceptible to native speakers of a language.

### 3.1 Term Selection

General Inquirer (Stone et al., 1966) provides a list of 1,621 positive and negative words from Osgood's seminal study on word meaning (Osgood et al., 1957). These are words commonly used in everyday English. We include all of these words. In addition, we include 1,586 high-frequency phrases formed by the Osgood words in combination with simple negators such as *no*, *don't*, and *never*, modals such as *can*, *might*, and *should*, or degree adverbs such as *very* and *fairly*.[4] The eligible adverbs are chosen manually from adverbs frequently occurring in the British National Corpus (BNC)[5]. Each phrase includes at least one modal, one negator, or one adverb; a phrase can include several modifiers (e.g., *would be very happy*). The modifiers and the phrases are chosen in such a way that the full set includes several phrases for each Osgood sentiment word and includes several phrases for each modifier. In total, sixty-four different (single or multi-word) modifiers are selected. The final list contains 3,207 terms.

---

[4]The complete lists of negators, modals, and degree adverbs used to create this dataset are available at http://www.saifmohammad.com/WebPages/SCL.html#NMA.

[5]The British National Corpus, version 3 (BNC XML Edition). 2007. Distributed by Oxford University Computing Services on behalf of the BNC Consortium. http://www.natcorp.ox.ac.uk/

## 3.2 Best–Worst Scaling

Best–Worst Scaling (BWS), also sometimes referred to as Maximum Difference Scaling (MaxDiff), is an annotation scheme that exploits the comparative approach to annotation (Louviere and Woodworth, 1990; Cohen, 2003; Louviere et al., 2015). Annotators are given four items (4-tuple) and asked which item is the Best (highest in terms of the property of interest) and which is the Worst (least in terms of the property of interest). These annotations can then be converted into real-valued scores and also a ranking of items as per their association with the property of interest through a simple counting procedure: For each item, its score is calculated as the percentage of times the item was chosen as the Best minus the percentage of times the item was chosen as the Worst (Orme, 2009; Flynn and Marley, 2014). The scores range from -1 to 1. Further details on Best–Worst Scaling and its application to the task of sentiment annotation can be found in (Kiritchenko and Mohammad, 2016a).

## 3.3 Annotation process

The complete list of 3,207 terms was randomly sampled (with replacement) to create 6,414 (2 x 3,207) 4-tuples that satisfy the following criteria:

1. no two 4-tuples have the same four terms;

2. no two terms within a 4-tuple are identical;

3. each term in the term list appears approximately in the same number of 4-tuples;

4. each pair of terms appears approximately in the same number of 4-tuples.

Next, the set of 4-tuples was annotated through a crowdsourcing platform, CrowdFlower. The annotators were presented with four terms (single words and multi-word phrases) at a time, and asked which term is the most positive (or least negative) and which is the most negative (or least positive).[6] Each 4-tuple was annotated by ten respondents. We determined accuracy of every annotator on a small set of check questions labeled by the authors of this paper. We discarded all annotations provided by an annotator if their accuracy on these check questions was less than 70%.

---

[6]The full set of instructions to annotators is available at http://www.saifmohammad.com/WebPages/SCL.html#NMA.

## 3.4 Quality of Annotations

Let *majority answer* refer to the option chosen most often for a question. 80% of the responses to the Best–Worst questions matched the majority answer.

We also tested the reliability of the aggregated scores by randomly dividing the sets of ten responses to each question into two halves and comparing the rankings obtained from these two groups of responses. The Spearman rank correlation coefficient between the two sets of rankings was found to be 0.98. (The Pearson correlation coefficient between the two sets of sentiment scores was also 0.98.) Thus, even though annotators might disagree about answers to individual questions, the aggregated scores produced by applying the counting procedure on the Best–Worst annotations are remarkably reliable at ranking terms by sentiment.

## 3.5 Least Perceptible Difference in Sentiment

In psychophysics, there is a notion of *least perceptible difference* (aka *just-noticeable difference*)—the amount by which something that can be measured (e.g., weight or sound intensity) needs to be changed in order for the difference to be noticeable by a human (Fechner, 1966). Analogously, we can measure the least perceptible difference in sentiment. If two words have close to identical sentiment associations, then it is expected that native speakers will choose each of the words about the same number of times when forced to pick a word that is more positive. However, as the difference in sentiment starts getting larger, the frequency with which the two terms are chosen as most positive begins to diverge. At one point, the frequencies diverge so much that we can say with high confidence that the two terms do not have the same sentiment associations. The average of this minimum difference in sentiment score is the least perceptible difference for sentiment.

To calculate the least perceptible difference, we first build a plot of the relationship between 'difference in the sentiment scores between two terms' and 'agreement among annotators' when asked which term is more positive. For each term pair $w_1$ and $w_2$ such that $d = score(w_1) - score(w_2) \geq 0$, we count the number of Best–Worst annotations from which we can infer that $w_1$ is more positive than $w_2$ and divide this number by the total number of annota-

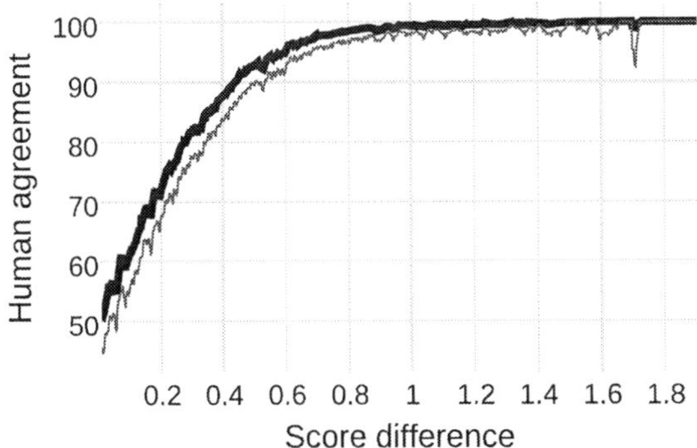



**Figure 1:** Human agreement on annotating term $w_1$ as more positive than term $w_2$ for pairs with difference in scores $d = score(w_1) - score(w_2)$. The x-axis represents $d$. The y-axis plots the avg. percentage of human annotations that judge term $w_1$ as more positive than term $w_2$ (thick line) and the corresponding 99.9%-confidence lower bound (thin blue line).

tions from which we can infer either that $w_1$ is more positive than $w_2$ or that $w_2$ is more positive than $w_1$. (We can infer that $w_1$ is more positive than $w_2$ if in a 4-tuple that has both $w_1$ and $w_2$ the annotator selected $w_1$ as the most positive or $w_2$ as the least positive. The case for $w_2$ being more positive than $w_1$ is similar.) This ratio is the human agreement for $w_1$ being more positive than $w_2$. To get more reliable estimates, we average the human agreement for all pairs of terms whose sentiment differs by $d \pm 0.01$. Figure 1 shows the resulting average human agreement. The thin blue line in the Figure depicts the 99.9%-confidence lower bounds on the agreement. The least perceptible difference is the point starting at which the lower bound consistently exceeds 50% threshold (i.e., the point starting at which we observe with 99.9% confidence that the human agreement is higher than chance). The least perceptible difference when calculated from SCL-NMA is 0.069. In the next section, we use the least perceptible difference to determine whether a modifier significantly impacts the sentiment of the word it composes with.

## 4 Impact of Negators, Modals, and Degree Adverbs on Sentiment

SCL-NMA contains many phrases formed by different types of modifiers—negators, modals, and degree adverbs. Thus, this lexicon is a good resource for studying the impact of these types of modifiers on sentiment. In the following, we compare the sen-

timent score of single-word term $w$ with the sentiment score for phrase *mod w*, where *mod* is a modifier from a particular group (negator, modal, or degree adverb). Table 2 shows the average effect of different modifier groups on sentiment. The columns show the average change in sentiment score between $w$ and *mod w*, the number of pairs (of $w$ and *mod w*) used to determine the average, the number of phrases *mod w* whose sentiment score is greater (↑) or less (↓) than the score of $w$ by at least 0.069 (the least perceptible difference). Since the impact of modifiers can be different depending on the sentiment of the modified word $w$, we present separate analyses for when $w$ is positive and when $w$ is negative. For the analysis in this section only, a word is considered positive if it has a sentiment score greater than or equal to 0.3, and considered negative if its sentiment score is less than or equal to -0.3.[7]

Observe that the most change in sentiment is caused by negation; it consistently decreases the scores of positive words, and increases the scores of negative words. The average score difference is substantial for both positive words (0.926 points) and negative words (0.791 points). Modals also tend to decrease the scores of positive words, and increase the scores of negative words, though to a much smaller extent than negators. As with negators, modals affect positive words more strongly than they do negative words. Degree adverbs show less consistency than negators and modals; they can both heighten or lower the sentiment of a word. Moreover, the same adverb can behave differently with different words from the same sentiment group (positive or negative). Therefore, we report the average *absolute* differences in scores for this modifier group. These average differences are substantially smaller than the ones reported for modals and negators; the effect of degree adverbs is minor. Besides, in contrast to modals and negators, for a large percentage of degree adverb phrases (for 35% of the positive-word phrases and for 37% of the negative-word phrases), the sentiment scores do not differ from the scores for the corresponding single words by the least perceptible difference (0.069 points). In the subsections below, we further examine the im-

---

[7]This threshold is somewhat arbitrary, and is chosen to discard neutral terms from the analysis, whose sentiment tends not to change much with these modifiers.

**Table 2:** The impact of different modifier groups on sentiment. 'Avg. diff.' is the average difference between the score of *mod w* and *w*. '# pairs' is the number of pairs (of *w* and *mod w*) used to determine the average. '# score ↑ (↓)' indicates the number of phrases for which $score(mod\ w)$ is greater (less) than $score(w)$ by at least 0.069 (the perceptible difference).

| Modifier Group | On positive words | | | | On negative words | | | |
|---|---|---|---|---|---|---|---|---|
| | Avg. diff. | # pairs | # score ↑ | # score ↓ | Avg. diff. | # pairs | # score ↑ | # score ↓ |
| negators | -0.926 | 265 | 1 | 264 | 0.791 | 71 | 71 | 0 |
| modals | -0.317 | 258 | 9 | 231 | 0.238 | 72 | 54 | 8 |
| degree adverbs (abs. diff.) | 0.201 | 435 | 106 | 212 | 0.166 | 163 | 42 | 68 |

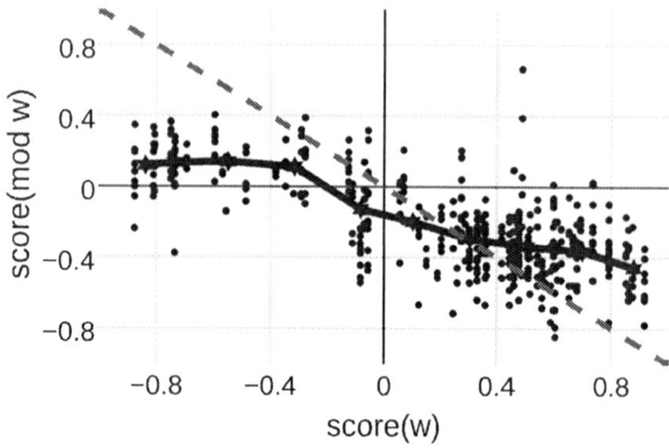

**Figure 2:** The impact of **negators** on sentiment. The x-axis is $score(w)$, the sentiment score of a term $w$; the y-axis is $score(mod\ w)$, the sentiment score of a term $w$ preceded by a negator. Each dot corresponds to one phrase *mod w*. The black line shows an average effect of the negators group. The dashed red line shows the reversing polarity hypothesis $score(mod\ w) = -score(w)$.

pact of each modifier category on the sentiment of its scope. Also, we provide rankings of different negators, modals, and degree adverbs as per the average change in sentiment score between $w$ and *mod w*. This would allow linguists and other researchers to better understand the behavior of different modifiers.

## 4.1 Negation

There exist two common approaches to incorporate the impact of negation in automatic systems: (1) *reversing polarity hypothesis*, where the sentiment score of a word '$score(w)$' is replaced with '$-score(w)$'; and (2) *shifting hypothesis*, where the sentiment score of a word '$score(w)$' is reduced by a fixed amount: '$score(w) - sign(score(w)) \times b$'. We will show that neither hypothesis accurately captures the impact of negation. We will also present an analysis of the overall impact of negation and the impact of individual negators (aka negation triggers).

In our dataset, the negators are formed by 'no' negation words like *no*, *not*, *never*, and *nothing* in combination with auxiliary and modal verbs. Figure 2 shows the overall impact of negation on sentiment of single words. Each dot in this figure corresponds to one negated phrase '*negator w*'. The x-axis corresponds to $score(w)$ (the sentiment score of a word $w$); the y-axis is $score(mod\ w)$ (the sentiment score of a word $w$ preceded by a negator). The black line shows an average effect of negation. The dashed red line shows the reversing polarity hypothesis: $score(mod\ w) = -score(w)$. Observe that on average negators tend to substantially down-shift the sentiment of positive words turning them into negative expressions. On the other hand, the scores of negative terms increase, but to a smaller extent than the scores of positive words. Words with high absolute sentiment values tend to experience the greatest shift. This is true for both positive and negative words. However, this shift is substantially smaller than is proposed by the reversing polarity hypothesis. Overall, the reversing polarity hypothesis fit is rather poor. The shifting hypothesis does not explain the data either. Another observation is that words with similar sentiment scores can form negated phrases with very different sentiment scores (appearing as columns of dots in the graph). This is mostly due to the effect of different negators. However, the same negator can sometimes have different effect on words with similar sentiment. For example, the three words *easy*, *good*, and *better* all have similar sentiment scores: $score(easy) = 0.598$, $score(good) = 0.556$, $score(better) = 0.486$. Yet, the corresponding negated phrases formed with the same negator *never* range from negative ($score(never\ good) = -0.542$), to slightly negative ($score(never\ easy) = -0.112$), to positive ($score(never\ better) = 0.666$).

**Table 3:** The impact of **negators** on sentiment.

| Modifier | Avg. diff. | # pairs | # score ↑ | # score ↓ |
|---|---|---|---|---|
| **On positive words** | | | | |
| will not be | -1.066 | 9 | 0 | 9 |
| cannot | -1.030 | 12 | 0 | 12 |
| did not | -0.978 | 13 | 0 | 13 |
| not very | -0.961 | 14 | 0 | 14 |
| not | -0.959 | 45 | 0 | 45 |
| no | -0.948 | 29 | 0 | 29 |
| was no | -0.939 | 14 | 0 | 14 |
| will not | -0.935 | 11 | 0 | 11 |
| was not | -0.928 | 29 | 0 | 29 |
| have no | -0.917 | 8 | 0 | 8 |
| does not | -0.907 | 13 | 0 | 13 |
| could not | -0.893 | 12 | 0 | 12 |
| would not | -0.869 | 11 | 0 | 11 |
| had no | -0.862 | 7 | 0 | 7 |
| would not be | -0.848 | 15 | 0 | 15 |
| may not | -0.758 | 6 | 0 | 6 |
| nothing | -0.755 | 6 | 0 | 6 |
| never | -0.650 | 7 | 1 | 6 |
| **On negative words** | | | | |
| will not | 0.878 | 5 | 5 | 0 |
| does not | 0.823 | 5 | 5 | 0 |
| was not | 0.786 | 10 | 10 | 0 |
| no | 0.768 | 8 | 8 | 0 |
| not | 0.735 | 14 | 14 | 0 |

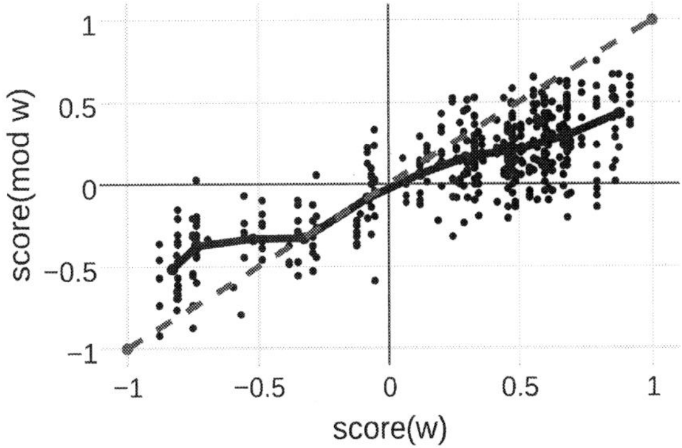

**Figure 3:** The impact of **modals** on sentiment. The x-axis is $score(w)$, the sentiment score of a term $w$; the y-axis is $score(mod\ w)$, the sentiment score of a term $w$ preceded by a modal verb. Each dot corresponds to one phrase $mod\ w$. The black line shows an average effect of the modals group. The dashed red line shows the function $score(mod\ w) = score(w)$.

## 4.2 Modals

In our dataset, the modal modifiers are formed by modal verbs *can, could, should, would, may, might,* and *must* in combination with auxiliary verbs. Figure 3 demonstrates the overall impact of modals on sentiment. One can observe that on average modals have a smoothing effect on sentiment: they make negative words less negative and positive words less positive. Words with high absolute sentiment values tend to experience the greatest shift; though, this shift is still quite small (around 0.4 points).

The effect of individual modal modifiers on positive and negative words is shown in Table 4. The most influential modal modifier is *would have been*. It consistently downshifts sentiment by a significant margin (about 0.5 points). Modifiers involving modals *could,* and *might* also affect sentiment in a consistent and noticeable way for both positive and negative words. Modals *can* and *would* form modifiers that have the smallest effect on sentiment of positive and negative words (with the exception of the modifier *would have been*).

## 4.3 Degree Adverbs

As mentioned earlier, the average differences in sentiment caused by degree adverbs are quite small; many differences are negligible. Furthermore, these modifiers are less consistent than negators and modals; there are many degree adverbs that increase

Next, we investigate the effect of individual negators. Table 3 shows the impact of negation triggered by different negators. The majority of the negation triggers have a large effect on both positive and negative words; the absolute difference in scores between a negated phrase and the corresponding sentiment word is 0.8-1.0 points on positive words and 0.7-0.9 points on negative words. The greatest shift in sentiment on positive words was observed for the modifier *will not be*, and on negative words for modifier *will not*. The weakest effect is caused by *may not*, *nothing*, and *never*. Verb tenses seem not to affect the behavior of negators significantly. For example, the average change in sentiment caused by *not* and by *was not* differs only by 0.03-0.05 points. The modal verbs *will* and *can* form strong negation phrases *will not*, *will not be*, and *cannot* that showed the most change in sentiment. Other modal verbs, such as *could*, *would*, and *may*, form negation phrases with smaller effect on sentiment.

49

Table 4: The impact of **modals** on sentiment.

| Modifier | Avg. diff. | # pairs | # score ↑ | # score ↓ |
|---|---|---|---|---|
| **On positive words** | | | | |
| would have been | -0.491 | 12 | 0 | 12 |
| could | -0.390 | 16 | 1 | 15 |
| might | -0.387 | 14 | 0 | 14 |
| may | -0.384 | 14 | 1 | 13 |
| should be | -0.365 | 22 | 0 | 22 |
| could be | -0.342 | 14 | 0 | 13 |
| must | -0.338 | 12 | 0 | 11 |
| should | -0.314 | 14 | 0 | 12 |
| may be | -0.300 | 20 | 2 | 18 |
| might be | -0.298 | 14 | 2 | 10 |
| must be | -0.287 | 19 | 0 | 17 |
| would | -0.284 | 16 | 0 | 15 |
| can be | -0.283 | 18 | 2 | 15 |
| would be | -0.261 | 29 | 0 | 25 |
| can | -0.208 | 16 | 1 | 13 |
| would be very | -0.186 | 8 | 0 | 6 |
| **On negative words** | | | | |
| could | 0.351 | 5 | 5 | 0 |
| could be | 0.268 | 8 | 7 | 1 |
| might be | 0.256 | 5 | 5 | 0 |
| can be | 0.249 | 6 | 4 | 0 |
| would be | 0.224 | 12 | 7 | 2 |
| can | 0.200 | 5 | 4 | 0 |
| may be | 0.169 | 8 | 5 | 2 |

the sentiment intensity of some words from one class (positive or negative) and decrease the sentiment intensity of other words from the same class. For example, *certainly* heightens the sentiment intensity of positive word *important* (by about 0.21 points), but lowers the sentiment intensity of another positive word *hope* (by about 0.31 points). We found that the only degree adverb in our set that affects sentiment to a large extent (0.835 points) is *less*; it consistently and significantly decreases the sentiment intensity of positive words. In fact, it acts as negator and reduces the sentiment intensity of positive words to a degree similar to that of negators. There are a few other modifiers that consistently reduce the sentiment intensity of positive words by a significant amount: *was too, too, probably, fairly,* and *relatively.* Only one intensifier, *highly,* consistently and significantly increase the sentiment of positive words. The sentiment of negative words is significantly lowered by intensifiers *extremely* and *very very.*

## 4.4 Interactive Visualization

As part of this project, we created an interactive visualization for SCL-NMA.[8] The visualization has several components that allow to investigate the effect of sentiment modifiers on individual words as well as to inspect the complete set in one scatter plot. The groups of modifiers are color-coded for ease of exploration. The full information for a phrase, including the sentiment scores of the phrase and its constituent content word, can be viewed by hovering over the point in the graph with the mouse. The scatter plot can be filtered to show phrases that include only a particular type of the modifiers (negators, modals, or degree adverbs). All the components are linked together so that by clicking on a point in one component one can highlight or filter the corresponding points shown in the other components. We hope that the users will find this visualization very helpful in exploring aspects of the data they are interested in.

## 5 Conclusions

We created a real-valued sentiment lexicon of phrases that include a variety of common sentiment modifiers such as negators, modals, and degree adverbs. Both phrases and their constituent content words are annotated manually using the Best–Worst Scaling technique. We showed that the obtained annotations are reliable—re-doing the annotation with different sets of annotators produces a very similar ranking of terms by sentiment. We use the annotations for the phrases to present an extensive analysis of how negators, modals, and degree adverbs impact the sentiment of other words in their scope. We demonstrate that these modifiers affect sentiment in complex ways so that their effect cannot be easily modeled with simple heuristics. In particular, we observe that the effect of a modifier is often determined not only by the type of the modifier (whether it is a negator, modal, or degree adverb) but also by the modifier word and the content word themselves. The created lexicon is made freely available to the research community to foster further research, especially towards automatic methods for sentiment composition and towards a better understanding of how sentiment is composed in the human brain.

---

[8]www.saifmohammad.com/WebPages/SCL.html#NMA

# References

Margaret M Bradley and Peter J Lang. 1999. Affective norms for English words (ANEW): Instruction manual and affective ratings. Technical report, The Center for Research in Psychophysiology, University of Florida.

Yejin Choi and Claire Cardie. 2008. Learning with compositional semantics as structural inference for subsentential sentiment analysis. In *Proceedings of the Conference on Empirical Methods in Natural Language Processing (EMNLP)*, pages 793–801.

Steven H. Cohen. 2003. Maximum difference scaling: Improved measures of importance and preference for segmentation. Sawtooth Software, Inc.

Herbert Aron David. 1963. *The method of paired comparisons.* Hafner Publishing Company, New York.

Gerard De Melo and Mohit Bansal. 2013. Good, great, excellent: Global inference of semantic intensities. *Transactions of the Association for Computational Linguistics*, 1:279–290.

Peter Sheridan Dodds, Kameron Decker Harris, Isabel M. Kloumann, Catherine A. Bliss, and Christopher M. Danforth. 2011. Temporal patterns of happiness and information in a global social network: Hedonometrics and Twitter. *PloS One*, 6(12):e26752.

Andrea Esuli and Fabrizio Sebastiani. 2006. SENTIWORDNET: A publicly available lexical resource for opinion mining. In *Proceedings of the 5th Conference on Language Resources and Evaluation (LREC)*, pages 417–422.

Gustav Fechner. 1966. *Elements of psychophysics. Vol. I.* New York: Holt, Rinehart and Winston.

T. N. Flynn and A. A. J. Marley. 2014. Best-worst scaling: theory and methods. In Stephane Hess and Andrew Daly, editors, *Handbook of Choice Modelling*, pages 178–201. Edward Elgar Publishing.

Yvette Graham, Nitika Mathur, and Timothy Baldwin. 2015. Accurate evaluation of segment-level machine translation metrics. In *Proceedings of the Annual Conference of the North American Chapter of the ACL (NAACL)*, pages 1183–1191.

Emily Grijalva, Daniel A. Newman, Louis Tay, M. Brent Donnellan, P.D. Harms, Richard W. Robins, and Taiyi Yan. 2015. Gender differences in narcissism: A meta-analytic review. *Psychological bulletin*, 141(2):261–310.

Marcus Hartner. 2013. The lingering after-effects in the reader's mind – an investigation into the affective dimension of literary reading. *Journal of Literary Theory Online.*

Minqing Hu and Bing Liu. 2004. Mining and summarizing customer reviews. In *Proceedings of the 10th ACM SIGKDD International Conference on Knowledge Discovery and Data Mining (KDD)*, pages 168–177, New York, NY, USA.

Lifeng Jia, Clement Yu, and Weiyi Meng. 2009. The effect of negation on sentiment analysis and retrieval effectiveness. In *Proceedings of the 18th ACM Conference on Information and Knowledge Management (CIKM)*, pages 1827–1830, New York, NY, USA.

Alistair Kennedy and Diana Inkpen. 2005. Sentiment classification of movie and product reviews using contextual valence shifters. In *Proceedings of the Workshop on the Analysis of Informal and Formal Information Exchange during Negotiations (FINEXIN)*, Ottawa, Ontario, Canada.

Svetlana Kiritchenko and Saif M. Mohammad. 2016a. Capturing reliable fine-grained sentiment associations by crowdsourcing and best–worst scaling. In *Proceedings of The 15th Annual Conference of the North American Chapter of the Association for Computational Linguistics: Human Language Technologies (NAACL)*, San Diego, California.

Svetlana Kiritchenko and Saif M. Mohammad. 2016b. Sentiment composition of words with opposing polarities. In *Proceedings of The 15th Annual Conference of the North American Chapter of the Association for Computational Linguistics: Human Language Technologies (NAACL)*, San Diego, California.

Svetlana Kiritchenko, Xiaodan Zhu, and Saif M. Mohammad. 2014. Sentiment analysis of short informal texts. *Journal of Artificial Intelligence Research*, 50:723–762.

Svetlana Kiritchenko, Saif M. Mohammad, and Mohammad Salameh. 2016. SemEval-2016 Task 7: Determining sentiment intensity of english and arabic phrases. In *Proceedings of the International Workshop on Semantic Evaluation (SemEval)*, San Diego, California, June.

Jochen Kleres. 2011. Emotions and narrative analysis: A methodological approach. *Journal for the Theory of Social Behaviour*, 41(2):182–202.

Emanuele Lapponi, Jonathon Read, and Lilja Ovrelid. 2012. Representing and resolving negation for sentiment analysis. In *Proceedings of the 12th IEEE International Conference on Data Mining Workshops*, pages 687–692.

Jingjing Liu and Stephanie Seneff. 2009. Review sentiment scoring via a parse-and-paraphrase paradigm. In *Proceedings of the Conference on Empirical Methods in Natural Language Processing*, pages 161–169.

Jordan J. Louviere and George G. Woodworth. 1990. Best-worst analysis. Working Paper. Department of Marketing and Economic Analysis, University of Alberta.

Jordan J. Louviere, Terry N. Flynn, and A. A. J. Marley. 2015. *Best-Worst Scaling: Theory, Methods and Applications.* Cambridge University Press.

Saif M. Mohammad and Svetlana Kiritchenko. 2015. Using hashtags to capture fine emotion categories from tweets. *Computational Intelligence*, 31(2):301–326.

Saif M. Mohammad and Peter D. Turney. 2013. Crowd-sourcing a word–emotion association lexicon. *Computational Intelligence*, 29(3):436–465.

Saif M. Mohammad, Svetlana Kiritchenko, and Xiaodan Zhu. 2013. NRC-Canada: Building the state-of-the-art in sentiment analysis of tweets. In *Proceedings of the International Workshop on Semantic Evaluation (SemEval)*, Atlanta, Georgia, USA, June.

Saif M. Mohammad, Svetlana Kiritchenko, Parinaz Sobhani, Xiaodan Zhu, and Colin Cherry. 2016a. A dataset for detecting stance in tweets. In *Proceedings of 10th edition of the the Language Resources and Evaluation Conference (LREC)*, Portorož, Slovenia.

Saif M. Mohammad, Parinaz Sobhani, and Svetlana Kiritchenko. 2016b. Stance and sentiment in tweets. *Special Section of the ACM Transactions on Internet Technology on Argumentation in Social Media*, Submitted.

Saif M Mohammad. 2012. From once upon a time to happily ever after: Tracking emotions in mail and books. *Decision Support Systems*, 53(4):730–741.

Saif M. Mohammad. 2016. Sentiment analysis: Detecting valence, emotions, and other affectual states from text. In Herb Meiselman, editor, *Emotion Measurement*. Elsevier.

Bryan Orme. 2009. Maxdiff analysis: Simple counting, individual-level logit, and HB. Sawtooth Software, Inc.

Charles E Osgood, George J Suci, and Percy Tannenbaum. 1957. *The measurement of meaning*. University of Illinois Press.

Livia Polanyi and Annie Zaenen. 2004. Contextual valence shifters. In *Proceedings of the Exploring Attitude and Affect in Text: Theories and Applications (AAAI Spring Symposium Series)*.

Maria Pontiki, Harris Papageorgiou, Dimitrios Galanis, Ion Androutsopoulos, John Pavlopoulos, and Suresh Manandhar. 2014. SemEval-2014 Task 4: Aspect based sentiment analysis. In *Proceedings of the 8th International Workshop on Semantic Evaluation (SemEval)*, Dublin, Ireland.

Sara Rosenthal, Preslav Nakov, Svetlana Kiritchenko, Saif Mohammad, Alan Ritter, and Veselin Stoyanov. 2015. SemEval-2015 task 10: Sentiment analysis in Twitter. In *Proceedings of the 9th International Workshop on Semantic Evaluation (SemEval)*, pages 450–462, Denver, Colorado.

Josef Ruppenhofer, Jasper Brandes, Petra Steiner, and Michael Wiegand. 2015. Ordering adverbs by their scaling effect on adjective intensity. In *Proceedings of Recent Advances in Natural Language Processing (RANLP)*, pages 545–554, Hissar, Bulgaria.

Philip Stone, Dexter C. Dunphy, Marshall S. Smith, Daniel M. Ogilvie, and associates. 1966. *The General Inquirer: A Computer Approach to Content Analysis*. The MIT Press.

Maite Taboada, Julian Brooke, Milan Tofiloski, Kimberly Voll, and Manfred Stede. 2011. Lexicon-based methods for sentiment analysis. *Computational Linguistics*, 37(2):267–307.

Duyu Tang, Furu Wei, Bing Qin, Ming Zhou, and Ting Liu. 2014. Building large-scale Twitter-specific sentiment lexicon: A representation learning approach. In *Proceedings of the International Conference on Computational Linguistics (COLING)*, pages 172–182.

Louis L. Thurstone. 1927. A law of comparative judgment. *Psychological review*, 34(4):273.

Peter Turney and Michael L Littman. 2003. Measuring praise and criticism: Inference of semantic orientation from association. *ACM Transactions on Information Systems*, 21(4).

Amy Beth Warriner, Victor Kuperman, and Marc Brysbaert. 2013. Norms of valence, arousal, and dominance for 13,915 English lemmas. *Behavior Research Methods*, 45(4):1191–1207.

Michael Wiegand, Alexandra Balahur, Benjamin Roth, Dietrich Klakow, and Andrés Montoyo. 2010. A survey on the role of negation in sentiment analysis. In *Proceedings of the Workshop on Negation and Speculation in Natural Language Processing (NeSp-NLP)*, pages 60–68, Stroudsburg, PA, USA.

Theresa Wilson, Janyce Wiebe, and Paul Hoffmann. 2005. Recognizing contextual polarity in phrase-level sentiment analysis. In *Proceedings of the Conference on Human Language Technology and Empirical Methods in Natural Language Processing*, pages 347–354, Stroudsburg, PA, USA.

Xiaodan Zhu, Hongyu Guo, Saif Mohammad, and Svetlana Kiritchenko. 2014. An empirical study on the effect of negation words on sentiment. In *Proceedings of the 52nd Annual Meeting of the Association for Computational Linguistics*, pages 304–313, Baltimore, Maryland, June.

# How can NLP Tasks Mutually Benefit Sentiment Analysis?
# A Holistic Approach to Sentiment Analysis


**Lingjia Deng**
Intelligent Systems Program


University of Pittsburgh
lid29@pitt.edu

**Janyce Wiebe**
Intelligent Systems Program
Department of Computer Science
University of Pittsburgh
wiebe@cs.pitt.edu



## Abstract

Existing opinion analysis techniques rely on the clues within the sentence that focus on the sentiment analysis task itself. However, the sentiment analysis task is not isolated from other NLP tasks (co-reference resolution, entity linking, etc) but they can benefit each other. In this paper, we define dependencies between sentiment analysis and other tasks, and express the dependencies in first order logic rules regardless of the representations of different tasks. The conceptual framework proposed in this paper using such dependency rules as constraints aims at exploiting information outside the sentence and outside the document to improve sentiment analysis. Further, the framework allows exception to the rules.


## 1 Introduction

Opinions are ubiquitous in language. Existing opinion analysis techniques rely on the clues in the sentence that focus on the sentiment analysis task itself. Consider, for example,

(Ex1) Oh no, the voters defeated the bill.

The sentiment lexicons are used to recognize *Oh no* as a negative opinion, the semantic role labeling features are used to recognize the target is the *defeating* event (Yang and Cardie, 2013), and the implicatures are used to recognize the writer is positive toward the bill since the writer is negative toward the defeating event which harms the bill (Deng et al., 2014; Deng and Wiebe, 2015). These work mainly

rely on the clues that directly indicate opinions (e.g., recognizing *On no* as a negative opinion), or indicate components of opinions (e.g., recognizng the target being *defeating*), or indicate other opinions based on the information within the sentence (e.g., recognizing a positive opinion toward *the bill*). They do not exploit the vast amount of knowledge outside the sentence, which are outputs from many NLP tasks. But the task of sentiment analysis may benefit from those tasks. Consider (Ex2), for example,

(Ex2) President Obama proposed the healthcare reform. I support him.

we recognize in the second the sentence that the writer (*I*) is positive toward *him*. Further, we recognize the writer is positive toward *President Obama* since by co-reference resolution we know that *him* refers to *President Obama*.

Meanwhile, other NLP tasks may benefit from sentiment analysis. Consider, for example,

(Ex3) The allies successfully defeated Nazi. They are really brave.

The sentiment analysis system may infer that the writer is positive toward the allies and negative toward Nazi. Based on this information, we can infer that the word *they* in the second sentence refers to the allies instead of Nazi. Thus the sentiment analysis outputs help the co-reference resolution task.

The relation of sentiment analysis and other NLP tasks cannot be easily modelled as a pipeline. For example, in (Ex2) a co-reference resolution needs to be run first to infer the writer is positive toward Obama, while in (Ex3) the positive sentiments needs

53


*Proceedings of NAACL-HLT 2016*, pages 53–59,
San Diego, California, June 12-17, 2016. ©2016 Association for Computational Linguistics

to be recognized first to infer the word *they* refer to the allies. Previous work (Deng et al., 2014; Deng and Wiebe, 2015) develop joint models to infer sentiments based on the implicature rules (e.g, (Ex1)). They first develop independent systems to recognize sentiments and components of sentiments. Then joint approaches are used to take the outputs from independent systems as input and globally infer sentiments based on all the input information. The implicature rules are used as constraints in the joint approaches. Similar to their method, we can use rules introduced in this paper as constraints in the joint models, and jointly resolve sentiment analysis and other NLP tasks. Furthermore, though the representations of knowledge that different tasks generate are various, the dependencies in this paper are expressed in a unified way: first order logic rules.

In summary, this paper presents a conceptual framework using the newly defined dependency rules as constraints of joint models to exploit various kinds of knowledge to make progress toward a deeper interpretation of subjective language. The background of joint models is given in Section 2. The dependency rules and corresponding NLP tasks are given in Section 3. Furthermore, the framework allows exceptions to the rules, which will be discussed in Section 4. Finally we give the conclusion.

## 2   Background

The ultimate goal of this paper is to improve sentiment analysis by exploiting various knowledge, each of which corresponds to an NLP task. We define atoms corresponding to the tasks in Table 1.

The primary task of sentiment analysis is to assign scores to the atoms $pos(X,Y)$ and $neg(X,Y)$ (i.e., assigning true or false, or numeric scores to the atoms). Most of previous work directly assign scores to $pos(X,Y)$ and $neg(X,Y)$ without any dependency rule. Some recent work (Deng et al., 2014; Deng and Wiebe, 2015) take the scores as local scores and maximize the sum of scores of all the Primary Task and Implicature Knowledge atoms in Table 1 w.r.t. the constraints defined by a subset of implicature rules in (Wiebe and Deng, 2014a). Their experiments have shown that the joint models are able to choose a better assignment of the scores to all the atoms globally rather than make individual decisions according to local scores only.

However, the previous conceptual framework (Wiebe and Deng, 2014b) only defines rules over the Implicature Knowledge atoms to only consider the information within the sentence. And they are limited to a particular type of event: +/-effect event. Instead, this paper introduces rules defined over the External Knowledge atoms to exploit knowledge outside the sentence and outside the document. Further, the atoms defined in this paper are general so that people can use these atoms to design more rules.

## 3   Dependency Rules and NLP Tasks

The dependency rules are expressed as first order logic rules. As a start, we represent one of the rules from (Wiebe and Deng, 2014a) in first order logic applied to (Ex1) in Section 1.

In (Ex1), we infer from the negative sentiment toward the defeated event that the writer is positive toward the bill. The defeated event is defined as a -effect event since it has negative effect on the theme, the bill (Deng et al., 2013). The instantiated rule is:

$$(R1)\ neg(writer, defeat) \wedge \text{-effect}(defeat)$$
$$\wedge\ theme(defeat, bill) \Rightarrow pos(writer, bill)$$

Different from the rules defined in (Wiebe and Deng, 2014a), we define new rules depicting the dependencies between sentiments (e.g., $pos(X,Y)$) and external knowledge outside the sentence (e.g., $posExternal(X,Y)$). We focus on two types of knowledge. The first involves knowledge from elsewhere within the same document, and the second involves document-external knowledge such as that stored in a knowledge base (e.g., Freebase).

For ease of understanding, a rule is presented as an instantiated rule applied to an example (as (R1) above). There are variations of the rules listed in this paper according to different context.[1]

### 3.1   Rules of Intra-Document Knowledge

**Co-reference Resolution.**   Recall (Ex2) in Section 1. The writer is positive toward Obama because the

---

[1]For example, a variation of (R1) is: pos(writer, defeat) $\wedge$ -effect(defeat) $\wedge$ theme(defeat, bill) $\Rightarrow$ neg(writer, bill)

| Primary Task | | |
| --- | --- | --- |
| pos(X,Y) | X has positive sentiment toward Y, evoked in the current sentence | |
| neg(X,Y) | X has negative sentiment toward Y, evoked in the current sentence | |

| Implicature Knowledge | | | | |
| --- | --- | --- | --- | --- |
| +sentiment(S) | S is a positive sentiment | +effect(T) | T is a +effect event |
| -sentiment(S) | S is a negative sentiment | -effect(T) | T is a -effect event |
| source(S,X) | the source of S is X | agent(T,X) | the agent of T is X |
| target(S,Y) | the target of S is Y | theme(T,Y) | the theme of T is Y |

| External Knowledge | |
| --- | --- |
| posExternal(X,Y) | X has positive sentiment toward Y, external to the sentence |
| negExternal(X,Y) | X has negative sentiment toward Y, external to the sentence |
| sameEntity(X,Y) | X and Y refer to same entity |
| altEntity(X,Y) | X and Y represent alternative entities |
| agree(X,Y) | X and Y agree with each other |
| reinforcing(X,Y) | X and Y are reinforcing sentiments |
| non-reinforcing(X,Y) | X and Y are non-reinforcing sentiments |
| ideology(X,I) | X holds ideology I |
| aspect(X,Y) | an aspect (feature) of X is Y |

**Table 1:** Atoms in the Rules.

word *him* refers to Obama. The instantiated rule is:

(R2) posExternal(writer,him) ∧
    sameEntity(him,Obama)
    ⇒ pos(writer,Obama)

**Agree.** We may also infer that the writer has the same sentiments as sources with whom he or she agrees. While much previous work detects agreement at the turn level in conversation (Michel Galley, 2004; Wang et al., 2011), or identifies participants who agree with one another (Hassan et al., 2012; Abu-Jbara et al., 2012; Park et al., 2011), there is recent work on detecting agreement within documents (Wang and Cardie, 2014; Abbott et al., 2011; Misra and Walker, 2013). Consider, *I agree with Paul. ... The plan is a brilliant idea.* The writer (I) agree with Paul, and the writer is positive toward the plan. Then we infer that probably Paul is positive toward the plan.

(R3) agree(writer,Paul) ∧ posExternal(writer,plan)
    ⇒ pos(Paul,plan)

**Opinion-oriented Discourse Models.** Furthermore, previous work have developed opinion-oriented discourse models (*OODMs*) (Somasundaran, 2010). The OODM models recognize toward which entities the writer's sentiments are the same (*sameEntity*), and toward which entities the writer's sentiments are opposite (*altEntity*). The discourse *sameEntity* relation covers not only identity, but also part-whole, synonymy, generalization, specialization, entity-attribute/aspect, instantiation, cause-effect, and implicit background topic, i.e., relations that have been studied by many researchers in the context of anaphora and co-reference (e.g. (Clark, 1975; Vieira and Poesio, 2000; Mueller and Strube, 2001)). Two entities are in an *altEntity* relation if they are mutually exclusive options in the context of the discourse. For example, in a debate about mobile phones, the iPhone and iOS are considered as *sameEntity*, while the Android and iPhone are considered as *altEntity*. In OODM models, same sentiments toward same entities express the same stance, and opposite sentiments toward alternative targets express the same overall stance (Somasundaran, 2010).

(R4) posExternal(writer,iOS) ∧
    sameEntity(iOS,iPhone) ⇒ pos(writer,iPhone)
(R5) posExternal(writer,iOS) ∧
    altEntity(iOS,Android) ⇒ neg(writer,Android)

However, the opinions throughout the documents

may not always be consistent. In the same document, a source may be both positive and negative toward a target. In this paper, we define **rules to explain conflicting opinions** in the document.

**Aspect-Based Sentiment Analysis.** In one case, the source has different opinions about different aspects of the same target. Consider *The iPhone display is beautiful. But it is too expensive.* The writer is positive toward the display while negative toward the price. Such case can be modelled via the rule:

(R6) posExternal(writer,iPhone) $\wedge$
    sameEntity(iPhone,it) $\wedge$ neg(writer,it) $\Leftrightarrow$
    aspect(iPhone,display) $\wedge$ aspect(it,price) $\wedge$
    posExternal(writer,display) $\wedge$ neg(writer,price)

Several researchers have focused on the task of mining data to discover aspects of products and sentiments toward different aspects (Liu, 2012).

**(Non-)Reinforcing Sentiment Analysis.** In the other case, people may be ambivalent, or change their minds in the course of a document. Two sentiments may be in *reinforcing* or *non-reinforcing* discourse scenarios. Reinforcing relations exist between opinions when they contribute to the same overall stance. Non-reinforcing relations exist between opinions that show ambivalence, which represents a discourse scenario in which inconsistent sentiments are expressed with respect to a stance (Somasundaran, 2010; Trivedi and Eisenstein, 2013; Bhatia et al., 2015). Consider, *It is expensive. ... However, I think it is worth a try if I loan to buy the phone.* Previous work (Somasundaran, 2010) may recognize that two non-reinforcing sentiments occur (indicated by the word *However*). *S1* represents the negative opinion in the first sentence expressed toward it, and *S2* represents the positive opinion in the second sentence expressed toward the phone.

(R7) non-reinforcing(S1,S2) $\wedge$
    source(S1,writer) $\wedge$ source(S2,writer) $\wedge$
    target(S1,It) $\wedge$ target(S2,the phone) $\wedge$
    sameEntity(It, the phone)
    $\wedge$ negExternal(writer,It) $\Rightarrow$ pos(writer,the phone)

Two non-reinforcing opinions can also be expressed toward alternative entities. Consider, *The iPhone is too expensive. ... But the price of Android cannot guarantee a satisfactorily smooth operating system.* *S1* represents the negative opinion in the first sentence expressed toward iPhone, and *S2* represents the negative opinion in the second sentence expressed toward Android.

(R8) non-reinforcing(S1,S2) $\wedge$
    source(S1,writer) $\wedge$ source(S2,writer) $\wedge$
    target(S1,iPhone) $\wedge$ target(S2,Android) $\wedge$
    altEntity(iPhone, Android)
    $\wedge$ negExternal(writer,iPhone)
    $\Rightarrow$ neg(writer,Android)

## 3.2 Rules of Extra-Document Knowledge

**Entity Linking.** Knowledge from outside the document is also important. For example, the work in entity linking maps entity mentions (e.g.,Obama, US President) in the text to entries in the knowledge base (e.g., BARACK OBAMA) (Ji and Grishman, 2011; Rao et al., 2013). Such information can be exploited to recognize *sameEntity*, as shown below.

(R9) sameEntity(Obama, BARACK OBAMA)
    $\wedge$ sameEntity(US President, BARACK OBAMA)
    $\Rightarrow$ sameEntity(Obama, US President)

Thus, we can use the knowledge base to enrich the recognition of *sameEntity* and help recognize more sentiments.

**Ideology.** Groups of people sharing the same ideology tend to have the same opinions about certain things. Suppose we have known that Donald Trump is conservative, and a conservative ideology is against the concept of gun control, then we probably infer that he is opposed to gun control in the context.

(R10) ideology(Donald Trump,CONSERVATIVE)
    $\wedge$ negExternal(CONSERVATIVE,GUN CONTROL)
    $\wedge$ sameEntity(GUN CONTROL, gun control)
    $\Rightarrow$ neg(Donald Trump,gun control)

Rather than attempt to computationally define a general notion of ideology, people in NLP tend to use data for which specific ideologies have been defined. Previous work have studied recognizing ideologies including political party affiliation (Iyyer et al., 2014), or labels such as *left*, *right*, and *center* (Sim et al., 2013), or use a proxy for ideology such as voting record (Gerrish and Blei, 2011).

## 4  Integrating Evidence Against Rules

The framework allows exceptions to the rules. The joint models implemented in the previous work (Deng et al., 2014; Deng and Wiebe, 2015) use implicature rules as soft constraints. However, previous work didn't investigate when the rules are blocked. In this section we introduce two types of evidences against the rules. [2] The first case is when the event is involuntarily conducted. Consider Ex(4A) below.

> (Ex4A) The insurance companies will increase their spending on health care improvement.
> (Ex4B) The insurance companies will **be required to** increase their spending on health care improvement.

Assuming that there is a positive sentiment toward health care improvement in (Ex4A), the implicature rules infer a positive sentiment toward the insurance companies since the companies are increasing the improvement. However, consider the variation (Ex4B). The implicature here is less strong and perhaps defeated. The reason is that the companies will be *forced* to increase their spending.

Another case is when an event is *accidental*. For example in (Ex5A),

> Ex(5A) John deleted the file I need.
> Ex(5B) John **accidentally** deleted the file I need.

the rules imply a negative sentiment toward John. However, this inference is weakened in the variation (Ex5B). To recognize these cases, lexical clues are important, such as unintentionally, involuntary. Given a list of seed words, resources such as WordNet, word embeddings (Mikolov et al., 2013) and paraphrase databases (e.g., PPDB (Ganitkevitch et al., 2013)) can be utilized to find semantically similar words and phrases.

---

[2]We realized these cases from the study of implicit sentiment in Greene and Resnik (Greene and Resnik, 2009).

Further, we can integrate the evidences against the rules into the rules themselves. For example, (R11) is the rule applied to (Ex4A). If we want to integrate evidences against rules to model cases such as (Ex4B), we can revised rule by incorporating the atom *initiative* representing whether an event is conducted initiatively, as (R11*) shows. If initiative(increase) is false, this inference is blocked.

(R11) pos(writer, increase) $\wedge$
    agent(company, increase)
     $\Rightarrow$ pos(writer, company)
(R11*) pos(writer, increase) $\wedge$
    agent(company, increase) $\wedge$ **initiative(increase)**
     $\Rightarrow$ pos(writer, company)

This shows that the rule is flexible to add or remove an atom. Also, the framework is flexible to block a rule in the context. Such flexibility allows the framework to model various context and adapt to different genres.

## 5  Conclusion

Sentiment analysis is not isolated from other NLP tasks. The conceptual framework in this paper aims at improving sentiment analysis by introducing dependency rules between sentiments and various knowledge provided from various NLP tasks including co-reference resolution, opinion discourse analysis, entity linking and ideology, etc. The framework uses dependency rules as constraints in the joint models. Further, the framework can block a rule in context by recognizing evidences against the instantiated rule. Though it is a conceptual framework, it bridges different tasks of sentiment analysis and various tasks in NLP together to provide a holistic approach to sentiment analysis and the other tasks as well.

## Acknowledgements.

This work was supported in part by DARPA-BAA-12-47 DEFT grant #12475008. We thank the anonymous reviewers for their helpful comments.

## References

Rob Abbott, Marilyn Walker, Pranav Anand, Jean E. Fox Tree, Robeson Bowmani, and Joseph King. 2011.

How can you say such things?!?: Recognizing disagreement in informal political argument. In *Proceedings of the Workshop on Language in Social Media (LSM 2011)*, pages 2–11, Portland, Oregon, June. Association for Computational Linguistics.

Amjad Abu-Jbara, Pradeep Dasigi, Mona Diab, and Dragomir Radev. 2012. Subgroup detection in ideological discussions. In *Proceedings of the 50th Annual Meeting of the Association for Computational Linguistics (Volume 1: Long Papers)*, pages 399–409, Jeju Island, Korea, July. Association for Computational Linguistics.

Parminder Bhatia, Yangfeng Ji, and Jacob Eisenstein. 2015. Better document-level sentiment analysis from rst discourse parsing. In *Proceedings of the 2015 Conference on Empirical Methods in Natural Language Processing*, pages 2212–2218, Lisbon, Portugal, September. Association for Computational Linguistics.

H. H. Clark. 1975. Bridging. *Theoretical issues in natural language processing . New York: Association for Computing Machinery*, page 6.

Lingjia Deng and Janyce Wiebe. 2015. Joint prediction for entity/event-level sentiment analysis using probabilistic soft logic models. In *Proceedings of the 2015 Conference on Empirical Methods in Natural Language Processing*, pages 179–189, Lisbon, Portugal, September. Association for Computational Linguistics.

Lingjia Deng, Yoonjung Choi, and Janyce Wiebe. 2013. Benefactive/malefactive event and writer attitude annotation. In *ACL 2013 (short paper)*. Association for Computational Linguistics.

Lingjia Deng, Janyce Wiebe, and Yoonjung Choi. 2014. Joint inference and disambiguation of implicit sentiments via implicature constraints. In *Proceedings of COLING 2014, the 25th International Conference on Computational Linguistics: Technical Papers*, pages 79–88, Dublin, Ireland, August. Dublin City University and Association for Computational Linguistics.

Juri Ganitkevitch, Benjamin Van Durme, and Chris Callison-Burch. 2013. Ppdb: The paraphrase database. In *Proceedings of the 2013 Conference of the North American Chapter of the Association for Computational Linguistics: Human Language Technologies*, pages 758–764, Atlanta, Georgia, June. Association for Computational Linguistics.

Sean Gerrish and David M. Blei. 2011. Predicting legislative roll calls from text. In *ICML*.

Stephan Greene and Philip Resnik. 2009. More than words: Syntactic packaging and implicit sentiment. In *Proceedings of Human Language Technologies: The 2009 Annual Conference of the North American Chapter of the Association for Computational Linguistics*,

pages 503–511, Boulder, Colorado, June. Association for Computational Linguistics.

Ahmed Hassan, Amjad Abu-Jbara, and Dragomir Radev. 2012. Detecting subgroups in online discussions by modeling positive and negative relations among participants. In *Proceedings of the 2012 Joint Conference on Empirical Methods in Natural Language Processing and Computational Natural Language Learning*, pages 59–70, Jeju Island, Korea, July. Association for Computational Linguistics.

Mohit Iyyer, Peter Enns, Jordan Boyd-Graber, and Philip Resnik. 2014. Political ideology detection using recursive neural networks. In *Proceedings of the 52nd Annual Meeting of the Association for Computational Linguistics (Volume 1: Long Papers)*, pages 1113–1122, Baltimore, Maryland, June. Association for Computational Linguistics.

Heng Ji and Ralph Grishman. 2011. Knowledge base population: Successful approaches and challenges. In *Proceedings of the 49th Annual Meeting of the Association for Computational Linguistics: Human Language Technologies-Volume 1*, pages 1148–1158. Association for Computational Linguistics.

Bing Liu. 2012. *Sentiment Analysis and Opinion Mining*. Synthesis Lectures on Human Language Technologies. Morgan & Claypool Publishers.

Julia Hirschberg Elizabeth Shriberg Michel Galley, Kathleen McKeown. 2004. Identifying agreement and disagreement in conversational speech: Use of bayesian networks to model pragmatic dependencies. In *Proceedings of the 42th Annual Meeting of the Association for Computational Linguistics (ACL-2004)*.

Tomas Mikolov, Ilya Sutskever, Kai Chen, Greg S Corrado, and Jeff Dean. 2013. Distributed representations of words and phrases and their compositionality. In *Advances in neural information processing systems*, pages 3111–3119.

Amita Misra and Marilyn Walker. 2013. Topic independent identification of agreement and disagreement in social media dialogue. In *Proceedings of the SIGDIAL 2013 Conference*, pages 41–50, Metz, France, August. Association for Computational Linguistics.

Christoph Mueller and Michael Strube. 2001. Annotating anaphoric and bridging relations with mmax. In *2nd SIGdial Workshop on Discourse and Dialogue*.

Souneil Park, Kyung Soon Lee, and Junehwa Song. 2011. Contrasting opposing views of news articles on contentious issues. In *Proceedings of the 49th Annual Meeting of the Association for Computational Linguistics: Human Language Technologies*, pages 340–349, Portland, Oregon, USA, June. Association for Computational Linguistics.

Delip Rao, Paul McNamee, and Mark Dredze. 2013. Entity linking: Finding extracted entities in a knowledge base. In *Multi-source, multilingual information extraction and summarization*, pages 93–115. Springer.

Yanchuan Sim, Brice D. L. Acree, Justin H. Gross, and Noah A. Smith. 2013. Measuring ideological proportions in political speeches. In *Proceedings of the 2013 Conference on Empirical Methods in Natural Language Processing*, pages 91–101, Seattle, Washington, USA, October. Association for Computational Linguistics.

Swapna Somasundaran. 2010. *Discourse-Level Relations for Opinion Analysis*. Ph.D. thesis, Department of Computer Science, University of Pittsburgh.

Rakshit Trivedi and Jacob Eisenstein. 2013. Discourse connectors for latent subjectivity in sentiment analysis. In *Proceedings of the 2013 Conference of the North American Chapter of the Association for Computational Linguistics: Human Language Technologies*, pages 808–813, Atlanta, Georgia, June. Association for Computational Linguistics.

Renata Vieira and Massimo Poesio. 2000. An empirically based system for processing definite descriptions. *Computational Linguistics*, 26(4):539–593.

Lu Wang and Claire Cardie. 2014. Improving agreement and disagreement identification in online discussions with a socially-tuned sentiment lexicon. In *Proceedings of the 5th Workshop on Computational Approaches to Subjectivity, Sentiment and Social Media Analysis*, pages 97–106, Baltimore, Maryland, June. Association for Computational Linguistics.

Wen Wang, Sibel Yaman, Kristin Precoda, Colleen Richey, and Geoffrey Raymond. 2011. Detection of agreement and disagreement in broadcast conversations. In *Proceedings of the 49th Annual Meeting of the Association for Computational Linguistics: Human Language Technologies*, pages 374–378, Portland, Oregon, USA, June. Association for Computational Linguistics.

Janyce Wiebe and Lingjia Deng. 2014a. An account of opinion implicatures. *arXiv*, 1404.6491[cs.CL].

Janyce Wiebe and Lingjia Deng. 2014b. A conceptual framework for inferring implicatures. In *Proceedings of the 5th Workshop on Computational Approaches to Subjectivity, Sentiment and Social Media Analysis*, pages 154–159, Baltimore, Maryland, June. Association for Computational Linguistics.

Bishan Yang and Claire Cardie. 2013. Joint inference for fine-grained opinion extraction. In *Proceedings of the 51st Annual Meeting of the Association for Computational Linguistics (Volume 1: Long Papers)*, pages 1640–1649, Sofia, Bulgaria, August. Association for Computational Linguistics.

# An Unsupervised System for Visual Exploration of Twitter Conversations

**Derrick Higgins, Michael Heilman, Adrianna Jelesnianska** and **Keith Ingersoll**

Civis Analytics

dhiggins@civisanalytics.com

## Abstract

Social media provides a wealth of information regarding users' perspectives on issues, public figures and brands, but it can be a time-consuming and labor-intensive process to develop data pipelines in which those perspectives are encoded, and to build visualizations that illuminate important developments. This paper describes a system for quickly developing a model of the conversation around an issue on Twitter, and a flexible visualization system that allows analysts to interactively explore key facets of the analysis.

## 1 Introduction

This paper introduces a visualization system designed to support deep analysis of Twitter conversations that persist over a long period of time (as well as inform decisions concerned with recent developments). Given a set of tweets that define the conversation to be modeled (and which may be selected by arbitrary criteria including keywords, users, and time frames of interest), Civis Analytics' web-based system provides a rich and interactive set of visualizations that illustrate

- the major themes of discussion and user perspectives,

- communities of users engaged in the conversation (and their centrality to it),

- how strongly users and user groups address particular themes,

- the activity of themes and user groups over time, and

- the activity of themes and user groups in different geographical regions.

We anticipate that an analyst can use this tool to quickly develop a high-level understanding of the dynamics of a given issue on Twitter, to drill down into the specifics of how particular users and tweets contribute to changes in the conversation, and to develop informed strategies for outreach or intervention. The tool takes advantage of current research in topic modeling and community analysis, and can easily incorporate domain-specific knowledge where it is available.

## 2 Related Work

Civis' system for visualizing the dynamics of social media conversations builds upon prior research in a number of areas.

### 2.1 Data processing technologies

First, there are a number of enabling technologies that are used to transform the unstructured data stream from Twitter into a structured representation that our system can use as the basis for visualization.

One such technology is topic modeling – unsupervised identification of major themes in a set of text documents. Since its introduction (Blei et al., 2003), topic modeling has been tailored to perform better on short texts such as microblogs. For example, the Dirichlet Multinomial Mixture Model (Yin and Wang, 2014) modifies the standard LDA model to constrain all words of a text to be generated by

60

*Proceedings of NAACL-HLT 2016*, pages 60–65,
San Diego, California, June 12-17, 2016. ©2016 Association for Computational Linguistics

the same mixture component (topic), and the Biterm Topic Model (Yan et al., 2015) combines adjacent terms to provide richer information about the subject of a short text. The topic modeling method incorporated into the Civis social listening tool builds upon this research to provide meaningful topic groupings on short texts, but currently does not make use of any tweet metadata such as author or time frame.

Similarly, much progress has been made in recent years in adapting sentiment analysis to microblog data. Promising methods include hybrid topic-sentiment models (Xiang and Zhou, 2014), the incorporation of tweet metadata into the model (Vosoughi et al., 2015), and the application of word sense disambiguation as a pre-processing step (Sumanth and Inkpen, 2015).

Finally, our visualization tool makes use of graph-based community analysis. We use the Louvain algorithm (Blondel et al., 2008) on the friend-follower graph to find coherent user communities in a Twitter conversation; a survey of modern methods for community analysis is given by Malliaros and Vazirgiannis (2013).

While the current version of the Civis visualization tool includes topic modeling, community inference, and sentiment analysis, it is agnostic as to the source of these data layers. Our data abstraction layer guarantees that the visualization too will work as long as the relevant model can assign numeric values to tweets (or, in the case of community analysis, categories to users).

### 2.2 Visualization research

We also build on previous work that has developed interfaces for visualizing microblog metadata derived using natural language tools. Xie et al. (2013) use high-frequency bar charts to demonstrate the activity associated with "bursty" topics identified by their algorithm, while Malik et al. (2013) conduct user studies to refine a Twitter topic exploration tool with multiple information displays.

In the area of sentiment analysis, many dashboards have been developed to show the time course of opinion associated with a particular topic or keyword. Hao et al. (2011) develop a system with more engaging displays than the standard line chart, including heatmaps embedded within calendars, and activity maps.

The tool we will present in our demonstration differs from these previous interfaces primarily in the flexibility it allows for faceting the analysis according to NLP-related features, location, user community, and time.

## 3 System Overview

Civis Analytics' system for visualizing conversations on Twitter is intended to allow an analyst to quickly develop a model of the most important themes of discussion on an issue, the parties involved in the conversation, and trends across time and space.

In our live demonstration of the system, we will show how it can be used to analyze a wide variety of issues, including climate change, data science, and education. To provide a clearer indication of the type of views the system supports, though, we focus here on an analysis of the 2015-16 US Presidential primary campaign. The dataset for our analysis consists of approximately 15 million tweets posted between May, 2015 and February, 2016. These tweets were selected to include references to one or more of the Republican or Democratic candidates for the presidency (by name or using a strongly associated hashtag).

We applied a version of topic modeling adapted to short texts to infer a set of 44 topics, which are not mutually exclusive. Some of these topics are associated with particular candidates, while others are related to issues or events in the campaign. An analyst manually labeled these topics by inspecting the words and tweets most strongly associated with each, and the resulting topic definitions are included in our visualization tool for reference; Figure 1 demonstrates how topic-word associations are shown to users for the first 5 topics in our set (alphabetically).

We also selected a set of the most-active and most-followed users in the conversation for community analysis. We automatically inferred a set of three communities of users, which roughly correspond to political orientation ("Conservatives", "Progressives", and "Media", with the last group also including some political centrists). In our visual interface, these user groupings can be explored using an interactive graph that shows user clusters projected into two dimensions (cf. Figure 2). The 2D projection is done using the t-SNE algorithm (van der Maaten and Hinton, 2008) so that users with similar friend-follower relationships generally appear near one another. Users can interactively explore the graph to identify key users in each community and access their profiles.

The Civis interface also allows users to access more information about particular Twitter accounts that are relatively central to the network for a particular issue (using a network centrality measure such as PageRank). We hypothesize that accounts with a central position in the friend-follower network restricted to a particular issue are likely to be important, and perhaps influential figures in the relevant Twitter community. As shown in Figure 3, the available metadata about these key accounts includes the number of followers, how active they are on a given issue, and their relative engagement across topics.

Our system also supports sentiment analysis; Figure 4 demonstrates the average sentiment polarity of tweets overlaid on the graph of relationships between Twitter users. While the activity of particular topics is often strongly indicative of sentiment on its own, the sentiment layer may sometimes encode independent information as well.

**Figure 4:** Overlay of sentiment on to user exploration view

Finally, given base data associated with each tweet regarding topics, sentiment, and user communities, the Civis social listening tool provides multiple visualizations that allow users to explore the inter-relationships among these variables (including crosstabs, maps, and time series charts). Figure 5 shows a sample line chart displaying the time course of activation of the Bernie Sanders, Hillary Clinton and Black Lives Matter topics, restricted to the subset of Twitter users who are classified as belonging to the Progressive community.

## 4 Discussion and Future Work

The Civis social listening tool provides a flexible environment in which an analyst can interactively explore selected dimensions of a Twitter conversation. We hope it will inspire future research on visualization techniques for social media, and we anticipate extending the tool in a number of directions in the near future.

First, we plan to extend the set of case studies we have developed in order to test and demonstrate its functionality. We have built out analyses of the 2016 US Presidential Primary, climate change, and data science, but we would like to extend this set to include a more diverse set of topic areas.

Second, we plan to conduct more formal usability studies to establish which parts of the interface are most useful, and which users may find confusing or superfluous.

Finally, we hope to broaden the source data behind the tool to include other social media platforms and text sources. Print news stories, blog posts, and data feeds from Instagram all represent extensions that could provide additional context for analysts to exploit, given the right tools for summarization of their content.

**Figure 1:** Visualization of words most strongly associated with selected topics

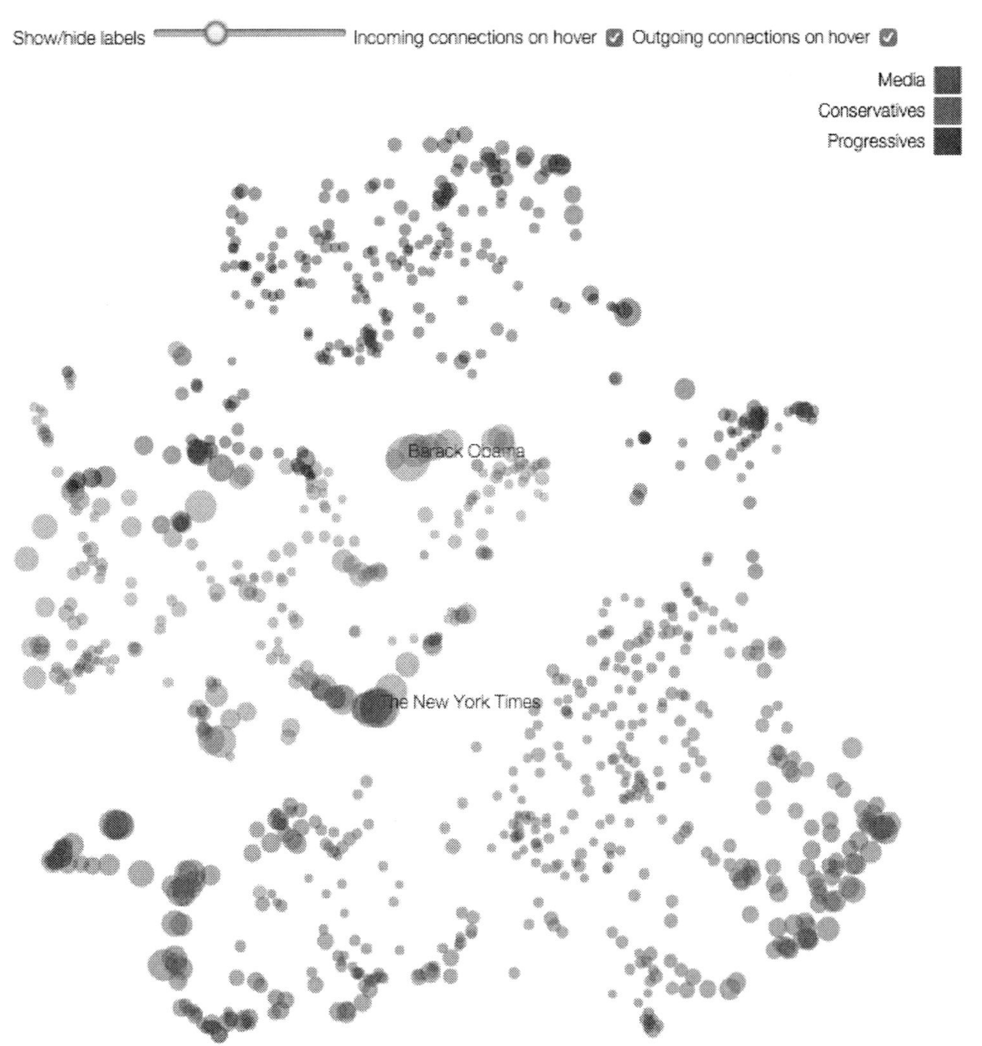


**Figure 2:** Interface for exploration of users and communities engaged in Twitter conversation (using a two-dimensional projection of friend-follower links)

**Figure 3:** List of most influential accounts from the Conservative community in the Presidential Primary analysis

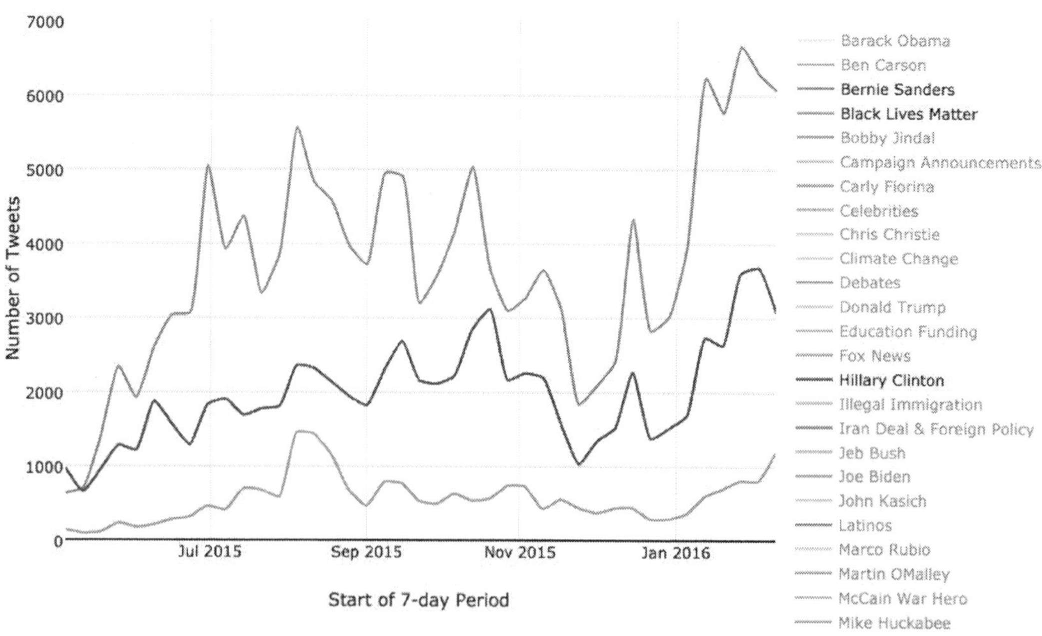


**Figure 5:** Visualization of trends in the Civis social listening interface, illustrated using the activity of Progressive users on the Bernie Sanders (top), Hillary Clinton (middle) and Black Lives Matter (bottom) topics

## References

David M. Blei, Andrew Y. Ng, and Michael I. Jordan. 2003. Latent Dirichlet allocation. *Journal of Machine Learning Research*, 3:993–1022, March.

Vincent D. Blondel, Jean-Loup Guillaume, Renaud Lambiotte, and Etienne Lefebvre. 2008. Fast unfolding of communities in large networks. *Journal of Statistical Mechanics: Theory and Experiment*, 2008(10):10008+, July.

Ming C. Hao, Christian Rohrdantz, Halldor Janetzko, Umeshwar Dayal, Daniel A. Keim, Lars-Erik Haug, and Meichun Hsu. 2011. Visual sentiment analysis on Twitter data streams. In *IEEE VAST*, pages 277–278. IEEE Computer Society.

Sana Malik, Alison Smith, Timothy Hawes, Panagis Papadatos, Jianyu Li, Cody Dunne, and Ben Shneiderman. 2013. TopicFlow: visualizing topic alignment of Twitter data over time. In Jon G. Rokne and Christos Faloutsos, editors, *ASONAM*, pages 720–726. ACM.

Fragkiskos D. Malliaros and Michalis Vazirgiannis. 2013. Clustering and community detection in directed networks: A survey. *Physics Reports*, 533(4):95 – 142. Clustering and Community Detection in Directed Networks: A Survey.

Chiraag Sumanth and Diana Inkpen. 2015. How much does word sense disambiguation help in sentiment analysis of micropost data? In *Proceedings of the 6th Workshop on Computational Approaches to Subjectivity, Sentiment and Social Media Analysis*, pages 115–121, Lisboa, Portugal, September. Association for Computational Linguistics.

Laurens van der Maaten and Geoffrey E. Hinton. 2008. Visualizing high-dimensional data using t-SNE. *Journal of Machine Learning Research*, 9:2579–2605.

Soroush Vosoughi, Helen Zhou, and deb roy. 2015. Enhanced Twitter sentiment classification using contextual information. In *Proceedings of the 6th Workshop on Computational Approaches to Subjectivity, Sentiment and Social Media Analysis*, pages 16–24, Lisboa, Portugal, September. Association for Computational Linguistics.

Bing Xiang and Liang Zhou. 2014. Improving Twitter sentiment analysis with topic-based mixture modeling and semi-supervised training. In *Proceedings of the 52nd Annual Meeting of the Association for Computational Linguistics (Volume 2: Short Papers)*, pages 434–439, Baltimore, Maryland, June. Association for Computational Linguistics.

Wei Xie, Feida Zhu, Jing Jiang, Ee-Peng Lim, and Ke Wang. 2013. TopicSketch: Real-time bursty topic detection from twitter. In Hui Xiong, George Karypis, Bhavani M. Thuraisingham, Diane J. Cook, and Xindong Wu, editors, *ICDM*, pages 837–846. IEEE Computer Society.

Xiaohui Yan, Jiafeng Guo, Yanyan Lan, Jun Xu, and Xueqi Cheng. 2015. A probabilistic model for bursty topic discovery in microblogs. In *The Twenty-Ninth AAAI Conference on Artificial Intelligence*.

Jianhua Yin and Jianyong Wang. 2014. A Dirichlet multinomial mixture model-based approach for short text clustering. In *Proceedings of the 20th ACM SIGKDD International Conference on Knowledge Discovery and Data Mining*, KDD '14, pages 233–242, New York, NY, USA. ACM.

# Threat detection in online discussions

**Aksel Wester**[1] and **Lilja Øvrelid**[1] and **Erik Velldal**[1] and **Hugo Lewi Hammer**[2]

[1] Department of Informatics
University of Oslo
{aksellw, liljao, erikve}@ifi.uio.no

[2] Department of Computer Science
Oslo and Akershus University College of Applied Sciences
hugo.hammer@hioa.no

## Abstract

This paper investigates the effect of various types of linguistic features (lexical, syntactic and semantic) for training classifiers to detect threats of violence in a corpus of YouTube comments. Our results show that combinations of lexical features outperform the use of more complex syntactic and semantic features for this task.

## 1  Introduction

Threats of violence constitute an increasingly common occurrence in online discussions. It disproportionately affects women and minorities, often to the point of effectively eliminating them from taking part in discussions online. Moderators of social networks operate on such a large scale that manually reading all posts is an insurmountable task. Methods for automatically detecting threats could therefore potentially be very helpful, both to moderators of social networks and to their members.

In this article, we evaluate different types of features for the task of detecting threats of violence in YouTube comments. We draw on both lexical, morphosyntactic and lexical semantic information sources and experiment with different machine learning algorithms. Our results indicate that successful detection of threats of violence is largely determined by lexical information.

## 2  Related work

There is little previous work specifically devoted to the detection of threats of violence in text. However, there is previous work which examines other types of closely related phenomena, such as 'cyberbullying' and hate-speech.

Dinakar et al. (2011) propose a method for the detection of cyberbullying by targeting combinations of profane or negative words, and words related to several predetermined sensitive topics. Their data set consists of over 50,000 YouTube comments taken from videos about controversial topics. The experiments reported accuracies from 0.63 to 0.80, but did not report precision or recall.

There has been quite a bit of work focused on the detection of threats in a data set of Dutch tweets (Oostdijk and van Halteren, 2013a; Oostdijk and van Halteren, 2013b), which consists of a collection of 5000 threatening tweets. In addition, a large number of random tweets were collected for development and testing. The system relies on manually constructed recognition patterns in the form of $n$-grams, but details about the strategy used to construct these patterns are not given. In Oostdijk and van Halteren (2013b), a manually crafted shallow parser is added to the system. This improves results to a precision of 0.39 and a recall of 0.59.

Warner and Hirschberg (2012) present a method for detecting hate speech in user-generated web text, which relies on machine learning in combination with template-based features. The task is approached as a word-sense disambiguation task, since the same words can be used in both hateful and non-hateful contexts. The features used in the classification were combinations of uni-, bi- and trigrams, part-of-speech-tags and Brown clusters. The best results were obtained using only unigram features,



*Proceedings of NAACL-HLT 2016*, pages 66–71,
San Diego, California, June 12-17, 2016. ©2016 Association for Computational Linguistics

|           | Comments | Sentences | Users posting |
| --------- | -------- | --------- | ------------- |
| Total     | 9,845    | 28,643    | 5,483         |
| Threats   | 1,285    | 1,384     | 992           |

**Table 1:** Number of comments, sentences and users in the YouTube threat data set.

with a precision of 0.67 and a recall of 0.60. The authors suggest that deeper parsing could reveal significant phrase patterns.

Most closely related to the current paper is the work of Hammer (2014), reporting on experiments on (a previous version of) the same corpus as used here. The method uses a logistic LASSO regression analysis on bigrams (skip-grams) of important words to classify sentences as either threats of violence or not. The system makes use of a list of words that are correlated with threats of violence. The article does not, however, describe exactly how these important words were selected, stating only that words were chosen that were significantly correlated with the response (violent/non-violent sentence). Results are reported only in terms of proportion of false positives for the two classes, and it is not clear how the data was split for training and evaluation, making it difficult to directly compare our results to those of Hammer (2014).

## 3 The YouTube threat corpus

The YouTube threat corpus[1] comprises user-written comments from eight different YouTube videos (Hammer, 2014). The videos cover religious and political topics like halal slaughter, immigration, Anders Behring Breivik, Jihad, etc. A given comment consists of a set of sentences, each of them manually annotated to be either a threat of violence (or support for a threat of violence), or not. The corpus also records usernames of the commenters.

As shown in Table 1, the corpus consists of 9,845 comments, comprising 28,643 sentences. There are 1,384 sentences containing threats, spread over 1,285 comments. Hammer (2014) reports inter-annotator agreement on this data set to be 98 %, as calculated on 120 of the comments, doubly annotated for evaluation.

---

[1] Please contact the authors if you want to obtain access to the corpus for your own research.

```
User #44
1      and i will kill every fucking
       muslim and arab!

User #88
0      Need a solution?
1      Drop one good ol' nuke on that
       black toilet in Mecca.
```

**Figure 1:** Example comments from the YouTube threat corpus.

Figure 1 provides some examples of comments from the corpus. The first line is the anonymized username, and the subsequent lines are the sentences of the comment. The sentences are annotated with a number indicating whether they contain a threat of violence (1) or not (0).

## 4 Experiments

Much of the previous related work presented in Section 2 made use of pre-compiled lists of correlated words and manually crafted patterns. Whereas these resources can be effective, they are highly task-specific and do not easily lend themselves to replication. Furthermore, while much of the previous work seem to highlight the effectiveness of lexical features, several of the authors also suggest that parsing may be beneficial for these tasks.

The approach followed in the current paper is to train a machine-learned model to automatically detect threats. We experiment with a range of different sources of linguistic information for defining our feature templates. We also generalize these features through a 'backoff' technique. Throughout, we make use of resources and tools that are freely available and reusable.

### 4.1 Experimental setup

**Pre-processing** Since threat annotation is performed on the sentence level, the corpus has been manually split into sentences as part of the annotation process. We performed tokenization, lemmatization, POS-tagging and dependency parsing using the spaCy NLP toolkit. SpaCy assigns both the standard Penn Treebank POS-tags (Marcus et al., 1993), as well as the more coarse-grained Universal POS tag set of Petrov et al. (2012). The dependency parser assigns an analysis in compliance with the

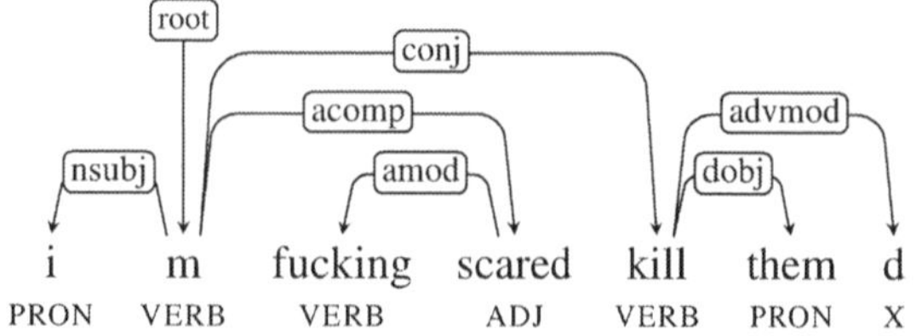


**Figure 2:** Dependency parse of example sentence from the corpus, with assigned uPOS tags.

ClearNLP converter (Choi and Palmer, 2012), see Figure 2 for an example dependency graph from the corpus. The corpus was further enriched with the cluster labels described in Turian et al. (2010), created using the Brown clustering algorithm (Brown et al., 1992) and induced from the Reuters corpus of English newswire text (RCV1). We vary the number of clusters to be either 100, 320, 1000 or 3200 clusters and use the full cluster label. We also make use of the WordNet resource (Fellbaum, 1998) to include information about the synset of a word, as well as its parent and grandparent synsets.

**Classifiers** We test three different classification frameworks in our development testing: Maximum Entropy (MaxEnt), Support Vector Machines (SVM), and Random Forests (RF). We approach the task as a binary classification task, using the implementations found in the scikit-learn toolkit (Pedregosa et al., 2011).

**Tuning** When tuning each model, we aim to maximize the F-score. For the MaxEnt and SVM classifiers we tune the regularization parameter (C), where a smaller value corresponds to stronger regularization. When tuning these classifiers, we start with C-values from 1 to 150 in 10-value increments, select the best performing C-value and repeat the process with decreasing increments, with the range of C-values centered on the best performing C-value thus far. After 6 iterations, we terminate the tuning, and select the best performing C-value. When tuning the Random Forest classifier, we perform a grid search over the number of trees, and the maximum number of features used when splitting a node in the tree. In the following experiments, we perform tuning on all feature sets.

**Features** Based on the enriched corpus, as described above, we experiment with the following sources of information for defining our features:

- Lexical:
  - Word form
  - Lemma
- Morphosyntactic:
  - Penn Treebank (PTB) POS
  - Universal POS (uPOS)
  - Dependency Relation
- Semantic:
  - Brown cluster label
  - WordNet synset, + parent and grandparent

The features are structured according to a set of *feature templates*, which record varying degrees of linear order and syntactic context: *bag-of* features (unordered), bigrams, trigrams and dependency triples. Examples of the latter, given the sentence in Figure 2, would be: {<m, nsubj, i>, <root, root, m>, <scared, amod, fucking>, ... }

Our lexicalized features are very specific and require the exact combination of two lexical items in order to apply to a new instance. Following Joshi and Penstein-Rose (2009), we therefore experiment with generalizing features by 'backing off' to a more general category, e.g., from word form to lemma or POS. For example, a dependency triple over word forms like <kill, dobj, them> would thus be generalized to <VERB, dobj, them> using *head-backoff*, and <kill, dobj, PRON> using *modifier-backoff*. These additional backoff features are included for bigrams and trigrams as well as dependency triples.

We impose a simple count-based reduction of the feature set; only features appearing at least twice in the training data are included in the model.

## 4.2 Development results

We start by defining an informed baseline system, empirically selecting an initial set of features and a classification framework to use as a basis and reference point for further development. The features for this initial round of tuning comprise basic lexical features; word forms and lemmas, in addition to $n$-grams defined over these.

In the second round of experiments we test combinations of these basic lexical feature types, be-

|                       | MaxEnt     | SVM        | RF         |
| --------------------- | ---------- | ---------- | ---------- |
| Bag-of-words          | **0.6123** | **0.6068** | **0.5918** |
| Bag-of-lemmas         | 0.5902     | 0.5982     | 0.5856     |
| Bigrams of word forms | 0.4856     | 0.4887     | 0.4944     |
| Trigrams of word forms| 0.2776     | 0.2856     | 0.2859     |

**Table 2:** Results for baseline system; F-score for bag-of lexical features (word form and lemma), and bigram and trigram templates over word forms. From left to right the columns correspond to Maximum Entropy classifiers, Support Vector Machines, and Random Forests.

| $n$-gram combination | BoW    | BoW+BoL    |
| -------------------- | ------ | ---------- |
| no $n$-grams         | 0.6123 | 0.6278     |
| +bigrams             | 0.6376 | 0.6577     |
| +trigrams            | 0.6180 | 0.6453     |
| +bi- and trigrams    | 0.6337 | **0.6656** |

**Table 3:** F-scores of the bag-of-words feature set, with different combinations of the other feature sets tested in Table 2, namely bag-of-lemmas and $n$-grams of word forms.

|          | $POS_{Lex}$ | $Dep_{Lex}$ | Synset | Brown  |
| -------- | ----------- | ----------- | ------ | ------ |
| BoF      | 0.6018      | 0.5655      | 0.4922 | 0.4688 |
| BoW+BoF  | 0.6071      | 0.6185      | 0.6176 | 0.6145 |

**Table 4:** F-scores of *bag-of* features (BoF) with and without bag-of-words (BoW). $POS_{Lex}$ and $Dep_{Lex}$ are lexicalized POS and dep-tags, respectively, where each feature is a tuple consisting of the tag and the word form of the token.

|                | bigram | trigram | bi+trigram |
| -------------- | ------ | ------- | ---------- |
| Lemma backoff  | 0.6611 | 0.6480  | **0.6649** |
| POS backoff    | 0.6410 | 0.6294  | 0.6320     |
| Dep backoff    | 0.6208 | 0.6194  | 0.6220     |
| Synset backoff | 0.6454 | 0.6448  | 0.6537     |
| Brown backoff  | 0.6285 | 0.6173  | 0.6335     |

**Table 5:** Backoff from different combinations of $n$-grams. The models also contain bag-of-words, and BoF for each feature, as in Table 4. Each backoff combination is the one that achieved the best result.

fore moving on to introduce more linguistic features, both syntactic and semantic, as *bag-of* features, and as backoff from word form $n$-grams. Finally, we will evaluate the inclusion of dependency triples.

Table 2 shows initial development results in terms of F-score for the the three different classifiers across four different feature sets; bags of word-forms and lemmas, as well as bigrams and trigrams over word forms. Generally, we see that feature sets containing lexical *bag-of* features outperform the $n$-gram features. The overall best result came from the MaxEnt classifier with the bag-of-word form feature set. This model yielded an F-score of 0.6123, with a precision of 0.6777 and a recall of 0.5585, using the MaxEnt classifier after tuning. This is the feature set we will use as our basic reference model in the next stage of our experiments is the bag-of-word forms. We will also only be using the the MaxEnt classifier for the remainder for reported development experiments. Besides acheiving the best result on the BoW feature set, MaxEnt also has a shorter training time than the other two classifiers.

We go on to test various combinations of these word form $n$-grams and the lexical *bag-of* features. As seen in Table 3, we test bag-of-words alone, and bag-of-words (BoW) with bag-of-lemmas (BoL), combined with the word form variants of bigrams,

trigrams and both. The best result without BoL comes from BoW with only bigrams, with an F-score of 0.6376, closely followed by BoW with both types of $n$-grams, which got an F-score of 0.6337. However, the best result overall came from the combination of BoW, BoL, and both types of $n$-grams, which got an F-score of 0.6656.

Next, we include feature types based on the other information sources listed above, i.e., POS, dependencies, WordNet synsets, and Brown clusters. All these features are instantiated both with the *bag-of* feature template on their own, and in combination with the bag-of-words features. As seen in Table 4, none of the feature types alone yield higher F-scores than bag-of-words. On the other hand, when combined with BoW, all feature types (except the lexicalized POS-tags) perform better than BoW alone. However, none of them outperform BoW and BoL combined (F=0.6278, cf. Table 3), or the combination of BoW+BoL with $n$-grams (F=0.6656).

Next, the $n$-grams and *bag-of* features are combined with generalized versions of $n$-gram features using the 'backoff' strategy described in the previous section. In Table 5 we see that the lemma backoff consistently outperform the other feature types, but that even lemma backoff does not improve upon the results without backoff features. We test all possible backoff combinations.

| Dependency backoff | BoW+dep | All |
|---|---|---|
| w/o backoff | 0.6240 | **0.6586** |
| Lemma | 0.6224 | 0.6507 |
| POS | **0.6298** | 0.6547 |
| Synset | 0.6234 | 0.6516 |
| Brown | 0.6299 | 0.6504 |

**Table 6:** Dependency triples with and without feature backoff, in combination with other features: 'BoW+dep' is the feature set containing bag-of-words and dependency triples. 'All' is the feature set containing BoW, BoL, bi- and trigrams and dependency triples. Each row backs off to a different feature type.

Lastly, we will test the addition of dependency triples to our models. We add dependency triples consisting of word forms, both alone, and in conjunction with feature backoffs. We test both head-backoff and modifier-backoff, and we report the variant that achieved the best results. As seen in Table 6, the inclusion of word form dependency triples improved upon the simplest model, with an F-score of 0.6240, compared to 0.6123 for bag-of-words alone. Dependency triples did not, however, improve upon the results achieved by our previous best performer (F=0.6656). The addition of backoff also did not improve the results above the previous best performer.

For the development data then, our best performer remains the feature set comprising bag-of-word forms, bag-of-lemmas, and word form bigrams and trigrams; with an F-score of 0.6656. We will refer to this model as 'lexical $n$-grams'.

The lexical $n$-gram feature set achieved a precision (P) of 0.7709 and a recall (R) of 0.5857. The performance of the same feature set improved slightly when using the SVM classifier (F=0.6667, P=0.7629, R=0.5920). Compared with our initial BoW system, which had P=0.6777 and R=0.5585, we see that the majority of the improvement comes from the increase in precision. The increases in both models compared with BoW are statistically significant, with p-values of 1.3e−11 and 8.6e−11 for the lexical $n$-gram system using MaxEnt and SVM, respectively, using the Wilcoxon signed-rank test. When reviewing a random sub-sample of the false positives and false negatives, we see that the noisy data has caused some problems for the pre-processor. Another source of errors, specifically for

|  | Precision | Recall | F-score |
|---|---|---|---|
| BoW | 0.7325 | 0.5943 | 0.6562 |
| Lexical $n$-grams, MaxEnt | **0.7532** | 0.6299 | 0.6860 |
| Lexical $n$-grams, SVM | 0.7490 | **0.6370** | **0.6885** |

**Table 7:** Precision, recall and F-score on the held-out test set for the basic BoW model and the best development feature set; the lexical $n$-gram model.

precision, are comments which use multiple typically threatening words in a non-threatening context.

### 4.3 Held-out results

We performed our final testing on the held-out test set using the basic BoW model and the lexical $n$-gram model, using both the MaxEnt and SVM classifiers. The held-out test set consists of 5,685 sentences, 281 of which are threats, and we train on the entire development set. As seen in Table 7, the $n$-gram models outperforms the BoW model by a good margin, with F-scores of 0.6885 (SVM), 0.6860 (MaxEnt), and 0.6562 (BoW). However, the difference in F-scores between the two feature sets is not as large as on the development data, and they are in fact not statistically significant, with p-values of 0.14 and 0.16, when comparing the MaxEnt and SVM lexical n-gram models, respectively, to BoW, using Wilcoxon. At the same time, we see that all the models actually achieves higher scores on the held-out data than the development data, and this effect is particularly strong for the BoW model (with the F-score going up from 0.6123 to 0.6562).

## 5   Conclusion

This paper has developed and compared several machine-learned models for automatically detecting threats of violence in online discussions. The data set comprises a manually annotated corpus of comments from YouTube videos. We have reported experimental results for different classification frameworks and a wide range of different linguistic features. The best performance was observed for combinations of simple lexical features (bag-of-words and lemmas, in combination with bi- and trigrams). Introducing more complex features – drawing on information from WordNet synsets, Brown clusters, POS tags and dependency parses – did not improve on the simpler surface-based feature set.

## References

Peter F. Brown, Peter V. deSouza, Robert L. Mercer, Vincent J. Della Pietra, and Jenifer C. Lai. 1992. Class-based n-gram models of natural language. *Computational Linguistics*, 18.

Jinho D. Choi and Martha Palmer. 2012. Guidelines for the clear style constituent to dependency conversion. Technical Report 01-12, Institute of Cognitive Science, University of Colorado Boulder.

Karthik Dinakar, Roi Reichart, and Henry Lieberman. 2011. Modeling the detection of textual cyberbullying. In *Proceedings of The Social Mobile Web*.

Christiane Fellbaum, editor. 1998. *WordNet: an electronic lexical database*. MIT Press, Cambridge, MA.

Hugo Lewi Hammer. 2014. Detecting threats of violence in online discussion using bigrams of important words. In *Proceedings of Intelligence and Security Informatics Conference (JISIC)*, pages 319–319.

Mahesh Joshi and Carolyn Penstein-Rose. 2009. Generalizing dependency features for opinion mining. In *Proceedings of the ACL-IJCNLP 2009 Conference Short Papers*, page 313–316.

Mitchell Marcus, Beatrice Santorini, and Mary Ann Marcinkiewicz. 1993. Building a large annotated corpora of English: The Penn Treebank. *Computational Linguistics*, 19:313–330.

Nelleke Oostdijk and Hans van Halteren. 2013a. N-gram-based recognition of threatening tweets. In *Proceedings of Computational Linguistics and Intelligent Text Processing*, pages 183–196. Springer.

Nelleke Oostdijk and Hans van Halteren. 2013b. Shallow parsing for recognizing threats in Dutch tweets. In *Proceedings of IEEE/ACM International Conference on Advances in Social Networks Analysis and Mining*, Niagara, Canada. ACM.

Fabian Pedregosa, Gaël Varoquaux, Alexandre Gramfort, Vincent Michel, Bertrand Thirion, Olivier Grisel, Mathieu Blondel, Peter Prettenhofer, Ron Weiss, Vincent Dubourg, Jake Vanderplas, Alexandre Passos, David Cournapeau, Matthieu Brucher, Matthieu Perrot, and Édouard Duchesnay. 2011. Scikit-learn: Machine learning in Python. *Journal of Machine Learning Research*, 12:2825–2830.

Slav Petrov, Dipanjan Das, and Ryan McDonald. 2012. A universal part-of-speech tagset. In *Proceedings of the International Conference on Language Resources and Evaluation (LREC)*, pages 2089–2096.

Joseph Turian, Lev Ratinov, and Yoshua Bengio. 2010. Word representations: a simple and general method for semi-supervised learning. In *Proceedings of the 48th Meeting of the Association for Computational Linguistics*, Uppsala, Sweden.

William Warner and Julia Hirschberg. 2012. Detecting hate speech on the world wide web. In *Proceedings of the Second Workshop on Language in Social Media*, pages 19–26, Montreal, Canada. Association for Computational Linguistics.

# Classification of comment helpfulness to improve knowledge sharing among medical practitioners.


**Pierre André Ménard**
Computer research institute of Montréal
`pierre-andre.menard@crim.ca`

**Caroline Barrière**
Computer research institute of Montréal
`caroline.barriere@crim.ca`



## Abstract

Clinical research article summaries called infoPOEMs (Patient-Oriented Evidence that Matters) are emailed by the Canadian Medical Association to family physicians who read them and answer the online Information Assessment Method (IAM) questionnaire which a free form textual opinion fields to comment on the value or content of the infoPOEM. This article presents results of a relevance evaluation study applied on these comments to automatically determine their helpfulness and consequently the interest of sharing them among the medical community. A dataset of 3,470 manually annotated comments provides a gold standard, containing structural, syntactic, and semantic features taken from the Unified Medical Language System and IAM questionnaire. Applied machine learning algorithms show a global f-measure improvement of 9.1% when compared to a binary occurrence bag-of-word baseline.


## 1 Introduction

The task of opinion mining has gained importance in the last years with our world being increasingly made of posted information with crowds commenting on such information. Such increased volume of crowd comments has led to text analysis research aiming at understanding and clustering the opinions found in those comments (e.g. see recent articles (Mukherjee and Liu, 2012; Turney, 2002; Chen and Zimbra, 2010)) and to help manage interactions within the online community (Huh et al., 2013).

An even more recent task is not so much on understanding comments content, but rather on evaluating comments value, impact or helpfulness for the community reading them. Most research addressing this task, as shown in the Related work section, uses comments on product information on Amazon. But the idea of evaluating comments helpfulness can be extended to other contexts such as community learning or sharing of knowledge. In the present research, we look particularly at the community of medical practitioners in the context of reading and commenting on scientific article summaries which are called infoPOEMs® (Patient-Oriented Evidence that Matters). Within this medical community, comments about an infoPOEM made by one practitioner could be useful to other practitioners regardless of the opinion expressed. The helpfulness dimension is not necessarily correlated with the opinion dimension with typical values being positive, negative or neutral. For example, the comment "good article" certainly has a different helpfulness value than the comment "this is a very good article since it shows for the first time that drug X can be useful in disease Y", even though both comments are positive.

The automatic identification of helpfulness becomes the subject of our research. Practitioners are not interested in reading all comments, only the valuable or "helpful" ones, and an automatic identification of helpfulness would provide a more efficient way for knowledge sharing among them.

## 2 Related Work

Assessing the helpfulness of comments made about recreational or informational items has been explored recently mainly for online products or movie reviews. Many studies look at Amazon data, which is perfectly suited for this task since it provides training data readily available. Besides the research work on Amazon data, we also mention one work on peer review in an educational context. We provide pretty extensive details on the features selected and results obtained for the different work to allow us to compare our feature


*Proceedings of NAACL-HLT 2016*, pages 72–81,
San Diego, California, June 12-17, 2016. ©2016 Association for Computational Linguistics

sets and our results to the ones mentioned here.

Within the Amazon studies, the most cited approach by Kim and Pantel (2006) uses machine learning algorithms with text-based features to rank the usefulness of products reviews from the Amazon.com website. They use a dataset of 25,841 reviews from 1,802 products (mp3 players and digital cameras). Their gold standard ranking is based on user responses, provided on the site, to the question "Was this review helpful to you?". Their features are divided into five sets: structural, lexical, syntactic, semantic and metadata. Structural features comprise total token number, number of sentences, average sentence length, percentage of question sentences, number of exclamation sentences, bold and line break html tags. Lexical features comprise tf-idf (Term Frequency-Inverse Document Frequency) of unigrams and bigrams. Syntactic features included percentage of open-class tokens, verb tokens, first person verbs, adjective and adverb. Semantic features comprise occurrences of product features in the review, as well as occurrences of positive and negative sentiment words. Metadata features comprise number of stars rating, difference between given star rating and average star rating of the product. Using these comments' derived features, they use a SVM-RBF algorithm to evaluate features' correlation. Their best result used only three features (comment's length, unigrams and star rating) providing a Spearman rank correlation of 0.66.

Ngo-Ye and Sinha (2012) also looks at Amazon.com reviews, using 2,718 reviews of 11 books. Rather than expanding the set of features, as with Kim and Pantel (2006), they limit themselves to the traditional bag-of-words approach. Their contribution is on dimensionality reduction using the regressional ReliefF algorithm in comparison with LSA, correlation feature selection (CFS) and two other dimension reduction methods. Using both binary occurrences of words and real frequency occurrences as features, they conclude that the use of regressional ReliefF dimension reduction algorithm outperform basic bag-of-word, LSA and CFS on every count.

Zhang and Tran (2008) suggests an information entropy-based bag-of-word model to predict the helpfulness of reviews. As training data, they use 9,955 gps and mp3 player reviews from Amazon. Contrarily to Kim and Pantel (2006) who attempted correlation with a gold standard rank-ing, they transform the problem into a binary classification problem using a consumer vote ratio threshold of $>60\%$ to consider a review as helpful. They compare their entropy-based method with three classifiers: Naive Bayes, Decision Tree and sequential minimal optimization (Platt, 1998). The resulting performances (77.2% for helpful and 77.5% for non-helpful) for their approach beat Naive Bayes (h:76.2% and n-h:75.2%) and Decision Tree (h:72.3% and n-h:75.3%) but of the same rank as an occurrence-base bag-of-word using the SMO classifier (h:76.1% and n-h:78.0%) when considering both value of the output class.

Other research also take place in other fields like educational peer-review systems. This is the case with Xiong and Litman (2011) who used a feature-based machine learning approach on peer-review assessments from an introductory collegial history class to evaluate their usefulness. They collected 267 comments made on 16 papers which evaluated the quality of the work (facts, clarity, argument structure and so on). While using the previously published features (Kim and Pantel, 2006) as a baseline, they introduced new features like problem localization ("Page 2 says ..."), new lexicon categories (modal verb, negation, positive and negative words, ...) and cognitive-science constructs (praise, problem, summary, solution, ...). The baseline using structural, unigrams and metadata features offered a 0.62 Pearson correlation (0.67 with new features). The context of this research is the nearest to ours as it targets the usefulness of comments for educational purposes.

## 3 Applicative context

The Canadian Medical Association (CMA) delivers by email clinical research article summaries called infoPOEMs (Patient-Oriented Evidence that Matters) to family physicians around the country. To transform the reading of infoPOEMs into an actual learning experience, research in education states the importance of having the reader (learner) reflect on the value of his reading by answering questions. While questions on the content only test short-term memory, questions on the value of the information for clinical practice can stimulate reflective learning. The impact of such practice and its validation have been researched in depth (Grad et al., 2006; Grad et al., 2008; Pluye et al., 2010a; Pluye et al., 2010b).

As part of their mandatory continuing education

program, physicians can answer an online questionnaire called Information Assessment Method or IAM (Grad et al., 2011). It contains many questions to gauge the impact of the infoPOEM's content on the physicians knowledge and practice: "Is your practice changed and improved?", "Are you motivated to learn more?", "Are you dissatisfied?", "Is this summary relevant for at least one of your patients?". In addition to the predefined questions, physicians can add comments about their reading experience targeting the quality of the overall infoPOEM information, the research, the methodology, and so on. The examples below illustrate how physicians' comments can fluctuate in length, content and targeted issues.

1. Content of drops not specified

2. Why was this study done when we have prev information regarding pot harms done with acute lowering of BP post stroke?

3. Good to hear this as CRP is a rather non-specific marker

4. very interesting

5. Cost of each Rx regime?

6. administrative physician

Comments can be related to missing information (1, 5), generic appreciation (4), critical disagreement (2), agreement with support (3), contextual information about inapplicability of the information (6), etc.

## 4 Methodology

Our research takes a similar approach as Kim and Pantel (2006) and Xiong and Litman (2011) on feature extraction and machine-learning, while looking at a closed system without clear "wisdom-of-the-crowd" indicators. We evaluate the impact of features based on textual analysis of the comment itself, but also features based on a comparison between the infoPOEM and the comment, as well as features relying on external domain-specific resources. Our methodology consists of (1) circumscribing the data and developing a gold standard, (2) defining a set of features that will best describe the data to be categorized, (3) experiment with machine learning approaches for categorization and (4) perform an evaluation using the gold standard.

### 4.1 Dataset and gold standard

The gold standard was annotated by three medical students with different experience levels. They were asked to read anonymous comments submitted by physicians and indicate if they found them valuable for their knowledge or practice. [1]

Each annotator was provided with a list of anonymous comments and their associated infoPOEM for reference. They could access, if needed, the full text of the infoPOEM if the comment was not clear to them. A preliminary annotation phase was done with 300 randomly selected comments to be annotated by the three annotators (100 each). This phase provided a better understanding of the problem to validate the annotation schema used for the main annotation task. The classification schema included three choices to annotate the helpfulness of a comment: "valuable", "non-valuable" or "I don't know". The annotators were asked to consider each comment independently and not let the reading of previous comments influence their choice.

The main annotation task was based on two batches of comments. A first one, relatively small, contained 250 comments and was given to all three reviewers and allowed us to calculate an inter-annotator agreement. A larger set of comments was split in three parts to have each comment annotated by a single reviewer. This provided a total of 3,470 comments associated with 327 randomly picked infoPOEMs. Of these comments, 1,586 (45.6%) were deemed valuable and 1,884 (54.3%) non-valuable. A dozen comments were tagged "I don't know" and removed from the dataset.

The 300 comments from the preliminary annotation step joined with the 250 comments for the inter-annotator agreement were used as the development dataset (550 unique comments) to define, develop, test and refine features presented in the next section but were not used in the dataset for the final evaluation. The other set of 3,470 comments was used as the evaluation dataset for performance assessment.

The size of the manually annotated dataset compares advantageously to the 1000 annotated comments of Ghose and Ipeirotis (2007) and the 267 of Xiong and Litman (2011). Using the first 250 comments annotated by the three annota-



---

[1]The anonymous comments were provided by the Canadian Medical Association under a non-disclosure agreement for research purposes only.

tors, an inter-annotator agreement of 0.4846 was computed using the Fleiss' Kappa method for multiple annotators with all three classes (valuable / non-valuable / i don't know). The inter-annotator agreement was recalculated using only the 247 comments with only the two main classes (valuable/non-valuable) which provided a score of 0.5004. The remaining data shows a stronger agreement on valuable comments than on non-valuable ones. The level of agreement calculated on this dataset is considered moderate according to Landis and Koch (1977) when compared to pure chance agreement and is of the same order as in Xiong and Litman (2011). Using each annotator as the gold standard versus others, the f-measures were 0.806 between annotators 1 and 2, 0.783 between 1 and 3 and 0.792 between 2 and 3.

The reason behind the average ratings for inter-annotator agreement score can be explained by one or many of the following points: coding instructions were interpreted differently by each annotator, coding decision is based on factors which are not present in textual data (like relevant prior knowledge, expertise domain or interest, personal taste or bias and so on), decision factors were present in the text but not correctly understood by the readers, etc. While it is difficult to provide a clear and proven diagnosis of the reason behind these scores, lower scores usually increase the difficulty to develop prediction systems. As such, the average agreement provides a contextualisation of potential performance for this task; a near-perfect classification of comments is not the goal as it would overfit the three annotator's classification.

## 4.2 Feature definition

The purpose of defining features is to capture as well as possible the characteristics of comments which would be representative of their helpfulness character. Inspired by previous research, we define a set of base features, focusing on standard text analysis techniques. But we apply these techniques not only to the comment's content itself, but also in a comparative setting looking at similarities between an infoPOEM and its comments. We present these base features first. Second, we look at metadata features from the infoPOEM itself. Third, we use the actual IAM questionnaire as a source of features. Fourth, inspired by our specific problem being in the medical domain, we define a set of features using a medical resource,

the UMLS (Unified Medical Language System). The feature extraction process was developed using GATE (Cunningham et al., 2011) with part-of-speech TreeTagger (Schmid, 1994) tool.

### 4.2.1 Base

The base set includes all features extracted using natural language processing techniques. It includes features and their representations used in previous researches like Kim and Pantel (2006; Xiong and Litman (2011) as well as new ones introduced in this article. They can be regrouped in the structural, syntactic and semantic subsets.

**Structural** Structural features target statistical properties of tokens contained in the comments. The total number of each one was added as separate features. Two features were also added for tokens: the standard deviation and a three-value discretization of the standard deviation to account for the length being within range of the average (*avg*) number of tokens of all comments, above (*high*) or under (*low*) it, using $\pm 1\sigma$ as the threshold.

**Syntactic** Following a part-of-speech tagging (attributing a syntactic role to each word), the number of stop words and content words were added as features, which summed up to the number of tokens from the structural feature. The standard variation and its discretization (as seen previously) were also added. The first and second person pronouns (ex: I, we, us, etc) were added as total count and binary occurrence (true if any occurrence are observed, false if none) features to the dataset to identify author related comments like accounts of personnal experiences, thoughts, preferences or opinions.

Then for each type of content words (verb, adverb, noun, adjective) found both in the comment and the corresponding infoPOEM, we added four similarity-based features. They were the total count of similar occurrences, the binary occurrence, the ratio between the total count and the total number of content words and finally the ratio between the total count and the total number of words.

**Semantic** To identify comments with strong opinions or impressions, we use specific verbs (e.g. admit, enjoy, deem, endorse, decline, concern, advise, ...) and match the infinitive form of these verbs in the comments following a part-of-speech tagging step. Negative indicators (not, never, neither, nor, can't, don't, etc) are also annotated to target potentially critical comments. As the comments were on infoPOEMs within a scientific discipline, terminology related to the scientific method (observation, qualitative, inference, ...), the statistical domain (population, marginal variable, match sample, ...) and to measurement (unit, cm, m, mg, ug, kg, ml, ...) were added separately as features. Finally, the five standard section's labels (title, clinical question, bottom line, study design, synopsis) from the infoPOEM were added as keywords to detect if a text was commenting on the specific section of the infoPOEM.

The number of instances and the binary occurrence for each of these semantic concepts (opinion verbs, domain terminology, negative indicators and localisation indicators) were added as features.

### 4.2.2  Metadata

To each infoPOEM is associated a code called the level of evidence (LOE). This code describes the type of research protocol used in therapy, diagnosis or prognosis research using one letter and one number (1a, 1b, 1c, ..., 2a, 2b, ...). A minus sign can be added at the end of the code to denote researches that cannot provide conclusive answers in cases where the confidence interval is too large or the heterogeneity of the population's sample used is problematic. We use this code and split it in 3 parts to provide 3 features: the type (first character, from 1 to 5), the subtype (second character, from A to C) and the presence of the minus indicator.

### 4.2.3  IAM

Each question from the IAM questionnaire was added as a feature. Most of the questions asked for a logical yes/no answer. A few questions accepted either yes, no or "possibly" as an answer. Only one question pertaining to the relevance of the information regarding the physician's patients, asked for an answer using three levels: "totally relevant", "partially relevant" or "not relevant". The possibility to answer some specific questions was also dependant on the answer on previous questions; i.e. questions #3 and #4 were only available if the totally or partially relevance was chosen at question #2. Regardless of this factor, all questions were added as individual and stand-alone features in the dataset.

### 4.2.4  UMLS

Unlike the work with Amazon data which relies on official product feature sources to find vocabulary representative of different products, we do not have access to such sources in this study. Instead, we extracted single words and multiword expressions from the Unified Medical Language System, a large medical ontology hosted at the National Library of Medicine (`http://umlsks.nlm.nih.gov/`) to analyse the domain specific nature of the reviews and infoPOEMs. The relevant part of this resource splits biomedical and related concepts into 13 groups and 94 types using themes like genes and molecular sequences, anatomy, living beings, physiology, procedures, disorders, organizations and so on, with each type related to one group.

For each type and group, the number of occurrences, the binary occurrence and the similarity occurrences were added as features. The similarity occurrence indicates how many expressions found in a comment were also found in the infoPOEM related to that comment. This type of feature was added to verify if an author was talking about domain-specific concepts from the infoPOEM. Because of the relation between groups and types, each matching expression was both represented with a type feature and its corresponding group feature. In addition, the global binary and total occurrence of UMLS expressions were added as two features to logically regroup all UMLS type and group features. Therefore, if a word was tagged as being part of 4 types and 3 groups, the global binary occurrence would be 1 and the global number would be 7.

## 5  Performance evaluation

### 5.1  Baseline

Two baselines were created using the bag-of-word model applied to the whole set of annotated comments. The preprocessing included a tokenizer, an English stop word filter and the Snowball English stemmer, using each stemmed token as a feature in the dataset. The bag-of-word baselines have been extracted and tested using the RapidMiner tool (Mierswa et al., 2006).

The first baseline follows the best replicable results from Kim and Pantel (2006) using the length in token of the comment and a unigram bag-of-words. The stemmed tokens were then weighted using the tf-idf measure. The resulting dataset was

Table 1: Weighted f-measure results for algorithms on each dataset.

| | B | B+I | B+U | B+I+U | 150R |
|---|---|---|---|---|---|
| BayesNet | 0.651 | **0.693** | 0.673 | 0.692 | 0.651 |
| Voted Percept. | 0.659 | 0.692 | 0.686 | 0.704 | **0.713** |
| JRip | 0.663 | 0.686 | 0.671 | 0.679 | **0.688** |
| LMT | 0.660 | 0.700 | 0.694 | 0.700 | **0.708** |

(B): Base, (I): IAM questionnaire, (U): UMLS,
(150R): B+I+U with selection of 150 features with Relief-F

processed with the SVM-RBF algorithm which provided a f-measure score of 63.6%.

The second baseline is based on the conclusion of Zhang and Tran (2008), which presented a method providing a weighted score equivalent to the SMO algorithm applied to a binary occurrences bag-of-words. The SMO (sequential minimal optimization algorithm for training a support vector classier) and binary bag-of-words method performed on our comment corpus yielded a 62.2% f-measure which is significantly lower than the 77.1% f-measure averaged from the helpful and not helpful classes using their product review dataset.

## 5.2 Helpfulness prediction

As the helpfulness evaluation was based on few annotators instead of large population like on Amazon, classification algorithms were used to predict the correct value instead of a rank correlation method. We used the ten-fold cross-validation to provide the recall, precision and f-measure estimation for each one. The feature sets were then combined with one another to verify which group gave the best results. Evaluation of machine-learning algorithms has been made using the Weka toolset (Hall et al., 2009).

To be able to test the relative strength of the feature sets from section 4.2, four datasets were created using the following feature sets: base (B), base and IAM questionnaire (B+I), base and UMLS (B+U) and all three sets together (B+I+U). The three metadata features they were included in the base feature set (B). Finally, as the UMLS set contains a large number of features, a fifth dataset (B+I+U-150R) was created using a smaller subset of features which were selected following Ngo-Ye and Sinha (2012) study, using the Relief-F algorithm to select the 150 top features, excluding the output class.

For each of the five datasets, a single algorithm from the four main families was tested: BayesNet (Friedman et al., 1997) (baysian), Voted Perceptron (Freund and Schapire, 1998) (function), JRip (Cohen, 1995) (rule-based) and Logistic model trees (Landwehr et al., 2005)(decision tree). Table 1 provides an overview of each algorithm applied on each of the 5 datasets with the corresponding f-measure. Numbers in bold indicate the dataset on which each algorithm best performed.The base feature set did better than the two baselines, increasing prediction quality by 2.7% and 4.1% respectively to 66.3%. Adding the UMLS to the base feature set (B+U) marginally increased the performance by 0.4%. The IAM feature set, when joined with the base (B+I), did better with 70.4%, an 1.4% increase. Finally, the dataset with the highest results is the Relief-F selected subset with a top scoring f-measure of 71.3%, which is an improvement of 0.9% over the 70.4% using the complete dataset (B+I+U), both attained with the voted perceptron algorithm.

## 5.3 Features relevance

The average absolute weight of each feature from the voted perceptron algorithm applied on the feature set B+I+U provided a ranking from the most discriminative feature to the least, for which the first 24 for each class are shown in Table 2. The first column, for the positive class (valuable), shows that the number of tokens still makes the top of the list with the five first features under different forms: number of content, any or stop tokens, percentage of similar (sim %) content tokens and number of sentence. The group (grp) and type (typ) UMLS features occupy almost half the list (10 out of 23) using similarity (sim) count, binary occurrence (bin) and number of occurrences (nbr). Five questions from the IAM questionnaire are also in the list, with three top ones being negative assessment from the physicians.

The second section shows for the negative class (non-valuable) that standard deviations (stddev) related to token length are the three most relevant features. 14 out of 24 features are from the UMLS resource with two-third (9 out of 13) using the similarity count. Three questions from the IAM questionnaire are also used. The rankings for the two output classes show that while length of comments is still a significant aspect of perceived value, features from the UMLS dataset are ranked high for their discriminative power. The similarity aspect is also used in half of the UMLs features

Table 2: Feature discriminative ranking from (B)ase, I(AM) and (U)MLS set

| Positive | Negative |
| --- | --- |
| (B) Content Tok. [nbr] | (B) Content tok. [stddev] |
| (B) Tok. [nbr] | (B) Tok. [stddev] |
| (B) Stop Tok. [nbr] | (B) Stop tok. [stddev] |
| (B) Content tok. [sim %] | (B) Person pronoun [nbr] |
| (B) Sentence [nbr] | (B) Stop tok. [nom stddev] |
| (U) Typ embryo struct. [bin] | (U) Typ Occup [sim] |
| (U) Typ molecul. func. [sim] | (I) Reminded already knew |
| (B) Stop tok. [%] | (I) Learned something new |
| (B) Tok. [stddev nom *low*] | (B) Tok. [stddev nom *high*] |
| (I) I disagree with content | (U) Typ receptor [sim] |
| (B) LOE subtype | (U) Typ acid [sim] |
| (U) Grp Objects [nbr] | (U) Typ amino acid [bin] |
| (U) Typ bacterium [bin] | (U) Typ bacterium [sim] |
| (B) Tok. [stddev nom *avg*] | (U) Typ regul activ. [bin] |
| (U) Typ manuf object [nbr] | (B) Person pronoun [bin] |
| (I) There is a problem | (U) Typ receptor [sim] |
| (U) Grp Physiology [bin] | (U) Typ hazard subst. [sim] |
| (I) Not enough information | (U) Typ neoplas proc. [sim] |
| (U) Typ event [sim] | (U) Typ biomed occ. [bin] |
| (U) Grp Procedures [bin] | (U) Typ receptor [nbr] |
| (U) Typ bacterium [nbr] | (U) Grp Activ. Behav. [sim] |
| (I) Therapeutic approach | (I) Dissatisfied |
| (B) Summary structure [nbr] | (U) Typ eukaryote [bin] |
| (I) Info relevant for patient | (U) Grp Physiology [sim] |

(11 out of all 23 UMLS features) which indicates the preponderant usefulness of this aspect over the other like binary occurrence and basic count.

An interesting observation on Table 2 is the type of IAM questions which prompt positive and negative value for the medical community. The top three IAM features used for the positive class (valuable) are from negative questions: "'I disagree with the content'", "'There is a problem with this infoPoem'", "'Not enough information'". The negative class exhibit the same occurrence, as questions like "'I learned something new'", "'Reminded of something I already knew'" and "'I learned something new'", which are supportive of the article, are used by the algorithm as highly discriminative features. This may suggest that comments shedding a negative view on article's comments are considered more relevant than supportive ones. This would supports the brilliant-but-cruel hypothesis (Amabile, 1983).

## 5.4 Applicability

While the experiments results show good improvement over previous methods, enforcing the straight-out application of the trained classification model might not be advisable in the spirit of knowledge sharing in a continuing education program. As previously shown, the average inter-annotator agreement might be used to seek a more lenient classification method to select which comments are to be shared among the physician's community and which are to be removed. One path to explore in this context is the opportunity that each algorithm can provide a confidence level which expresses the certainty of the algorithm regarding the chosen prediction class. It is usually based on the similarity rating between the features in the assessed entry and the ones in the trained model.

These results were generated using the voted perceptron algorithm. The dataset used for training was the 300 comments from the first step, combined with the 250 comments used for the inter-annotator agreement evaluation, using a majority vote to choose a relevant class. Finally, 450 randomly picked comments from the main dataset (3,470 comments) were added to these comments to provide a 1,000 comments dataset to the voted perceptron algorithm. The remaining 3,020 comments (3,470 minus the 450 retained for training) from the main dataset were used for evaluation purpose.

Table 3 shows the results for levels of confidence ranking from 75% to 95% for each individual class by providing the total number of comments classified as such, the number of errors (wrongfully classified comments) and the resulting prediction ratio. For example, the algorithm at a confidence level of 80% classifies 575 comments as being non-valuable. In these 575 comments, 65 were in fact classified by the annotator as belonging to the other class, resulting in a 88.7% success ratio, which is significantly higher than the best result from Table 1.

It can be observed in this table that while the non-valuable class provides a better success rate at the 95% confidence level, they all degrade to approximately 83% at 70% confidence rating. The non-valuable class shows better results but classifies a smaller amount of comments at the two higher confidence levels. It then drops to the same level for lower confidence than the valuable class, but progressively classifying more comments.

These new results could be used in two main scenarios for knowledge sharing among the medical practitioners. The first scenario is to use an arbitrarily chosen confidence level (for example, 80%) to filter out most of the non-valuable comments from the dataset. Physicians could then browse the remaining comments which would have a higher chance of being helpful. The sec-

Table 3: Precision performance per confidence level.

| Confidence level | Overall | | | Non-helpful | | | Helpful | | |
|---|---|---|---|---|---|---|---|---|---|
| | Precision % | Errors | Total | Precision % | Errors | Total | Precision % | Errors | Total |
| 95 | 96.50 | 5 | 143 | 1 | 0 | 23 | 95.83 | 5 | 120 |
| 90 | 94,46 | 19 | 343 | 97,56 | 3 | 123 | 92,73 | 16 | 220 |
| 85 | 91,32 | 57 | 657 | 92,05 | 26 | 327 | 90,61 | 31 | 330 |
| 80 | 88,10 | 122 | 1,025 | 88,70 | 65 | 575 | 87,33 | 57 | 450 |
| 75 | 86,20 | 191 | 1,384 | 86,11 | 115 | 828 | 86,33 | 76 | 556 |

ond scenario is to use the confidence level as a ranking for all comments. Comments classified as valuable with a high confidence rating would be presented at the top of the list, followed by comments classified with a slightly lower confidence score and so on.

This second scenario provides more flexibility in an education context. The bottom of this list would be the top confidence scored comments for the non-valuable class, which could still be offered. This second scenario provides more flexibility in an education context. Even if most readers would only look at the top of the list, the curiosity driven readers would have access to the complete listing of comments which could be useful for topics relevant to their practice.

## 6 Discussion and Conclusion

Our applicative setting is one of information sharing in a context of continuing education for medical practitioners. This is certainly far from product review, but still the same problem exists that many comments are made by users, and these comments are not all useful to other users. Nevertheless, because of this applicative difference, performance comparison with other publications is not straightforward as we are not in a typical social media-based interactive setting, which means that typical data like star rating (used in Kim and Pantel (2006)) and relationship between reviews (like for Zhang et al. (2012)) is not available. Still, it can be observed in our performance evaluation that the basic unigram bag-of-word approach did not perform as well as our more complex features.

The UMLS features did not improve the overall performance when coupled with the base or the base+IAM questionnaire feature sets, probably because of the less relevant features which made data noisier. This is correlated with the increase of performance seen when the complete dataset was reduced to the 150 most discriminative features with the Relief-F feature selection algorithm. The IAM questionnaire, which physician are not

obliged to answer completely, may suffer from the same problem of missing information on star rating for new products. Even if it is successfully used by classification algorithm, other features should be prioritized when possible. This could lead to more stable performances which are not dependent on the completeness of an external source of information.

As seen in the top negative features in Table 2, standard deviation was a useful measure for classification. The discretization of these features was also useful for both output classes. Although, while length can be a good predictor as shown in previous study (Kim and Pantel, 2006) and allows to discard useless short comments ("very good", "thanks", etc.), it will undeniably wrongly classify comments like "N?" (indicating the missing population size of a study) as useless. This is an extreme difficult case.

In conclusion, this research explored a textual feature extraction process with machine-learning classification to predict the helpfulness of comments in a context of continuing education for family physicians. Our research is well anchored in previous research on the topic, and we make further contributions by introducing similarity-based features to compare comments and infoPOEMs. We also introduce the use of an external domain specific resource to provide a measure of domain appropriateness for the comment, which is playing a role in its evaluation of helpfulness.

We showed that our method improved two previous baselines by 7.7% and 9.1% to a final 71.3% with the voted perceptron algorithm applied over a dataset of 150 features selected using the Relief-F algorithm. Since the categorization is far from perfect even if it gives good results (far above chance), we also suggested two confidence-based scenarios to make the categorization applicable in a real-world knowledge sharing context among medical practitioners.

# References

TM Amabile. 1983. Brilliant but cruel: Perceptions of negative evaluators. *Journal of Experimental Social Psychology*, 19:146–156.

Hsinchun Chen and David Zimbra. 2010. AI and Opinion Mining. *IEEE Intelligent Systems*, 25(3):74–80, May.

William W. Cohen. 1995. Fast effective rule induction. In *Twelfth International Conference on Machine Learning*, pages 115–123. Morgan Kaufmann.

Hamish Cunningham, Diana Maynard, Kalina Bontcheva, Valentin Tablan, Niraj Aswani, Ian Roberts, Genevieve Gorrell, Adam Funk, Angus Roberts, Danica Damljanovic, Thomas Heitz, Mark A Greenwood, Horacio Saggion, Johann Petrak, Yaoyong Li, and Wim Peters. 2011. *Text Processing with GATE (Version 6)*.

Y. Freund and R. E. Schapire. 1998. Large margin classification using the perceptron algorithm. In *11th Annual Conference on Computational Learning Theory*, pages 209–217, New York, NY. ACM Press.

N. Friedman, D. Geiger, and M. Goldszmidt. 1997. Bayesian network classifiers. *Machine Learning*, 29(2-3):131–163.

Anindya Ghose and Panagiotis G. Ipeirotis. 2007. Designing novel review ranking systems: Predicting the Usefulness and Impact of Reviews. In *Proceedings of the ninth international conference on Electronic commerce - ICEC '07*, page 303, New York, New York, USA. ACM Press.

R Grad, P Pluye, and ME Beauchamp. 2006. Validation of a Method to Assess the Clinical Impact of Electronic Knowledge Resources. *E-Service journal*.

RM Grad, P Pluye, and J Mercer. 2008. Impact of research-based synopses delivered as daily e-mail: a prospective observational study. *Journal of the American Medical Informatics Association*.

Roland Grad, Pierre Pluye, Vera Granikov, Janique Johnson-Lafleur, Michael Shulha, Soumya Bindiganavile Sridhar, Jonathan L. Moscovici, Gillian Bartlett, Alain C. Vandal, Bernard Marlow, and Lorie Kloda. 2011. Physicians' assessment of the value of clinical information: Operationalization of a theoretical model. *Journal of the American Society for Information Science and Technology*, 62(10):1884–1891.

M Hall, E Frank, G Holmes, and B Pfahringer. 2009. The WEKA data mining software: an update. *SIGKDD Explorations*, 11(1).

Jina Huh, Meliha Yetisgen-Yildiz, and Wanda Pratt. 2013. Text classification for assisting moderators in online health communities. *Journal of Biomedical Informatics*, (0):–.

SM Kim and Patrick Pantel. 2006. Automatically assessing review helpfulness. In *Proceedings of the 2006 Conference on Empirical Methods in Natural Language Processing*, number July, pages 423–430.

JR Landis and GG Koch. 1977. The measurement of observer agreement for categorical data. *Biometrics*.

Niels Landwehr, Mark Hall, and Eibe Frank. 2005. Logistic model trees. *Machine Learning*, 59(1-2):161–205.

Ingo Mierswa, Michael Wurst, Ralf Klinkenberg, Martin Scholz, and Timm Euler. 2006. YALE: Rapid Prototyping for Complex Data Mining Tasks. In *Proceedings of the 12th ACM SIGKDD international conference on Knowledge discovery and data mining - KDD '06*, page 935, New York, New York, USA. ACM Press.

Arjun Mukherjee and Bing Liu. 2012. Modeling Review Comments. In *Proceedings of 50th Anunal Meeting of the Association for Computational Linguistics*.

Thomas L. Ngo-Ye and Atish P. Sinha. 2012. Analyzing Online Review Helpfulness Using a Regressional ReliefF-Enhanced Text Mining Method. *ACM Transactions on Management Information Systems*, 3(2).

John C. Platt. 1998. Sequential minimal optimization: A fast algorithm for training support vector machines.

Pierre Pluye, Roland M. Grad, Vera Granikov, Justin Jagosh, and Kit Leung. 2010a. Evaluation of email alerts in practice: Part 1. Review of the literature on clinical emailing channels. *Journal of Evaluation in Clinical Practice*, 16(6):1227–1235, December.

Pierre Pluye, Roland M. Grad, Janique Johnson-Lafleur, Tara Bambrick, Bernard Burnand, Jay Mercer, Bernard Marlow, and Craig Campbell. 2010b. Evaluation of email alerts in practice: Part 2 - Validation of the information assessment method. *Journal of Evaluation in Clinical Practice*, 16(6):1236–1243.

H Schmid. 1994. Probabilistic part-of-speech tagging using decision trees. *Proceedings of the International Conference on New Methods in Language Processing*, pages 44–49.

PD Turney. 2002. Thumbs up or thumbs down?: semantic orientation applied to unsupervised classification of reviews. *Proceedings of the 40th Annual Meeting on Association for Computational Linguistics*, (July):417–424.

Wenting Xiong and Diane Litman. 2011. Automatically predicting peer-review helpfulness. In *Proceedings of the 49th Annual Meeting of the Association for Computational Linguistics: Human Language Technologies*, number 2009, pages 502–507.

Richong Zhang and Thomas Tran. 2008. An Entropy-Based Model for Discovering the Usefulness of Online Product Reviews. *2008 IEEE/WIC/ACM International Conference on Web Intelligence and Intelligent Agent Technology*, pages 759–762, December.

Kunpeng Zhang, Yu Cheng, Wei-keng Liao, and Alok Choudhary. 2012. Mining millions of reviews: a technique to rank products based on importance of reviews. In *Proceedings of the 13th International Conference on Electronic Commerce - ICEC '11*, pages 1–8, New York, New York, USA. ACM Press.

# Political Issue Extraction Model: A Novel Hierarchical Topic Model That Uses Tweets By Political And Non-Political Authors

**Aditya Joshi**[1,2,3]    **Pushpak Bhattacharyya**[1]    **Mark Carman**[2]
[1]IIT Bombay, India
[2]Monash University, Australia
[3]IITB-Monash Research Academy, India
{adityaj, pb}@cse.iitb.ac.in, mark.carman@monash.edu

## Abstract

People often use social media to discuss opinions, including political ones. We refer to relevant topics in these discussions as political issues, and the alternate stands towards these topics as political positions. We present a Political Issue Extraction (PIE) model that is capable of discovering political issues and positions from an unlabeled dataset of tweets. A strength of this model is that it uses twitter timelines of political and non-political authors, and affiliation information of only political authors. The model estimates word-specific distributions (that denote political issues and positions) and hierarchical author/group-specific distributions (that show how these issues divide people). Our experiments using a dataset of 2.4 million tweets from the US show that this model effectively captures the desired properties (with respect to words and groups) of political discussions. We also evaluate the two components of the model by experimenting with: (a) Use to alternate strategies to classify words, and (b) Value addition due to incorporation of group membership information. Estimated distributions are then used to predict political affiliation with 68% accuracy.

## 1   Introduction

Political discussions in social media contain contentious topics (called '**political issues**'), and alternate stands with respect to these issues (called '**positions**'). We present a topic model that discovers political issues and positions in tweets. Our model is called **Political Issue Extraction (PIE)**

**model**. The input is the twitter timelines of authors (*i.e.*, the user who created the tweet), and political affiliation information for a subset of authors (*i.e.*, political authors. Antonym: Non-political authors). Political and non-political authors contribute to formation of topics, whereas only political authors contribute to position that a group is likely to take. Since our dataset consists of tweets from the US, political affiliation can be one of the three groups: '*Democrats*', '*Republicans*' or '*Unknown*'.

For every tweet, we estimate two latent variables: issue and position. To discover topics related to issues and positions, we classify words in a tweet in three categories: issue words, position words and emoticons. Instead of document-specific distributions as in LDA, we include a hierarchy of author-specific and group-specific position distributions in our model. This hierarchy estimates three distributions for each topic: global position, position of a given political group and position of a specific author.

We evaluate our model by (a) validating our topics against standard topic lists, (b) considering different strategies of splitting words into the three categories, and (c) validating how the model benefits from the group information. Finally, we use our model to predict political affiliation of authors.

Models based on LDA by Jo and Oh (2011), Mei et al. (2007); Lin and He (2009) extract sentiment-coherent topics. Past work related to political opinion has been reported by Gayo-Avello, Metaxas, and Mustafaraj (2011); Conover et al. (2011); O'Connor et al. (2010); Wong et al. (2013); Yano, Cohen, and Smith (2009); Lin, Xing, and Hauptmann (2008);



*Proceedings of NAACL-HLT 2016*, pages 82–90,
San Diego, California, June 12-17, 2016. ©2016 Association for Computational Linguistics

Wang, Mohanty, and McCallum (2005), and more recently by Benton et al. (2016). Two of them close to our work are by Grimmer (2010); Fang et al. (2012). Our model improves upon them in three ways:

1. In PIE model, position words depend on both issue and position latent variables (as opposed to only the latter in prior work),

2. In PIE model, a novel hierarchical author/group-wise distribution is considered instead of document-wise distribution.

3. To the best of our knowledge, PIE model is the first that operates at the author level by using complete author timelines of both political and non-political authors, and affiliation information of a subset of authors (only political authors).

The rest of the paper is organized as follows. We present the structure and estimation procedure of PIE model in Section 3 and discuss our experiment setup in Section 4. The evaluation is in Section 5. Finally, we conclude and point to future work in Section 6.

## 2 Related Work

Our model is based on Latent Dirichlet Allocation (LDA) given by Blei, Ng, and Jordan (2003). Models based on LDA by Jo and Oh (2011), Mei et al. (2007), Lin and He (2009), and Zhao et al. (2010) present approaches to extract sentiment-coherent topics in datasets.

The past work in analytics related to political opinion can be broadly classified in three categories. The first category predicts the outcome of an election. Gayo-Avello, Metaxas, and Mustafaraj (2011) predict the election outcome for a pair of Democrat and Republican candidates, while Metaxas, Mustafaraj, and Gayo-Avello (2011) aggregate sentiment in tweets in order to map it to votes. Conover et al. (2011) use a network graph of authors and their known political orientations, in order to predict the political orientation. The second category of work in the political domain deals with correlation of sentiment with real-world events. O'Connor et al. (2010) correlate sentiment expressed in text to time series of real-world events. Wong et al. (2013) derive the consistency between tweeting and retweeting behaviour and real-world sentiment about an event. Gerrish and Blei (2011) present the ideal point topic model that correlates votes by legislators to bills being passed along with sentiment in the texts of these bills.

Our PIE model falls in the third category: extraction of political topics from a dataset. In this respect, the work closest to ours is by Grimmer (2010) and Fang et al. (2012). Grimmer (2010) present a hierarchical topic model to understand how senators explain their work in their press releases. Assuming a single topic per press release, the topic of a document is derived from an author-specific distribution over topics. Fang et al. (2012) divide words in a political statement as topic words and opinion words, based on POS tags, and assume different distributions for the two. Like these two works, we assume a single topic per tweet, and divide words into categories based on POS tags. Our model improves upon these two works in the following key ways:

- A richer latent variable structure. In our model, the opinion words depend on BOTH topic and opinion latent variables (as opposed to only the latter). This structure allows our model to generate topics corresponding to political positions, which is not achieved in the past work.

- The author-topic distribution and hierarchy of author-sentiment distributions (as noted in Section 1). In case of our models, authors are arranged into groups and this group-wise distribution is tightly linked to the structure of the model.

## 3 PIE Model

In this section, we introduce the PIE model. We first discuss the rationale behind the design. We then describe the structure of the model. Following that, we present details of the input/output and the method for estimation of distributions.

### 3.1 Design Rationale

The primary goal of the model is to discover topics related to political issues and two positions per issue. To be able to discover issues and corresponding positions, PIE model considers two latent variables

$p$ and $i$. Topic $i$ represents the identifier for a political issue while the pair $p\text{-}i$ represents the identifier for a position.

The first component of the model is derived from the **nature of data**. A tweet contains two kinds of content words: "objective" words that describe an entity and "subjective" words that express opinion towards an entity. Emoticons can be thought of as a third category of sentiment words. We represent these three kinds of words as three observed variables: topic words $t$, opinion words $o$ and emoticons $e$. A topic word $t$ is derived from the topic $i$, an opinion word is derived from the topic $i$ and sentiment $p$ pair while an emoticon $e$ is derived from sentiment $p$ alone.

The second component of the model is derived from the **nature of the problem**. In a political setting, people are organized in political groups while the opinion of a group towards a topic is a result of individual users in the group. To model this nature, we use a hierarchical structure that relates global sentiment, group-wise sentiment and author-specific sentiment. Our model contains a hierarchy of distributions $\psi_i$, $\psi_{ig}$ and $\psi_{iu}$ indicating global, group-wise and author-specific sentiment respectively, towards political issue indicated by $z$ for a user $u$ who belongs to group $g$.

### 3.2 Structure

The model is shown in Figure 1. The **input** is a dataset of $T$ tweets, each annotated with one among $U$ authors(/users of twitter). Also, each author has exactly one out of $G$ political affiliations. We represent a tweet as a collection of three types of words: (a) *Issue words* that describe a political issue, (b) *Position words* that express a position towards the issue, and (c) *Emoticons*. We do not consider hashtags as a special case because of  Cohen and Ruths (2013) who show that hashtags are not strong indicators of political orientation. Two latent variables are defined for each tweet: issue $i$ and position $p$. **The topics corresponding to issue $i$ represent political issues, while topics corresponding to pairs of issue $i$ and position $p$ represent political positions.** The assumption that a tweet has exactly one issue and position is reasonable due to limited length of tweets. The arrows from $i$ and $p$ that lead to $t$, $o$ and $e$ realize the role of the three categories of content terms as follows:

1. The topic words $t$ describe a political issue and hence, are based only on the topic $i$.

2. The opinion words $o$ express position towards a political issue and hence, are based on both the issue $i$ and position $p$.

3. The sentiment of an emoticon $e$ does not depend on the issue being talked about and hence, is based only on position $p$.

The model estimates two sets of distributions: one for words and another for the user groups. The three categories of words lead to three distributions that are estimated by the model: (a) **Issue word-issue distribution** $\vec{\eta}_i$, (b) **Position word-issue-position distribution** $\vec{\phi}_{ip}$, and (c) **Emoticon-position distribution** $\vec{\chi}_e$. Since an emoticon may not completely belong to either of the political positions, we do not rely on a mapping to a position but consider a distribution of emoticons over positions. This incorporates more intricate forms of opinion expression like sarcasm. In addition to these term-specific distributions, the PIE model estimates author/group-specific distributions: (a) **Author-Issue distributions**: $\vec{\theta}_g$ is the probability of an issue with respect to a group $g$, $\vec{\theta}_u$ is the probability of an issue with respect to an author $u$, (b) **Author-position distributions**: $\vec{\psi}_i$ is the probability of a position with respect to an issue $i$, $\vec{\psi}_{ig}$ is the probability of a position with respect to an issue $i$ and group $g$, while $\vec{\psi}_{iu}$ is the probability of a position with respect to issue $i$ and author $u$. Variables and distributions in the model are in Table 1.

The generative process of the corpus can be described as follows[1]:

---

[1] 'Dir' in the generative process denotes a Dirichlet prior.

1. *For each issue $i$, select*
   $\vec{\eta}_i \sim Dir(\gamma)$, *and* $\vec{\psi}_i \sim Dir(\beta_1)$

2. *For each position $p$ select*
   $\vec{\phi}_p \sim Dir(\delta_1)$, $\vec{\phi}_{ip} \sim Dir(\delta_2 \vec{\phi}_p)$, *and* $\vec{\chi}_p \sim Dir(\epsilon)$

3. *For each group $g$ select*
   $\vec{\theta}_g \sim Dir(\alpha_1)$, *and* $\vec{\psi}_{ig} \sim Dir(\beta_2 \vec{\psi}_i)$

4. *For each author $u$ select*
   $\vec{\theta}_u \sim Dir(\alpha_2 \vec{\theta}_g)$, *and* $\vec{\psi}_{iu} \sim Dir(\beta_3 \vec{\psi}_{ig})$

5. *For each tweet $k$ select*
   (a) *topic $i_k \sim \vec{\theta}_{u_k}$ and sentiment $p_k \sim \vec{\psi}_{i_k, u_k}$*
   (b) *all topic words, $t_{kj} \sim \vec{\eta}_{i_k}$*
   (c) *all opinion words, $o_{kj} \sim \vec{\phi}_{i_k, p_k}$*
   (d) *all emoticons, $e_{kj} \sim \vec{\chi}_{p_k}$*

## 3.3 Estimation

In the PIE Model, we need to estimate word-topic distributions namely $\vec{\eta}_i$, $\vec{\chi}_e$ and $\vec{\phi}_o$ and author-specific distributions $\vec{\theta}_u$ and $\vec{\psi}_{i,u}$. The estimation of the joint probability distribution is computationally intractable. Hence, we use Gibbs sampling by Casella and George (1992) to estimate the underlying distributions. For computational efficiency, we use moment matching for estimation. The sampling algorithm runs for a pre-determined number of iterations. We implement a block sampler based on Heinrich (2005) that samples $p_k$ and $i_k$ of the $k^{th}$ tweet together and results in faster convergence. The joint probability of $p_k$ and $i_k$ is given by:

$$P(p_k, i_k | u_k, \vec{p}_{-k}, i_{-k}) \propto$$

$$\theta_{i_k | u_k} \psi_{p_k | i_k, u_k} (\prod_j \eta_{t_{kj} | i_k})(\prod_j \phi_{o_{kj} | p_k, i_k})(\prod_j \chi_{e_{kj} | p_k})$$

where all parameters $\theta, \psi, \eta, \phi$ and $\chi$ are estimated withholding information regarding the previous assignment to the $k^{th}$ tweet. The generative story is omitted in the current version, due to lack of space.

The word-specific distributions are estimated as:

$$\hat{\eta}_{t|i} = \frac{N_{t,i}^{(n)} + \gamma \frac{1}{V^{(n)}}}{N_i^{(n)} + \gamma}$$

$$\hat{\theta}_{i|u} = \frac{N_{i,u}^{(i)} + \alpha_2 \theta_{i|g(u)}}{N_u^{(i)} + \alpha_2}, \quad \hat{\theta}_{i|g} = \frac{N_{i,g}^{(i)} + \alpha_1 \frac{1}{V()}}{N_g^{(i)} + \alpha_1}$$

$$\hat{\phi}_{o|p,i} = \frac{N_{o,p,i}^{(o)} + \delta_2 \phi_{o|p}}{N_{p,i}^{(o)} + \delta_2}, \quad \hat{\phi}_{o|p} = \frac{N_{o,p}^{(o)} + \delta_1 \frac{1}{V^{(o)}}}{N_p^{(o)} + \delta_1}$$

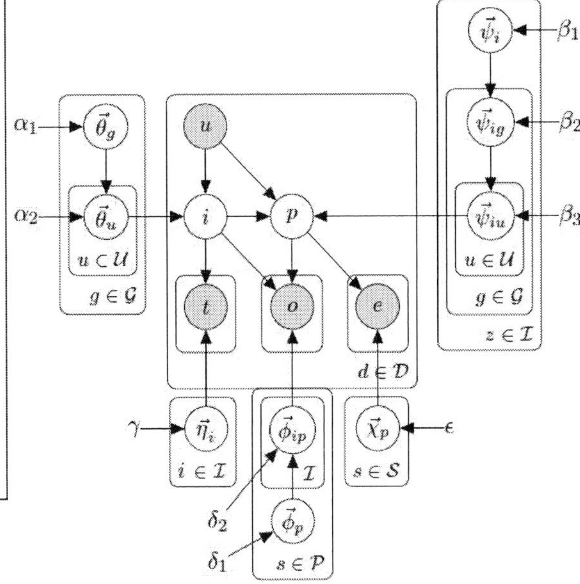

**Figure 1:** PIE Model: Plate Diagram

| Random Variables | |
|---|---|
| $u, g$ | Author of a tweet and Group of the author |
| $i, p$ | Issue and position of a tweet |
| $t, o$ | Issue/Position-word in a tweet |
| $e$ | Emoticon in a tweet |

| Distributions | |
|---|---|
| $\vec{\theta}_{u/g}$ | Dist. over issues for author $u$ / group $g$ |
| $\vec{\psi}_{i,u/g}$ | Dist. over positions for issue $i$ and author/group |
| $\vec{\eta}_i$ | Dist. over topic-words for issue $i$ |
| $\vec{\phi}_{i,p}$ | Dist. over opinion-words for issue-position pair |
| $\vec{\chi}_p$ | Dist. over emoticons for position $p$ |

| Hyper-parameters | |
|---|---|
| $\alpha, \beta$ | Concentration par. issue/position dist. |
| $\gamma$ | Concentration par. for issue-word dist. |
| $\delta$ | Concentration par. for position-word dist. |
| $\epsilon$ | Concentration par. for emoticon dist. |

| Counts | |
|---|---|
| $N_{t,i}^{(t)}$ | Frequency of topic-word $t$ in tweets for topic $i$ |
| $N_{i,u}^{(i)}$ | Frequency of tweets on topic $i$ by author $u$ |
| $V^{(t)}$ | Vocabulary size for topic words |

**Table 1:** Glossary of Variables/Distributions used

$$\hat{\chi}_{e|p} = \frac{N_{e,p}^{(e)} + \epsilon \frac{1}{V^{(e)}}}{N_p^{(e)} + \epsilon}$$

where the count notation can be read as follows:

$N_{e,p}^{(e)}$ denotes the number of times emoticon $e$ occurs within tweets assigned to position $p$ across the corpus and $V^{(e)}$ is the size of the emoticon vocabulary. The equations show that for speed and ease of implementation, we use a simple approximation to the group-wide Dirichlet mean parameter $\vec{\phi}_{o|p}$ rather than estimating expected table counts within a Chinese Restaurant Process as given by Griffiths and Tenenbaum (2004). (We leave an investigation of more precise parameter estimation to future work.)

The author/group-specific distributions are estimated in a hierarchical manner as follows:

$$\hat{\theta}_{i|u} = \frac{N_{i,u}^{(i)} + \alpha_2 \theta_{i|g(u)}}{N_u^{(i)} + \alpha_2}, \quad \hat{\theta}_{i|g} = \frac{N_{i,g}^{(i)} + \alpha_1 \frac{1}{V^{(i)}}}{N_g^{(i)} + \alpha_1}$$

$$\hat{\psi}_{p|i,u} = \frac{N_{p,i,u}^{(p)} + \beta_3 \psi_{p|i,g(u)}}{N_{i,u}^{(p)} + \beta_3}, where :$$

$$\hat{\psi}_{p|i,g} = \frac{N_{p,i,g}^{(p)} + \beta_2 \psi_{p|i}}{N_{i,g}^{(p)} + \beta_2}, \quad \hat{\psi}_{p|i} = \frac{N_{p,i}^{(p)} + \beta_1 \frac{1}{V^{(p)}}}{N_i^{(p)} + \beta_1}$$

The notation here is the same as for the word-issue distributions, except that the counts are now at the "tweet-level" rather than the "word-level", i.e. $N_{i,u}^{(i)}$ indicates number of tweets by author $u$ assigned the topic $i$. Note again the use of simple estimates for the group-wide parameters $\vec{\theta}_g$ and $\vec{\psi}_{z,g}$.

## 4  Experiment Setup

We create a dataset of tweets using Twitter API (https://dev.twitter.com/). The authors whose timelines will be downloaded are obtained as follows. We first obtain a list of famous Democrats and Republicans using sources like about.com, The Guardian and Fanpagelist. This results in a list of 32 Republicans and 46 Democrats. We expand this list by adding randomly selected friends of these twitter handles. (The choice of "friends" as opposed to "followers" is intentional.) We then download complete twitter timelines of all authors (Twitter sets the upper limit to 3200 tweets). The resultant dataset consists of 2441058 tweets. Dirichlet hyperparameters and values of $I$=35 and $P$=2 are experimentally determined. We set priors on position words using a word list of 6789 words given by McAuley and Leskovec (2013). Function words and 25 most frequent words are removed.

| Segregation strategy | Coherence |
|---|---|
| POS-based | **0.468** |
| POS-based+PMI Collocns. | 0.436 |
| Subjectivity-based | 0.451 |
| POS+Subjectivity-based | 0.457 |

**Table 2:** Average topic coherence per topic for different strategies of word segregation

## 5  Evaluation

To validate the efficacy of our model, our evaluation addresses the following questions:

- What impact do components of the model have, on its ability to discover these issues and positions? *(Section 5.1)*

- What political issues and positions does the model discover? *(Section 5.2)*

- Once we discovered political issues, positions and group-wise distribution, can the model be used to predict political affiliation? *(Section 5.3)*

### 5.1  Impact of Model Components on Performance

We evaluate two key components of PIE model, namely, segregation of words and hierarchy of author-group distributions.

**Segregation of words**: A key component of PIE model is the strategy to decide whether a word is an issue word or position word. We experiment with following alternatives to do this: (a) **POS-based segregation** as done in Fang et al. (2012) using twitter POS tagger Bontcheva et al. (2013). We experimentally determine the optimal split as: nouns as issue words, and adjectives, verbs and adverbs as position words, (b) **POS-based+PMI-based collocation handler** to include n-grams, using Bird (2006), (c) **Subjectivity-based segregation** classifies words present in the subjectivity word list by McAuley and Leskovec (2013) as position words, (d) **POS+Subjectivity-based segregation** where we first categorize nouns as issue words, and then look for other words in the subjectivity word list. In order to select the best strategy of segregation, we compute topic coherence metric $Cv$ using Palmetto by Röder, Both, and Hinneburg

| | Average cosine similarity | | $\Delta$ |
|---|---|---|---|
| | **With** | **Without** | |
| **Within members of the same group** | | | |
| Demo.-Demo. | **0.261** | 0.253 | 0.01 |
| Repub.-Repub. | **0.014** | 0.013 | 0.001 |
| **Within members of different groups** | | | |
| Demo.-Repub. | **0.108** | 0.113 | -0.005 |
| Repub.-Demo. | **0.040** | 0.042 | -0.002 |

**Table 3:** Average cosine similarity between author-position distributions, with and without group membership information

(2015) for all topics. This metric uses normalized PMI. Average coherence per topic is shown in Table 2. We observe the highest value of 0.468 in case of the POS-based strategy. The remaining subsections report results for our experiments with this strategy.

**Efficacy of author-group distributions**: To evaluate the benefit of our hierarchy of distributions, we obtain average cosine similarity between author-position distributions of the two political groups. For every author with known political affiliation, we first obtain the cosine similarity between the $\psi_{iu}$ of the author and the $\psi_{iu}$ of other authors belonging to his/her own political group. This is then averaged over all authors. This value indicates how different/similar authors of a affiliation are. Table 3 shows these values for different combinations. The columns indicate two scenarios: when political affiliation information is used ('with') and when it is not used ('without') during the estimation. The rows indicate the four possible scenarios. The average cosine similarities are not symmetric, by design. The sign on $\Delta$ shows that incorporation of political affiliation information makes authors of the same group more similar to each other, and authors of different groups less similar to each other, as desired.

## 5.2 Qualitative Evaluation

The issues extracted from our model are represented by the topics formed using topic words. We list some of the topics extracted using PIE model in Table 4. Each cell contains top 5 words of each topic with a manually assigned description in boldface. These topics are the political issues underlying our dataset. The issues discovered are *"health in-*

| Insurance | Gun laws | Crime |
|---|---|---|
| health | people | scene |
| insurance | gun | police |
| people | laws | man |
| care | guns | fire |
| plan | control | suspect |
| **Abortion** | **Security/War** | **Employment** |
| abortion | attack | workers |
| baby | video | job |
| babies | security | wages |
| freedom | police | jobs |
| women | forces | people |
| **Immigration** | **Economy** | **Climate** |
| workers | tax | climate |
| immigration | jobs | people |
| stories | debt | change |
| patriot | taxes | warming |
| politics | spending | years |
| **Marriage** | **Election** | **Disasters** |
| people | bill | acres |
| freedom | vote | fire |
| marriage | campaign | weather |
| rights | state | snow |
| women | election | storm |

**Table 4:** Top words in Political Issues discovered by PIE

*surance, abortion, security, employment, gun laws, immigration, economy, climate, marriage, election, disasters, crime and government"*. In addition to these, topics beyond political issues are also observed, as expected. These include **sports** (*game, team, season, year, football*), **promotional online content** ({*blog, showcase, article, courtesy, support*} or {*photo, photos, video, entry, album*}), etc. Manual identification of political issues from the set of retrieved topics is necessary because approaches like considering top-k probable topics may not work. For example, social media concepts such as followers or promotional online content occur more frequently than immigration and abortion. We validate that **our political issues appear in at least one out of three online lists of issues** from Gallup.com, About.com and Ontheissues.com in Table 5.

The alternate positions that people take, are shown in Table 6. Each box consists of a political issue written in boldface and top five words in topics corresponding to alternate sentiment. These topics show what we mean by *"alternate"* positions and that they are not merely positive or negative. In case of the political issue *"abortion"*, the con-

| | A | Gallup | O | | A | G | O | | A | G | O |
|---|---|---|---|---|---|---|---|---|---|---|---|
| Abortion | | ✓ | ✓ | Government | | ✓ | | Economy | ✓ | ✓ | |
| Climate | ✓ | ✓ | | Gun Laws | ✓ | | ✓ | Election | | | |
| Crime | | | ✓ | Immigration | | ✓ | ✓ | Employment | | ✓ | ✓ |
| Disasters | ✓ | | | Insurance | | ✓ | ✓ | Security/War | ✓ | | ✓ |
| Marriage | ✓ | ✓ | ✓ | | | | | | | | |

**Table 5:** Comparison of Our Political Issues with three Online Lists of Political Issues from About.com (A), Gallup (G) and OnTheIssues (O)

| Abortion | | Security/War | |
|---|---|---|---|
| Join | Prolife | Killed | Military |
| Religious | Killed | Syrian | Illegal |
| Stand | Born | Military | Russian |
| Support | Unborn | Fast | Targeting |
| Conservative | Aborted | Furious | Back |

| Gun laws | | Immigration | |
|---|---|---|---|
| Illegal | Dont | Join | Top |
| Free | Free | Support | Enter |
| Dont | Stop | Back | Check |
| Vote | Illegal | Stand | Stop |
| Stop | Give | Proud | Join |

| Insurance | | Marriage | |
|---|---|---|---|
| Pay | Check | Back | Gay |
| Federal | Hear | Don | Religious |
| Signed | Here | Lost | Political |
| Paid | Call | Liberal | Free |
| Uninsured | Hope | Great | ** |

**Table 6:** Top words in Political Positions Discovered by PIE;
** is a popular twitter handle

trasting positions correspond to topics given by *join, religious, stand, support, conservative* and *prolife, killed, born, unborn, aborted*. It can be seen that the first position gives a religious view whereas the second position presents an emotional appeal with respect to abortion. Similarly, consider the box for "*immigration*". One position corresponds to "*support*" and "*stand*" by immigrants while the opposing position corresponds to "*check*" or "*stop*" immigration. In case of "*insurance*", authors are divided into ones who talk about "*paying*" and the ones who see "*hope*" in revised insurance policies. Finally, look at the box corresponding to "*gun laws*". Both positions contain topics with negative words but differ in a way that one position talks about a "*vote*" while the opposite position mentions "*give*".

Figure 2 shows the absolute difference between the $P(p|i, g)$ for a topic-party pair. The observations

are intuitive since the issues with **least difference are *employment and disasters*** while the most contentious are *abortion, election and immigration*.

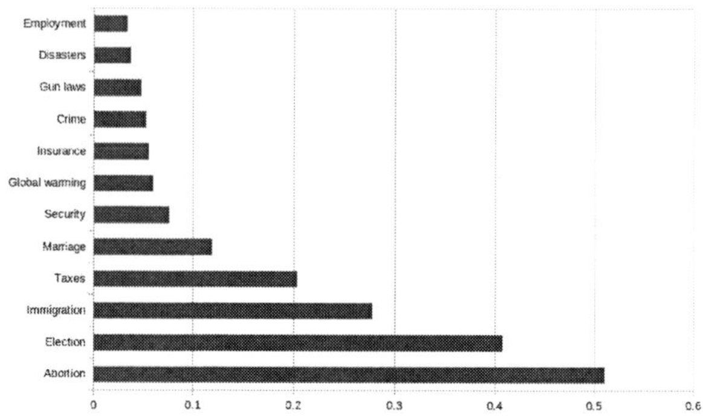


**Figure 2:** Difference between Political Positions

| Approach | Accuracy (%) |
|---|---|
| Baseline: *Gottipati et al. (2013)* | 60 |
| Log likelihood-based | 68 |

**Table 7:** Comparison of PIE model with past approaches for prediction of Political Affiliation

### 5.3 Application: Prediction of Political Affiliation

Obtaining a set of non-political authors with reliable political affiliation is challenging. We first select authors who were labeled as '*Unknown*'. This means that PIE model did not know about their political affiliation during training. Among these authors, we select ones who have mentioned their political affiliation in their profile description. This results in 25 test authors (out of which 6 are Democrats). We consider two approaches to predict political affiliation:

1. **Baseline**: This baseline is similar to Gottipati et al. (2013) except that the vectors in our case

are based on PIE model. We calculate cosine similarities between estimated author-position distribution $\psi_{iu}$ for test authors and each of the group-position distributions $\psi_{ig}$ for the two political groups. The predicted affiliation is the group with greater similarity value.

2. **Log likelihood-based**: We use the distribution for words and groups, that have been computed during training. For each test author, we again run our estimation on their tweets twice, once for each group. The goal is to learn $\psi_{iu}$ and $\theta_u$ and compute two log-likelihood values, once for each group, and predict the more likely affiliation.

Table 7 compares our approach with a past approach. The log likelihood approach results in the best accuracy of 68%.

## 6 Conclusion & Future Work

In this paper, we presented a Political Issue Extraction (PIE) model to discover political issues and two positions per issue, using a dataset of tweets by US politicians and civilians. Our PIE model represented a tweet as three sets of words: topic words, opinion words and emoticons. To model author-specific distributions, we considered a hierarchical set of distributions.

To evaluate PIE model, we compared multiple strategies to classify words into three categories and showed that POS-based classification gives highest topic coherence. Our model was able to identify: a) topics corresponding to political issues, b) alternate positions that the two parties may take, and c) the issues that are likely to be the most *"contentious"*. We estimated twelve political issues (such as security, disasters, immigration, etc.) and positions within each. Using cosine similarity within groups, we showed that our model placed members of the same group closer to each other than the ones from the other group, when group information was provided. Our PIE model discovers that abortion, immigration and marriage are among the most contentious political issues. Finally, we also presented findings of a pilot study to predict political affiliation of authors using PIE model, and achieved an accuracy of 68%.

As future work, we wish to be able to automatically identify which of the topics extracted from our model are political issues. Although the current model can be used for extraction more than two positions in principle, we would like to see if any additional challenges come up in that case. This model can be mapped to identification of controversial topics, brand loyalty, etc.

## References


About.com. Political Issues, url = http://uspolitics.about.com/od/electionissues/.

Benton, A.; Paul, M. J.; Hancock, B.; and Dredze, M. 2016. Collective supervision of topic models for predicting surveys with social media. In *Proceedings of AAAI Conference*.

Bird, S. 2006. Nltk: the natural language toolkit. In *Proceedings of the COLING-ACL on Interactive presentation sessions*, 69–72. Association for Computational Linguistics.

Blei, D. M.; Ng, A. Y.; and Jordan, M. I. 2003. Latent dirichlet allocation. *the Journal of machine Learning research* 3:993–1022.

Bontcheva, K.; Derczynski, L.; Funk, A.; Greenwood, M. A.; Maynard, D.; and Aswani, N. 2013. TwitIE: An open-source information extraction pipeline for microblog text. In *Proceedings of the International Conference on Recent Advances in Natural Language Processing*. Association for Computational Linguistics.

Casella, G., and George, E. I. 1992. Explaining the gibbs sampler. *The American Statistician* 46(3):167–174.

Cohen, R., and Ruths, D. 2013. Classifying political orientation on twitter: It's not easy! In *ICWSM*.

Conover, M. D.; Gonçalves, B.; Ratkiewicz, J.; Flammini, A.; and Menczer, F. 2011. Predicting the political alignment of twitter users. In *Privacy, security, risk and trust, 2011 IEEE third international conference on social computing*, 192–199. IEEE.

Fang, Y.; Si, L.; Somasundaram, N.; and Yu, Z. 2012. Mining contrastive opinions on political texts using cross-perspective topic model. In *Proceedings of the fifth ACM international conference on Web search and data mining*, 63–72. ACM.

Gallup.com. Jobs, Government, and Economy remain top US problems, url = http://www.gallup.com/poll/169289/jobs-government-economy-remain-top-problems.aspx.

Gayo-Avello, D.; Metaxas, P. T.; and Mustafaraj, E. 2011. Limits of electoral predictions using twitter. In *ICWSM*.

Gerrish, S., and Blei, D. M. 2011. Predicting legislative roll calls from text. In *Proceedings of the 28th international conference on machine learning (icml-11)*, 489–496.

Gottipati, S.; Qiu, M.; Yang, L.; Zhu, F.; and Jiang, J. 2013. Predicting users political party using ideological stances. In *Social Informatics*. Springer. 177–191.

Griffiths, D., and Tenenbaum, M. 2004. Hierarchical topic models and the nested chinese restaurant process. *Advances in neural information processing systems* 16:17.

Grimmer, J. 2010. A bayesian hierarchical topic model for political texts: Measuring expressed agendas in senate press releases. *Political Analysis* 18(1):1–35.

Heinrich, G. 2005. Parameter estimation for text analysis. Technical report, Technical report.

Jo, Y., and Oh, A. H. 2011. Aspect and sentiment unification model for online review analysis. In *Proceedings of the fourth ACM international conference on Web search and data mining*, 815–824. ACM.

Lin, C., and He, Y. 2009. Joint sentiment/topic model for sentiment analysis. In *Proceedings of the 18th ACM conference on Information and knowledge management*, 375–384. ACM.

Lin, W.-H.; Xing, E.; and Hauptmann, A. 2008. A joint topic and perspective model for ideological discourse. In *Machine Learning and Knowledge Discovery in Databases*. Springer. 17–32.

McAuley, J. J., and Leskovec, J. 2013. From amateurs to connoisseurs: modeling the evolution of user expertise through online reviews. In *Proceedings of the 22nd international conference on World Wide Web*, 897–908. International World Wide Web Conferences Steering Committee.

Mei, Q.; Ling, X.; Wondra, M.; Su, H.; and Zhai, C. 2007. Topic sentiment mixture: modeling facets and opinions in weblogs. In *Proceedings of the 16th international conference on World Wide Web*, 171–180. ACM.

Metaxas, P. T.; Mustafaraj, E.; and Gayo-Avello, D. 2011. How (not) to predict elections. In *Privacy, security, risk and trust (PASSAT), 2011 IEEE third international conference on and 2011 IEEE third international conference on social computing (SocialCom)*, 165–171. IEEE.

O'Connor, B.; Balasubramanyan, R.; Routledge, B. R.; and Smith, N. A. 2010. From tweets to polls: Linking text sentiment to public opinion time series. *ICWSM* 11:122–129.

Ontheissues.com. Candidates on the Issues, url = http://www.ontheissues.org/default.htm.

Röder, M.; Both, A.; and Hinneburg, A. 2015. Exploring the space of topic coherence measures. In *Proceedings of the eight International Conference on Web Search and Data Mining, Shanghai, February 2-6*.

Wang, X.; Mohanty, N.; and McCallum, A. 2005. Group and topic discovery from relations and text. In *Proceedings of the 3rd international workshop on Link discovery*, 28–35. ACM.

Wong, F. M. F.; Tan, C. W.; Sen, S.; and Chiang, M. 2013. Quantifying political leaning from tweets and retweets. In *ICWSM*.

Yano, T.; Cohen, W. W.; and Smith, N. A. 2009. Predicting response to political blog posts with topic models. In *Proceedings of Human Language Technologies: The 2009 Annual Conference of the North American Chapter of the Association for Computational Linguistics*, 477–485. Association for Computational Linguistics.

Zhao, W. X.; Jiang, J.; Yan, H.; and Li, X. 2010. Jointly modeling aspects and opinions with a maxent-lda hybrid. In *Proceedings of the 2010 Conference on Empirical Methods in Natural Language Processing*, 56–65. Association for Computational Linguistics.

# Early text classification: a Naïve solution[*]


**Hugo Jair Escalante**
INAOE
Puebla, 72840, Mexico
hugojair@inaoep.mx

**Manuel Montes y Gomez**
INAOE
Puebla, 72840, Mexico
mmontesg@inaoep.mx

**Luis Villaseñor Pineda**
INAOE
Puebla, 72840, Mexico
villasen@inaoep.mx

**Marcelo L. Errecalde**
Universidad Nacional de San Luis
San Luis, D5700HHW, Argentina
merrecalde@gmail.com


## Abstract


Text classification is a widely studied problem, and it can be considered *solved* for some domains and under certain circumstances. There are scenarios, however, that have received little or no attention at all, despite its relevance and applicability. One of such scenarios is early text classification, where one needs to know the category of a document by using partial information only. A document is processed as a sequence of terms, and the goal is to devise a method that can make predictions as fast as possible. The importance of this variant of the text classification problem is evident in domains like sexual predator detection, where one wants to identify an offender as early as possible. This paper analyzes the suitability of the standard naïve Bayes classifier for approaching this problem. Specifically, we assess its performance when classifying documents after seeing an increasingly number of terms. A simple modification to the standard naïve Bayes implementation allows us to make predictions with partial information. To the best of our knowledge Naïve Bayes has not been used for this purpose before. Throughout an extensive experimental evaluation we show the effectiveness of the classifier for early text classification. What is more, we show that this simple solution is very competitive when compared with state of the art methodologies that are more elaborated. We foresee our work will pave the way for the development of more effective early text classification techniques based in the naïve Bayes formulation.



[*]This work was supported by CONACyT grants No. CB-2014-241306 and PN-247870.


## 1 Introduction

Text classification is the task of assigning documents to its correct categories (Sebastiani, 2008). This is one of the most studied topics within natural language processing. Advances in the last two decades have made significant progress and nowadays the text classification problem is considered to be solved in some scenarios and under certain circumstances (e.g., news classification with plenty of data). There are, however, settings of the text classification problem that have received little attention despite the wide applicability they may have. One of such scenarios is that of *early text classification*, which deals with the development of predictive models that are capable of determining the class a document belongs to as soon as possible. A text is assumed to be processed sequentially, starting at the beginning of the document and reading input words one by one. It is desired to make predictions with as low information as possible.

The early text classification topic has received little attention in the community, and there exist only a few works that have approached similar scenarios (Dulac-Arnold et al., 2011) (please note that in this work the problem is not stated as one of early recognition). Despite its low popularity, this topic has a major potential in practical applications. For instance, consider the problem of detecting sexual predators in chat conversations. Here, the goal is to sequentially read a conversation and to determine as fast as possible whenever a sexual predator is involved; clearly, a detection using the whole conversation can only be used for forensics rather than for prevention. Other sample applications include,




*Proceedings of NAACL-HLT 2016*, pages 91–99,
San Diego, California, June 12-17, 2016. ©2016 Association for Computational Linguistics

any kind of conversation analysis that requires of a fast response, (e.g., cyber-bullying prevention, adaptive/intelligent answering systems); trending-topic discovery (e.g., analyzing comments on social networks and determining as soon as possible whenever a topic will become a trend); content filtering (e.g., filtering inappropriate/ilegal content in local networks), author profiling (e.g., knowing the age, gender or interest of a person by using as few written information as possible) etcetera.

This paper explores the suitability of one of the most popular methods for text classification, i.e., naïve Bayes (McCallum and Nigam, 1998; Sebastiani, 2008), to approach the early-classification setting: *early naïve Bayes*. Specifically, we evaluate the capabilities of this classifier to make predictions when *seeing* an increasing number of terms from documents. A simple modification to the standard naïve Bayes implementation allows us to make predictions with partial information. Despite its simplicity, the proposed extension obtains competitive performance in standard text classification tasks and in sexual predator detection. In fact we show that the proposed modification compares favorably with the only existing work that addresses a similar task. Hopefully, our work will motivate research on further extensions to this classifier for early text classification.

The remainder of this paper is organized as follows. Next section reviews related work on early text classification and on extensions to naïve Bayes to face closely related problems. Then, Section 3 describes naïve Bayes classifier and the modification we propose to make early predictions. Section 4 reports experimental results that show the effectiveness of the proposal. Section 5 presents conclusions and discusses future work directions.

## 2    Related work

This section reviews related work on both: early text classification and extensions to naïve Bayes to face similar problems.

### 2.1    Early text classification

To the best of our knowledge, the early text categorization problem has been approached only in (Dulac-Arnold et al., 2011); although the authors'

main focus was not on making predictions earlier but on improving the classification performance with a *sequential reading approach*. In that work, the authors process documents in a sentence-level basis. Every time $t$, the authors read a sentence and attempt to determine the class of the document, where multi-label classification is allowed. They proposed a Markov decision process (MDP) to approach the problem, where two possible actions were allowed: read next sentence, or classify. Each sentence has to be represented by its *tfidf* representation and a classifier is trained to learn good/bad state-action pairs (10,000 examples were randomly generated) on a high-dimensional space.

The performance of their method was evaluated in standard text classification data sets. Although the performance of such method is competitive (it was compared to a SVM classifier), it remains unknown whether a much more simpler approach would be as effective as the complex procedure in (Dulac-Arnold et al., 2011). In Section 4 we compare the proposed extension of naïve Bayes with the previous work. We show our proposal is competitive in terms of performance, but also has the following advantages: it is scalable in the number of categories (the MDP evaluated every possible state after reading each sentence, ours simply adds probabilities); it is able to make predictions with as low information as no-word (using priors-only information, but the most important aspect is that it can make predictions at anytime); it process documents in a word-level basis (i.e., one word added at a time, while the MDP requires processing whole sentences); training is much more efficient (same training complexity as an standard naïve Bayes classifier, the MDP requires of high-complexity training procedures) and the resultant model is way more simple.

Although the early text classification problem has not been studied elsewhere, it is worth mentioning works that have approached related tasks. In (Denoyer et al., 2001), the authors propose a hidden Markov model (HMM) to classify passages within documents. The task is information retrieval and a document is considered as relevant or irrelevant (i.e. two classes) to a given category/query. The document is decomposed into passages, each of which is considered by the HMM as relevant or irrelevant to the classification. No attempt is made to perform classification early, although it is interesting that the proposed model is a generalization of the multinomial naïve Bayes we consider in this work (again, for the two-class whole-document classification problem).

In (Dulac-Arnold et al., 2012) the authors extend the MDP proposed for sequential text classification to deal with any other type of data. The formulation is almost the same as in (Dulac-Arnold et al., 2011), although this time the MDP can decide what feature to sample from the instance under analysis (i.e., there is no sequential input). Furthermore, the MDP is equipped with a mechanism that aims to minimize the number of features to use for classification. Clearly, this extended MDP is not applicable to the early text classification domain (words cannot be chosen from documents, they appear sequentially).

Summarizing, it is remarkable the little attention that early text classification has received so far, this may be due to the fact that not so many applications in the past required to cope with this problem. Nowadays, however, the *online status* of the world population, requires of technology that can anticipate the prediction of certain events with the goal of preventing undesired effects or, on the other hand, to act as fast as possible to take the leadership on information technology.

## 2.2 Extending naïve Bayes

Naïve Bayes has been used extensively in text mining and within machine learning in general, because of its high performance in several domains, several modifications and extensions have been proposed to augment the scope of the classifier. Related to our work, the following extensions have been reported in the literature:

- **Alleviating independence assumption of Naïve Bayes.** This is perhaps the most studied topic in terms of extending the mentioned classifier. The independence assumption may be too strong for some domains/applications, therefore, several works have been proposed that try to relax it. Most notably TAN (Friedman et al., 1997), AODE (Webb et al., 2005), and WANBIA (Zaidi et al., 2013) extensions have reported outstanding results. Neverthe-

less, the focus here is on relaxing the attribute independence assumption, and not on working with partial information. One should note, however, that this extended versions of naïve Bayes can be well suited for early text classification, as attribute-dependency information can help the algorithm to classify texts earlier.

- **Anytime naïve Bayes.** The goal of this type of extensions is to provide naïve Bayes with mechanisms that allow it to make predictions at anytime (Yang et al., 2007; Hui et al., 2009). This means that the algorithm has to be ready to provide a prediction under time constraints: the classifier can spent increasing amounts of time for doing inference, but it must provide an answer when requested; usually accuracy increases as more time is allowed. This type of methods is related to our proposal in that the system has to be ready to make predictions at anytime, however, the granularity of information processing is different: in anytime classification a whole instance is seen, whereas in early text classification, part of an instance is available.

- **Incremental naïve Bayes.** Refers to developing learning and inference mechanisms to allow the classifier be trained in an online learning setting (Alcobé, 2002; Klawonn and Angelov, 2006). That is, reading a sample (or batch of samples at a time), the model makes predictions for the incoming samples and then it is provided with the correct labels, next, model parameters have to be updated accordingly. This type of methods are related to our proposal in that partial information is processed incrementally, although one should note that information units are instances and not words/attributes.

- **Naïve Bayes for incomplete information.** These extensions aim at helping naïve Bayes to deal with missing information, usually, at the attribute level. For instance by equipping the classifiers with mechanisms to work under highly-sparse representations (e.g., in short text categorization) (Shen et al., 2009; Cabrera et al., 2013; He and Ding, 2007; Yuan et al., 2012). These methods are mostly based on smoothing attribute-class probabilities and often use co-occurrence statistics. Although not dealing with early text classification, this type of methods are relevant because smoothing plays a key role when working with partial information (everything not seen so far has to be smoothed).

Summarizing, there have been many attempts to improve and extend naïve Bayes to be robust against several limitations, however, to the best of our knowledge, it has not been used for early text classification before. This is somewhat surprising given that, as shown in the next section, the naïve Bayes classifiers can naturally deal with partial information.

## 3 Early text classification with Naïve Bayes

This section describes the way we use naïve Bayes classifier for early text classification.

### 3.1 Naïve Bayes classifier

We first describe the standard naïve Bayes classifier. Consider a data set: $\mathcal{D} = (\mathbf{x}_i, y_i)_{\{1,\ldots,N\}}$ with $N$ pairs of instances ($\mathbf{x}_i$) and labels ($y_i$) associated to a supervised classification problem. Assuming that $\mathbf{x}_i \in \mathbb{R}^q$ and $y_i \in C = \{1, \ldots, K\}$ we have a $K-$class classification problem with numeric[1] attributes.

Under the naïve Bayes classifier, the class for an unseen instance $\mathbf{x}_T = \langle x_{T,1}, \ldots, x_{T,q} \rangle$ is given by:

$$\hat{C} = \arg\max_{C_i} P(C_i | \mathbf{x}_T) \tag{1}$$

From Bayes' theorem it follows that the posterior probability above can be estimated as:

$$P(C_i | \mathbf{x}_T) = \frac{P(\mathbf{x}_T | C_i) P(C_i)}{P(\mathbf{x}_T)} \tag{2}$$

The denominator can be removed from Equation (1) as it does not affect the decision:

$$P(C_i | \mathbf{x}_T) \approx P(\mathbf{x}_T | C_i) P(C_i) \tag{3}$$

---

[1]One should note that in text classification we can transform any document to a numeric vector with the bag of words representation, i.e., a vector of length $q$, where $q$ is the vocabulary size and each element of the vector indicates the relevance of a term for describing the content of the document.

The assumption of naïve Bayes is that the probability of occurrence of attributes of $\mathbf{x}_T$ is independent given its class, that is:

$$P(C_i | \mathbf{x}_T) \approx \prod_{j=1}^{q} P(x_{T,j} | C_i) P(C_i) \tag{4}$$

The maximum likelihood estimation for the prior of class $C_i$ is given by:

$$\hat{P}(C_i) = \frac{|X_i|}{N} \tag{5}$$

where $X_i$ is the set of all instances in $\mathcal{D}$ that are labeled with class $C_i$. Hence, the key of the naïve Bayes classifier lies in the estimation of $P(\mathbf{x}_T | C_i)$, or more precisely of $\prod_{j=1}^{q} P(x_{T,j} | C_i)$. Depending on the type of data (e.g., binary, discrete, or real) a different distribution may be assumed for computing $P(x_{T,j} | C_i)$ (e.g., Bernoulli, Multinomial, or Gaussian, respectively). In text classification one of the most effective implementations is based in the multinomial distribution, when documents are represented by its term-frequency representation (i.e., we know for each document, the number of times each term from the vocabulary occurs) (McCallum and Nigam, 1998; Kibriya et al., 2005). Accordingly, we focus in this implementation, this means we assume w.l.o.g.: $\mathbf{x}_i \in \mathbb{Z}_+^q$ (i.e. the representation of a document is a vector of frequency values / integers).

Assuming a multinomial distribution for the model we have that the maximum likelihood estimation for the term of interest is:

$$P(\mathbf{x}_T | C_i) \approx \prod_{j=1}^{q} \hat{P}(x_{T,j} | C_i)^{f_{j,T}} \tag{6}$$

where $f_{j,T}$ is the value of the $j^{th}$ attribute in instance $\mathbf{x}_T$ (in text classification $f_{j,T}$ is the frequency of occurrence of the $j^{th}$ term in document $T$), and

$$\hat{P}(x_{T,j} | C_i) = \frac{1 + F_{j,C_i}}{q + \sum_k^q F_{k,C_i}} \tag{7}$$

where $F_{l,C_i}$ is the sum of values of the $l^{th}$ attribute in documents of class $C_i$. The derivation from Equation (6) removes factorial terms that do not affect the final decision. For more details we refer the reader

to (McCallum and Nigam, 1998; Kibriya et al.,
2005). In the description above we did not assume
a text categorization problem because the same results apply to any type of (multinomial-distributed)
attributes. In the following we use text-mining terminology, but we emphasize the description is gen-
eralizable to other problems.

### 3.2  Early Naïve Bayes

In early text classification we assume that during
training we have full documents, therefore, the same
training procedure as the standard naïve Bayes classifier is performed for estimating the necessary probabilities[2]. The difference comes at inference time:
when classifying a new document we assume we
read it in sequential order starting from the beginning (i.e. the first word from top to bottom and from
left to right). W.l.o.g.[3], at time $t$ we assume we
have read the first $t-$terms in the document (i.e., one
word is read at each time). Let $d_T$ denote the document we want to classify, where it contains $M_{d_T}$
words, then, $d_T = w_1, w_2, \ldots, w_{M_{d_T}}$.

We notice from Equations (5-7) that in fact we
can make predictions for document $d_T$ regardless
the amount of information we have read from it: at
time $t$ we know that $d_T = w_1, \ldots, w_t$, therefore, we
can generate a bag-of-words $\mathbf{x}_T$ representation for
$d_T$ as follows $\mathbf{x}_T = \langle \mathbf{x}_{T,1}, \ldots, \mathbf{x}_{T,q} \rangle$, where $\mathbf{x}_{T,j}$
indicates the frequency of occurrence of the $j^{th}$ term
in document $d_T$ (i.e., a *tf* weighting scheme). Terms
not occurring the $d_T$ or not seen so far at time $t$ are
assigned values of $\mathbf{x}_{T,j} = 0$. With this representation we can use Equation (3) directly to classify
the document. Actually, we can attempt to classify
document $d_T$ without having read any information!
(i.e., with $t = 0$), of course the probability will be
dominated by the priors, see Equation (5). Simply as
this, we can use naïve Bayes to perform early classification.

We now briefly analyze what are the main components in play when making predictions early. At

---

[2]One may also train naïve Bayes with partial documents,
however, in that case the probability estimates associated to the
model are not reliable because they are obtained from reduced
documents. In preliminary experiments we corroborated this
fact.

[3]One should note that we can take steps of any length, instead of processing word-by-word.

time $t$ one can rewrite Equation (4) as:

$$P(C_i|\mathbf{x}_T) \approx P(C_i) \prod_{j:j \in d_T} P(x_{T,j}|C_i) \prod_{k:k \notin d_T} P(x_{T,k}|C_i)$$

(8)

the second product (over $j \in d_T$) accounts for
the terms appearing in the document (probabilities
are affected by the frequency of occurrence of such
terms in $d_T$ so far); the third product (on $k \notin d_T$)
simply reduces to 1 (because of the exponent in
Equation (6)). Therefore, for small values of $t$, the
priors dominate the decision, as $t$ increases the content of the document will dominate the other products. Therefore, the way these three components are
estimated can be crucial for improving the performance of naïve Bayes in early classification.

Despite the simplicity of this early text classification approach, we will see in the next section that
it compares favorably with a more complicated solution from the state of the art. We show its validity in a variety of problems. This paper motivates
further work on extending this model for early text
classification. For instance, one can define/modify
adaptive priors that change as the value of $t$ increases; we can implement the same idea with methods that take into account term-dependencies (see
e.g., (Friedman et al., 1997; Webb et al., 2005;
Zaidi et al., 2013)) in order to increase the predictive power of the classifier; also one can adopt ad-
vanced/alternative smoothing techniques to account
for partial and missing information properly (Shen et
al., 2009; Cabrera et al., 2013; He and Ding, 2007);
as well as many other possibilities. The main goal of
this paper is to show that naïve Bayes can be used for
early text classification and that its performance is
competitive with the single existing solution to this
problem. We foresee our work will pave the way for
development of a new type of models.

## 4  Experiments and results

For experimentation we considered the data sets
described in Table 1. We considered three standard thematic text categorization tasks (also used
in (Dulac-Arnold et al., 2011)) and a data set for sexual predator detection (Inches and Crestani, 2012).
All of the data and our code will be made available
under request for future comparisons. In the subsections below we provide details on each data set

and report the corresponding experimental results obtained with them.

| Text categorization | | | | | |
|---|---|---|---|---|---|
| **Data set** | **Classes** | **Terms** | **Red.V.** | **Train** | **Test** |
| Reuters-8 | 8 | 23583 | 2483 | 5339 | 2333 |
| 20-Newsgroup | 20 | 61188 | 6894 | 11269 | 7505 |
| WebKB | 4 | 7770 | 3727 | 2458 | 1709 |
| **Sexual predator detection** | | | | | |
| SPD | 2 | 155886 | 6770 | 6588 | 15329 |

**Table 1:** Data sets considered for experimentation. Red. V. is the number of terms when a reduced vocabulary is used.

Text data sets were processed as follows: stop words were removed, then stemming was applied, next the bag-of-words representation was obtained using the TMG toolbox, a term-frequency (*tf*) weighting scheme was used (Zeimpekis and Gallopoulos, 2006). All of the data were processed in Matlab$^R$. For most experiments we used reduced vocabularies, that is, we used only a subset of the most frequent words/terms (see column 4 in Table 1), we proceeded like this for efficiency, nevertheless we also report results with full-vocabularies in text categorization data sets.

In addition to the comparison to the state of the art, we considered a linear SVM classifier as baseline, since this is a *mandatory* baseline in text classification (Joachims, 2008; Sebastiani, 2008). SVM was used in early classification similarly as the naïve Bayes model: it was trained with complete documents, and for making predictions, the bag of words of a document up to time $t$ is obtained and feeded to the SVM classifier. In preliminary experimentation we compared SVM with *tf* and *tfidf* weighting schemes, we report the performance of SVM with the latter scheme because we obtained better results with this configuration.

In all of our experiments we report the performance of the early text classifiers when varying the percentage of the words in test documents (same procedure as in (Dulac-Arnold et al., 2011)). Macro-average $f_1$ measure was used for multiclass text categorization problems and $f_1$ of the minority class (i.e., predators) for the sexual predator detection data set. Ideally, the performance of a good early text classifier should draw a curve close to the $y-axis$ (see figures below): i.e., better performance with less information. A different problem, not evaluated in this paper, is that of triggering a prediction

whenever the classifier is sure about the class of a document. Please note, however, that simple triggering mechanisms can be derived for our proposed formulation, e.g., after seeing a predefined number of words, or when the difference between the most probable and the second most probable class exceeds a threshold, and so on.

## 4.1 Early text categorization

First we analyze the performance of early naïve Bayes on thematic text classification. The first three data sets from Table 1 were considered, these are widely used benchmark data sets for text categorization; standard training/testing partitions[4] were used. Results of this experiment are shown in Figure 1.

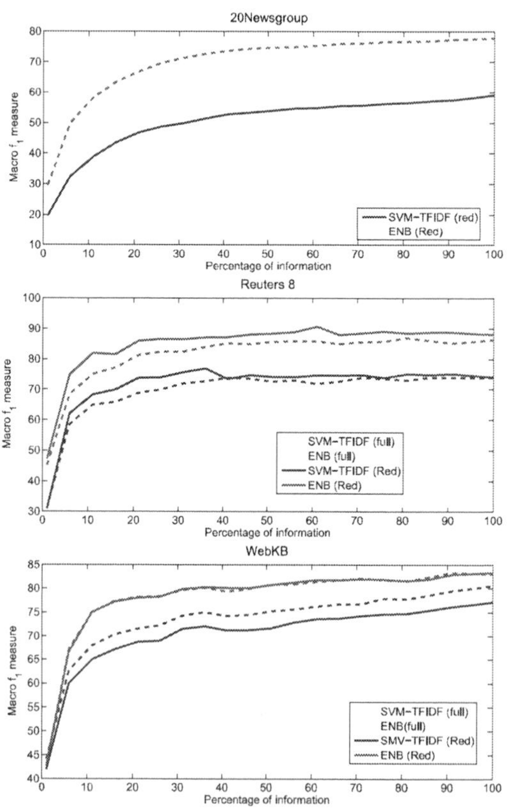

**Figure 1:** Early text classification on standard data sets.

It can be seen in the top plot that the early naïve Bayes (ENB hereafter) classifier outperforms considerably the SVM baseline for the 20Newsgrup data set. For both methods, the performance in-

---

[4] As reported in: http://web.ist.utl.pt/acardoso/datasets/

creased monotonically and, as expected, better performance was obtained when more information is considered.

The middle and bottom plots in Figure 1 show results for Reuters 8 and WebKB, respectively; in these plots we show the performance of both methods, ENB and SVM, and when using all of the vocabulary (*full*) and a reduced one (for 20Newsgrup data set we were not able to run an experiment with the full vocabulary in reasonable times). Regardless of the vocabulary used, ENB outperforms SVM. However, using the full vocabulary had opposed effects in the two data sets. In Reuters 8, using the whole vocabulary reduced the performance of both methods mainly when using less than 50% of information; in WebKB the performance of ENB is virtually the same, but the performance of SVM increased when using the full vocabulary. This can be due to the specific characteristics of the data. Finally, in the three data sets it is somewhat evident that the predictive performance of ENB presents low variations after processing about 50% of the texts.

## 4.2 Comparison with related work

In this section we compare the performance of naïve Bayes with the MDP introduced in (Dulac-Arnold et al., 2011) using the same data sets from the previous section. For this comparison we replicated the experiment reported by the authors of (Dulac-Arnold et al., 2011). For each of the data sets, we used different percentages, $\{1\%, 5\%, 10\%, 30\%, 50\%, 90\%\}$, of documents for the training set and the remainder for the test set (this was not our choice, but the setting proposed by the authors of the reference paper). Five runs were performed, in each run the documents for training were randomly chosen. Average results are shown in Figure 2. The results of ENB are shown as graphs, whereas for the reference method we report the single-best reported result (shown as markers, one per training set size). Please note that in (Dulac-Arnold et al., 2011) the authors optimized the parameters of their method, called STC, whereas we have used default implementation/parameters for ENB.

From Figure 2, it can be seen that the percentage of training documents used for learning the model affects considerably the performance of ENB. In all

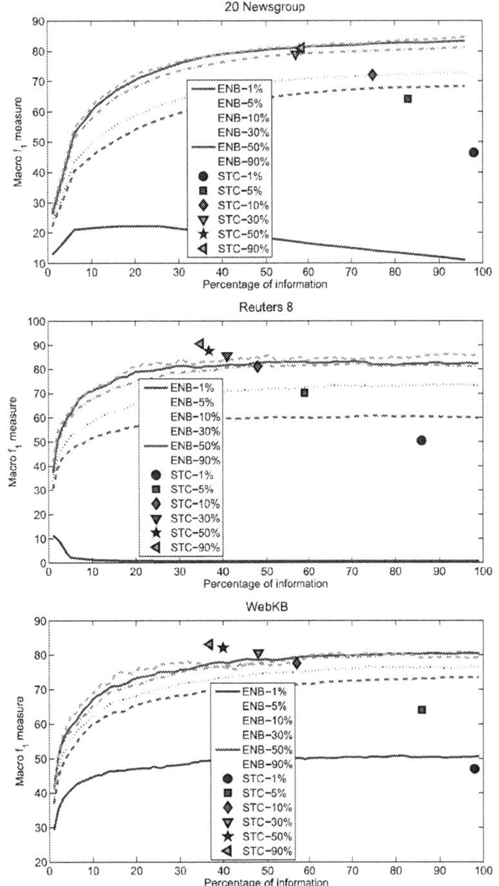

**Figure 2:** Comparison of ENB and the reference method STC.

three cases, using less than 30% of the samples for training results in low performance. This can be due to the fact that with small amounts of training documents, the estimated probabilities are not very representative of the classification task (and so, it is not convenient to estimate probabilities from partial information only). The best results were obtained when using 50% or 90% of instances for training the model. Also we can notice that the performance stabilizes after 40% of the information has been processed.

When comparing the ENB approach with the sequential text classification technique (STC) from (Dulac-Arnold et al., 2011), it can be seen that the MDP from the reference work and our ENB perform very similar (even when we only show best/optimized results for STC). This is a very interesting result: we obtained comparable performance to a more complex model, with a much more simpler and efficient technique.

### 4.3 Sexual predator detection

We now evaluate the performance of ENB on the task of sexual predator detection. We used the development / test partitions of the data set used in the sexual predator competition from PAN'12 (Inches and Crestani, 2012), see Table 1. This corpus contains a large number of chat conversations, some of which include a sexual predator trying to approach a child[5]. The problem approached in the original competition was to identify sexual predators from many chat conversations. However, in this work, we approach the problem of detecting conversations with potential sexual predators in it. We proceeded in this way because the original task was one of forensic analysis: detect predators offline using all of the conversations in which they were involved (see (Villatoro-Tello et al., 2012) for our solution that obtained the best result in that challenge). Our ultimate goal, on the other hand, is to detect, as early as possible, conversations in which a sexual predator is involved, in such a way that sexual-attacks can be prevented and an alert for parents/police officers can be emitted. Based on our previous results from (Villatoro-Tello et al., 2012), and on the literature on non-thematic text classification we decided to represent chat conversations with 3-grams of characters (i.e., terms in this data set are sequences of 3-letters extracted from the training corpus); with this data set we used a reduced vocabulary and preprocessing processes described in (Villatoro-Tello et al., 2012). As suggested in (Inches and Crestani, 2012), for this experiment we report $f_1$ measure on the minority class (i.e., predators). Results of this experiment are shown in Figure 3.

On the one hand, we can see that this is a very difficult task, the performance of both models, SVM and ENB, is somewhat low, even when the whole information from documents is used (the highest performance is lower than 70% of $f_1$ measure). This is not a surprising result if we notice that this problem is highly imbalanced: the imbalance ratio for training and test partitions is of 12.1 and 9.56, respectively. Furthermore, the reduction of the vocabulary

---

<sup>5</sup>Police officers acted as children, predators are real.

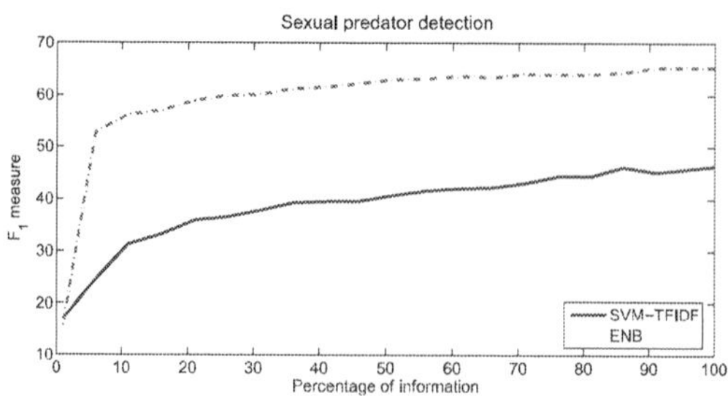

**Figure 3:** Early classification performance on detection of sexual predators.

may affect significantly this particular domain (the jargon used in chat conversations is quite diverse and rich). Despite the difficulty of the problem, we can see that again the ENB method outperforms the SVM model in most cases. Results shown in this section make evident the need of better methods for early text classification.

## 5 Conclusions

We described the use of naïve Bayes for early text classification. A minor modification to naïve Bayes allows us to make predictions using partial information. We show the effectiveness of this simple approach in three types of problems and compare its performance with the only existing state-of-the-art method. Our method compares favorably in terms of both effectiveness and earliness performance with the reference method, a much more complex model. Also, our method consistently outperformed an SVM baseline. Furthermore, we are the first in approaching the early classification of chat conversations for detecting sexual predators. Although results are encouraging, there is too much work to do yet. We foresee our work will pave the way for the development of more elaborated techniques based on naïve Bayes for early classification.

Future work is vast, for instance, exploiting research advances in extensions of naïve Bayes (see Section 2) for early text classification. Also, it is very important to develop spotting mechanisms that can be combined with the early naïve Bayes technique. Finally, theoretical analyses of the problem and the proposed method are very much needed.

## References

J. R. Alcobé. 2002. Incremental learning of tree augmented naive bayes classifiers. In *IBERAMIA'02*, volume 2527 of *LNCS*, pages 32–41. Springer.

J. M. Cabrera, H. J. Escalante, and M. Montes y Gómez. 2013. Distributional term representations for short-text categorization. In *Proc. of CICLING*, volume 7817 of *LNCS*, pages 335–346. Springer.

L. Denoyer, H. Zaragoza, and P. Gallinari. 2001. Hmm–based passage models for document classification and ranking. In *Proc. of 23rd European Colloquium on Information Retrieval Research (ECIR'01)*.

G. Dulac-Arnold, L. Denoyer, and P. Gallinari. 2011. Text classification: A sequential reading approach. In *Advances in Information Retrieval, Proc. of 33rd European Conference on IR Research, (ECIR'11)*, volume 6611 of *LNCS*, pages 411–423. Springers.

G. Dulac-Arnold, L. Denoyer, P. Preux, and P. Gallinari. 2012. Sequential approaches for learning datum-wise sparse representations. *Machine Learning*, 89:87–122.

N. Friedman, D. Geiger, and M. Goldszmidt. 1997. Bayesian network classifiers. *Machine Learning*, 29(2):131–163.

F. He and X. Ding. 2007. Improving naive bayes text classifier using smoothing methods. In *Proc. ECIR'07 Proceedings of the 29th European conference on IR research*, volume 4425 of *LNCS*, pages 703–707. Springer.

B. Hui, Y. Yang, and G. I. Webb. 2009. Anytime classification for a pool of instances. *Machine Learning*, 77:61–102.

G. Inches and F. Crestani. 2012. Overview of the international sexual predator identification competition at pan-2012. In *CEUR Workshop Proceedings, Working Notes for CLEF 2012 Conference*, volume 1178. CEUR.

T. Joachims. 2008. Text categorization with support vector machines: Learning with many relevant features. In *Proceedings of ECML-98*, volume 1398 of *LNCS*, pages 137–142. Springer.

A. M. Kibriya, E. Frank, B. Pfahringer, and G. Holmes. 2005. Multinomial naive bayes for text categorization revisited. In *AI 2004: Adv. Artificial Intelligence*, volume 3339 of *LNCS*, pages 488–499. Springer.

F. Klawonn and P. Angelov. 2006. Evolving extended naïve bayes classifiers. In *Proc. of Sixth IEEE International Conference on Data Mining Workshops, ICDM Workshops*, pages 643–647. IEEE.

A. McCallum and K. Nigam. 1998. A comparison of event models for naive bayes text classification. In *Proc. of AAAI/ICML-98 Workshop on Learning for Text Categorization*, pages 41–48. AAAI.

F. Sebastiani. 2008. Machine learning in automated text categorization. *ACM Computer Surveys*, 34(1):1–47.

D. Shen, J. Wu, B. Cao, J.T. Sun, Q. Yang, Z. Chen, and Y. Li. 2009. Exploiting term relationship to boost text classification. In *Proc. of the 18th ACM Conference on Information and Knowledge Management*, CIKM '09, pages 1637–1640. ACM.

E. Villatoro-Tello, A. Juarez-Gonzalez, H. J. Escalante, M. Montes y Gomez, and L. Villase nor Pineda. 2012. A two-step approach for effective detection of misbehaving users in chats. In *CLEF 2012 Evaluation Labs and Workshop - Working Notes Papers*.

G. Webb, J. R. Boughton, and Z. Wang. 2005. Not so naive bayes: Aggregating one-dependence estimators. *Machine Learning*, 58:5–24.

Y. Yang, G. I. Webb, K. Korb, and K.M. Ting. 2007. Classifying under computational resource constraints: anytime classification using probabilistic estimators. *Machine Learning*, 69:35–53.

Q. Yuan, G. Cong, and N. M. Thalmann. 2012. Enhancing naive bayes with various smoothing methods for short text classification. In *Proc. of WWW Companion*.

N. A. Zaidi, J. Cerquides, M. J. Carman, and G. I. Webb. 2013. Alleviating naive bayes attribute independence assumption by attribute weighting. *Journal of Machine Learning Research*, 14:1947–1988.

D. Zeimpekis and E. Gallopoulos, 2006. *Grouping Multidimensional Data: Recent Advances in Clustering*, chapter TMG: A MATLAB toolbox for generating term-document matrices from text collections, pages 187–210. Springer.

# Semi-supervised and Unsupervised Categorization of Posts in Web Discussion Forums using Part-of-Speech Information and Minimal Features


**Krish Perumal**
Department of Computer Science
University of Toronto
Toronto, ON, M5S 3G4, Canada
krish@cs.toronto.edu

**Graeme Hirst**
Department of Computer Science
University of Toronto
Toronto, ON, M5S 3G4, Canada
gh@cs.toronto.edu



## Abstract

Web discussion forums typically contain posts that fall into different categories such as *question, solution, feedback, spam,* etc. Automatic identification of these categories can aid information retrieval that is tailored for specific user requirements. Previously, a number of supervised methods have attempted to solve this problem; however, these depend on the availability of abundant training data. A few existing unsupervised and semi-supervised approaches are either focused on identifying only one or two categories, or do not discuss category-specific performance. In contrast, this work proposes methods for identifying multiple categories, and also analyzes the category-specific performance. These methods are based on sequence models (specifically, hidden Markov Models) that can model language for each category using both probabilistic word and part-of-speech information, and minimal manually specified features. The unsupervised version initializes the models using clustering, whereas the semi-supervised version uses few manually labeled forum posts. Empirical evaluations demonstrate that these methods are more accurate than previous ones.


## 1 Introduction

Web discussion forums are platforms where people converse with one another to collaboratively solve problems and discuss issues. These are useful for existing users who participate in the discussion; however, new users need to read the entire forum thread for obtaining a solution or a summary of all opinions. This problem becomes much more pronounced in cases where threads contain tens or hundreds of posts, and reading the entire thread becomes impractical[1]. In such cases, labeling the purpose of each post can guide the user towards useful posts (i.e., containing solutions) and away from trivial posts (i.e., containing feedback or off-topic discussions). Moreover, current information retrieval techniques return entire threads as results to search queries. But by being sensitized to these annotations, they can return targeted results containing only the relevant posts. Further, user-contributed information contained in these forums can be better structured and can contribute towards the development of domain-specific knowledge bases. With these motivations in mind, this work aims to automatically annotate each post in a discussion forum with its purpose in the conversation thread. Our methods are not tailored for a specific domain or tagset. However, to demonstrate the objective of this work, Table 1 shows an example thread in which all posts are manually tagged with their purpose in the conversation.

## 2 Related Work

Categorizing forum posts is closely related to the task of *dialogue act tagging*, which is defined as the identification of the meaning of an utterance at the level of illocutionary force (Stolcke et al., 2000); for example, an utterance could be identified as falling

---

[1]For example, the JeepForum thread http://www.jeepforum.com/forum/f15/mud-tires-119948/ contains more than 500 posts discussing popular brands of tires.

100


*Proceedings of NAACL-HLT 2016*, pages 100–108,
San Diego, California, June 12-17, 2016. ©2016 Association for Computational Linguistics

| Post | Purpose |
|---|---|
| *User 15JKU*: Hey Guys, Im looking to get 35s tires with either 18s or 20s as it will be more of a daily driver and sometimes go mudding. My only concern is how they will perform in mud? Also, how loud would they for a daily driven jeep? Also, would A/T tires work for mudding? | *Question* |
| *User mschi772*: You need to more accurately convey what your true priorities are. You're asking for too much from one tire. | *Request for Clarification* |
| *User 15JKU*: Just asking if anyone knows how loud they are. My main concern is how they'll do on mud and if i should go with different tire. | *Clarification* |
| *User mschi772*: Nitto Trail Grapplers are a "classic" MT design. This is a very popular design for people who frequently go offroading but want to maintain some street manners. | *Solution* |
| *User JcArnold*: I've got 37" trails and they are not noisy. I don't know about mud but they are great tires in the rocks and snow. | *Solution* |
| *User 15JKU*: Thanks guys! Truly appreciate it. | *Feedback* |

Table 1: Example forum thread manually tagged with each post's purpose in the conversation. (Adapted from: `http://www.jeepforum.com/forum/f15/tire-recommendations-3455674/`)

into one or more categories such as *question*, *solution*, *clarification*, *feedback*, *command*, *request*, etc.

Most previous work has concentrated on supervised machine learning methods (Catherine et al., 2012; Bhatia et al., 2012; Wang et al., 2010; Kim et al., 2010; Sondhi et al., 2010) using manually annotated data in order to predict the annotations of unseen data. Apart from being constrained by the requirement of manually annotated data for training, these methods are also limited in applicability to the domains they are trained on. In contrast, unsupervised methods overcome these drawbacks by identifying unlabeled clusters of data, each of which could potentially be mapped to a target category that one wants to identify. To the best of our knowledge, three unsupervised techniques have been previously proposed for categorization of posts in Web forums. Out of these, Deepak and Visweswariah (2014) identified only *answer* posts, and Cong et al. (2008) additionally extracted *question* posts. The more difficult task of identifying multiple categories was tackled only by Joty et al. (2011). They used a combination of HMMs and Gaussian Mixture Models (GMMs) in order to classify forum posts into 12 dialogue act categories. This model is similar to the content and conversation models used for other tasks by Ritter et al. (2010) and Barzilay and Lee (2004) respectively. In addition to the probability distribution of word $n$-grams, they use some structural features such as the chronological position of a post in the thread, the number of tokens in the post, and author identity. The motivation for this approach is that HMMs can model the sequential nature of dialogue acts well. For example, the fact that a *solution* is more likely to follow a *question*, as opposed to any other category, can be implicitly encoded in the HMMs. Our approach is inspired by the same idea.

One major drawback of unsupervised methods is that they often generate clusters unrelated to the target categories. For example, clustering of forum posts on the travel domain might lead to a cluster containing posts pertaining to New York City sightseeing alone. This cluster is irrelevant when the purpose is to find clusters of post categories such as *question, answer, feedback*, etc. Moreover, because the clusters are unlabeled, post-processing is necessary to map the clusters to the target categories. Semi-supervised methods can overcome the drawbacks of both unsupervised and supervised methods by using a minimal amount of labeled data (which is costly to obtain) and a large amount of unlabeled data (which is easily available). To our knowledge, there exist only two semi-supervised methods for categorization of posts in Web forums and they identify only *answer* posts. Catherine et al. (2013) employed the co-training framework, whereas Jeong et al. (2009) used domain adaptation from labeled spoken dialogue datasets by means of a sub-tree pattern mining algorithm. In experiments, we show that our methods outperform the former work; however, the unavailability of code and data prevents empirical comparison with the latter.

# 3 Proposed Methods

## 3.1 Conversation Model

As discussed previously, our models derive inspiration from the work of Joty et al. (2011). Our underlying model is the same but differs in several important details. Our conversation model is a Hidden Markov Model (HMM), in which hidden (unobserved) states correspond to post categories, and emissions (observed) correspond to bags of post $n$-grams. Here, a thread $T_k$ consists of a sequence of category labels, and each category label $C_i$ emits a bag of word $n$-grams $N_i$ of the $i^{\text{th}}$ chronological post in the thread. The learning algorithm (Algorithm 1) of the conversation model uses iterative Expectation Maximization (EM) to maximize the expected probability of a post given a state, repeating until convergence of the sum of all observation probabilities. During the expectation step (E-step), a word $n$-gram language model is constructed for each state. Using this state-specific language model, the emission probability of an observation (or post) can be calculated. During the maximization step (M-step), the most likely state sequence is calculated using Viterbi algorithm. The language model for each state is constructed using smoothed $n$-gram frequency counts (using a smoothing parameter, $\delta_1$). The parameter, *lmType*, determines the use of either unigrams or bigrams. The initial state probabilities and state transition probabilities are estimated using smoothed frequency counts of initial states and state transitions respectively (using a smoothing parameter of $\delta_2$). The calculation of these estimates is based on work by Barzilay and Lee (2004) (and are different from those of Joty et al. (2011)). A more detailed explanation of this model is made available by Perumal (2016).

In the HMM, the probability of a post $P_i$, given a state $S_k$, is calculated as a categorical probability of its word $n$-grams, as shown in Equation 1.

$$p(P_i|S_k) = \prod_j p(W_{i,j}|L_k) \qquad (1)$$

where $W_{i,j}$ is the $j^{\text{th}}$ (in no particular order) word $n$-gram in post $P_i$, and $L_k$ is the language model for state $S_k$.

### 3.1.1 Unsupervised Version

In the unsupervised version, the prior probabilities of the model are derived from a two-step process (based on the work of Barzilay and Lee (2004)): (i) every post is represented as a vector of word $n$-gram frequency counts, and (ii) the vectors are clustered using hierarchical clustering. The resultant cluster labels are used to calculate the frequency counts of initial HMM states and state transitions, and hence the corresponding probabilities. The priors are optionally calculated using an additional concept of *insertion states*. These are the states which contain a number of posts fewer than a fixed threshold, called *state size threshold*. This concept is used to account for small noise states that pertain to no meaningful target category. If used, all insertion states are merged into a single state, representing a noise state.

### 3.1.2 Semi-Supervised Version

Instead of using unsupervised clustering, we propose to derive the priors (i.e., the language model, the initial state probabilities and state transition probabilities) using smoothed frequency counts of post labels in few manually labeled threads. The rationale of this process is to form a better real-world estimate of the model parameters in the first EM iteration, and thereby reduce errors in the final predictions.

## 3.2 Conversation Model with Part-of-Speech Tags

Since the conversation models of Ritter et al. (2010) take only word $n$-gram language models into account, it is likely that they output clusters of posts that are topically related, without reflecting the posts' purpose or intention. To overcome this limitation, we enhance the plain conversation model by modeling HMM emissions partially from part-of-speech (POS) tags of words. This idea is based on the assumption that posts belonging to the same category are likely to be syntactically similar. For example, *question* posts are very likely to contain POS tags such as *WDT*, *WP*, *WP$*, and *WRB*[2]. Our model uses POS $n$-gram language models in addition to word $n$-gram language models, and calculates the HMM emission probability of a post given its

---

[2]These tags can be seen in the Penn Treebank project (Marcus et al., 1993).

state using a linear combination of both. Here, the probability of a post $P_i$, given a state $S_k$, is calculated as shown in Equation 2.

$$p(P_i|S_k) = \frac{\prod_j \left[ \lambda \times p(W_{i,j}|L_k) + (1-\lambda) \times p(POS_{i,j}|PL_k) \right]}{Z}$$

$$0 \leq \lambda \leq 1 \qquad (2)$$

$$Z = \sum_{i,k} \left[ \prod_j \left[ \lambda \times p(W_{i,j}|L_k) + (1-\lambda) \times p(POS_{i,j}|PL_k) \right] \right]$$

where $POS_{i,j}$ is the $j^{\text{th}}$ (in no particular order) POS $n$-gram in post $P_i$, $PL_k$ is the POS $n$-gram language model for state $S_k$, $\lambda$ is the parameter that controls the proportion of probability arising from the word and POS language models (using $\lambda = 1$ is equivalent to the conversation model), and $Z$ is the normalizing constant.

### 3.3 Conversation Model with Features

As a further enhancement to the conversation models, we incorporate discriminative features that might be useful for generating clusters that better represent the desired categories. For example, the chronological position of a post in a thread might be a useful feature, because a post is more likely to be a *question* if it is the first post in a thread as opposed to any other position. The following features are used: post position, post length, presence of question mark(s) (*?*, *???*, etc.) in current and preceding post, presence of *thank* or *thanks*, presence of *same* or *similar*, presence of *did*, presence of exclamation mark(s) (*!*, *!!!*, etc.), average cosine similarity with other posts in thread, cosine similarity with initial post, current post's author identity, whether previous post is by same author, number of previous posts by current author, and total number of posts by current author. All feature values are discretized. Joty et al. (2011) also use a few specific features in their model, but our approach is more general and can accommodate a variable number of features. The probability of a post $P_i$, given a state $S_k$, is calculated as shown in equation 3.

$$p(P_i|S_k) = \prod_j p(W_{i,j}|L_k) \prod_f p(F_{i,f}|FL_k) \qquad (3)$$

where $F_{i,f}$ is the $f^{\text{th}}$ (in no particular order) discrete-valued feature in post $P_i$, and $FL_k$ is the feature model for state $S_k$.

---

**Ubuntu** (Bhatia et al., 2012)
    Domain: Computer technical
    Tagset: *Question, Repeat Question,*
        *Clarification, Solution, Further Details,*
        *Positive Feedback, Negative Feedback, Spam*
    Number of threads: 100

**TripAdvisor-NYC** (Bhatia et al., 2012)
    Domain: Travel
    Tagset: Same as **Ubuntu**
    Number of threads: 100

**Apple** (Catherine et al., 2012)
    Domain: Computer technical
    Tagset: *Answer*
    Number of threads: 300 labeled and 140,000 unlabeled

Table 2: Discussion forum datasets used in the current work's experiments.

### 3.4 Mapping of Clusters to Categories in Unsupervised Methods

Unsupervised methods output cluster labels for each post, not a specific category label. In order to pair them with an observed category label, a one-to-one mapping is obtained using the Kuhn-Munkres algorithm for maximal weighting in a bipartite graph (Kuhn, 1955; Munkres, 1957). The nodes of the graph correspond to the predicted cluster labels and gold labels, and the weights correspond to the number of overlapping posts between them. In this procedure, one set of disjoint nodes of the bipartite graph corresponds to the set of predicted cluster labels, and the other set corresponds to the set of manually obtained gold labels. The weight of an edge from cluster label $c$ to gold label $g$ is calculated as the number of posts which are predicted as $c$ and also have a gold label $g$. Joty et al. (2011) follow the same procedure.

## 4 Experiments

### 4.1 Datasets

For our experiments, we use forum datasets from previous work. Details of their tagsets, sizes, and domains are listed in Table 2.

---

**Algorithm 1** Conversation model

---

**Input**: A list of threads $T$, each containing a list of posts $P$ (in chronological order)
**Parameters**: *initialNumClusters, mergeInsertionStates, stateSizeThreshold, maxNumIterations, lmType*, $\delta_1$, $\delta_2$
**Output**: A list of cluster labels $CL$ for each post in each thread (in the order of the input)

1: **for all** thread $T_x$ **do**
2:     **for all** post $P_{x,y} \in T_x$ **do**
3:         $V_{x,y} := vectorize(P_{x,y})$      // $V_{x,y}$ is the vector of post $P_{x,y}$
4:     **end for**
5: **end for**
6: $ICL := cluster(V, initialNumClusters)$     // $ICL$ is the list of initial cluster labels for each post ($ICL_{x,y}$ is the initial cluster label for post $P_{x,y}$ in thread $T_x$)
7: $S := ICL$     // $S$ is the list of states for all posts; at this step, it is the same as the initial cluster labels
8: **for** $n = 1 \rightarrow maxNumIterations$ **do**
9:     **if** *mergeInsertionStates* is *true* **then**
10:         $[S, numStates] := merge\_small\_states(S, stateSizeThreshold)$
11:     **end if**
12:     **for** $i = 1 \rightarrow numStates$ **do**
13:         $SP_i = \emptyset$
14:         **for all** state $S_{x,y}$ **do**
15:             **if** $S_{x,y} = i$ **then**
16:                 $SP_i := SP_i \cup P_{x,y}$     // $SP_i$ is the set of all posts that belong to state $i$
17:             **end if**
18:         **end for**
19:         $L_i := language\_model(SP_i, lmType, \delta_1)$
20:     **end for**
21:     **for** $i = 1 \rightarrow numStates$ **do**
22:         $init\_counts_i := \Sigma_{T_x} \mathbb{1} S_{x,1} = i$     // $S_{x,1}$ is the state of the first post in thread $T_x$
23:     **end for**
24:     **for** $i = 1 \rightarrow numStates$ **do**
25:         $\pi_i := (init\_counts_i + \delta_2)/(\Sigma_k(init\_counts_k) + \delta_2 \times numStates)$     // $\pi_i$ is the probability that initial state is $i$
26:     **end for**
27:     **for** $i = 1 \rightarrow numStates$ **do**
28:         **for** $j = 1 \rightarrow numStates$ **do**
29:             $trans\_counts_{i,j} := \Sigma_{T_x} \sum_{a=1}^{|T_x|-1} \mathbb{1} S_{x,a} = i, S_{x,a+1} = j$
30:         **end for**
31:     **end for**
32:     **for** $i = 1 \rightarrow numStates$ **do**
33:         **for** $j = 1 \rightarrow numStates$ **do**
34:             $\phi_{i,j} := (trans\_counts_{i,j} + \delta_2)/(\Sigma_{k,l}(trans\_counts_{k,l}) + \delta_2 \times numStates^2)$     // $\phi_{i,j}$ is the probability of transitioning from state $i$ to state $j$
35:         **end for**
36:     **end for**
37:     $S := Viterbi\_algorithm(\pi, \phi, L)$
38:     **if** sum of observation probabilities converged **then**
39:         **break**
40:     **end if**
41: **end for**
42: $CL := S$

---

### 4.2 Preprocessing and Configuration Parameters

Initially, all forum posts were tokenized by sentence and word, followed by POS tagging and stemming — all using Stanford CoreNLP Toolkit (Manning et al., 2014). Stopword removal was found to degrade performance; hence, it was not used. Forum conversations often consist of informal English language text, along with the use of domain-specific abbreviations and non-standard special characters such as ellipses and emoticons. Hence, some errors are introduced in all the previous steps. However, no effort was made to overcome them, and this is accepted as a limitation of the current work.

All methods require the conversion of posts to vectors of $n$-grams. For this purpose, we experimented with both unigrams and bigrams, and the former was found to produce better performance. The maximum number of iterations of Expectation Maximization was set to 100, which was sufficient because all experimental runs were completed in fewer than 100 iterations. The values of both smoothing parameters (i.e., $\delta_1$ and $\delta_2$) were varied in the range of $10^{-1}$ to $10^{-9}$. Subsequently, $10^{-2}$ and $10^{-9}$ were found to be the best values for $\delta_1$ and $\delta_2$ respectively. The value of the POS model's $\lambda$ was varied between $10^{-6}$ and $1 - 10^{-6}$, and the value of 0.999 was found to be the best. Since the unigram/bigram vocabulary size is much larger than the POS tag vocabulary size, the former probability distribution is much more fine-grained. For example, each word unigram's probability value in the NYC dataset is of the order of $10^{-4}$ (since the unigram vocabulary size is 5000), whereas each POS unigram's probability value is of the order of $10^{-2}$ (since the POS vocabulary size is 42). So, the value of 0.999 for word unigrams and 0.001 for POS unigrams can be viewed as a scaling factor to ensure that both contribute almost equally towards discriminating between post categories. The parameters, *initialNumClusters* and *stateSizeThreshold*, directly affect the resulting number of clusters. In all experimental runs, both these parameters were varied in the range of 1 to 100, and those which did not output the desired number of clusters (i.e., number of distinct gold labels) were ignored. In each case,

different parameter values were best suited; however, only the best performing results are reported.

For semi-supervised methods, experiments were carried out in a randomized $n$-fold cross-validation setup. The dataset was randomly divided (by sampling from the uniform distribution) into $n$ equal-sized folds, and the experiment was run $n$ times. In each run, one fold was used for initializing the priors of the models, and the remaining $n - 1$ folds were used for evaluation. In the case of language models, different datasets benefited from using one of word/POS unigram or bigram models. Hence, experiments were run using both, and results are reported for the better performing alternative.

### 4.3 Baselines

The *random baseline* randomly assigns category labels to every post (by sampling from the uniform distribution). The *majority baseline* assigns the most commonly occurring gold category label to every post, which is *solution* for all the datasets used in this work. Two other baselines are heuristic in nature, and are both based on the assumption that the first post in the thread is very likely to be a *question*. The first of these, called *question-solution heuristic 1*, assigns *question* to the first post in the thread, *spam/other* to the last post, and *solution* to the rest. It assumes that the last post in the thread is very likely to be unrelated to the main thread topic and that many of the preceding posts are likely to be *solution*. The second heuristic baseline, called *question-solution heuristic 2*, assigns *question* to the first post in the thread, *solution* to the second post, and *spam/other* to the rest. It assumes that the second post is very likely to be a *solution* in direct response to the first *question* post, and many of the following posts are likely to be *spam/other*.

### 4.4 Main Results

Table 3 lists the accuracy values from experiments using all possible combinations of the implemented models for the Ubuntu and NYC datasets. For the unsupervised methods, the mean 1-to-1 accuracy values are reported using the procedure described in section 3.4. For the baselines and the semi-supervised methods, the reported accuracy values are averages over all categories.

| | Accuracy (%) | |
|---|---|---|
| **Method** | **Ubuntu** | **NYC** |
| *Baselines* | | |
| **Random** | 78.11 | 77.71 |
| **Majority** | 85.37 | 87.91 |
| **Problem-Solution Heuristic 1** | 87.71 | 89.06 |
| **Problem-Solution Heuristic 2** | 82.88 | 80.69 |
| *Unsupervised* | | |
| **HMM+Mix** | 83.30 | 87.91 |
| **CONV** | 88.85 | 90.06 |
| **CONV + POS** | 88.85 | 90.06 |
| **CONV + FEAT** | 89.26 | 90.83 |
| **CONV + POS + FEAT** | 89.26 | 90.83 |
| *Semi-Supervised* | | |
| **HMM+Mix** | 82.33 | 86.91 |
| **CONV** | 88.45 | 90.74 |
| **CONV + POS** | 88.29 | 90.86 |
| **CONV + FEAT** | 89.08 | 91.31 |
| **CONV + POS + FEAT** | 89.10 | 91.72 |

Table 3: Experimental results for the Ubuntu and NYC datasets using all the possible combinations of models in both unsupervised and semi-supervised settings (CONV: Conversation model; POS: Part-of-speech tags; FEAT: Features).

Joty et al. (2011) reported results of their best performing HMM+Mix model for dialogue act classification on email and forum thread datasets. The code and datasets are not available to other researchers; hence, we implemented the HMM+Mix, while also accommodating the additional features that we used for our methods.

Our unsupervised methods beat all the baselines, in contrast to Joty et al. (2011)'s HMM+Mix, which beats only the random baseline. The use of both POS tags and features results in the best overall performance, whereas the use of POS tags does not make any difference in performance. The semi-supervised adaptation of the existing HMM+Mix model outperforms only the random baseline. However, all of our semi-supervised methods beat all the baselines. In this case, the sole use of POS tags or features results in improved performance. But the use of both in combination leads to the best performance overall. Specifically, for the Ubuntu dataset, the best average accuracy value is 89.10%. In case of the NYC dataset, the corresponding best value is 91.72%. The corresponding absolute accuracy values are 56.40%

| **Method** | **P** | **R** | **F$_1$** |
|---|---|---|---|
| Catherine et al. (2013) | 0.57 | 0.84 | 0.68 |
| CONV + POS + FEAT | 0.66 | 0.73 | 0.69 |

Table 4: Experimental results comparing the performance of an existing semi-supervised answer extraction method with our best semi-supervised method (i.e., conversation model with POS tags and features).

| **Category** | **P** | **R** | **F$_1$** |
|---|---|---|---|
| *Question* | 83.81 | 73.95 | 78.57 |
| *Repeat Question* | 0.00 | 0.00 | 0.00 |
| *Clarification* | 78.57 | 22.45 | 34.92 |
| *Further Details* | 40.00 | 8.51 | 14.04 |
| *Solution* | 66.05 | 96.56 | 78.44 |
| *+ve Feedback* | 0.00 | 0.00 | 0.00 |
| *-ve Feedback* | 60.78 | 30.10 | 40.26 |
| *Junk* | 33.33 | 4.00 | 7.14 |

Table 5: Experimental results of semi-supervised conversation model with POS tags and features for one of the folds in a 10-fold cross-validation setup using the NYC dataset.

and 66.86% respectively. The reported results using semi-supervised methods are averages over 10 runs of a randomized 10-fold cross-validation setup.

Catherine et al. (2013) reported the performance of their semi-supervised *answer* extraction approach on 300 labeled threads of the Apple discussion forums dataset. They trained using only three training threads; however, the identities of these three are not known. The code is also unavailable. Hence, the methods can only be compared indirectly. For the methods of Catherine et al. (2013), precision, recall and $F_1$-measure values are obtained from their paper. The same values are reported for our best method (i.e., the semi-supervised conversation models with POS tags and features), using a 100-fold cross-validation setup; i.e., out of 300 labeled threads, 3 were used for training, and 297 were used for testing in each fold. Table 4 shows that our method performs better in terms of $F_1$-measure and precision.

## 4.5 Category-wise Performance and Error Analysis

Table 5 shows the category-wise performance of one of the runs of 10-fold cross-validation for the NYC dataset using the semi-supervised conversation

|  | Predicted | | | | | | | |
|---|---|---|---|---|---|---|---|---|
| | **Q** | **RQ** | **C** | **FD** | **S** | **F+** | **F-** | **J** |
| **Q** | 104 | 0 | 5 | 0 | 7 | 0 | 2 | 1 |
| **RQ** | 1 | 0 | 0 | 0 | 1 | 0 | 0 | 0 |
| **C** | 2 | 0 | 11 | 0 | 40 | 0 | 0 | 2 |
| **FD** | 16 | 0 | 1 | 1 | 20 | 0 | 12 | 1 |
| **S** | 10 | 0 | 1 | 1 | 374 | 0 | 6 | 10 |
| **F+** | 0 | 0 | 0 | 0 | 0 | 0 | 0 | 0 |
| **F-** | 21 | 0 | 1 | 1 | 35 | 0 | 43 | 2 |
| **J** | 2 | 0 | 1 | 0 | 17 | 0 | 11 | 10 |

Table 6: Confusion matrix of the semi-supervised conversation model with POS tags and features, for one of the folds in a 10-fold cross-validation setup using the NYC dataset (Q: Question; RQ: Repeat Question; C: Clarification; FD: Further Details; S: Solution; F+: Positive Feedback; F-: Negative Feedback; J: Junk).

model with POS tags and features. Table 6 shows the confusion matrix of the same experiment. The confusion matrix for the Ubuntu dataset is similar. Predictions of *question*, *solution*, *clarification* and *negative feedback* are the best in terms of precision values; however, the recall values of the two latter categories are not practically useful. The most common error is the prediction of a non-*solution* category as *solution*, indicating a bias towards predicting the majority category. Overall, the predictions of minority categories are not practically useful, because they were less accurate than the predictions using the random baseline. Specifically, there are no predictions of *repeat question* and *positive feedback*, owing to the minuscule number of posts with these labels. Since previous literature ignores the analysis of category-wise performance altogether, a direct comparison is not possible. But this confusion matrix indicates a major weakness of current semi-supervised and unsupervised approaches in classifying minority categories.

## 5 Conclusions and Future Work

Our experimental results indicate that our unsupervised methods are not adequate for tackling a task as complex as forum post categorization. However, they are able to capture some useful sequential dependencies, as observed from the fact that they outperformed the random and majority baselines. Also, knowledge of POS tags and simple textual features provided more context for classification, and thus enabled the technique to classify more accurately. The novel proposal of incorporating a few labeled examples for initializing the model priors led to better performance than the *question-solution heuristic* baselines in most cases. Our experiments demonstrate that these methods perform better than previous methods. Prediction of *question* and *solution* categories were the most accurate, followed by *clarification* and *negative feedback*. However, predictions of the minority categories are not accurate enough to be practically useful.

Discussion forum posts often contain multiple dialogue categories, i.e., a post could start with some sentence(s) mentioning a *solution* to a previous *question*, and end with some sentence(s) posing a new *question*. Such cases can be tackled by employing a 2-tier hierarchical HMM which models the transition between sentence categories within a single post (in addition to the higher-level post category transitions). However, this proposal is dependent on the availability of datasets that are annotated by category at the sentence level. The lack of knowledge of long-range dependencies between different categories is another drawback of current methods. Consequently, they are unable to learn that a post cannot be classified as *solution*, without any *question* post before it. This problem can be addressed by using higher-order Markov chains, but this would lead to much greater run-time and space complexity as well as specially tailored algorithms for inference. Instead, the use of heuristics to flag certain categories, based on prior post categories in the thread, could resolve this problem more efficiently. Moreover, effort should be made to balance the distribution of categories that are used for initializing and training the methods. We leave these ideas for exploration in future work.

## Acknowledgments

This research was supported by the Natural Sciences and Engineering Research Council of Canada under the Engage grant (no. EGP 477227-14). We thank Afsaneh Fazly and Mohamed Abdalla for their valuable contributions, and thank the anonymous reviewers for their constructive feedback.

## References

Regina Barzilay and Lillian Lee. 2004. Catching the drift: Probabilistic content models, with applications to generation and summarization. In *Proceedings of the 2nd Human Language Technology Conference and Annual Meeting of the North American Chapter of the Association for Computational Linguistics*, pages 113–120.

Sumit Bhatia, Prakhar Biyani, and Prasenjit Mitra. 2012. Classifying user messages for managing Web forum data. In *Proceedings of the 15th International Workshop on the Web and Databases (WebDB'12)*, pages 13–18.

Rose Catherine, Amit Singh, Rashmi Gangadharaiah, Dinesh Raghu, and Karthik Visweswariah. 2012. Does similarity matter? The case of answer extraction from technical discussion forums. In *Proceedings of the 24th International Conference on Computational Linguistics (COLING)*, pages 175–184.

Rose Catherine, Rashmi Gangadharaiah, Karthik Visweswariah, and Dinesh Raghu. 2013. Semi-supervised answer extraction from discussion forums. In *Proceedings of the 6th International Joint Conference on Natural Language Processing (IJCNLP)*, pages 1–9.

Gao Cong, Long Wang, Chin-Yew Lin, Young-In Song, and Yueheng Sun. 2008. Finding question-answer pairs from online forums. In *Proceedings of the 31st Annual International ACM SIGIR Conference*, pages 467–474.

P Deepak and Karthik Visweswariah. 2014. Unsupervised solution post identification from discussion forums. In *Proceedings of the 52nd Annual Meeting of the Association for Computational Linguistics*, pages 155–164.

Minwoo Jeong, CY Lin, and GG Lee. 2009. Semi-supervised speech act recognition in emails and forums. In *Proceedings of the 2009 Conference on Empirical Methods in Natural Language Processing (EMNLP)*, pages 1250–1259.

Shafiq Joty, Giuseppe Carenini, and Chin Yew Lin. 2011. Unsupervised modeling of dialog acts in asynchronous conversations. In *Proceedings of the 22nd International Joint Conference on Artificial Intelligence (IJCAI)*, pages 1807–1813.

Su Nam Kim, Li Wang, and Timothy Baldwin. 2010. Tagging and linking web forum posts. In *Proceedings of the 14th Conference on Computational Natural Language Learning (CoNLL)*, pages 192–202.

Harold W Kuhn. 1955. The Hungarian method for the assignment problem. *Naval Research Logistics Quarterly*, 2(1-2):83–97.

Christopher D. Manning, Mihai Surdeanu, John Bauer, Jenny Finkel, Steven J. Bethard, and David McClosky. 2014. The Stanford CoreNLP natural language processing toolkit. In *Proceedings of the 52nd Annual Meeting of the Association for Computational Linguistics: System Demonstrations*, pages 55–60.

Mitchell P Marcus, Mary Ann Marcinkiewicz, and Beatrice Santorini. 1993. Building a large annotated corpus of English: The Penn Treebank. *Computational linguistics*, 19(2):313–330.

James Munkres. 1957. Algorithms for the assignment and transportation problems. *Journal of the Society for Industrial and Applied Mathematics*, 5(1):32–38.

Krish Perumal. 2016. Semi-supervised and unsupervised methods for categorizing posts in web discussion forums. Master's thesis, University of Toronto. http://ftp.cs.toronto.edu/pub/gh/Perumal-MSc-2016.pdf.

Alan Ritter, Colin Cherry, and Bill Dolan. 2010. Unsupervised modeling of Twitter conversations. In *Proceedings of the 2010 Annual Conference of the North American Chapter of the Association for Computational Linguistics*, pages 172–180.

Parikshit Sondhi, Manish Gupta, ChengXiang Zhai, and Julia Hockenmaier. 2010. Shallow information extraction from medical forum data. In *Proceedings of the 23rd International Conference on Computational Linguistics (COLING)*, pages 1158–1166.

Andreas Stolcke, Klaus Ries, Noah Coccaro, Elizabeth Shriberg, Rebecca Bates, Daniel Jurafsky, Paul Taylor, Rachel Martin, Carol Van Ess-Dykema, and Marie Meteer. 2000. Dialogue act modeling for automatic tagging and recognition of conversational speech. *Computational Linguistics*, 26(3):339–373.

Li Wang, Su Nam Kim, and Timothy Baldwin. 2010. Thread-level analysis over technical user forum data. In *Proceedings of the Australasian Language Technology Association Workshop*, pages 27–31.

# Linguistic Understanding of Complaints and Praises in User Reviews

**Kavita Ganesan**
Github Inc.
88 Colin P Kelly Jr St
San Francisco, CA 94107
kganes2@github.com

**Guangyu Zhou**
Department of Computer Science
University of Illinois at Urbana-Champaign
Urbana, IL 61801
gzhou6@illinois.edu

## Abstract

Traditional sentiment analysis has been focused on predicting the polarity of texts as *positive* or *negative* at different granularity. This broad categorization does not account for informativeness of the underlying text. For many real-world applications such as social listening, brand monitoring and e-commerce platforms, the opinions that really matter are the informative opinions describing why something is good or bad. In this paper, we try to understand the properties of *complaints* and *praises* which is an informative subset of the negative and positive categories. Our analysis in the context of user reviews shows that complaints and praises have distinct properties that differentiate it from positive only or negative only sentences.

## 1 Introduction

Over the last two decades, sentiment analysis research has been focused on predicting *positive* and *negative* polarity ratings at different granularity - at the passage level, sentence level as well as aspect or phrasal level (Pontiki et al., 2015; Wang et al., 2015; Pontiki and Manandhar, 2014; Pang et al., 2002; Pang and Lee, 2008; Wilson et al., 2005; Wang et al., 2010; Snyder and Barzilay, 2007; Titov and McDonald, 2008; Lu et al., 2009; Wang, 2015; Diao et al., 2014). While such ratings provide a general sense of 'what people think', it does not take into account the informativeness of the comments that contribute towards those ratings as long as the comments have some form of desired subjectivity (e.g. should contain a noun and an adjective). Consider the following sentences about the *Xbox* :

1. *The Xbox is way too expensive!*

2. *I really hate the Xbox!*

In the traditional sense, both these sentences would be considered negative comments of equal importance. However, sentence (1) is actually more informative than (2). This difference is critical in many application scenarios. For example, if a business analyst wants to analyze the complaints or pain points of a product, a comment such as '*I really hate the Xbox!*' does not increase the understanding of the analyst. However, the comment '*The Xbox is way too expensive!*' informs the analyst that one of the problems of the Xbox is that it is not affordable. Another example is in competitive intelligence. A company will learn more about a competitor's product from a comment such as '*Wow! the Xbox is very user-friendly!*' as opposed to '*The Xbox is just awesome.*' as the former provides a concrete reason.

The goal of this paper, is to study the linguistic properties of *complaint* and *praise* sentences which we define as an informative subset of the more general negative and positive categories, providing reasons for a topic or aspect being positive or negative. We perform our study in the context of user reviews as user generated reviews tend to have informative subjective content inter-mingled with non-informative subjective content and factual or neutral utterances. We investigate several properties, including the length property, noun and adjective usage, past tense and negation usage and finally the usage of intensifiers and causal links. We contrast the properties of *complaint* and *praise* sentences with *negative only* or *positive only* sentences.

Our study shows several distinct properties of complaints and praises in contrast to positive only and negative only sentences. We believe that this study would set a foundation for improving existing sentiment classification and opinion summarization systems. The data set used for this study is publicly available at http://kavita-ganesan. com/complaints-and-praises[1].

---

[1]You can also reference: https://github.com/ kganes2/complaints-and-praises



*Proceedings of NAACL-HLT 2016*, pages 109–114,
San Diego, California, June 12-17, 2016. ©2016 Association for Computational Linguistics

| negative only | complaint | positive only | praise |
|---|---|---|---|
| ~~This is not a good **com-pany**~~, stay away! | This **company** takes your payment but on the *day of the scheduled job, they don't appear.* | I really love that **restaurant**, its awesome. | This **restaurant** has *delicious tacos and the ambience is amazing!* |
| The **phone's screen** is very disappointing :( | Unhappy with this **phone**, the *screen is not clear and the fonts are way too small.* | Nice **phone**, love it and totally recommend it! | I like the fact that the **phone** *fits right in your pocket* |

Table 1: Examples of *negative only* and *positive only* sentences as well *complaint* and *praise* sentences. Bolded text are the topics and the italicized text answer 'why' the topic is positive or negative.

## 2   Related Work

While there are many systems attempting to predict finer granularity of sentiment ratings at the aspect or phrasal level (Pontiki et al., 2015; Pontiki and Manandhar, 2014; Wang et al., 2015; Wang et al., 2010; Snyder and Barzilay, 2007; Titov and McDonald, 2008; Lu et al., 2009; Wilson et al., 2005; Wang, 2015; Diao et al., 2014), these systems still do not have a clear understanding on what makes a sentence informative enough linguistically to be used for mining fine grained sentiments. The common assumption is that a subjective sentence should contain a *noun* and an *adjective*. In addition, these systems consider all negative and positive expressions as equal contributors. For example, the phrases *'screen is bad', 'the screen is way too small'* and *'the screen is too big'* would all equally affect ratings on the *screen* aspect. In reality, the first phrase is a general negative statement compared to the second and third phrases which are much more informative, providing reasons for the screen being bad. Having the option of analyzing only the informative subset would add significant value to sentiment analysis applications. For this purpose, there has to be a good understanding on how to distinguish between the different types of subjective comments.

In the work of (Kim and Hovy, 2006), the authors attempt to train a classifier to predict 'pro' and 'con' reasons in user reviews. However, there is a lack of definition on what 'pros' or 'cons' represent and how they can be linguistically identified. Our study thus bridges this gap by providing insights into key linguistic properties of *complaint* and *praise* sentences in contrast to plain *negative only* and *positive only* sentences.

## 3   Defining Complaints and Praises

In this section, we formally define the concept of a *complaint* and a *praise*. Given a sentence, $S$, we refer to this sentence as a *positive* sentence if its connotation is positive and a *negative* sentence if its connotation is negative. We refer to a negative sentence as a **complaint** if it has a negative connotation with *supplemental information*, answering the question of why a topic or aspect is negative. We refer to a sentence as **negative only** if it is negative with no such supplemental information. Similarly, we refer to a positive sentence as a **praise**, if the sentence has a positive connotation with *supplemental information*, clearly indicating what makes the topic or aspect positive. A sentence is considered **positive only** if it is positive with no such supplemental information.

Our definition of supplemental information refers to any information in an opinionated sentence that answers the question of 'why' the like or dislike for a topic, improving the user's understanding for that topic. For example, the sentence *"Xbox is just bad...I hate it."* is considered *negative only* and not a complaint because if does not have information explaining why the user dislikes the Xbox. However, the sentence *"The Xbox is awfully expensive, I would not recommend it"* would qualify as a *complaint* as it answers 'why' the user has a negative opinion about the Xbox which in turn improves a user's understanding about the Xbox (that it is expensive). Table 1, shows examples of negative only, positive only, complaint and praise sentences.

## 4   Dataset

To conduct our analysis, we collected 2500 reviews from various sources including TripAdvisor, Yelp, Walmart and Sephora. We then recruited 4 students to manually categorize sentences from the user reviews into 1 of 5 categories. The categories are: *NegativeOnly, Complaint, PositiveOnly, Praise,* and *Irrelevant.* The sentences were randomly assigned to the students. Students were asked to perform categorization based on the

| Category | Avg. # of words | Avg. length |
|---|---|---|
| Complaint | 15.75 | 80.88 |
| **Difference** | **+53.66%** | **+%55.69** |
| PositiveOnly | 10.33 | 53.13 |
| Praise | 15.54 | 82.45 |
| **Difference** | **+50.44%** | **+55.19%** |

Table 2: Average number words and average length per sentence in the dataset.

formal definition of a complaint and a praise sentence as described in Section 3. Non-opinion containing sentences and noise were placed in the *Irrelevant* category. We use the four main categories - *NegativeOnly*, *Complaint*, *PositiveOnly* and *Praise* for our study. For a fair comparison, we ensured that we only used 500 randomly picked sentences within each category.

## 5 Sentence Length Analysis

Our first analysis deals with understanding the general length of *complaints* and *praises* in contrast to *negative only* or *positive only* sentences. In Table 2, we report the average length and number of words in a sentence within each sentiment category. On average, a *praise* or *complaint* sentence is at least 50% longer than a *positive only* or *negative only* sentence. The average number of words in a *praise* sentence is 15.54 and a *positive only* sentence it is 10.33. The average number of words in a *complaint* sentence is 15.75 and a *negative only* sentence it is 10.25. Intuitively, this makes sense since *complaints* and *praises* require elaboration on why something is good or bad but in the case of *negative only* or *positive only* sentences, the statements can be fairly general.

## 6 Noun and Adjective Usage

Nouns and adjectives are essential parts of speech within subjective sentences as these together are key indicators of sentiment (Hu and Liu, 2004; Pang and Lee, 2008; Kim et al., 2011). For example, a negative only sentence such as *'the screen is bad'* or a complaint such as *'the screen is not clear'* both have nouns ('screen') and adjectives ('bad' and 'clear'). Both the noun and adjectives play a role in indicating negative sentiment. To better understand if there is a difference in adjective and noun usage in a *complaint* or a *praise* versus a *negative only* or *positive only* sentence, we obtained the mean, mode and median of nouns and adjectives in our manually categorized dataset. We also noted the counts of nouns appearing near ad-

jectives within a 3 word window. We report the results in Table 3.

**Noun analysis:** Based on Table 3, we see that with the NegativeOnly and PositiveOnly categories, most sentences have 1 noun per sentence (see mode in Table 3). However, in the Complaint and Praise categories, most sentences use 3 nouns per sentence. This is because a *complaint* or a *praise* sentence describes 'what' was good or bad about a topic requiring more use of nouns. For example, if a praise was about the food at a restaurant, the *tacos*, *salsas* and *chips* could have been outstanding.

**Adjective analysis:** In terms of adjectives, the first point to observe is that most *praise* sentences use 2 or more adjectives while most *complaint* sentences use a single adjective. Upon further investigation, we realized that in a *praise* sentence, user's tend to compliment more than one aspect of a topic within a single sentence. For example, consider the following praise sentence: *This is a really lightweight machine and it is easy to assemble'*. The user is complimenting two aspects of the machine within a single sentence: (1) weight and (2) assembly. For this same reason, the adjective+nouns have the highest occurrence within the praise category as multiple positive sentiments are coupled within a single sentence.

This is different from *complaints*, where within complaints, users tend to elaborate why a single aspect of a topic is bad. For example, consider the following complaint: *'This machine was really hard to put together, the screws don't fit so I sent it back'*. This sentence only describes a single aspect which is the fact that the product was hard to assemble, why that was the case and what the user did to address it. This appears to be the common nature of complaints. This is why most *complaints* use no more adjectives than *negative only* sentences.

## 7 Past Tense Analysis

One observation that we made while visually analyzing our manually constructed dataset is that complaints seemed to use more past tense than the other three categories. To validate our observation, we did a count of occurrence of past tense words in each category of our dataset. The average past tense counts per sentence and the top 6 past tense words used is reported in Table 4. From this, it is evident that complaints have the highest past tense usage compared to the other three cate-

| Nouns | Mean | Mode | Median | Adjectives | Mean | Mode | Median | Noun + Adjective | Mean | Mode | Median |
|---|---|---|---|---|---|---|---|---|---|---|---|
| NegativeOnly | 1.87 | 1.00 | 1.00 | NegativeOnly | 0.972 | 1.00 | 1.00 | NegativeOnly | 0.60 | 0.00 | 0.00 |
| Complaint | 3.36 | 3.00 | 3.00 | Complaint | 1.500 | 1.00 | 1.00 | Complaint | 1.00 | 0.00 | 1.00 |
| **Difference** | **+1.49** | **+2.00** | **+2.00** | **Difference** | **+0.528** | **0.00** | **0.00** | **Difference** | **+0.40** | **0.00** | **0.00** |
| PositiveOnly | 2.16 | 1.00 | 2.00 | PositiveOnly | 1.164 | 1.00 | 1.00 | PositiveOnly | 0.75 | 0.00 | 1.00 |
| Praise | 3.56 | 3.00 | 3.00 | Praise | 2.086 | 2.00 | 2.00 | Praise | **1.50** | **1.00** | **1.00** |
| **Difference** | **+1.40** | **+2.00** | **+1.00** | **Difference** | **+0.922** | **+1.00** | **+1.00** | **Difference** | **+0.75** | **+1.00** | **0.00** |

Table 3: Mean, mode and median of nouns and adjectives computed on a per sentence basis.

| PositiveOnly | Praise | NegativeOnly | Complaint |
|---|---|---|---|
| 0.55 | 0.68 | 0.63 | **1.26** |

| Category | Top 6 past tense with counts |
|---|---|
| **PositiveOnly** | was 56, had 23, been 14, were 13, loved 8, tried 8 |
| **Praise** | was 86, were 32, had 22, made 9, been 7, got 6 |
| **NegativeOnly** | was 61, had 24, did 19, got 11, were 11, been 9, |
| **Complaint** | was 155, had 40, were 35, did 23, got 20, made 14 |

Table 4: Average # of past tense words and top 6 past tense words in each category

| Category | Avg # Nega-tions | %Sentences with Negations | Top 6 Negation Words |
|---|---|---|---|
| PositiveOnly | 0.094 | 8.8% | not 16, no 9, don't 6, can't 5, never 4, didn't 3 |
| Praise | 0.208 | 18.6% | not 46, no 15, don't 13, didn't 8, wouldn't 6, can't 4 |
| NegativeOnly | **0.538** | **48.8%** | not 131, don't 33, never 27, no 16, didn't 13, nothing 9 |
| Complaint | 0.428 | 37.8% | not 88, no 36, didn't 28, don't 17, never 9, wasn't 9 |

Table 5: Distribution of negations and top 6 negation words per category.

gories. On average, every complaint sentence uses at least 1 past tense. As we investigated further, we found that this is related to our observation from the previous section where within a complaint, a user is often explaining away why something was bad and what their actions were in response to the situation, which is usually something in the past.

As we looked into the actual past tense words used, we noticed that there is no significant difference in the top past tense words used across categories which can be seen from Table 4. What remains evident is that the complaint category uses more of these words than any of the other categories.

## 8 Negation Analysis

When we want to say that something is not true or is not the case, we use negative words, phrases or clauses. Negation can happen in a number of ways, most commonly, when we use a negative word such as *no, not, never, none, nobody*, etc. In sentiment analysis tasks, negation words are typically associated with the negative category. However, since we are interested in a finer granularity of the negative class (i.e. negative only and complaint) as well as the positive class (positive only and praise), we try to get an understanding of how negations are used across the 4 categories. For this analysis, we used a list of common negation words (e.g. not, no, never) along with words that end

with "n't" (e.g. doesn't, hasn't, haven't) and did a count of these words to determine percentage of sentences containing negations as well as the average number of negations per sentence. We also noted the top negation words in each category and the results are reported in Table 5.

Based on Table 5, we see that while positive only sentences rarely use negations, the praise sentences use negations to a certain extent (∼20% of sentences contain negations). Manual inspection revealed that negations were primarily used to describe a positive aspect of a topic. For example, consider the negation in the following sentence: *this lasts all night and feels really great on my skin not oily cakey or heavy*". The negation here is used to describe the fact that the product does not feel bad on the skin.

Another interesting finding is that the NegativeOnly category has the highest use of negations with almost 50% of the sentences containing at least one negation word. This number is even higher than the complaint category where the sentences are generally longer. Through visual inspection, we found that this happens because negative only sentences have limited description on why something is 'not good'. Therefore, clear indication of *disapproval* is with the use of negations. The following sentences from our dataset

| Category | % sentences containing intensifiers |
|---|---|
| PositiveOnly | 14.80% |
| Praise | **20.60%** |
| NegativeOnly | 13.40% |
| Complaint | 16.80% |

Table 6: Intensifier usage across categories.

are negative only sentences with clear indication of dislike with the use of negations:

*"i would <u>not</u> recommend dinner here at all "*

*"<u>never</u> going back"*

*"<u>don't</u> stay there "*

*"for the price it just <u>wasn't</u> worth it"*

## 9   Intensifier Usage

Intensifiers are words that strengthen the meaning of other expressions and show emphasis. Common intensifiers include *absolutely, completely, extremely, highly, rather, really,* and etc. We noticed that intensifiers are heavily used in user generated opinions to emphasize appreciation or in some cases dissatisfaction. For example, to express appreciation on some restaurant service one may say *'The service was extremely fast and the food was super delicious!'*. The intensifiers in this sentence clearly adds strength to the user's opinion. To understand which category of sentences are more inclined towards using intensifiers, we computed the percentage of sentences that contain at least one intensifier. We used a list of 35 intensifiers, expanding on the list published in (Ganesan and Zhai, 2012).

Based on Table 6, we can see that intensifiers are mostly used in praise sentences with almost 20% of the sentences containing at least one intensifier. The use of intensifiers is less prominent in the other 3 categories. Based on manual analysis, we found two reasons for this. First, is the fact that praise sentences tend to couple multiple positive aspects into a single sentence as pointed out in Section 6. So there is more use of intensifiers with the adjectives. The second reason stems from the fact that users tend to over emphasize positive points and state negative points more in a matter of fact fashion. The words *'very'* and *'really'* are the top intensifier words used across all four categories.

## 10   Causal Transitions

As complaint and praise sentences contain explanation of 'why' a particular topic is good or bad,

| Category | % sentences containing all causal transitions | % sentences containing 'because' and 'since' |
|---|---|---|
| PositiveOnly | 16.60% | 2.4% |
| Praise | 23.80% | 2.4% |
| NegativeOnly | 16.40% | 2.2% |
| Complaint | **28.20%** | **4.6%** |

Table 7: Causal transitions used across categories.

there will be natural occurrences of cause and effect, known as causal transitions. For example, the sentence *'Seems like this phone is poorly designed as the screen keeps blurring out and the buttons keep getting stuck'* shows clear cause and reason. Causal transition words include *because, since, therefore, as, as a result, for this reason, consequently, thus* and etc. We used 20 such words covering *cause and reason, effect and result* as well as *consequence* to understand if such words have a stronger occurrence in one category than another.

Table 7 shows percentage of sentences containing causal transitions within each category. Notice that while approximately 17% of the *positive only* and *negative only* sentences use causal transitions, there is a much stronger relationship between causal transitions and the *complaints* category with 28% of the sentences carrying causal links. This tells us that complaints tend to have more explicit description on what caused something to be bad or reaction in response to something negative. For example, within user reviews, it would be more common to see an expression such as *'I returned the vacuum because it was broken'* as opposed to *'I love the vacuum because it works really well'*. To further understand this behavior, we looked at occurrences of strong causal expressions (i.e. sentences with 'because' and 'since') to validate that there indeed is more explicit use of causation in the complaints category. Based on Table 7, we can see that there is clearly a higher use of strong causal expressions in the complaints category compared to the other three categories.

## 11   Conclusion and Future Work

In this paper, we sought to understand the linguistic properties of *complaints* and *praises* which we define as an informative subset of the more general negative and positive polarity with **reasons** or **explanation** on what makes a topic negative/positive. Our study in the context of user reviews has shown several interesting findings.

We first showed that, *complaint* and *praise* sentences are in general longer and use more nouns than adjectives compared to a *positive only* or a *negative only* sentence. Even though subjective sentences are assumed to contain nouns and adjectives we now have evidence that nouns appear more frequently than adjectives in more informative subjective sentences. We also showed that *praise* sentences tend to use more adjectives and intensifiers compared to *complaint* sentences. The higher use of adjectives can be attributed to the fact that people were more likely to compliment several aspects of a topic within a single sentence as opposed to complaints, where people explain away the reason for the dislike or disapproval. Intensifiers play a more significant role in praise sentences as users tend to over emphasize positive points. Our study also shows that there is a stronger link between causation and *complaints* compared to the other categories.

In the future, we would like to test the power of some of the prominent features in our study to understand the value of these features in developing a fine-grained sentiment classifier.

# References


[Diao et al.2014] Qiming Diao, Minghui Qiu, Chao-Yuan Wu, Alexander J Smola, Jing Jiang, and Chong Wang. 2014. Jointly modeling aspects, ratings and sentiments for movie recommendation (jmars). In *Proceedings of the 20th ACM SIGKDD international conference on Knowledge discovery and data mining*, pages 193–202. ACM.

[Ganesan and Zhai2012] Kavita Ganesan and ChengXiang Zhai. 2012. Opinion-based entity ranking. *Information retrieval*, 15(2):116–150.

[Hu and Liu2004] Minqing Hu and Bing Liu. 2004. Mining and summarizing customer reviews. In *Proceedings of the tenth ACM SIGKDD international conference on Knowledge discovery and data mining*, pages 168–177. ACM.

[Kim and Hovy2006] Soo-Min Kim and Eduard Hovy. 2006. Automatic identification of pro and con reasons in online reviews. In *Proceedings of the COLING/ACL on Main Conference Poster Sessions*, COLING-ACL '06, pages 483–490, Stroudsburg, PA, USA. Association for Computational Linguistics.

[Kim et al.2011] Hyun Duk Kim, Kavita Ganesan, Parikshit Sondhi, and ChengXiang Zhai. 2011. Comprehensive review of opinion summarization (opinion mining survey).

[Lu et al.2009] Yue Lu, ChengXiang Zhai, and Neel Sundaresan. 2009. Rated aspect summarization of short comments. In *Proceedings of the 18th international conference on World wide web*, pages 131–140. ACM.

[Pang and Lee2008] Bo Pang and Lillian Lee. 2008. Opinion mining and sentiment analysis. *Foundations and trends in information retrieval*, 2(1-2):1–135.

[Pang et al.2002] Bo Pang, Lillian Lee, and Shivakumar Vaithyanathan. 2002. Thumbs up?: sentiment classification using machine learning techniques. In *Proceedings of the ACL-02 conference on Empirical methods in natural language processing-Volume 10*, pages 79–86. Association for Computational Linguistics.

[Pontiki and Manandhar2014] Maria Pontiki and Suresh Manandhar. 2014. Semeval-2014 task 4: Aspect based sentiment analysis.

[Pontiki et al.2015] Maria Pontiki, Dimitrios Galanis, Haris Papageorgiou, Suresh Manandhar, and Ion Androutsopoulos. 2015. Semeval-2015 task 12: Aspect based sentiment analysis.

[Snyder and Barzilay2007] Benjamin Snyder and Regina Barzilay. 2007. Multiple aspect ranking using the good grief algorithm.

[Titov and McDonald2008] Ivan Titov and Ryan T McDonald. 2008. A joint model of text and aspect ratings for sentiment summarization. Citeseer.

[Wang et al.2010] Hongning Wang, Yue Lu, and Chengxiang Zhai. 2010. Latent aspect rating analysis on review text data: a rating regression approach. In *Proceedings of the 16th ACM SIGKDD international conference on Knowledge discovery and data mining*, pages 783–792. ACM.

[Wang et al.2015] Linlin Wang, Kang Liu, Zhu Cao, Jun Zhao, and Gerard de Melo. 2015. Sentiment-aspect extraction based on restricted boltzmann machines. In *Proceedings of ACL 2015*.

[Wang2015] Hao Wang. 2015. *Sentiment-aligned Topic Models for Product Aspect Rating Prediction*. Ph.D. thesis, Applied Sciences: School of Computing Science.

[Wilson et al.2005] Theresa Wilson, Janyce Wiebe, and Paul Hoffmann. 2005. Recognizing contextual polarity in phrase-level sentiment analysis. In *Proceedings of the conference on human language technology and empirical methods in natural language processing*, pages 347–354. Association for Computational Linguistics.

# Reputation System: Evaluating Reputation among All Good Sellers

**Vandana Jha, Savitha R, P Deepa Shenoy** and **Venugopal K R**
Department of Computer Science and Engineering,
University Visvesvaraya College of Engineering,
Bangalore University, Bangalore, India
Email: vjvandanajha@gmail.com

## Abstract

A reputation system assists people selecting whom to trust. The "all good reputation" problem is common in e-commerce domain, making it difficult for buyers to choose credible sellers. Observing high growth of online data in Hindi language, in this paper, we propose a reputation system in this language. The functions of this system include 1) review mining for different criteria of online transactions 2) calculation of reputation rating and reputation weight for each criteria from user reviews and 3) ranking sellers based on computed reputation score. Extensive simulations conducted on eBay dataset show its effectiveness in solving "all good reputation" problem. So far as our knowledge is concerned, this is the first work in Hindi language on reputation system.

## 1 Introduction

Reputation is an estimation of the trust the community has built in you. It is a complex and context-dependent opinion of the community about any entity in question. It is highly influencial in e-commerce applications. In traditional transactions, the product is physically available for inspection whereas in online transactions, the people transact among strangers, without any physical manifestation. The consumer is forced to pay for the goods and services before receiving/trying them. Reputation is crucial for the success of e-commerce systems. Reputation system calculates and reports reputation score for an entity based on opinions from other members of the community having direct interaction with the entity in question. These opinions are collected in the form of ratings and/or free text reviews. Reputation scores are publicly available to all the members of the community so that participants can decide about future transactions. Reputation systems are used for third-party sellers by various e-commerce sites, such as, eBay and Amazon. For example on eBay, the reputation score is calculated on the total number of positive and negative feedback ratings for transactions using the formula: $\frac{\#Positive\_Ratings}{\#Positive\_Ratings+\#Negative\_Ratings}$ for feedbacks left in the last 1 month, 6 months and 12 months[1].

There is an overview of studies and experiments on eBay reputation system in (Resnick et al., 2006). Surprisingly, most of the feedback ratings on eBay are positives (99% on average) (Resnick et al., 2001) which lead to an issue known as "all good reputation" issue (Resnick et al., 2001), (Resnick and Zeckhauser, 2002). Even though detailed seller ratings are available on eBay site based on four criteria, *item as described, communication, shipping time* and *shipping and handling charges* (as shown in Figure 1) but these are also positively biased. This is misleading and does not help buyer in taking decision for the transaction. Although the ratings or scores are positively biased but the feedback comments (from now onwards called as reviews) expressed in the form of free text give the clear picture of the disappointments for some criteria during transaction (O'Donovan et al., 2007). For example, *smooth transaction, great product* but *slow delivery*, with a positive reputation score. We can extract buyers' experience about all the criteria of transactions by mining the knowledge embedded in their reviews

---

[1] `http://pages.ebay.in/help/feedback/`
`allaboutfeedback.html`



*Proceedings of NAACL-HLT 2016*, pages 115–121,
San Diego, California, June 12-17, 2016. ©2016 Association for Computational Linguistics

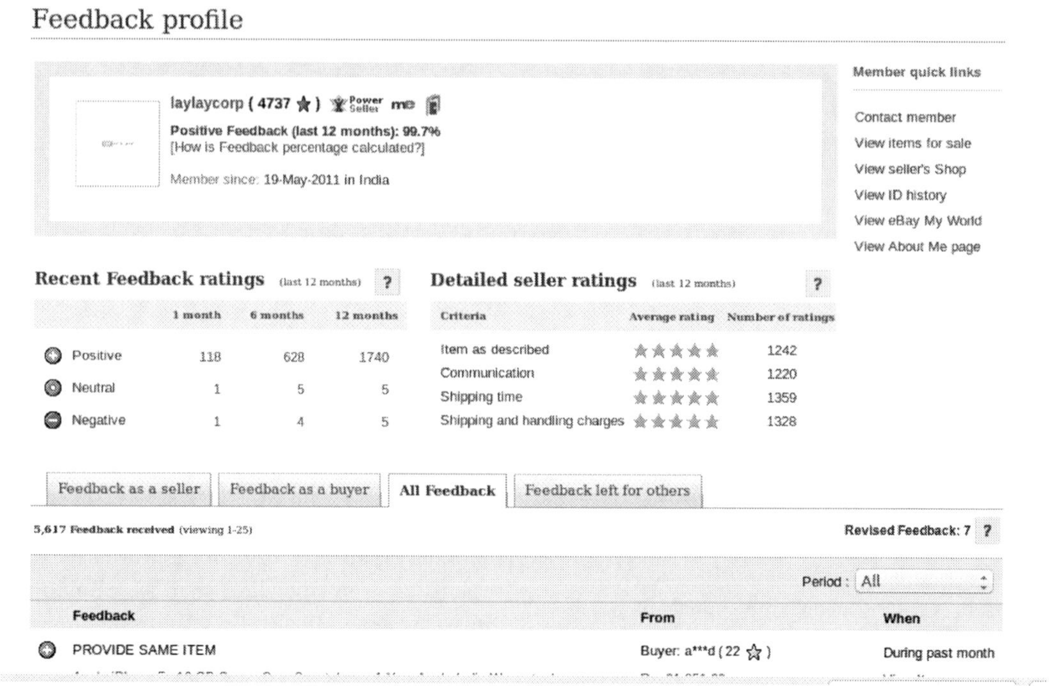

Feedback profile

**Figure 1:** Feedback profile of a seller (laylaycorp) from `www.ebay.in` with 99.7% positive feedback score, Detailed seller ratings and Feeback comments

and calculate broad and complete reputation score for sellers.

## 1.1 Motivation

Online shopping through these e-commerce sites (`www.ebay.in`, `www.amazon.in` etc.) are gaining popularity in India. This popularity is increasing more because of their mobile applications accessed on smart phone. Smart phone has made one more thing possible, that is, writing in someone's own language using language selector. Both the benefits of smart phone get combined together and give the advantage of buying products from e-commerce sites and leaving reviews in Hindi, Bengali, Tamil etc. The proposed reputation system is for Hindi language. Hindi, the 4th largest spoken language, makes 4.7% of the world population[2]. It is the official language of India. English is understandable only by 25.9% of Internet users[3] so research in other languages is the need of the hour.

---

[2]`http://en.wikipedia.org/wiki/List_of_languages_by_number_of_native_speakers`

[3]`http://www.internetworldstats.com/stats7.htm`

## 1.2 Contribution

A reputation system is proposed in this paper, which can evaluate reputation and rank sellers by review mining. Here "all good reputation" sellers, with more than 90% reputation score, are considered. Reputation system calculates a comprehensive reputation profile for sellers which include criteria based scores and weights, as well as total reputation scores by adding all the criteria scores. This approach combines opinion mining techniques (Pang and Lee, 2008), (Liu, 2012) with Natural Language Processing techniques. Our reputation weights are calculated by using criteria based opinion expressions, unlike other methods (Lu et al., 2009), (Wang et al., 2011), (Wang et al., 2010), to reduce positive biasing in ranking of sellers. The simulations conducted on eBay dataset show its effectiveness in solving "all good reputation" issue.

The organization of the paper is as follows: A brief overview of the related work is in section 2. Section 3 describes the proposed reputation system. Simulation runs on eBay datasets and all the results concerned are discussed in section 4. Conclusions are given in section 5.

## 2 Related Work

So far our knowledge is concerned, this is the first work on reputation system in Hindi language so we are unable to provide related work specifically in this language. Following is the state of art about reputation system in other languages and the methods applied to compute it.

Related Work can be branched into two main parts: 1) Review analysis and mining and 2) Review mining for computing reputation and trust. Reviews can be movie reviews, product reviews or other forms of free text.

### 2.1 Review analysis and mining

There have been works focussing on sentiment classification. (O'Donovan et al., 2007) and (Gamon, 2004) showed that reviews, in the form of free text, are noisy and mining knowledge out of it, is a challenging task. (Hijikata et al., 2007) focuses on summarizing the reviews and deleted 80.8% of courteous comments saying that these comments contain almost no information. (Lu et al., 2009) focuses on summarising short comments, each associated with an overall rating. (Hu and Liu, 2004) focuses on developing opinion lexicon for identifying opinion orientation for product reviews. (Qiu et al., 2011) focuses on applying syntactic relations for improving the accuracy of aspect extraction. (Zhuang et al., 2006) focuses on a multi-knowledge based approach, which integrates WordNet, statistical analysis and movie knowledge. But these works are neither in Hindi language nor use the concept of grouping opinion expressions.

Review mining in Hindi Language for polarity detection is the center point for (Jha et al., 2015c), (Jha et al., 2015a), (Jha et al., 2015b), (Jha et al., 2016), (Bakliwal et al., 2012), (Narayan et al., 2002).

### 2.2 Review mining for computing reputation and trust

Literatures (Resnick et al., 2001), (Resnick and Zeckhauser, 2002) and (O'Donovan et al., 2007) are available which focus on reputation systems and shown strong biasing towards positive rating. Even though sufficient solution to this problem has not been suggested, paper (O'Donovan et al., 2007) has proposed to analyse review comments. Paper

(Jøsang et al., 2007) is a survey on all the systems which can be used to find trust and reputation in e-commerce domain. Various statistical methods like the Beta reputation (Jsang and Ismail, 2002), Rating aggregation algorithm (Resnick et al., 2006) and Kalman inference (Wang et al., 2012) are also proposed for computing trust.

## 3 Reputation System

We have considered buyers' reviews from *eBay* dataset for eight sellers ($s = 8$). The reputation score is the weighted summation of criteria based reputation ratings for each seller and calculated by the following formula:

$$ReputationScore = \sum_{i=1}^{c} R_i * W_i, \qquad (1)$$

where $R_i$ and $W_i$ are reputation rating and weight respectively for criteria $c$. Here, $c = 4$, i.e., *Item as described (I)*, *Communication (C)*, *Shipping time (S)* and *Shipping and handling charges (Cost)*.

### 3.1 Criteria Based Reputation Rating

We calculated criteria based reputation rating using Bayesian method given in (Jøsang et al., 2007). Reputation rating for each criteria can be computed from the count of positive and negative ratings for that criteria. According to Bayes rule, the updated (posteriori) reputation rating is estimated from previous (priori) reputation ratings (Jsang and Ismail, 2002). The reputation rating can be defined by the beta probability density functions parameter tuple ($\alpha$, $\beta$) (where $\alpha$ and $\beta$ are the count of positive and negative ratings respectively). It is denoted by $beta(p|\alpha, \beta)$ and can be declared using the gamma function $\Gamma$ as:

$$beta(p|\alpha, \beta) = \frac{\Gamma(\alpha+\beta)}{\Gamma(\alpha)\Gamma(\beta)} p^{\alpha-1}(1 - p)^{\beta-1}$$

The probability expectation value of the beta distribution, $\alpha/(\alpha + \beta)$, is linearly combined with the mean, $y/n$, to compute reputation rating (Heinrich, 2008) i.e., $R_i = \frac{y+\alpha}{n+\alpha+\beta}$, where $y$ is the number of positive ratings and $n$ is the total number of ratings. When there is no prior ratings, then $\alpha = \beta$. Let's assume, $\alpha + \beta = c$, then $\alpha = \beta = 1/2 * c$ and $R_i$ can be defined as:

$$R_i = \frac{y + 1/2 * c}{n + c} \qquad (2)$$

| S | SellerName | ProductType | #Reviews | #P | #N | Pos (%) | DSR (Number of ratings) | | | |
|---|---|---|---|---|---|---|---|---|---|---|
| | | | | | | | I | C | S | Cost |
| 1 | uniqcorp | Mob.Acc. | 47 | 44 | 3 | 93.6170 | 4.5 (40) | 4.4 (41) | 4.2 (40) | 5(44) |
| 2 | Jeelus-com | Mob.Acc. | 58 | 54 | 4 | 93.1034 | 4.5 (51) | 4.4 (51) | 4.3 (53) | 5(58) |
| 3 | exclusiveretail | Mob.Acc. | 70 | 69 | 1 | 98.5714 | 4.8 (66) | 4.8 (63) | 4.9 (63) | 5(67) |
| 4 | aaa999acessoriesshop | Mob.Acc. | 63 | 57 | 6 | 90.4762 | 4.5 (55) | 4.3 (51) | 4.2 (54) | 5(64) |
| 5 | rkaquafreshindia2015 | HomApp. | 84 | 79 | 5 | 94.0476 | 4.3 (79) | 4.3 (76) | 4.1 (74) | 5(98) |
| 6 | xiting.deals | HomApp. | 49 | 47 | 2 | 95.9183 | 4.5 (30) | 4.4 (28) | 4.2 (29) | 5(30) |
| 7 | Stallions-elex | HomApp. | 49 | 47 | 2 | 95.9183 | 4.6 (51) | 4.5 (50) | 4.6 (50) | 5(47) |
| 8 | trinitronestore | HomApp. | 49 | 47 | 2 | 95.9183 | 4.4 (41) | 3.9 (40) | 3.8 (40) | 5(42) |

**Table 1:** Seller Dataset from *www.ebay.in*

## 3.2 Criteria Based Weight

In this step, the reviews are tokenized and Part-Of-Speech (POS) tagging is performed using hindi-pos-tagger[4]. The typed dependency relation representation (De Marneffe and Manning, 2008) concept is used for extracting opinion expressions from the reviews. These expressions are clustered for each criteria and criteria based weight is computed.

The typed dependency relation representation (De Marneffe and Manning, 2008) provides a straightforward description of grammatical relations in sentences. A sentence can be depicted by a group of dependency relations between pairs of words using (head, dependent), where criteria or criteria words are represented by heads and related words or modifiers become dependent on heads. This can be accomplished using hindi-dependency-parser-2.0[5]. After parsing, words with adjective, noun, verb and adverb POS tags are separated as these only express subjectivity (Turney, 2002). The pairs like adjectives and nouns, and adverbs and verbs, express opinion expression where nouns or verbs represent criteria words and adjectives or adverbs represent opinion towards these criteria. Next, we generate clusters for each criteria. These clusters are formed by matching words in the reviews with criteria words (cword). If the match occurs then one word before and after criteria word is tested for being a modifier or not being a criteria word. The words which satisfy this condition, are clustered together for that criteria.

The dependency relations are used to compute criteria based weight based on LDA topic modelling technique (Blei et al., 2003). We are taking the results from Gibbs sampler for LDA (Heinrich, 2008), (Griffiths and Steyvers, 2004) for determining weight of the words. $W_i$ can be computed as follows:

$$CriteriaWeight = \sum_{i=1}^{t} \frac{(n-m)}{(n+m)},$$

where $t$ is the number of cluster words in each criteria, $n$= count of number of words which are *otherthanWordOtherthanCriteria*, $m$=count of number of words which are *otherthanWordSameCriteria*.

$$W_i = \frac{CriteriaWeight}{Wordcount} \tag{3}$$

## 4 Performance Evaluation

### 4.1 Datasets

We have crawled 477 buyer's reviews for eight eBay sellers from *www.ebay.in*, where four sellers are randomly selected for each of two categories namely Mobile Accessories (Mob.Acc.) and Home Appliances (HomApp.) from "Shop by category" list. These reviews are converted into Hindi language using translator[6]. Further machine translation is corrected manually by one native speaker. The preprocessed reviews are stored as Reviews file. We have also extracted the feedback profile for each seller for the evaluation of our reputation system[7] (Figure 1). It consist of following informations for a seller:

- The *Feedback score (#P)*, which is the total number of positive ratings for transactions in the past.

---

| Seller | CriteriaReputationRating | | | |
|---|---|---|---|---|
| | I | C | S | Cost |
| 1 | 0.8636 | 0.8462 | 0.8091 | 0.9583 |
| 2 | 0.8709 | 0.8524 | 0.8347 | 0.9677 |
| 3 | 0.9337 | 0.9325 | 0.9513 | 0.9718 |
| 4 | 0.8729 | 0.8338 | 0.8166 | 0.9706 |
| 5 | 0.8427 | 0.8420 | 0.8036 | 0.9804 |
| 6 | 0.8529 | 0.8325 | 0.7988 | 0.9412 |
| 7 | 0.8895 | 0.8704 | 0.8889 | 0.9608 |
| 8 | 0.8462 | 0.7545 | 0.7364 | 0.9565 |

**(a)** Criteria based ReputationRating

| Seller | CriteriaWeight | | | |
|---|---|---|---|---|
| | I | C | S | Cost |
| 1 | 0.1530 | 0.1917 | 0.1601 | 0.3707 |
| 2 | 0.0924 | 0.3241 | 0.1060 | 0.4076 |
| 3 | 0.1787 | 0.3479 | 0.0446 | 0.2737 |
| 4 | 0.3578 | 0.2570 | 0.2689 | 0.2262 |
| 5 | 0.0898 | 0.3403 | 0.1285 | 0.2667 |
| 6 | 0.2586 | 0.2835 | 0.1545 | 0.4393 |
| 7 | 0.1928 | 0.4433 | 0.1524 | 0.3146 |
| 8 | 0.1453 | 0.3530 | 0.2083 | 0.3362 |

**(b)** Criteria based Weights

**Table 2:** The computed results of CriteriaReputationRating and CriteriaWeight for eight sellers

- The *Positive Feedback percentage (Pos (%))*, which is calculated as $\frac{\#Positive\_Ratings}{\#Positive\_Ratings + \#Negative\_Ratings}$ for transactions in the past 12 months.

- The *Detailed seller ratings (DSR)*, which consists of four criteria for the transaction: *I*, *C*, *S* and *Cost* together with Average rating (in the form of five-star ratings) and Number of ratings for each criteria.

Table 1 shows the details of this dataset.

### 4.2 Evaluation Results

Table 2 shows the results of computing CriteriaReputationRating, $R_i$ and CriteriaWeight, $W_i$ for sellers. $R_i$ is calculated using DSR, these are the star ratings given by the users, without considering opinions expressed in the reviews. $W_i$ is computed using opinion expressions present in the reviews. $W_i$ is normalized to keep reputation score between 0 and 1. This is required for its comparison with *Pos (%)* to evaluate ranking among sellers. Our reputation system uses both the informations i.e., DSR star ratings as well as opinion expressions from the reviews and calculate *ReputationScore* (equation 1).

Table 3 shows seller 6, seller 7 and seller 8 have same value for *Pos (%)* which is $0.9592$ but each has different value for DSR. In this case, if *Pos (%)* is considered alone then these sellers (seller 6, seller 7 and seller 8) should be at the same rank, which is inaccurate as they have different DSR values. If only DSR value is considered for ranking then three sellers (seller 1, seller 4 and seller 6) should be at the same rank, as shown by underlined equal values (=

| Seller | Pos (%) | DSR | ReputationScore | Rank |
|---|---|---|---|---|
| 1 | 0.9362 | 4.5 | 0.7790 | 7 |
| 2 | 0.9310 | 4.6 | 0.8396 | 5 |
| 3 | 0.9857 | 4.9 | 0.7997 | 6 |
| 4 | 0.9048 | 4.5 | 0.9657 | 3 |
| 5 | 0.9405 | 4.4 | 0.7269 | 8 |
| 6 | 0.9592 | 4.5 | 0.9935 | 2 |
| 7 | 0.9592 | 4.7 | 0.9951 | 1 |
| 8 | 0.9592 | 4.3 | 0.8643 | 4 |

**Table 3:** Comparision between existing Reputation Score from `www.ebay.in` and computed Reputation Score by our system

4.5). Our reputation system rank them at different levels by considering their DSR values as well as opinions expressed in their reviews.

## 5 Conclusion

Reputation systems are commonly used in online transactions but they are suffering from "all good reputation" problem. The high reputation score of every seller makes it difficult for the buyers' to choose amongst them for the transaction. We have proposed a reputation system combining the concepts of Natural Language Processing, Opinion Mining and Summarisation Methods to compute reputation score and rank the sellers effectively. Our reputation score is the weighted summation of criteria based reputation ratings for each seller. This combines the knowledge out of user ratings given in the form of five-star ratings and the opinions expressed in the form of reviews. The effectiveness of the system is shown by the simulations conducted on eBay dataset. This is able to solve "all good reputation" problem.

# References


Akshat Bakliwal, Piyush Arora, and Vasudeva Varma. 2012. Hindi subjective lexicon: A lexical resource for hindi polarity classification. In *Proceedings of the Eight International Conference on Language Resources and Evaluation (LREC)*.

David M Blei, Andrew Y Ng, and Michael I Jordan. 2003. Latent dirichlet allocation. *the Journal of machine Learning research*, 3:993–1022.

Marie-Catherine De Marneffe and Christopher D Manning. 2008. The stanford typed dependencies representation. In *Coling 2008: Proceedings of the workshop on Cross-Framework and Cross-Domain Parser Evaluation*, pages 1–8. Association for Computational Linguistics.

Michael Gamon. 2004. Sentiment classification on customer feedback data: noisy data, large feature vectors, and the role of linguistic analysis. In *Proceedings of the 20th international conference on Computational Linguistics*, page 841. Association for Computational Linguistics.

Thomas L Griffiths and Mark Steyvers. 2004. Finding scientific topics. *Proceedings of the National Academy of Sciences*, 101(suppl 1):5228–5235.

Gregor Heinrich. 2008. Parameter estimation for text analysis. *University of Leipzig, Tech. Rep.*

Yoshinori Hijikata, Hanako Ohno, Yukitaka Kusumura, and Shogo Nishida. 2007. Social summarization of text feedback for online auctions and interactive presentation of the summary. *Knowledge-Based Systems*, 20(6):527–541.

Minqing Hu and Bing Liu. 2004. Mining and summarizing customer reviews. In *Proceedings of the tenth ACM SIGKDD international conference on Knowledge discovery and data mining*, pages 168–177. ACM.

V Jha, R Savitha, SS Hebbar, PD Shenoy, and KR Venugopal. 2015a. Hmdsad: Hindi multi-domain sentiment aware dictionary. In *Computing and Network Communications (CoCoNet), 2015 International Conference on*, pages 241–247. IEEE.

Vandana Jha, N Manjunath, P Deepa Shenoy, and KR Venugopal. 2015b. Hsas: Hindi subjectivity analysis system. In *2015 Annual IEEE India Conference (INDICON), (IEEE INDICON 2015)*, pages 312–317. IEEE.

Vandana Jha, N Manjunath, P Deepa Shenoy, KR Venugopal, and LM Patnaik. 2015c. Homs: Hindi opinion mining system. In *Recent Trends in Information Systems (ReTIS), 2015 IEEE 2nd International Conference on*, pages 366–371. IEEE.

Vandana Jha, N Manjunath, P Deepa Shenoy, and KR Venugopal. 2016. Hsra: Hindi stopword removal algorithm. In *2016 IEEE International Conference on Microelectronics, Computing and Communications (MicroCom 2016)*, National Institute of Technology Durgapur, India. IEEE.

Audun Jøsang, Roslan Ismail, and Colin Boyd. 2007. A survey of trust and reputation systems for online service provision. *Decision support systems*, 43(2):618–644.

Audun Jsang and Roslan Ismail. 2002. The beta reputation system. In *Proceedings of the 15th bled electronic commerce conference*, volume 5, pages 2502–2511.

Bing Liu. 2012. Sentiment analysis and opinion mining. *Synthesis Lectures on Human Language Technologies*, 5(1):1–167.

Yue Lu, ChengXiang Zhai, and Neel Sundaresan. 2009. Rated aspect summarization of short comments. In *Proceedings of the 18th international conference on World wide web*, pages 131–140. ACM.

Dipak Narayan, Debasri Chakrabarti, Prabhakar Pande, and Pushpak Bhattacharyya. 2002. An experience in building the indo wordnet-a wordnet for hindi. In *First International Conference on Global WordNet, Mysore, India*.

John O'Donovan, Barry Smyth, Vesile Evrim, and Dennis McLeod. 2007. Extracting and visualizing trust relationships from online auction feedback comments. In *IJCAI*, pages 2826–2831.

Bo Pang and Lillian Lee. 2008. Opinion mining and sentiment analysis. *Foundations and trends in information retrieval*, 2(1-2):1–135.

Guang Qiu, Bing Liu, Jiajun Bu, and Chun Chen. 2011. Opinion word expansion and target extraction through double propagation. *Computational linguistics*, 37(1):9–27.

Paul Resnick and Richard Zeckhauser. 2002. Trust among strangers in internet transactions: Empirical analysis of ebays reputation system. *The Economics of the Internet and E-commerce*, 11(2):23–25.

P Resnick, R Zeckhauser, E Friedman, and K Kuwabara. 2001. Reputation systems: Facilitating trust in internet interactions. working paper, mimeo.

Paul Resnick, Richard Zeckhauser, John Swanson, and Kate Lockwood. 2006. The value of reputation on ebay: A controlled experiment. *Experimental Economics*, 9(2):79–101.

Peter D Turney. 2002. Thumbs up or thumbs down? semantic orientation applied to unsupervised classification of reviews. In *Proceedings of the 40th annual meeting on association for computational linguistics*, pages 417–424. Association for Computational Linguistics.

Hongning Wang, Yue Lu, and Chengxiang Zhai. 2010. Latent aspect rating analysis on review text data: a rating regression approach. In *Proceedings of the 16th*

*ACM SIGKDD international conference on Knowledge discovery and data mining*, pages 783–792. ACM.

Hongning Wang, Yue Lu, and ChengXiang Zhai. 2011. Latent aspect rating analysis without aspect keyword supervision. In *Proceedings of the 17th ACM SIGKDD international conference on Knowledge discovery and data mining*, pages 618–626. ACM.

Xiaofeng Wang, Ling Liu, and Jinshu Su. 2012. Rlm: A general model for trust representation and aggregation. *Services Computing, IEEE Transactions on*, 5(1):131–143.

Li Zhuang, Feng Jing, and Xiao-Yan Zhu. 2006. Movie review mining and summarization. In *Proceedings of the 15th ACM international conference on Information and knowledge management*, pages 43–50. ACM.

# Improve Sentiment Analysis of Citations with Author Modelling

Zheng Ma[1], Jinseok Nam[1] and Karsten Weihe[2]

[1] *{ma,nam}@kdsl.informatik.tu-darmstadt.de*
[1]Information Center for Education, German Institute for Educational Research (DIPF)
Schloßstraße 29, 60486 Frankfurt, Germany

[2] *weihe@cs.tu-darmstadt.de*
[1,2] Computer Science Department, Technische Universität Darmstadt
Hochschulstrasse 10, 64283 Darmstadt, Germany

## Abstract

In this paper, we introduce a novel approach to sentiment polarity classification of citations, which integrates data about the authors' reputation. More specifically, our method extends the h-index with citation polarities and utilizes it in sentiment classification of citation sentences. Our computational results show that our method yields significant improvement in terms of classification performance.

## 1 Introduction

### 1.1 Background

Citation count between scientific publications have been the primary metric to measure importance and impact of articles or authors for decades. The advantage is simplicity and effectiveness. However, with the progress of machine learning, NLP and other disciplines, researchers developed various techniques to improve the quality of citation analysis and hence the quality of scholarly importance measurement. One of the efforts was to apply PageRank in citation network, which introduces weight on citation links for more accurate measurement (Ding, 2011). Although, this type of weighting is widely criticized (Alvarez and Soriano, 2014). Recent bibliometric studies showed that "there is no bad publicity in science", because criticized and controversial papers tend to be highly cited too (Radicch, 2012; Perc, 2014). Consequently, these controversial papers are positively estimated according to citation-count-based metrics, for example, impact factor and h-index. As Bonzi (1982) argued that if a cited work is criticized, it should consequently carry lower or even negative weight for bibliometric measures (Athar and Teufel, 2011).

### 1.2 Our contribution

Sentiment analysis of citation sentence makes this kind of fine-grained bibliometric measures possible. Augmented with polarized citation links, the citation network can be weighted more accurately by using negative weights. We introduce the p-index, which is the h-index extended by citation polarities.

Our assumption is that papers from prominent researchers are more probable to be cited in a positive manner than the papers from controversial researchers. Generally, if we know more about a researcher, it should be easier to determine the polarity of citations his/her paper receives. Our research question is whether or not the performance of citation sentiment analysis can be improved with better author modelling, in particular modeling with citation polarity.

In this paper, we report our on-going work on the citation sentiment analysis task. The rest of the paper is structured as follows: the next section briefly reviews some important work in this field. Then we introduce our method. In section 4, we present our experiment details. Preliminary experiment results and discussions about the results are structured in section 5 and 6. Finally, we summarize our work and discuss possible directions of future work.

## 2 Related Work

Teufel et al. (2006) was one of the pioneers in the field of citation classification. She proposed a classification scheme of 12 citation functions and used supervised technique for the classification task.



*Proceedings of NAACL-HLT 2016*, pages 122–127,
San Diego, California, June 12-17, 2016. ©2016 Association for Computational Linguistics

Athar (2011) continued this thread of research and focused in polarity classification of citations. They experimented the SVM classifier with rich features, such as negation, sentence splitting and dependency features. Athar (2012) published the Citation Sentiment Corpus, which contains 8736 annotated sentences.

Jochim (2012) used the following facet scheme to describe the nature of a citation: conceptual vs. operational; organic vs. perfunctory; evolutionary vs. juxtapositional; based on vs. alternative work; confirmative vs. negational.

Dong (2011) performed semi-supervised classification over categories: background, fundamental idea, technical basis and performance comparison. They have also developed the ACL Anthology Searchbench, which provides very practical paper search functionality with graphical presentation of local citation network of searched paper.[1]

Abu-jbara et al. (2013) has also contributed to this field by working on citation context identification, citation purpose classification and citation polarity identification. Their method achieved good performance by using SVM with linear kernel on a rich feature set.

## 3  Methodology

### 3.1  The Basis: The H-Index

There are several metrics to measure the impact of researchers. H-index (Hirsch, 2005) and g-index (Egghe, 2006) are two popular ones. These metrics and their variations are all based purely on citation counts. The h-index is defined as follows:

"A scientist has index h if h of his or her Np papers have at least h citations each and the other (Np − h) papers have ≤ h citations each." (Hirsch, 2005)

Mathematically, it can be represented as formula (1):

$$h\_index(f) = \max_{i} \min(f(i), i) \qquad (1)$$

where f is the function that corresponds to the number of citations for each publication, sorted in descending order.[2]

Obviously, h-index finds a balance point between publication amount and the citation count of each

publication. It is however not able to model the different polarities of citations.

### 3.2  Our Extension: The P-Index

In order to embed the polarity information in author modelling, we introduce the p-index, where p stands for polarity:

$$p\_index(f) = h\_index(f) \cdot p^{\alpha} \cdot n^{\beta} \qquad (2)$$

where p is the amount of positive citations the author receives. and n is the amount of negative citations, with positive citation coefficient $\alpha$ and negative citation coefficient $\beta$. Since P-index is an indicator positively correlated with an author's academic performance and reputation, higher value corresponds to better performance and reputation. Thus, $\alpha$ as an exponential coefficient is defined to be greater than 1. Similarly, the negative citation exponential is defined in the range: $0 < \beta < 1$.

The polarity of citation reflects the opinion of peers. The controversial authors that receive a lot of negative citations can be distinguished with the p-index. Thus the p-index combines scholar's performance information measured by h-index and the reputation information measured by citation polarity distribution. In general, the author is better modeled with p-index.

## 4  Experiment

### 4.1  Corpus

In the experiments, we used the Citation Sentiment Corpus (Athar, 2012) with ACL Anthology Network (Abu-jbara et al., 2013). ACL Anthology Network (AAN) is a widely used corpus containing computational linguistic publications. It contains more than 21,212 papers, 17,792 authors and 110,975 citation links. The Citation Sentiment Corpus contains 8,736 citation sentences extracted from AAN. Theses citation sentences are manually annotated into three classes: positive, negative, objective (neutral).

### 4.2  Preprocessing

Basically, we only performed two preprocessing steps, which we call text cleaning and citation mention replacement. In the text cleaning step, we solely removed erroneous characters and corrected the

---

[1] http://aclasb.dfki.de/

[2] https://en.wikipedia.org/wiki/H-index

spacing. In the citation mention replacement step, we use regular expressions to replace the target citation mention in the sentence with the label "TARGETREF", and other citation mentions with the label "REF", as shown in the following example:

```
Original:
A94-1008       A92-1018      o      "The two systems we use are ENGCG
(Karlsson et al. , 1994) and the Xerox Tagger (Cutting et al. , 1992)."

Replaced:
A94-1008       A92-1018      o      "The two systems we use are ENGCG
REF and the Xerox Tagger TARGETREF."
```

*Figure 1 An Example of Citation Mention Replacement*[3]

This way, the machine learning algorithm will be able to identify the position of the target reference and learn the semantic pattern between the target reference and the other tokens of the sentence. However, a few citation mentions cannot be automatically recognized. In our experiment, we ignore those citation sentences, in which the citation mentions cannot be replaced by TARGETREF or REF.

In order to exclude possible bias, we randomized the ordering of the data instances in the Citation Sentiment Corpus.

## 4.3   Features

In our experiments, each citation sentence is taken as one data instance, along with a set of features. We used the following feature set:

- Tf-IDF weighted unigram: straightforward feature for text classification tasks
- Polarity distribution of the target paper: the numbers of positive, negative and objective citations that the target paper receives. This is a kind of polarity modelling on paper level.
- Author ID: the author ID of the target paper as provided in AAN. We use the string form of author ID
- Affiliation ID: the author's affiliation ID of the target paper, also string form. To the best of our knowledge, our approach is the first attempt to utilize affiliation information in a citation sentiment analysis task.
- H-index/ P-index: the author's h-index or p-index of the target paper. The original h-index is provided in AAN and used by us as a

baseline. P-index is calculated from h-index using formula (2) and we use it to improve the performance of citation sentiment classification.

## 4.4   Experimental Setup

In our experimental implementation, we used the Python module SciKit-Learn[4] for machine learning, feature extraction and evaluation. Support Vector Machine (SVM) is chosen as the classification algorithm. SVM is a widely used algorithm for text classification (Athar, 2012 and Abu-jbara, 2013).

Since our main contribution is improving classification performance using p-index, we mainly focus on the effects caused by replacing the h-index by the p-index. The SVM hyper-parameter is one of the settings that stay identical in all experiments. Therefore, in our on-going work, we have not broadly explored the parameter grid of penalty parameter C and kernel coefficient $\gamma$, which are the main parameters of SVM with Radial Basis Function (RBF) kernel (Hsu et al., 2006).

In order to answer our research question in section 1, we performed the experiment in a comparative manner. Firstly, we partition the corpus into 10 subsets and prepare 10 pairs of train and test sets. Then, for each pair, we perform the following procedure:

1. Run the classifier with h-index to obtain the baseline performance, denoted by $F1_b$ in the following.

2. Calculate the p-indices of authors as defined in Formula (2).

3. Update data instances of both train and test set: replace h-index value with p-index

4. Run the classifier on the new train and test set. It yields the test result $F1_t$.

5. Calculate the relative improvement from baseline to test result as:

$$\delta = \frac{F1_t - F1_b}{F1_b} \tag{3}$$

---

[3] In this instance, "A94-1008" is the AAN paper ID of the citing paper and "A92-1018" is the ID of the cited paper.

"O" is the sentiment annotation, meaning "objective" (neutral).
[4] http://www.scikit-learn.org

This procedure is applied to all the train and test set pairs. Next we calculate the average of all of these relative improvement. This is the final result of one experiment; it measures the effectiveness of our method under one specific setting.

Since the p-index depends on the positive and negative citation coefficients, $\alpha$ and $\beta$, the final relative improvement depends significantly on the choice of $\alpha$ and $\beta$. Systematic results are presented in the following section.

## 5 Result

### 5.1 Evaluation metric

In the field of text classification, Macro-F1 is widely used to evaluate the performance. It is especially suitable for our work, because the Citation Sentiment Corpus is highly imbalanced.

We did not compare our results with others. As a consequence of different data preparation, algorithm setting and many other detailed factors, it is nontrivial to reproduce the results reported in other work.

Moreover, in principle, our work is to examine the effectiveness of a novel feature on author level, which is independent to the utilization of other features on sentence level, etc. (Athar, 2011 and Abujbara et al., 2013).

### 5.2 Search the Setting Space

We performed numerous experiments with various settings. The dimensions of setting space are:

- Whether to enable feature: polarity distribution of the target paper
- Whether to enable feature: affiliation ID
- Whether to enable feature: author ID
- Positive citation coefficient $\alpha$. We have sparsely explored the range of $1 < \alpha < 100$.
- Negative citation coefficient $\beta$. It has a relatively narrower definition range, $0 < \beta < 1$, which allows us to search more thoroughly.

It is a considerably large setting space to explore. We treated the first 3 dimensions as a group and the

| Pol P | Af. ID | Au. ID | Imprv. |
|---|---|---|---|
| - | - | - | 9.3% |
| Enabled | - | - | 2.6% |
| - | Enabled | - | 6.2% |
| - | - | Enabled | 9.6% |
| Enabled | Enabled | - | 6.2% |
| Enabled | - | Enabled | 9.6% |
| - | Enabled | Enabled | 11.2% |
| Enabled | Enabled | Enabled | 11.2% |

**Table 1:** Relative Improvements under different settings

last 2 dimensions as another. In this way, we reduced the dimensionality of the setting space and made the exploration more practical.

Initially, we fixed the first setting group and search for the best values of the second setting group. After a coarse search, we found that the best settings of exponential coefficients are around the point ( $\alpha = 1.1, \beta = 0.7$ ). Then a more intense search is performed in a small space surrounding this point. The best result achieved so far is at ($\alpha = 1.085, \beta = 0.727$).

Subsequently, we fixed $\alpha$ and $\beta$ at these values and test the 8 possible combinations of the 3 boolean settings in the first group. The best results are obtained with both affiliation ID and author ID features enabled.

Thus we have spotted one local maxima in the settings space: {Polarity of Paper Feature: Disabled; Affiliation ID Feature: Enabled; Author ID Feature: Enabled; $\alpha = 1.085$; $\beta = 0.727$}. This produces the most significant result so far: 11.2% relative improvement of Macro-F1 in the citation sentiment classification over the baseline: avg. Macro-F1=0.535. The baseline is obtained with the same system using h-index instead of the p-index.

### 5.3 Observation

Table 1 illustrates the relative improvement achieved under different feature selections. Each row represents an experiment. The first three columns indicate which features are enabled in an experiment and the last column reveals the relative improvement under this setting.

The first observation is that the polarity distribution of a paper (first column in the table) is not a helpful feature. When combined with other features, it hardly contributes to the system. When used alone, it decreases the performance.

In comparison, the affiliation ID is a better feature. Although it also causes some performance decline when used alone. But when combined with author ID, it makes positive contribution.

The best feature among these three is the author ID. The presence of author ID always boosts the performance of the system.

It is also worth mentioning that under this pair of exponential coefficients, all these possible feature selections deliver positive improvements.

## 5.4 Negative results

In the preceding sub section, we have reported the results from successful experiments. We have certainly tried other settings too, which are not as fruitful as the ones above.

Before we improved the sentiment classification by modelling the authors, we initially tried to improve it by modeling the papers. We applied python-igraph[5] implementation of the PageRank algorithm (Page et al., 1999) on the paper citation network. We used the PageRank value as a feature to model the target paper. However, in our experiments, this feature barely improved classification.

As for the p-index, we also tried different definitions. Instead of the exponential calculation, we tried linear and logarithm calculations too. The exponential version is proved to be the best.

Another variation of the p-index was to use $\log(p - index)$ in the place of p-index. Because when an author has a high positive citation count with relatively low negative citation count, her/his p-index will be considerably high. We presumed that suppressing it might be beneficial. However, experiment results support the p-index without logarithm.

Besides, we also tried out different settings of the machine learning classifier. We briefly tested SVM with linear kernel. Unlike reported by other work (Athar, 2011 and Abu-jbara et al., 2013), SVM with linear kernel performs worse than with RBF kernel in our experiments.

## 6 Discussion

As described in section 5, we answered our research question by comparing the Macro-F1 score between the baseline algorithm with h-index and the test algorithm with p-index. Significant improvement of classification performance verifies that the performance of citation sentiment analysis can be improved with better author modelling, in particular modeling with citation polarity.

Moreover, both good features observed in section 5.3 are the ones that describe some aspect of the author – namely, the affiliation of author or merely the ID of author. This straightforwardly supports our hypothesis that the better modeling of author is advantageous in citation sentiment analysis.

On the other hand, the feature "polarity distribution of paper" also models reputation, but on the paper level, which makes it useless for classification.

In the experiments, SVM with RBF kernel works better than SVM with linear kernel. The reason could be that the new features we introduced in this work needs non-linear separation in the hyper space. Another possible reason is that our parameter search is not adequately complete.

## 7 Conclusion and Future work

In this work, we answered our research question that polarity modeling of author significantly improves the citation sentiment analysis performance.

We believe that this approach can also contribute to sentiment analysis on social media or other domains. Generally, if the author's reputation can be modeled using polarized links, the sentiment analysis should benefit from utilizing this model.

For example, if some online forum facilitates rating functions, e.g. "thumb-up" and "thumb-down" button, its users' reputation can be modeled with polarity distribution. This model could assist the sentiment analysis of replies on the forum. Under the assumption that respected forum users are more likely to be replied in a positive sense.

With the current result as a proof of concept, we plan to further test our method by modeling the author with other methods, like PageRank on author citation network (Ding, 2011). We will also consider utilizing some popular semantic features to make our result more comparable to other systems.

## Acknowledgments

This work has been supported by the German Institute for Educational Research (DIPF) as part of the

---

[5] http://igraph.org/python

graduate program "Knowledge Discovery in Scientific Literature (KDSL).

## References


Amjad Abu-jbara, Jefferson Ezra. 2013 and Dragomir Radev. Purpose and polarity of citation: Towards NLP-based bibliometrics. In *Proceedings of NAACL-HLT*, pages 596–606.

Myriam H. Alvarez. and Jose M. Soriano. 2014. Sentiment,Polarity and Function Analysis in Bibiometrics: A Review, In *Proceedings of the First Workshop on Argumentation Mining, pages 102-3*, ACL

Awais Athar. 2011. Sentiment analysis of citations using sentence structure-based features. In *Proceedings of the ACL 2011 student session*. Pages 81-87. ACL.

Awais Athar and Simone Teufel. 2012. Context-enhanced citation sentiment detection. In *Proceedings of the 2012 Conference of the North American Chapter of the Association for Computational Linguistics: Human Language Technologies*. Pages 597-601. ACL.

Susan Bonzi. 1982. Characteristics of a literature as predictors of relatedness between cited and citing works. *Journal of the American Society for Information Science,* 33(4):208–216.

Ying Ding. 2011. Applying weighted PageRank to author citation networks. *Journal of the American Society for Information Science and Technology* 62.2 (2011): 236-245.

Cailing Dong, and Ulrich Schäfer. 2011. Ensemble-style Self-training on Citation Classification. *IJCNLP*. Page 623-631.

Leo Egghe. 2006 "Theory and practise of the g-index." *Scientometrics* 69.1 (2006): 131-152.

Jorge E. Hirsch. 2005. An index to quantify an individual's scientific research output. In *Proceedings of the National academy of Sciences of the United States of America, 102*(46), 16569-16572.

Chih-Wei Hsu, Chih-Chung Chang, and Chih-Jen Lin. 2003. A practical guide to support vector classification. Technical Report, National Taiwan University.

Charles Jochim and Hinrich Schütze. 2012. Towards a generic and flexible citation classifier based on a faceted classification scheme. In *Proceedings of the 2012 International Conference on Computational Linguistics*, pages 1343–1358

Lawrence Page, Sergey Brin, Rajeev Motwani & Terry Winograd. 1999. The PageRank citation ranking: bringing order to the web. Technical Report, Stanford University.

Matjaz Perc. 2014.. The Matthew effect in empirical data. *Journal of The Royal Society Interface,* 11(98):20140378.

Filippo Radicchi. 2012. In science "there is no bad publicity": Papers criticized in comments have high scientific impact. *Scientific Reports 2*

Simone Teufel, Advaith Siddharthan, and Dan Tidhar. 2006. Automatic classification of citation function. In *Proceedings of the 2006 conference on empirical methods in natural language processing*. ACL.

# Implicit Aspect Detection in Restaurant Reviews

R. Panchendrarajan, M. N. Nazick Ahamed, B. Murugaiah, S. Prakhash,
S. Ranathunga, A. Pemasiri
Department of Computer Science and Engineering
University of Moratuwa
Katubedda 10400, Sri Lanka

## Abstract

For aspect-level sentiment analysis, the important first step is to identify the aspects and their associated entities present in customer reviews. Aspects can be either explicit or implicit, where the identification of the latter is more difficult. For restaurant reviews, this difficulty is escalated due to the vast number of entities and aspects present in reviews. The problem of implicit aspect identification has been studied for customer reviews in different domains, including restaurant reviews. However, the existing work for implicit aspect identification in customer reviews has the limitation of choosing at most one implicit aspect for each sentence. Furthermore, they deal only with a limited set of aspects related to a particular domain, thus have not faced the problem of ambiguity that arises when an opinion word is used to describe different aspects. This paper presents a novel approach for implicit aspect detection, which overcomes these two limitations. Our approach yields an F1-measure of 0.842 when applied for a set of restaurant reviews collected from Yelp.

## 1 Introduction

Entities in a restaurant refer to products (e.g. food), services, individuals, events etc., and the aspects are the attributes or components of these entities (Zhang and Liu, 2014). For example, *smell* is an aspect of the food entity. As the customers go to restaurants for various purposes, rating values for individual aspects related to a restaurant are important as well as the overall rating value of the restaurant. For example, if someone is trying to select a restaurant to have a party, she will be interested in the rating value of parking facilities.

To determine the opinion on an aspect expressed in reviews, aspect-level sentiment analysis (or opinion mining) should be carried out. This consists of two core parts: detecting aspects and classifying sentiment score for each aspect (Schouten et al., 2015). Sentiment score is calculated using the positive or negative sentiments indicated by opinion words such as good, excellent, poor, and bad. Opinions are associated with opinion targets, which are entities on which opinions are expressed (Qiu et al., 2011). For example, in the sentence "Staff was very kind", the *staff* entity is the target of the opinion *kind*.

Rating value for an aspect is obtained by aggregating all the sentiment scores assigned for that aspect across the reviews. However, restaurant domain deals with a vast number of aspects such as food, individual food item, drink, appetizer, furniture, staffs, different places or areas, and offers, which are interrelated. When the relationships are modeled, one entity becomes the aspect of another. For example, entities food items, drinks, desserts and appetizers come under the category of food entity as its sub-aspects and each of those aspect has sub-aspects such as taste, quality, and price. Therefore the rating value of an aspect has a significant



*Proceedings of NAACL-HLT 2016*, pages 128–136,
San Diego, California, June 12-17, 2016. ©2016 Association for Computational Linguistics

impact on the rating value of its parent aspect(s). This behavior of different aspects can be modeled as hierarchical relationships so that the rating value of an aspect can be calculated as a composite score of its sub-aspects.

Aspects can be explicit or implicit. When aspects are mentioned literally in a text, they are called explicit aspects, whereas implicit aspects are only implied by the sentence but not literally mentioned (Schouten et al., 2015). For example consider the sentences, "Taste of food in that restaurant is great" and "Food is delicious in that restaurant". In the first sentence, aspect *taste* of food entity is explicitly mentioned and in the second one we can infer that it refers to the aspect *taste* of food entity, even though it is not explicitly mentioned. In the data set we considered, an average of 15.6% of the sentences contains one or more implicit aspects.

When compared with explicit aspect identification, identifying implicit aspects is much difficult. The problems escalate with the possibility to associate an aspect with multiple entities. For example, in the sentences "Pizza is very small" and "Pizza size is very small", aspect *size* is associated with the entity food item. In the sentences "Restaurant is small" and "Restaurant size is small", same aspect *size* is associated with the entity *Restaurant*. Similarly, the opinion word *small* that gets attached to the aspect *size* refers to size of pizza in the first two sentences, and to size of restaurant in the second two sentences, thus leading to ambiguity. This problem escalates when we deal with a large number of aspects

There can even be aspects that do not have a direct attachment to any entity. For example, in the sentences "I would recommend this restaurant" and "I will definitely be back", the overall experience of the customer is the aspect, however this aspect does not have any directly associated entity.

Customers also have a tendency to mention multiple aspects in a single sentence. For example, consider the sentences, "Even though food is expensive it was delicious" and "Food was delicious in that small restaurant". In the first sentence, two different aspects - *price* and *taste* of food are mentioned implicitly. The second one mentions two different aspects belonging to two different entities.

Implicit aspect identification is not a problem specific to restaurant reviews. Previous research has explored solutions for the same, for domains such as mobile phone reviews (Hai et al, 2011; Wang et al., 2013; Zhang and Zhu, 2013; Schouten et al., 2014, Schouten et al. 2015), restaurant reviews (Schouten et al., 2014, Schouten et al. 2015) and clothing reviews (Zhang and Zhu, 2013). However, none of this research is capable of identifying multiple implicit aspects appearing in a sentence. Moreover, they have dealt with only a limited number of high-level aspects, disregarding the hierarchical relationships they may have with other aspects.

This paper presents a method to detect implicit aspects mentioned in restaurant reviews. It is capable of identifying multiple implicit aspects appearing in a sentence. In our approach, each opinion word is considered as implying an implicit aspect. Using a model trained using manually tagged data, a list of aspects that can be implied by each of these opinions are identified. These aspects are given a score using the co-occurrence between opinion word and other words in the sentence. This is achieved by extending the work of Schouten et al. (2014) that identifies at most one implicit aspect in a given sentence. Aspect with the highest score is chosen as the potential candidate aspect. Opinion targets and opinions are extracted and checked whether they have any relationship with (parent or sibling) the predicted aspect.

In order to identify the relationships, different entities with different aspects are modeled as a hierarchy. Such a comprehensive model cannot be found in related literature for the restaurant domain. This hierarchy enables to verify whether the predicted implicit aspect is correct or not by utilizing two different relationships between aspects: aspect-parent and aspect-sibling. Such a verification technique cannot be found in the existing literature.

The rest of the paper is organized as follows. Section 2 discusses previous research related to implicit aspect identification, and Section 3 discusses our approach for the same. Section 4 presents the model we developed to capture the hierarchical relationships between aspects in the restaurant domain. Section 5 evaluates our system, and section 6 concludes the paper.

## 2 Related Work

As mentioned earlier, implicit aspect identification has been explored in the context of customer reviews for different domains. To identify implicit aspects, most of the previous research uses association between aspects and opinion words occurring in a sentence, where the aspect is implied by the opinion word.

Hu and Liu (2005) have used association rules and generate patterns to identify both explicit and implicit aspects. Popescu and Etzioni (2005) suggest an approach using Point wise Mutual Information (PMI) based semantic association analysis. No quantitative experimental results have been reported in this work. Su et al. (2008) propose a similar approach that clusters aspects as well as the opinions to generate association rules that map a set of aspects to opinions. However, this approach considers only adjectives as opinion words and no quantitative results are given.

Hai et al. (2011) propose a two-phase approach based on co-occurrence association rule mining (coAR) and the experiment was carried out for a set of Chinese mobile phone reviews. Main deficiency in their work is, they use only the co-occurrence of opinion words to identify an implicit aspect. A hybrid association rule mining technique proposed by Wang et al. (2013) overcomes this issue, by extracting indicators for aspects. They experimented on a Chinese data set of mobile phone reviews. These indicators are both opinion words and other words. Zhang and Zhu (2013) overcome the same issue by making use of the associations between an aspect and the rest of the notional words in the clause. A corpus of mobile phone reviews in Chinese and a collection of clothes reviews in Chinese were used in the research.

All these approaches have a drawback of identifying an implicit aspect only if it is available explicitly in the training data set. Schouten et al. (2014) overcome this issue by utilizing the co-occurrence between notional words and either the explicit or implicit aspect so that an implicit aspect can be identified even if it does not appear explicitly. The authors later extended this work by employing word sense disambiguation and utilizing the semantic relations between words (Schouten et al., 2015). Restaurant reviews and product reviews were used for the experiment purposes in both

studies. However, both these works are only capable of choosing at most one implicit aspect for each sentence. Furthermore they identify implicit aspects only of five categories, food, service, ambience, price, and anecdotes/miscellaneous. They do not consider different types of entities with different aspects, and their relationships.

In summary, none of this previous work is capable of identifying multiple implicit aspects occurring in a sentence. Moreover, they deal with only a limited number of aspects of the respective domain, and ignore the relationships between aspects at different levels. Thus they have not faced the problem of ambiguity when predicting an implicit aspect, in cases where the same opinion can be associated with different aspects.

## 3 Implicit Aspect Identification

This section presents our implicit aspect identification method that overcomes the following limitations discussed in section 2.

- Finding implicit aspects only of a set of limited categories in restaurant domain, thus ignoring the ambiguity in attaching opinions to aspects
- Finding only one implicit aspect in a sentence

Two models are created to identify implicit and explicit aspects separately. Both use a training data set with explicit and implicit aspects manually labeled. First model uses maximum entropy classification technique to identify explicit aspects. Second model identifies opinion words in a sentence and predicts the implicit aspect implied by that opinion word using the co-occurrence of words. Accuracy of the identified implicit aspect prediction is checked using a set of rules and the hierarchical relationships among aspects.

### 3.1 Training Data Set

In the data set, aspects (both explicit and implicit) and entities are manually labeled. For example, in the sentence "Pizza was small in that big restaurant", *pizza* and *restaurant* are identified as entities or explicit aspects and are labeled as *Food item* and *Restaurant*, respectively. *small* and *big* are opinion words that identify implicit aspects. Therefore the opinion words are labeled with the implicit aspect they indicate. For example, in the above sentence *small* and *big* are labeled as *Food_item_size* and *Environment_size*, respectively.

## 3.2 Training Phase

In the training phase, two models are separately trained to identify explicit aspects and implicit aspects. For explicit aspect identification, a standard maximum entropy classifier (Opennlp.apache.org, 2016) is used to create the model M1 using our annotated corpus. N-grams are used as features where n varies from 2 to 5.

In order to train the next model M2, training data set is scanned and a list of opinion words O is created by identifying the opinion words labeled as implicit aspects. In the second iteration of scanning, only the sentences with implicit aspects are extracted. Words labeled as explicit aspects in those extracted sentences are replaced with their explicit aspect label or entity label. For example, the sentence "Pizza was small in that big restaurant" is modified as "Food_item was small in that big restaurant". Modified sentences are stored under each identified opinion word along with their label. For example, the modified sentence "Food item was small in that big Restaurant" is stored under both opinion words *small* and *big* with the candidate aspect labels *Food_item_size* and *Environment_size*, respectively. All the possible aspects that can be implied by an opinion word are now available in the model as aspect-sentence pairs. For example, consider another sentence "Restaurant is not suitable for parties as it is very small". Here "Restaurant" and "it" are replaced by the explicit aspect tag *Restaurant*. This sentence is stored in the model under the opinion word *small* along with the candidate aspect label *Environment_size*. Finally model appears as follows for these two sentences:

**small**

*Food item_size* – Food_item was small in that big Restaurant

*Environment_size*- Restaurant is not suitable for parties as Restaurant is very small

## 3.3 Testing Phase

When a new restaurant review is given, explicit aspects and entities are identified using the trained model M1. Same as the training phase, words identified as entities or explicit aspects in the test data are replaced with their predicted explicit aspect or entity label. Modified test data are processed word by word within a sentence for opinion words available in the list O. For each identified opinion word in a sentence, the list of candidate aspects A is extracted using the model M2. With the list of candidate aspects, identifying the winning implicit aspect is a two-step process as described below.

### 3.3.1 Step 1

As the first step, one implicit aspect from the list of candidate aspects is chosen as the potential candidate aspect using the co-occurrence between the opinion word and other words in the sentence. If there is only one candidate aspect, it is chosen as the potential candidate. Otherwise, for each candidate aspect Ai, a score is computed using equation (1). This equation is a modified version of the equation used by Schouten et al. (2014). The limitation of Schouten et al.'s equation is, it does not consider the distance between an opinion word and other words in the sentence while calculating the co-occurrence of words to obtain the score. In our modified equation, we add a weight when calculating the sum of co-occurrence frequency of words. Distance between the opinion word and other words in the sentence are used as the weight, thus removing the impact of faraway words on the sum of co-occurrence. Co-occurrence frequency between opinion word and other words in the sentence is calculated using the sentences attached to the opinion words in model M2 for a particular candidate aspect.

$$\text{Score } A_i = 1/n \sum C_{ij}/f_j * 1/d_j \qquad (1)$$

In equation (1), n is the number of words in the given sentence, $A_i$ is the $i^{th}$ candidate aspect in A for which the score is computed, j represents $j^{th}$ word in the sentence, $C_{ij}$ is the co-occurrence frequency of aspect $A_i$ and $i^{th}$ word, $f_i$ is the frequency of the $i^{th}$ word and $d_j$ is the distance between the $j^{th}$ word and the opinion word. $1/d_j$ operates as weight.

Co-occurrence of stop words is not considered to get the sum. Highest scoring aspect that exceeds the threshold becomes the potential aspect for the next step. If the highest score is lower than the threshold, identified opinion word is discarded. Optimal threshold is identified based on the training data using a simple linear search. Threshold is

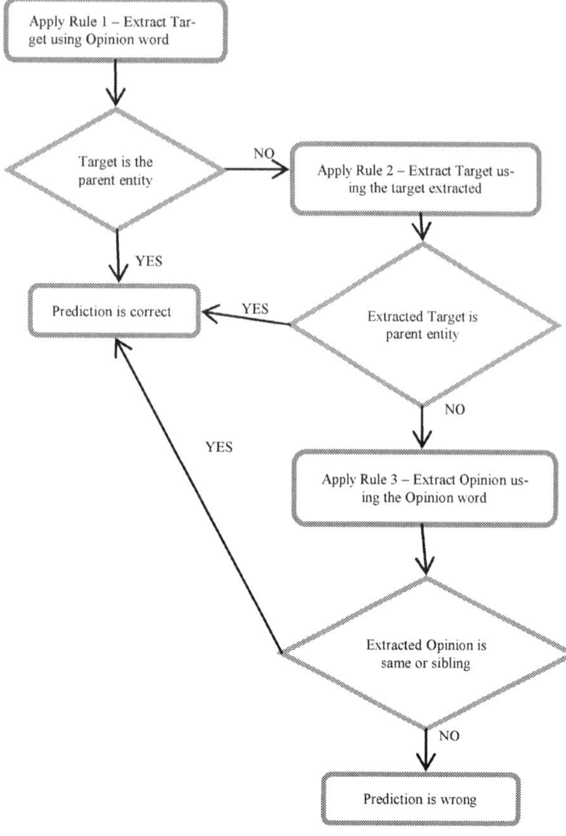

**Figure 1**:Flow of Step 2

increased from 0 by a step size of 0.01 until the optimum value for F1-measure is obtained.

However, evaluations (Table 1 – row 3) showed that step 1 is not sufficient to identify and discard wrong predictions for the aspect implied by an opinion word. For example, consider the sentence, "We came as a small group for the dinner". Here, opinion word *small* describes the size of the group. However while processing this sentence, *small* is identified as an opinion word available in O. Suppose either *Food_item_size* or *Environment_size* is chosen as the winning candidate entity. If the process stops at that point, *small* will be identified as either *Food_item_size* or *Environment_size*.

### 3.3.2 Step 2

In this step we validate the predicted implicit aspect implied by an opinion word. Step 2 works as the flow shown in Figure 1. Once the potential candidate aspect is chosen, next step is to extract its opinion target to check whether the prediction is correct or not. If the opinion target is the parent of the potential candidate, it is chosen as the winning candidate. Otherwise the potential candidate aspect is discarded. Opinion targets are extracted using the double propagation approach proposed by Qui et al (2011), which propagates information back and forth between opinion words and targets using grammar rules.

These grammar rules are based on the dependency relations between words. The dependency relations describe relations between opinion words and targets. We used the dependency relations mod, pnmod, subj, s, obj, obj2 and desc as defined by Qiu et al. (2011). Following are the rules we used:

**Rule 1** - Using the given opinion word, target is extracted using grammar rules. Example: In the sentence "staff were very kind", staff is identified as the target using the rule *kind -> mod -> Staff.*

**Rule 2**–Target extracted using Rule 1 is used to extract further targets in the sentence using grammar rules. Example: In the sentence "food and desserts are tasty in that restaurant", when the opinion word *tasty* is processed, dessert is identified as its target in the previous step. However, it is not the parent of *Food_item_Taste*. Therefore the flow moves to Rule 2 and *Food* is identified as target using the rule *Dessert ->conj ->Food*. Since *Food* is the grand parent of *Food_item_Taste* it is chosen as the winning candidate aspect.

**Rule 3** - Using the identified sibling or the same type of implicit aspects, opinion words are identified using grammar rules. Example: In the sentence "Staff was kind and available", *kind* is identified as *Staff_behaviour*. When *available* is processed, *kind* is identified as an opinion word using the rule *kind ->conj -> available*. Since both *Staff_behaviour* and *Staff_availability* are siblings in the hierarchy of aspects, *Staff_availability* is chosen as the winning aspect for the opinion word available.

Rules are applied one after other and checked whether the prediction is correct or not. If the prediction fails in all three rules aspect is discarded. In order to record these hierarchical relationships between aspects, we developed a comprehensive model for the restaurant domain, as described in Section 4.

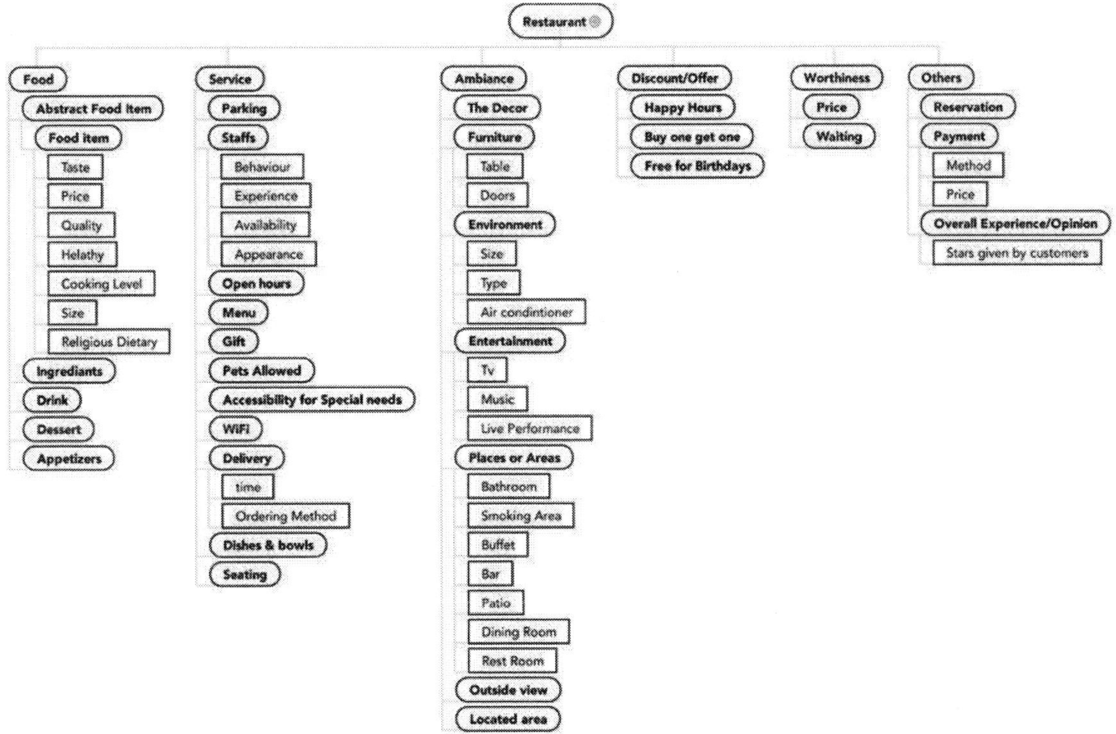

Figure 2: Hierarchy of Aspects

We also tried out two modifications for the above approach that we implemented: (1) implement Step 1 only where the chosen potential candidate aspect is considered as the winning aspect (i.e. do not execute step 2). (2) Consider the occurrence of stop words while calculating the weighted sum of co-occurrence.

## 4    Modeling the Hierarchy of Aspects

Restaurant industry deals with a vast number of entities such as food items, drinks, furniture, staff, offers, etc. which are interrelated to each other.

Figure 2 shows the model we developed to represent the hierarchical relationships between different entities and aspects. This model was manually developed using a random sample of 400 reviews and was validated and refined using another set of 400 reviews collected from Yelp (2016).

Model consists of aspects up to four levels. Level 1 one is restaurant and it has six sub main sub aspects as food, service, ambience, offers, worthiness and other aspects. Each sub aspect is further categorized. For example, aspect *Service* has *Staff* as its one of the sub aspects which has four sub aspects, *Behavior, Experience, Appearance and Availability*.

As discussed in section 3, identifying the relationship between various aspects enable to check whether the predicted implicit aspect is correct or not. For example consider the two sentences, "Food item was very expensive" and "Food was really delicious". In both sentences, aspects *Food_item_Price* and *Food_item_Taste* will be identified as implicit aspects, respectively. In order to check whether the prediction is correct or not, the opinion targets are extracted. In the above example, the opinion targets of *expensive* and *delicious* are *Food_item* and *Food* respectively. Since those are the parent and grandparent of the aspects *Food_item_Price* and *Food_item_Taste* respectively, *Food_item_Price* is chosen as the winning aspectfor the opinion word *expensive,* and *Food_item_Taste*is chosen as the winning aspect for the opinion word*delicious.*

Now consider the earlier discussed example, "I am a big fan of that restaurant". Here, "I" is identified as the opinion target of the opinion word *big* with the prediction of either *Food item_Size* or *Environment_Size*as higher scoring one will be cho-

133

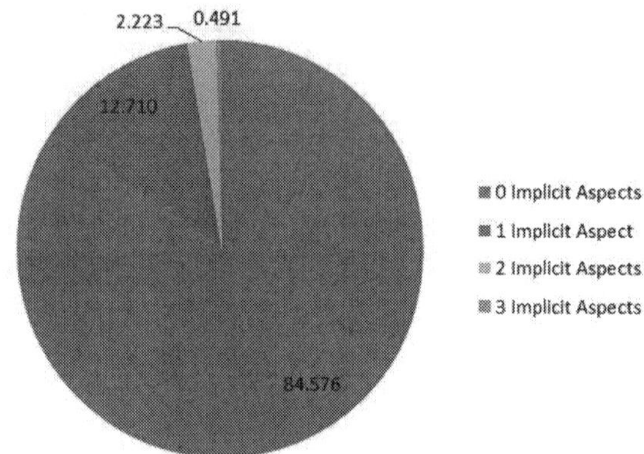

**Figure 3:** Average distribution of sentences in the restaurant review data set, according to the number of implicit features they contain in 1000 reviews.

sen as the potential candidate aspect. However, this prediction will be discarded as the opinion target is not even an entity in the model.

## 5 Data Set and Initial Analysis

1000 restaurant reviews collected from Yelp (2016) are used as the training data set. Both explicit and implicit aspects were labeled manually in this data set. Even though the restaurant domain deals with a vast amount of entities with various aspects, not all the sentences in restaurant reviews contain implicit aspects. As shown in Figure 3, 15.6% of the sentences contain one or more implicit aspects in 1000 restaurant reviews.

However it is essential to identify that small fraction of sentences and all the aspects mentioned implicitly in those sentences since important aspects are most likely to be used in the sentence implicitly. For example, more than 92% of aspects of staff entity appear implicitly in restaurant reviews, as it can be seen in Figure 4.

Figure 5 shows the distribution of Level 2 aspects (food, service, ambience, offers, worthiness and others) by considering all the aspects as sub aspects of level 2 aspects. Distribution of an aspect was obtained by calculating the frequency of occurrence of an aspect and its sub aspects in the training data set.

## 6 Evaluation

Evaluations are performed using 10-fold-cross validation with a training data set of 1000 reviews.

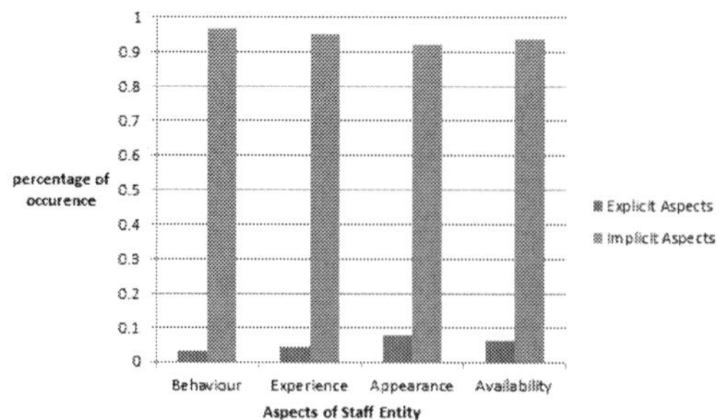

**Figure 4:** Percentage of aspects of Staff entity appearing explicitly or implicitly in 1000 reviews

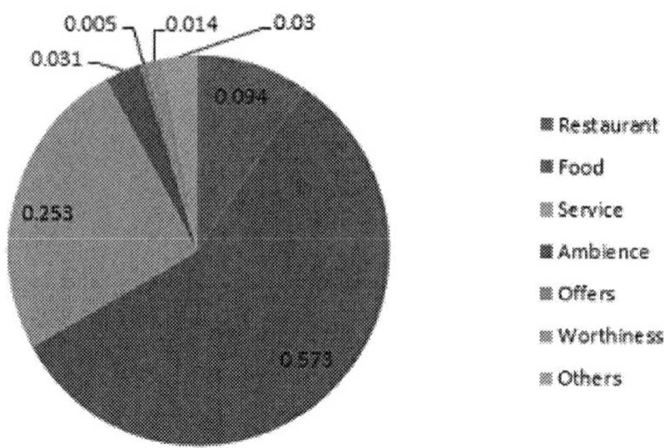

**Figure 5:** Distribution of level 2 aspects and restaurant in the training data set

For each instance of the algorithm, 900 reviews are used as the training set and the remaining 100 reviews are used for testing.

Table 1 shows the evaluation results of 10-fold-cross validation for the several methods. Methods 1 to 4 assume that the model M1 can identify explicit aspects and entities with an accuracy of 100%. Method 5 shows the results for our approach by using the trained model M1.

The accuracy of the M1 model was tested using an additional tagged set of 400 reviews. Model M1 identified explicit aspects with an F1-Measure of 0.88 (Precision – 0.931, Recall, 0.835).

| Method | Precision | Recall | F1-Measure |
|---|---|---|---|
| 1. Initially given solution | **0.947** | **0.758** | **0.842** |
| 2.Using the approach suggested by Schouten et al. [6] | 0.495 | 0.929 | 0.645 |
| 3. Modification 1 | 0.916 | 0.752 | 0.826 |
| 4. Modification 2 | 0.931 | 0.754 | 0.834 |

| 5. Initially given solution with the trained model M1 | 0.886 | 0.694 | 0.779 |
|---|---|---|---|

Table 1: Evaluation Results

It can be seen in Table 1 that our approach gives the best result. Moreover it is worth noting that the precision drops drastically from 0.947 to 0.529 in Modification 2 as it does not execute Step 2.

Moreover the approach suggested by Schouten et al. (2014) fails in the case of identifying large number of inter-related implicit aspects. Therefore adding step 2 to Schouten's work (Modification 1) improves precision from 0.49 to 0.91. The result for our approach is slightly higher than this, as it considers the distance between opinion words and other words in the sentence. Moreover, the occurrence of stop words does not have any impact as the F1-Measure obtained using Modification 2 is very close to the same obtained using proposed solution.

Table 2 shows the evaluation results for 10-fold-cross validation of our solution for sentences with more than one aspect and it can be observed that the F1-Measure is above 0.82.

| sentence type | Precision | Recall | F1-Measure |
|---|---|---|---|
| 1. Sentences with two implicit aspects | 0.978 | 0.709 | 0.822 |
| 2. Sentences with more than two implicit aspects | 0.975 | 0.725 | 0.832 |

Table 2: Evaluation results for sentences with multiple implicit aspects

In order to measure the inter-rater-reliability (IRR) of aspect annotation, three data sets, each with 100 reviews were picked. Each set was tagged by two different annotators. Two types of measure of consistency were computed; absolute agreement, and Kappa coefficient. The absolute agreement was calculated by dividing the total number of times all annotators agreed on a tag over the total number of tags. Kappa coefficient (Carletta, 1996) is calculated as follows,

Kappa Coefficient = P(A) - P(E)/(1 - P(E))    (2)

where P(A) is the proportion of times the annotators actually agree and P(E) is the proportion of times the annotators are expected to agree due to chance.

| File | Absolute Agreement | Cohen's Kappa |
|---|---|---|
| 1. Test data set 1 | 0.93 | 0.861 |
| 2. Test data set 2 | 0.928 | 0.855 |
| 3. Test data set 3 | 0.893 | 0.785 |
| Average | **0.917** | **0.834** |

Table 3: Annotator Agreement Test Results

An acceptable agreement for Cohen's Kappa value for most NLP classification tasks lies between 0.7 and 0.8 (Carletta, 1996). Table 3 shows the results for IRR test and it can be seen that average Kappa coefficient value for the test data sets is 0.83. Therefore the training data set with aspects labeled is acceptable.

## 7    Conclusion

This paper presented an approach to identify multiple implicit aspects in a sentence. Co-occurrence between opinion word and other words in the sentence is used to identify an aspect that is implied in an opinion word. Double propagation technique is used to extract opinion target to check whether the identified aspect is correct or not. Relationships between different entities with different aspects are modeled as a hierarchy, which helps in improving the accuracy of implicit aspect identification in the presence of a large number of inter-related aspects.

As future work, it would be interesting to extend this work dynamically to improve the model, as new entities and aspects are found. Furthermore, this work can be extended to other domains as well by identifying relationships between aspects specific to a domain and modeling them as a hierarchy.

## References


Carletta, J. Assessing Agreement on Classification Tasks: The Kappa Statistic. Computational Linguistics Volume 22 Issue 2, pages 248-254, 1996.

Hai, Z., Chang, K. and Kim, J. Implicit Feature Identification via Co-occurrence Association Rule Mining. In 12th International Conference on Computational Linguistics and Intelligent Text processing, volume 6608, pages 393–404. Springer, 2011.

Hu, M., Liu, B. and Cheng, J. Opinion Observer: Analyzing and Comparing Opinions on the Web. In Proceedings of the 14th International Conference on World Wide Web, pages 342–351. ACM, 2005.

Opennlp.apache.org,. "Apache Opennlp - Welcome To Apache Opennlp". N.p., 2016. Web. 7 Jan. 2016.

Popescu, A. and Etzioni, O. OPINE: Extracting Product Features and Opinions from Reviews. In Proceedings of HLT/EMNLP (Demonstration Abstracts), pages 32–33. Vancouver, 2005.

Qiu, G., Liu, B., Bu, J. and Chen, C. Opinion Word Expansion and Target Extraction through Double Propagation. Computational Linguistics, volume 37, pages 9–27, 2011.

Schouten, K. and Frasincar, F. Finding Implicit Features in Consumer Reviews for Sentiment Analysis. In 14th International Conference on Web Engineering, volume 8541, pages 130–144. Springer, 2014.

Schouten et al., Semantics-Driven Implicit Aspect Detection in Consumer Reviews. In Proceedings of the 24th International Conference on World Wide Web, pages 109-110. ACM, 2015.

Su, Q., Xu, X., Guo, H., Guo, Z., Wu, X., Zhang, X., Swen, B. and Su, Z. Hidden Sentiment Association in Chinese Web Opinion Mining. In Proceedings of the 17th International Conference on World Wide Web, pages 959–968. ACM, 2008.

Wang, W., Xu., H. and Wan, H. Implicit Feature Identification via Hybrid Association Rule Mining. Expert Systems with Applications: An International Journal Volume 40 Issue 9, pages 3518-3531, 2013.

Yelp,. "Yelp". N.p., 2016. Web. 7 Jan. 2016.

Zhang,L.and Liu, B.Aspect and Entity Extraction for Opinion Mining, Data Mining and Knowledge Discovery for Big Data, Volume 1, pages 1-49. Springer, 2014.

Zhang, Y. and Zhu, W. Extracting Implicit Features in Online Customer Reviews for Opinion Mining. In Proceedings of the 22nd International Conference on World Wide Web, pages 103–104. ACM, 2013.

# Domain Adaptation of Polarity Lexicon combining Term Frequency and Bootstrapping


**Salud M. Jiménez-Zafra, M. Teresa Martín-Valdivia,**
**M. Dolores Molina-Gonzalez and L. Alfonso Ureña-López**
Department of Computer Science, Universidad de Jaén (Spain)
Campus Las Lagunillas, E-23071, Jaén, Spain
{sjzafra, maite, mdmolina, laurena}@ujaen.es



## Abstract

In this paper we study several approaches to adapting a polarity lexicon to a specific domain. On the one hand, the domain adaptation using Term Frequency (TF) and on the other hand, the domain adaptation using pattern matching with a BootStrapping algorithm (BS). Both methods are corpus based and start with the same polarity lexicon, but the first one requires an annotated collection of documents while the second one only needs a corpus where it looks for linguistic patterns. The performance of both methods overcomes the baseline system using the general polarity lexicon iSOL. However, although the TF approach achieves very promising results, the BS strategy does not give as much improvement as we expected. For this reason, we have combined both methods in order to take advantage of the positive aspects of each one. With this new approach the results obtained are even better that those with the systems applied individually. Actually, we have achieved a significant improvement of 11.50% (in terms of accuracy) in the polarity classification of the movie reviews with respect to the results achieved with the general purpose lexicon iSOL.


## 1 Introduction

Sentiment Analysis (SA) is a discipline that combines Natural Language Processing (NLP) and data mining techniques to deal with the subjectivity in textual information. Several tasks have been studied but perhaps Polarity Classification is the most well known that focuses on determining the semantic orientation of a document: positive, negative or neutral.

Although different approaches have been applied to the field of polarity classification, the mainstream basically consists of two major methodologies. On the one hand, the Machine Learning (ML) approach that is based on using a collection of data to train the classifiers (Pang et al., 2002). On the other hand, the approach based on Semantic Orientation (SO) that does not need prior training but takes into account the orientation of words, positive or negative (Turney, 2002). In this paper we focus on semantic orientation in order to tackle one of the open issues related to polarity classification: domain adaptation.

Our main goal is to propose a method for automatically adapting a general polarity lexicon to a specific domain. Specifically, we are going to work with the movie domain because, as several papers demonstrate, this is a very difficult domain to deal with and adapt in SA (Turney, 2002; Taboada et al., 2009; Molina-González et al., 2015b). In addition, we will focus on Spanish since we consider that a language other than English is a more challenging task in the NLP area in general, and in SA in particular, due to the scarcity of resources.

Different methods have been proposed for tackling the domain adaptation problem by automatically generating polarity lexicons. One of the primary studies related to SA is (Blitzer et al., 2007). They note that the polarity of a particular word can carry opposing sentiments depending on the domain, so the general purpose lexicon should be adapted to the specific domain in order to improve

137


*Proceedings of NAACL-HLT 2016*, pages 137–146,
San Diego, California, June 12-17, 2016. ©2016 Association for Computational Linguistics

the effectiveness. Two main approaches to creating polarity lexicons automatically have been studied: dictionary-based and corpus-based. Dictionary-based approaches use external resources such as thesaurus or dictionaries in order to enrich a set of polar terms by aggregating new subjective words (Esuli and Sebastiani, 2006; Hu and Liu, 2004; Molina-González et al., 2013). On the other hand, corpus-based approaches also start from a set of polar terms but instead of using dictionaries, which are domain dependant and usually difficult to find in some languages, they try to integrate external knowledge from document collections (Hatzivassiloglou and McKeown, 1997; Turney, 2002; Molina-González et al., 2015b).

In this paper we investigate two corpus-based methods used to adapt a polarity lexicon to a specific domain. On the one hand, domain adaptation using Term Frequency (TF) and on the other hand, domain adaptation using pattern matching with a BootStrapping algorithm (BS). Both methods are corpus based and start with the same polarity lexicon, but the first one requires an annotated collection of documents while the second one only needs a corpus where it seeks the specific patterns. The performance obtained with both methods significantly overcomes the baseline system using the general polarity lexicon. Finally, we propose an approach that combines both domain adaptation methods and the results obtained are even better that those with the systems applied individually.

Most studies usually start with a very small set of polar terms and then apply some methods to extract and append new subjective words to the original list. However, in this paper we use a very large general lexicon as our starting point. Specifically, in the two approaches presented in the paper, we have used as seed the Spanish polarity lexicon iSOL (Molina-González et al., 2013). This lexicon has been successfully applied in several studies, showing a very good performance in Spanish SA (González et al., 2015a; Martínez-Cámara et al., 2014; Cruz et al., 2014). In addition, we have carried out our experiments with the Spanish movie corpus MuchoCine (Cruz et al., 2008).

Regarding the domain approaches applied, the first one is based on the Term Frequency (TF) in an annotated corpus. This approach has already been applied in previous studies using different domains (Molina-González et al., 2015b; Molina-González et al., 2014; González et al., 2015c). However, although in all the cases the results are improved, we have noted that some polar terms are wrongly added and sometimes some noise is introduced into the systems. Thus, in this paper we investigate a new method that not only adds new words but also, if some terms are detected to be highly subjective, they are eliminated from the adapted lexicon. This is the second approach used in this paper and it is based on detecting patterns in a corpus and applying a bootstrapping algorithm in order to enrich and clean the polarity lexicon. We will call this approach Boot-Strapping (BS). One of the best points of this second method is that we do not need any annotated corpus to adapt the system. We only need a polarity lexicon and a corpus of documents. From this corpus, we extract patterns using the information in the lexicon and we apply the bootstrapping algorithm in order to append or eliminate polar terms from the original lexicon. In this paper we only look for patterns including adjectives, because according to several studies this kind of word is the best clue to express subjectivity in documents (Wiegand et al., 2013).

As we will show in Section 5, the results obtained with the TF approach are very promising although the method requires an annotated corpus. On the other hand, although the results with the BS strategy also surpass the baseline system with the general opinion lexicon, the improvement is lower than we would hope. For this reason, we have decided to combine both methods in order to take advantage of them. Thus, we first apply the TF approach obtaining a new adapted polarity lexicon. This new list is used as the seed of polar terms for the BS algorithm. In this way, our method not only appends terms that are adapted to the domain but it also eliminates polar terms that can be considered highly subjective in this specific domain. The results achieved with this combined method improve on the performance of both approaches when they are applied individually.

The rest of the paper is organised as follows: The following section presents a review of the main methods of domain adaptation, focusing mainly on the corpus-based approaches and commenting on some studies that deal with Spanish. Section 3 introduces the methodology of adaptation based on term frequency and Section 4 presents domain adaptation using bootstrapping. Section 5 exhibits the resources employed and shows the results obtained. In addition, we propose the combination of both methods in order to achieve an improvement in the final system. Section 6 discusses the different results obtained and analyses the systems proposed showing their advantages and disadvantages. Finally, in Section 7 conclusions and future work are presented.

## 2 Background

In this paper we focus on Spanish domain adaptation. We follow two different corpus based methods and then we combine both of them. Our work is based on the papers briefly described below.

### 2.1 Methods using Bootstrapping (BS)

One of the first learning studies to extract linguistic patterns for determining the polarity of sentences was (Hatzivassiloglou and McKeown, 1997). They consider only adjectives and using a large corpus classify the new extracted terms as positive or negative. Turney (2002) follows the same approach but includes adverbs along with adjectives, and uses Pointwise Mutual Information and Information Retrieval to estimate the semantic orientation. Riloff et al. (2003) present a bootstrapping algorithm that learns subjective nouns from an unannotated corpus. The approach uses two high precision classifiers (HP-Subj and HP-Obj) to automatically identify subjective and objective sentences. These classifiers give very high precision but low recall. The extracted sentences are then added to the training data to learn patterns. The learned patterns are then used to automatically identify more subjective and objective sentences. The bootstrapping algorithm increases the recall of the final system while high precision is maintained.

Regarding the studies dealing with Spanish documents, (Vázquez et al., 2012) is one of the first works applying a bootstrapping algorithm to discover new subjective adjectives in a Spanish corpus, following the same approach as Hatzivassiloglou and McKeown (1997). However, they use a small set of polar seeds that they have previously shown to be domain independent (Vázquez and Bel, 2012). Actually, they introduce the concept of "highly sub-

jective adjectives" as those adjectives which can be considered not only positive for one domain and negative for another ("predictable steering" in car domain vs "predictable plot" in movie domain), but which could also change their prior polarity even within the same domain ("antique car" can be positive for a classic person and negative for a modern person).

Our method using a bootstrapping algorithm is based on this idea of "highly subjective adjectives". We first identify and extract the adjectives learned by the linguistic patterns, but before being included in the original lexicon, we first check whether the adjective must be eliminated or included in a set of "highly subjective adjectives".

### 2.2 Methods using Term Frequency (TF)

The method based on term frequency proposed in this paper has already been applied, although the domain and corpora used are different. For example, the proposed approach in (Du et al., 2010) is based on the idea that a word must be negative (or positive) if it appears in many negative (or positive) documents, among other assumptions. The authors select three datasets of different domains, and from the relationships between them, they generate two labelled sentiment lexicons (domain independent and domain dependent) for each domain. In (Dehkharghani et al., 2012) a method is proposed for building a domain-dependent polarity classification system. The hotel and movie domains are selected by the authors. Each review is represented by a set of domain-independent features and a set of domain-dependent ones. The domain independent features are extracted from SentiWordNet (Baccianella et al., 2010). To build the set of domain-dependent features the authors propose taking the lexicon built by Hu and Liu (2004) and choosing those positive/negative words that occur in a significant number of positive/negative reviews of the training corpus used for the experimentation.

For Spanish domain adaptation, García et al. (2012) develop a polarity classification system based on the use of a list of opinion words generated by the authors. The corpus used for the evaluation is a set of hotel reviews written in Spanish and gathered from TripAdvisor. The method consists of counting the number of positive and negative words that appear in the text. Molina-González et al. (2014) propose a method taking as a base the iSOL lexicon and then enrich it with the most frequent words in positive/negative reviews from a Spanish corpus in the tourism domain (subset of SFU corpus[1]). They implement an automatic method to determine the best ratio between positive and negative words in order to integrate them into the new adapted lexicon. The system is tested on a different corpus of Spanish hotel reviews composed of more than 32,000 opinions. The results obtained improve greatly on the result with other general purpose lexicon. Afterward, the same approach is extended to the 8 different domains present in the Spanish SFU corpus (Molina-González et al., 2015b). In this paper we have applied the same approach as Molina-González et al. (2014), but instead of focusing on the tourism domain we have applied the method to the movie domain. We have also carried out several experiments in order to determine the best ratio between positive and negative terms to consider polar terms.

## 3   Domain adaptation based on Bootstrapping

The bootstrapping algorithm implemented in this paper follows the approach described in (Vázquez et al., 2012) that proposes the use of a bootstrapping method to automatically create lists of polar adjectives relevant for a domain and to detect "highly subjective adjectives" (that is, adjectives that could change their polarity even in the same domain). It is a corpus-based method that only needs a set of linguistic patterns extracted from a corpus and a seed polarity lexicon. The hypothesis of this algorithm is that there are some linguistic patterns that provide evidence of the semantic orientation of the words, and therefore this information can be iteratively used to identify the polarity of new words. The patterns selected by Vázquez et al. (2012) are the ones corresponding in Spanish to those presented in Hatzivassiloglou and McKeown (1997) where the authors hypothesize that the conjunction "and" ("y"/"e") joins adjectives of the same orientation while the conjunction "but" ("pero"/"aunque") joins adjectives of different orientation. As seed words, they use a set of

28 positive and 7 negative adjectives that five human annotators manually labeled as domain independent (Vázquez and Bel, 2012). They test the effectiveness of the proposed approach over a set of 200 Spanish documents manually tagged with the polar adjectives that should be in the final polarity lexicon. From all the adjectives labeled by the bootstrapping algorithm (67% of the total are identified), 97.6% of the positive adjectives and 71.5% of the negatives adjectives are correctly tagged. The authors validate the method and obtain promising results, but they do not test the generated sentiment lexicon in the task of polarity classification, therefore we have decided to use it in our experimentation to check how it works.

The bootstrapping algorithm operates as follows. In first place, all the pairs of adjectives that match with any of the patterns defined (adj1 **"y"/"e"** adj2, adj1 **"pero"/"aunque"** adj2) are extracted from the training corpus. After this, the following process is iteratively repeated until there are no changes (insertion or removal) in the polarity lexicon.

For each pattern found, if any of the adjectives is in the seed polarity lexicon we proceed as follows:

- If the adjectives are joined by "y"/"e" and the polarity of one of them is unknown (that is, the adjective is not in the polarity lexicon yet), then the unknown adjective has the **same** semantic orientation as the other adjective and consequently it is added to the polarity lexicon with its corresponding polarity.

- If the adjectives are connected by "y"/"e" and the polarity of the two is known; if both have the same polarity all is well, but if they have opposite polarity (positive adj "y"/"e" negative adj, negative adj "y"/"e" positive adj), the two adjectives will be added to the list of highly subjective adjectives and both will be removed from the polarity lexicon.

- If the adjectives are joined by the conjunction "pero"/"aunque" and the polarity of one of them is unknown, then the unknown adjective has the **opposite** semantic orientation as the other adjective and consequently it is added to the polarity lexicon with its corresponding polarity.

---

[1] https://www.sfu.ca/~mtaboada/download/ downloadCorpusSpa.html

- If the adjectives are joined by "pero"/"aunque" and the polarity of the two is known; if both have opposite polarity all is well, but if they have the same polarity (positive adj "pero"/"aunque" positive adj, negative adj "pero"/"aunque" negative adj), the two adjectives will be added to the list of highly subjective adjectives and both will be removed from the polarity lexicon.

We first applied this approach directly using the 35 adjectives proposed by Vázquez and Bel (2012) over the MuchoCine Corpus. However, the results were very poor and, thus, we decided to start from the iSOL lexicon as seed for the BS algorithm.

The main advantages of this approach are that it does not need a corpus previously tagged with the semantic orientation of each text, it can be applied to any domain and it not only adds adjectives to the seed sentiment lexicon but also cleans it by removing the highly subjective adjectives. However, we also find some disadvantages. It only takes into account one part of speech, the adjective. Furthermore, it removes an adjective if it appears in a contradictory construction[2] without considering that the adjective could appear in more correct constructions than in those that are contradictory. For example, a user can make a mistake and write "clean and dirty", then the algorithm will remove both adjectives from the positive and negative lists respectively, but if it took into account that there are a great quantity of correct constructions for the adjective "dirty" (for example, "dirty and ugly", "dirty and dusty"...) it should not be removed from the negative list. Thus, we should consider other parameters before removing a specific polar term.

## 4 Domain adaptation based on Term Frequency

In order to implement the Term Frequency approach, we have followed the same assumptions as Du et al. (2010). According to this strategy, a word must be negative (or positive) if it appears in many negative (or positive) documents. Therefore, we have implemented an automatic method to determine the

groups of terms in order to integrate them into the new adapted lexicons. The groups of words are selected using the following equation:

$$
polarity(word) = \begin{cases} pos & \text{if } (f^- = 0 \wedge f^+ \geq n) \vee (\frac{f^+}{f^-} \geq n) \\ neg & \text{if } (f^+ = 0 \wedge f^- \geq n) \vee (\frac{f^-}{f^+} \geq n) \end{cases}
$$

$$(1)$$

Where $f^+$ is the absolute frequency of the occurrences of a given word in positive reviews and $f^-$ is the absolute frequency of the occurrences of a given word in negative reviews. Therefore, n is the ratio between the amount of positive and negative words.

The main advantage of this method is its simplicity and quick implementation. Nevertheless, we find several disadvantages. On the one hand, the task of finding available corpora labelled with polarity at the document level is sometimes difficult, particularly for certain domains and languages. On the other hand, the inclusion in the adapted lexicon of all types of words without any discrimination, depending only on a ratio, sometimes introduces noise that does not improve the result in polarity classification.

## 5 Experimental framework and results

We tested two corpus-based approaches and the combination of them for the domain adaptation of a polarity lexicon in Spanish. The list of opinion words taken as a starting point was iSOL (Molina-González et al., 2013). iSOL is a Spanish polarity lexicon generated from the automatic translation of the Bing Liu Lexicon (Hu and Liu, 2004) and the manual revision of it. It is composed of 2,509 positive and 5,626 negative words.

For the adaptation of this lexicon and for testing the TF and BS approaches we used the Spanish MuchoCine corpus (MC) (Cruz et al., 2008). This dataset consists of 3,878 movie reviews collected from the MuchoCine website. The reviews are written by web users, therefore the sentences found in the reviews may include spelling mistakes or informal expressions and they may not always be grammatically correct. The dataset contains about 2 million words and an average of 546 words per review. The opinions in the corpus are rated on a scale from 1 to 5. A rank of 1 means that the opinion is very

---

[2]Positive adj + "y"/"e" + negative adj; negative adj + "y"/"e" + positive adj; positive adj "pero"/"aunque" + positive adj; negative adj + "pero"/"aunque" + negative adj

bad and 5 means very good. Reviews with a rating of 3 can be categorized as "neutral", which means that the user considers the movie is neither bad nor good. In our experiments the neutral reviews were not taken into account, the opinions with ratings of 1 or 2 were considered as negative and those with ratings of 4 or 5 as positive (in total 1,351 positive and 1,274 negative reviews). The 60% of these reviews (781 positive and 794 negative reviews) were employed for the domain adaptation of iSOL and the remaining 40% (570 positive and 480 negative reviews) were used for testing the resultant lists in the task of polarity classification.

In order to apply the method based on frequency (TF), the punctuations and the stopwords of the documents were first removed. After this, the absolute frequency of each word in the positive and negative reviews was determined. Subsequently, several experiments were carried out to add to iSOL those words of the corpus that verify Equation 1, considering different ratios in order to fix the best ratio between positive and negative terms to consider polar terms.

In the case of the approach based on bootstrapping (BS), the documents were first tokenized and splitted into sentences and each token was tagged with its pertinent part of speech, using Freeling[3] (Carreras et al., 2004). Afterwards, the pairs of adjectives that matched with any of the defined patterns were extracted using regular expressions. Finally, two experiments were performed. In the first one, the bootstrapping algorithm was applied using as seed the opinion lexicon iSOL, and in the second the opinion lexicon resultant from applying the TF method with the best ratio (eSOLMovie) was employed as seed.

In order to evaluate the experiments we used the traditional measures employed in text classification: precision (P), recall (R), F1 and Accuracy. On the other hand, to calculate the polarity (p) of a review (r) with each lexicon, we take into account the total number of positive words (#positive) and the total number of negative words (#negative) within the review, according to the following strategy:

$$polarity(review) = \begin{cases} 1 & \text{if } (\#positive > \#negative) \\ -1 & \text{if } (\#positive \leq \#negative) \end{cases} \qquad (2)$$

As the baseline of our experimentation we took the general purpose lexicon iSOL, in order to adapt it to the movie domain with the proposed approaches and with the combination of them. The result of the polarity classification of the documents following the strategy defined previously and using iSOL is of 62.95%, in terms of accuracy.

Regarding the Term Frequency methodology, we first carried out different experiments in order to determine the best ratio to use in our final experiment combining both strategies. Thus, after testing several ratios we determined that the best one is obtained using the ratio n=4 (Figure 1). Therefore, this lexicon was taken as the seed list for the combined experiment with bootstrapping. Table 1 shows the results obtained over the MC corpus using iSOL (domain independent) and eSOLMovie$^n$ lexicons (adapted to the movie domain with the ratios n=3,4,5,6).

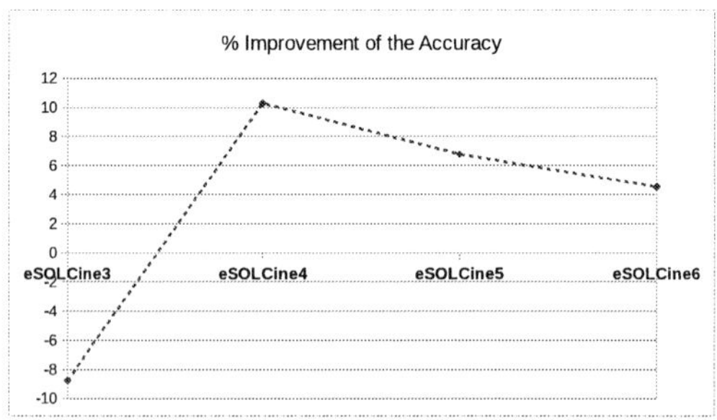


**Figure 1:** Improvement of the Accuracy respect to iSOL with the different eSOLMovie$^n$ lexicons.

In relation to the Bootstraping strategy, it found 1,841 "y"/"e" patterns and 39 "pero"/"aunque" patterns and it was tested using iSOL and eSOLMovie$^4$ as seeds. The experiment with iSOL detected 292 highly subjective adjectives, inserted 659 adjectives, removed 110 adjectives and converged in 5 iterations, achieving 63.71% of accuracy in the polarity classification of the corpus. On the other hand, the experiment with eSOLMovie4 detected 296 highly subjective adjectives, appended 626 adjectives, deleted 228 adjectives and converged in 4 iterations, achieving 70.19% of accuracy. Table 2

---

[3] http://nlp.lsi.upc.edu/freeling/

| Resource | Macro-P | Macro-R | Macro-F1 | Accuracy | Improvement Macro-F1 | Improvement Accuracy |
|---|---|---|---|---|---|---|
| iSOL | 62.59% | 62.28% | 62.43% | 62.95% | - | - |
| eSOLMovie$^3$ | 70.51% | 60.51% | 65.13% | *57.43% | 4.32% | -8.77% |
| **eSOLMovie$^4$** | **69.74%** | **68.39%** | **69.06%** | ***69.43%** | **10.62%** | **10.29%** |
| eSOLMovie$^5$ | 67.40% | 66.16% | 66.77% | *67.24% | 6.95% | 6.80% |
| eSOLMovie$^6$ | 65.56% | 65.09% | 65.33% | 65.81% | 4.65% | 4.54% |

**Table 1:** Results obtained using the different lexicons eSOLMovie$^n$.
An asterisk (*) means significantly different according to the Chi-square test ($\alpha = 0.05$) compared to the result with the baseline approach (iSOL).

| Resource | Macro-P | Macro-R | Macro-F1 | Accuracy | Improvement Macro-F1 | Improvement Accuracy |
|---|---|---|---|---|---|---|
| iSOL | 62.59% | 62.28% | 62.43% | 62.95% | - | - |
| iSOL+Bootstrapping | 63.63% | 62.55% | 63.09% | 63.71% | 1.06% | 1.21% |
| eSOLMovie$^4$ | 69.74% | 68.39% | 69.06% | *69.43% | 10.62% | 10.29% |
| **eSOLMovie$^4$+Bootstrapping** | **70.45%** | **69.22%** | **69.83%** | ***70.19%** | **11.85%** | **11.50%** |

**Table 2:** Results obtained with the different approaches.

shows the results achieved in the classification at the document level of the MC corpus using iSOL (domain independent) adapted to the movie domain with the BS approach, with the TF method (using the best ratio) and with the combination of both strategies (the bootstrapping algorithm over eSOLMovie4).

## 6 Results analysis

Table 3 shows a summary of the results obtained and Table 4 presents the total number of positive and negative polar terms inserted and eliminated from the original lexicon after applying each method. As we can see, the results obtained with the TF method (eSOLMovie$^n$) are very promising. It improves the accuracy of the classification with respect to the general purpose lexicon (iSOL) by 10.29%, inserting only 132 positive words and 126 negative words (Table 3 and 4). However, the restriction of this approach is that we need a corpus previously tagged with the polarity of the documents. Moreover, this strategy only appends new words to the original lexicon and sometimes the new terms introduce noise (for example, we consider that the words "fácil" (easy) and "rápido" (fast) could not be indicators of negative opinion in the movie domain, see Table 5).

Therefore, we also decided to conduct experiments with a technique based on bootstrapping that does not require an annotated corpus and that not only appends words but also removes some of them. The application of the BS approach for the adap-

tation of iSOL to the movie domain also achieves an improvement in the classification (iSOL + bootstrapping) over the baseline (iSOL), although this improvement is not as great as we expected (it is only about 1.21%, see Table 3). We think that one of the reasons could be that in this approach we have only used patterns for the extraction of adjectives, while the TF method appends a word independently of its PoS. Furthermore, we think that the fact of not only inserting but also removing adjectives would be promising but if we take a look at some of the words removed (Table 5), there are adjectives that a priori it seems they should not have been eliminated (for example, the adjectives "agradable" (pleasant) and "espectacular" (spectacular) of the positive list).

Due to this fact, we decided to combine both methods in order to take advantage of them. Thereby, the list generated with the TF method (eSOLMovie$^4$) was used as input in the BS algorithm and the resultant list (eSOLMovie$^4$ + Bootstrapping) was employed for the classification of the movie reviews, achieving an improvement with respect to the baseline (iSOL) of 11.50%, in terms of accuracy (Table 3). Moreover, the results obtained with this combined method improve on the performance of both approaches (iSOL + bootstrapping and eSOLMovie$^4$) when applied individually.

## 7 Conclusions and future work

In this paper we have presented two corpus-based approaches for the domain adaptation of a polarity

143

| Resource | #positive words | #negative words | Accuracy | Improvement Accuracy |
|---|---|---|---|---|
| iSOL | 2509 | 5626 | 62.95% | - |
| iSOL+Bootstrapping | 2743 | 5839 | 63.71% | 1.21% |
| eSOLMovie[4] | 2641 | 5752 | *69.43% | 10.29% |
| eSOLMovie[4]+Bootstrapping | 2857 | 5934 | *70.19% | 11.50% |

**Table 3:** Results summary.

| Resource | #positive words inserted | #negative words inserted | #positive words removed | #negative words removed |
|---|---|---|---|---|
| iSOL+Bootstrapping | 339 | 320 | 105 | 105% |
| eSOLMovie[4] | 132 | 126 | - | -% |
| eSOLMovie[4]+Bootstrapping | 326 | 300 | 110 | 118% |

**Table 4:** Total of positive/negative words inserted into iSOL and removed from iSOL with the different approaches.

| | iSOL+Bootstrapping | eSOLMovie[4] | eSOLMovie[4]+Bootstrapping |
|---|---|---|---|
| Example of positive words inserted | Relevante(relevant), amena(pleasant), azul(blue), humilde(humble), útlima(last), expectante(expectant), destacable(remarkable), talentosa(talented)... | Debut(debut), imprescindible(essential), peliculón(great movie), cruda(crude), sorprendente(surprising), impactante(impressive), cruel(cruel), catelera(billboard)... | Orgulloso(proud), llamativa(striking), anecdótica(anecdotal), original(original), atrapadora(trapping), breve(short), familiar(familiar), desgarrador(heartbreaking)... |
| Example of negative words inserted | Maquiavélica(machiavellian), asquerosilla(disgusting), simplona(simpleton), peculiar(peculiar), repelente(repellent), extraordinaria(axtraordinary), predecible(predictable), horroroso(horrifying)... | Fallida(failed), previsible(foreseeable), montón(be an average), secuela(sequel), exceso(excess), experimento(experiment), fácil(easy), rápido(fast)... | Cansino(tiresome), aburridisimo(very boring), gigantes(giants), claustrofóbica(claustrophobic), intrascendente(trivial), asfixiante(stifling), bochornosa(embarrassing), tétrica(gloomy)... |
| Example of positive words removed | Sensacional(sensational), poderoso(powerful), interesante(interesting), agradable(pleasant), espectacular(spectacular), consistente(consistent), primera(first), realista(realistic)... | | Cruel(cruel), brillante(brilliant), aceptable(acceptable), recomendable(recommendable), rico(rich), espectacular(spectacular), accesible(accessible), vital(vital)... |
| Example of negative words removed | Violentos(violents), extraña(strange), amenazante(threatening), sangrienta(bloody), despiadado(ruthless), terrible(terrible), enfermo(sick), doloroso(painful)... | | Rápido(fast), fácil(easy), perverso(perverse), gris(grey), trágica(tragic), misteriosa(mysterious), última(last), inesperado(unexpected)... |

**Table 5:** Examples of the words inserted into iSOL and removed from iSOL in the different experiments.

lexicon. Both methods are language independent and can be applied to any domain. One of them, the based on term frequency (TF), needs a corpus previously tagged with the polarity of the documents and the other one, the based on a bootstrapping algorithm (BS), does not require an annotated corpus, it only needs as input a set of patterns and a seed sentiment lexicon. The TF approach achieves very promising results while the BS strategy, although it improves on the baseline system with the general purpose lexicon, does not improve as much as we expected. Due to this fact we have combined both methods, in order to take advantage of the positive aspects of each of them. With this new lexicon we have achieved an improvement of 11.50% (in terms of accuracy) in the polarity classification of the movie reviews with respect to the results achieved with the general purpose lexicon iSOL.

In future work, we consider adding some improvements to the domain adaptation approach based on bootstrapping in order to solve one of the main disadvantages detected and to strengthen its main advantage. Thus, we plan to consider a different approach to remove an adjective from the sentiment lexicon, for example, if two adjectives are in contradictory constructions before removing them it could be a good idea to check the number of correct and contradictory constructions in which each of them appear, and remove them only if the number of contradictory constructions exceeds the number of correct constructions in a threshold. We also plan to check, before adding a new adjective to the sentiment lexicon, its polarity according to other important lexical resources (such as SentiWordNet using Multilingual Central Repository (Gonzalez-Agirre et al., 2012) to map sentiment labels to Spanish). Moreover, we will incorporate new patterns to the algorithm in order to extract polar words with another PoS (not only adjectives) such as nouns, verbs and adverbs.

## Acknowledgments

This work has been partially supported by a Grant from the Ministerio de Educación, Cultura y Deporte (MECD - scholarship FPU014/00983) and REDES project (TIN2015-65136-C2-1-R) from the Ministerio de Economía y Competitividad.

## References

Stefano Baccianella, Andrea Esuli, and Fabrizio Sebastiani. 2010. Sentiwordnet 3.0: An enhanced lexical resource for sentiment analysis and opinion mining. In *LREC*, volume 10, pages 2200–2204.

John Blitzer, Mark Dredze, Fernando Pereira, et al. 2007. Biographies, bollywood, boom-boxes and blenders: Domain adaptation for sentiment classification. In *Proceedings of the 45th annual meeting of the association of computational linguistics*, volume 7, pages 440–447, Prague, Czech Republic. Association for Computational Linguistics.

Xavier Carreras, Isaac Chao, Lluis Padró, and Muntsa Padró. 2004. Freeling: An open-source suite of language analyzers. In *LREC*.

Fermín L Cruz, José A Troyano, Fernando Enriquez, and Javier Ortega. 2008. Clasificación de documentos basada en la opinión: experimentos con un corpus de críticas de cine en español. *Procesamiento de Lenguaje Natural*, 41.

Fermín L Cruz, José A Troyano, Beatriz Pontes, and F Javier Ortega. 2014. Building layered, multilingual sentiment lexicons at synset and lemma levels. *Expert Systems with Applications*, 41(13):5984–5994.

Rahim Dehkharghani, Benin Yanikoglu, Dilek Tapucu, and Yucel Saygin. 2012. Adaptation and use of subjectivity lexicons for domain dependent sentiment classification. In *Data Mining Workshops (ICDMW), 2012 IEEE 12th International Conference on*, pages 669–673. IEEE.

Weifu Du, Songbo Tan, Xueqi Cheng, and Xiaochun Yun. 2010. Adapting information bottleneck method for automatic construction of domain-oriented sentiment lexicon. In *Proceedings of the third ACM international conference on Web search and data mining*, pages 111–120. ACM.

Andrea Esuli and Fabrizio Sebastiani. 2006. Sentiwordnet: A publicly available lexical resource for opinion mining. In *Proceedings of LREC*, volume 6, pages 417–422. Citeseer.

Aitor García, Sean Gaines, Maria Teresa Linaza, et al. 2012. A lexicon based sentiment analysis retrieval system for tourism domain. *Expert Syst Appl Int J*, 39(10):9166–9180.

Aitor Gonzalez-Agirre, Egoitz Laparra, and German Rigau. 2012. Multilingual central repository version 3.0. In *LREC*, pages 2525–2529.

M Dolores Molina González, Eugenio Martínez Cámara, and M Teresa Martín Valdivia. 2015a. Crisol: Base de conocimiento de opiniones para el español. *Procesamiento del Lenguaje Natural*, 55:143–150.

M Dolores Molina González, Eugenio Martínez Cámara, M Teresa Martín Valdivia, and Salud M Jiménez Zafra. 2015c. esolhotel: Generación de un lexicón de opinión en español adaptado al dominio turístico. *Procesamiento del Lenguaje Natural*, 54:21–28.

Vasileios Hatzivassiloglou and Kathleen R McKeown. 1997. Predicting the semantic orientation of adjectives. In *Proceedings of the 35th annual meeting of the association for computational linguistics and eighth conference of the european chapter of the association for computational linguistics*, pages 174–181. Association for Computational Linguistics.

Minqing Hu and Bing Liu. 2004. Mining and summarizing customer reviews. In *Proceedings of the Tenth ACM SIGKDD International Conference on Knowledge Discovery and Data Mining*, KDD '04, pages 168–177, New York, NY, USA. ACM.

Eugenio Martínez-Cámara, M Teresa Martín-Valdivia, M Dolores Molina-González, and José M Perea-Ortega. 2014. Integrating Spanish lexical resources by meta-classifiers for polarity classification. *Journal of Information Science*, page 0165551514535710.

M Dolores Molina-González, Eugenio Martínez-Cámara, María-Teresa Martín-Valdivia, and José M Perea-Ortega. 2013. Semantic orientation for polarity classification in Spanish reviews. *Expert Systems with Applications*, 40(18):7250–7257.

M Dolores Molina-González, Eugenio Martínez-Cámara, M Teresa Martín-Valdivia, and L Alfonso Urena-López. 2014. Cross-domain sentiment analysis using Spanish opinionated words. In *Natural Language Processing and Information Systems*, pages 214–219. Springer.

M Dolores Molina-González, Eugenio Martínez-Cámara, M Teresa Martín-Valdivia, and L Alfonso Ureña-López. 2015b. A Spanish semantic orientation approach to domain adaptation for polarity classification. *Information Processing & Management*, 51(4):520–531.

Bo Pang, Lillian Lee, and Shivakumar Vaithyanathan. 2002. Thumbs up?: Sentiment classification using machine learning techniques. In *Proceedings of the ACL-02 Conference on Empirical Methods in Natural Language Processing - Volume 10*, EMNLP '02, pages 79–86, Stroudsburg, PA, USA. Association for Computational Linguistics.

Ellen Riloff, Janyce Wiebe, and Theresa Wilson. 2003. Learning subjective nouns using extraction pattern bootstrapping. In *Proceedings of the seventh conference on Natural language learning at HLT-NAACL 2003-Volume 4*, pages 25–32. Association for Computational Linguistics.

Maite Taboada, Julian Brooke, and Manfred Stede. 2009. Genre-based paragraph classification for sentiment analysis. In *Proceedings of the SIGDIAL 2009 Conference: The 10th Annual Meeting of the Special Interest Group on Discourse and Dialogue*, pages 62–70. Association for Computational Linguistics.

Peter D. Turney. 2002. Thumbs up or thumbs down?: Semantic orientation applied to unsupervised classification of reviews. In *Proceedings of the 40th Annual Meeting on Association for Computational Linguistics*, ACL '02, pages 417–424, Stroudsburg, PA, USA. Association for Computational Linguistics.

Silvia Vázquez and Núria Bel. 2012. A classification of adjectives for polarity lexicons enhancement. In *Calzolari N, Choukri K, Declerck T (et al.), editors. Proceedings of the Eight International Conference on Language Resources and Evaluation (LREC'12)*, pages 3557–3561.

Silvia Vázquez, Muntsa Padró, Núria Bel, and Julio Gonzalo. 2012. Automatic extraction of polar adjectives for the creation of polarity lexicons. In *Kay M, Boitet C, editors. Proceedings of COLING 2012: Posters: 24th International Conference on Computational Linguistics COLING 2012; 2012 December 8-15; Mumbai, India. Mumbai: The COLING 2012 Organizing Committee; 2012. p. 1271-1280.*, pages 1271–1280. ACL (Association for Computational Linguistics).

Michael Wiegand, Manfred Klenner, and Dietrich Klakow. 2013. Bootstrapping polarity classifiers with rule-based classification. *Language resources and evaluation*, 47(4):1049–1088.

# Do Enterprises Have Emotions?

**Sven Buechel** and **Udo Hahn**
Jena University Language & Information Engineering (JULIE) Lab
Friedrich-Schiller-Universität Jena
Jena, Germany
`http://www.julielab.de`


**Jan Goldenstein** and **Sebastian G. M. Händschke** and **Peter Walgenbach**
School of Economics and Business Administration
Friedrich-Schiller-Universität Jena
Jena, Germany
`http://www.orga.uni-jena.de`


## Abstract


Emotional language of human individuals has been studied for quite a while dealing with opinions and value judgments people have and share with others. In our work, we take a different stance and investigate whether large organizations, such as major industrial players, have and communicate emotions, as well. Such an anthropomorphic perspective has recently been advocated in management and organization studies which consider organizations as social actors. We studied this assumption by analyzing 1,676 annual business and sustainability reports from 90 top-performing enterprises in the United States, Great Britain and Germany. We compared the measurements of emotions in this homogeneous corporate text corpus with those from RCV1, a heterogeneous Reuters newswire corpus. From this, we gathered empirical evidence that business reports compare well with typical emotion-neutral economic news, whereas sustainability reports are much more emotionally loaded, similar to emotion-heavy sports and fashion news from Reuters. Furthermore, our data suggest that these emotions are distinctive and relatively stable over time per organization, thus constituting an emotional profile for enterprises.


## 1   Introduction

In the past years, we have witnessed an enormous upsurge of research activities in the field of NLP related to affective language use in social networks. This work has mostly focused on subjective, often evaluative language of individual or informal ad-hoc groups of human actors in a multitude of social media platforms (Pang and Lee, 2008; Liu, 2015). Overall, this research analyzes language *about* organizations (e.g., opinions about the products they offer) rather than the language *of* organizations.

Quite recently, some areas of management and organization studies started modeling formal organizations in an anthropomorphic way, as social actors with human-like traits (King et al., 2010). Management and organization researchers following this approach claim that organizations have their own, persistent, human-like identity, play social roles and assume responsibility for their doings in the societies they are embedded in (Whetten, 2006). One of the far-reaching implications of granting organizations the status of social actors is, by default, their unequivocal submission to juridical standards as legal entities liable for violations of law in the same way as individual citizens are.

It is exactly this shift in the modeling of organizations (and thus business corporations, such as large enterprises) as social actors, which led us to our research questions. Within the new paradigm of computational social science (DiMaggio, 2015), we investigate whether organizations can also be attributed behavioral traits and properties typically associated with humans, such as attitudes, affects, emotions, etc.—a question which is, to the best of our knowledge, so far untackled despite its theoretical and empirical relevance (King et al., 2010).

147

*Proceedings of NAACL-HLT 2016*, pages 147–153,
San Diego, California, June 12-17, 2016. ©2016 Association for Computational Linguistics

## 2  Related Work

*Subjectivity analysis* is typically used as an umbrella term for NLP approaches concerned with all sorts of affective language use in which speakers' emotions play a crucial role. The most widespread subtask of subjectivity analysis is sentiment analysis or opinion mining (both terms are used interchangeably) (Pang and Lee, 2008). Most often, *sentiment* refers to the semantic orientation (or polarity), the positiveness or negativeness, of a sentence or a document. More recently, another subtask has attracted a lot of attention, namely emotion detection. Unlike (bipolar) sentiments, *emotion* describes a much more complex type of affective state typically associated with phenomena such as sadness, fear or joy. Yet its exact definition and distinction from other affective phenomena is an open issue (Munezero et al., 2014).

The more complex nature of emotion implies that both subtasks—sentiment analysis and emotion detection—need distinct analytic resources, especially lexicons. The number of general-language sentiment lexicons is, compared to the number of emotion lexicons, relatively large, including well-known resources such as SENTIWORDNET (Esuli and Sebastiani, 2006; Baccianella et al., 2010). Another notable resource is WORDNET-AFFECT which contains both, sentiment assessments (positive, negative, neutral and ambiguous) and a hierarchy of various emotion categories (Strapparava and Valitutti, 2004; Strapparava et al., 2006). Lately, however, an increasing number of emotion lexicons have been developed—within the fields of NLP (Mohammad and Turney, 2013; Staiano and Guerini, 2014), as well as cognitive psychology (Bestgen and Vincze, 2012; Warriner et al., 2013). As far as studies of sentiment in the economic area are concerned, Loughran and McDonald (2011) adapted the *Harvard Psychosociological Dictionary* to better fit the word usage of the finance domain. The resulting resource comprises six word lists (two of which refer to positive and negative words), thus forming a finance-specific sentiment lexicon.

Researchers in NLP and cognitive psychology have devised a multitude of different models of emotion which can be roughly subdivided into categorical and dimensional models (Scherer, 2000; Calvo and Kim, 2013). In computational studies, categor-ical models most often employ Ekman's (1992) six basic emotions or a derivative therefrom. According to this psychological theory, all human beings share a common set of (basic) emotions so that each emotional state of an individual can be unambiguously classified as one of these. Dimensional approaches, on the other hand, often refer to Russell and Mehrabian's (1977) Valence-Arousal-Dominance (VAD) model. According to this model, emotional states can be described relative to three fundamental emotional dimensions: valence (the degree of pleasure of an emotion), arousal (level of mental activity, ranging from low engagement to ecstasy) and dominance (extent of control felt in a given situation). Accordingly, emotions are characterized on three dimensions, each of which spans an interval of real-valued numbers indicating the strength and orientation of each dimension. Hence, other than in categorical approaches with a usually small (up to nine) and finite number of states, an infinite number of emotional states can be represented in dimensional approaches.

Subjective language use has also been a topic of interest in the business and economy domain. A common theme is here whether the linguistic 'tone' of public mass media's coverage of enterprises or publications authored by individual enterprises themselves are indicative of the companies' future economic performance, and can thus, e.g., be useful for stock trading strategies (for a recent survey, cf. Nassirtoussi et al. (2014)).

Early work on subjective language use in newspapers as predictors for companies' accounting earnings and stock returns (Tetlock et al., 2008) or in quarterly company reports for stock market performance prediction (Kloptchenko et al., 2004) reveals that such linguistic analysis uncover otherwise hard-to-quantify aspects of firms' fundamentals. The potential of news-driven sentiment analysis is elucidated in a recent study by Uhl (2014) who finds evidence that polarity measurements on Reuters news can explain and predict changes in stock returns better than macroeconomic factors, in isolation.

Bollen et al. (2011) examine to what extent subjective language on the social media platform TWITTER can be interpreted as a predictor of stock market prizes. They find that the predictive power of certain emotion categories exceeds that of the semantic orientation, leading to a significant improvement of basic stock market forecasting models. Their study reveals the possible benefits of the additional information emotion detection might contribute in contrast to (less expressive) sentiment analysis.

In a similar vein, Généreux et al. (2011) investigate the impact of financial news items on the stock price of companies. They treat short financial news snippets about companies as if they were carrying implicit sentiment about the future market direction made explicit by the vocabulary they employ. They investigate how this sentiment vocabulary can be automatically extracted from texts and subsequently be used for classification. This resembles previous work by Devitt and Ahmad (2007) who explored a computable metric of positive or negative polarity in financial news text which is consistent with human judgments and can be used in a quantitative analysis of news sentiment impact on financial markets.

Unlike sentiment analysis of informal communication pieces from social or mass media material, Kogan et al. (2009) were the first in company-centric text analysis to focus on official statements from enterprises on a larger scale (pioneering work was conducted by Kloptchenko et al. (2004), as mentioned above). They built up the *10-K Corpus*, a collection of 54,379 annual business reports (from 10,492 different publicly traded companies) published over the period from 1996 to 2006. They exploited this corpus to predict the volatility of stock returns, an established empirical measure of financial risk, using regression models. The economic assessments are derived from the distribution of unigrams and bigrams in the reports incorporating TF and TF-IDF-based measures for a bag-of-word (BOW) model.

Wang et al. (2013), in a follow-up study, reused the 10-K Corpus by incorporating Loughran and McDonald's (2011) finance-specific sentiment dictionary. The models they learn suggest strong correlations between financial sentiment words and risk in terms of stock return volatility. Using basically the same experimental set-up as the former study, Hájek et al. (2013) go one step further and demonstrate that by combining qualitative sentiment information of annual reports with quantitative financial indicators (e.g. market capitalization, profitability, etc.) the resulting stock price forecasting model is more accurate than using quantitative indicators alone. These findings are further supported by Kazemian et al. (2014) who present empirical data which indicate to act cautiously with respect to stock trading strategies based on sentiment analysis of linguistic data only (they propose to consider actual market returns, in addition). Interestingly, the study by Hájek et al. (2013) points out that the *change* in sentiment (rather than its specific value in some point of time) seems to be an important determinant of stock price development in the long run.

## 3  Experimental Set-up

In order to test the assumption whether enterprises can be attributed an emotional status as part of their identity as social actors, we, first, compiled a text corpus composed of annual business and sustainability reports of the thirty top-performing corporations in the United States, Great Britain and Germany. These enterprises were selected based on their listing in the Dow Jones, the FTSE 100, and the DAX Index, respectively. The global economic power of these corporations is quite impressive since, in 2014, their revenues comprised about 7% of the worldwide GDP, an equivalent of 5.4 trillion USD.

For these 90 corporations, we collected the English versions of all annual business and sustainability reports (also called corporate social responsibility (CSR) reports (Matten and Moon, 2008)) available online. This corpus amounts to 1,676 reports (3,798,070 sentences; 128,145,063 text tokens) divided into 1,087 annual and 589 sustainability reports covering the time span from 1992 to 2015.

We compared business reports (which we thought to be emotionally mostly neutral) to sustainability reports (which we thought to be much more emotionally loaded). This comparison is based on a simple vectorial BOW text analysis engine whose novel feature is an attached emotion word lexicon composed of 13,915 lexical entries (Warriner et al., 2013). Each of its lexical entries carries empirically determined (crowd-sourced) real-valued assessments for the three fundamental emotion dimensions of the VAD model (cf. Table 1 for illustrative lexicon entries and associated VAD values).

So far, this model—though among the most popular models of emotion in cognitive psychology—has found only very scant attention in the field of text-based subjectivity analysis (Calvo and Kim, 2013).

| Lemma | V | A | D |
|---|---|---|---|
| sunshine | 3.14 | 0.32 | 0.43 |
| leukemia | -3.53 | 0.75 | -2.17 |
| terrorism | -3.40 | 2.42 | -2.31 |
| calm | 1.89 | -3.33 | 2.44 |
| successful | 2.76 | 0.08 | 2.71 |
| uncontrollable | -1.16 | 0.81 | -2.82 |

**Table 1:** Lexicon entries from the VAD lexicon (adapted via scale transformation from Warriner et al. (2013)) with considerably high (low) valence, arousal or dominance values.

In the lexicon used in our experiments, valence, arousal and dominance are balanced in the interval of $[-4, 4]$ (in the original VAD lexicon (Warriner et al., 2013), values range in the interval of $[1, 9]$).

The basic processing cycle is as follows: A term-vector representation (stop word-free, lemmatized) is built up for each of the 1,676 reports. Each term component of the 1,676 vectors is matched with all of the 13,915 entries of the VAD lexicon. If a match occurs, i.e., the lexical item at the $i$-th vector component matches an entry in the VAD lexicon, the 3D emotion values of that item (cf. Table 1) are multiplied with the number of occurrences of this item in the underlying document. Finally, the emotion values for all matched entries per document are summed up and divided by the number of matches. This average yields the *emotion value* of a given document on the three principle emotional dimensions of the VAD scheme.

## 4 Results of the Experiments

In general, we found valence and dominance values around 0.6 and arousal values at $-1.0$. The fact that the latter is considerably lower than the former two is partially derived from the statistical properties of the emotion word lexicon we employ. Another noteworthy characteristic is the strong correlation between the valence and the dominance values ($r = 0.87$) as shown in Figure 1(b). This correlation can also be observed in the lexicon as well as in other corpora (see below) although it is pronouncedly higher in the enterprise corpus. The correlation's strength might be a suitable measure for the appreciation of control as expressed in the individual documents. This is so because high correlation hints at frequent co-occurrences of words having high (low) valence ratings and words having high (low) dominance ratings or a high frequency of words having both, high (low) valence and high (low) dominance ratings. According to this, the results can be interpreted as pointing out the great concernment corporations place on control.

Next, we investigated the role of the two text genres. First of all, in Figure 1, both genres can clearly be distinguished, in particular in Figures 1(b) and 1(c). We find that sustainability reports are on average way more positive (valence: 0.70) and dominant (0.68) than annual reports (0.62 and 0.59, respectively). The differences in both emotional dimensions are significant (two-tailed t-test: $p < 0.001$) and show large effect sizes (Cohen's $d > |0.7|$). This tendency may be due to the fact that annual reports have to comply with numerous external constraints corporations have to respect (e.g., themes and data required by legal prescriptions, etc.), whereas in sustainability reports corporations have full control over phrasing and contents and may focus on their voluntary activities.

To relate these findings to external resources and thus gather evidence for the validity of our approach, we compared our results from the enterprise data set to those from a Reuters corpus which contains newswire material (RCV1 (Lewis et al., 2004)). We found slightly lower valence and dominance values than in the enterprise data but standard deviation in the corporation corpus was half as high as in RCV1—this points out that the enterprise corpus is emotionally more homogeneous than Reuters.

Figure 2 depicts the localization of the two enterprise text genres relative to several newswire categories from the Reuters corpus in the VAD space. As can be seen, the enterprise documents compare well with Reuters business- and economy-related categories (in green), CCAT in particular, which contains corporate and industrial topics. The emotional values of business reports are thus shown to come close to that of newspaper articles of the corresponding content categories—these similarities seem to indicate that the measures we use are valid.

On the arousal dimension, sustainability reports reveal only a minor distance relative to Reuters business and economic categories and the enterprises' annual reports. Yet, on the valence and dominance dimensions, they correspond very closely to highly emotional fashion and sports news (GFAS

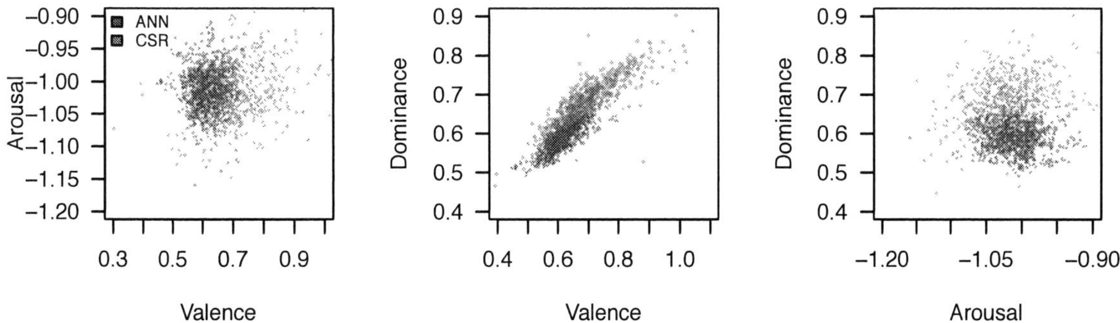

**Figure 1:** Scatter plots of the emotional values of the 1,676 enterprise reports—1,087 annual reports (ANN: blue) and 589 sustainability reports (CSR: red)—of the corporation corpus in the VAD space.

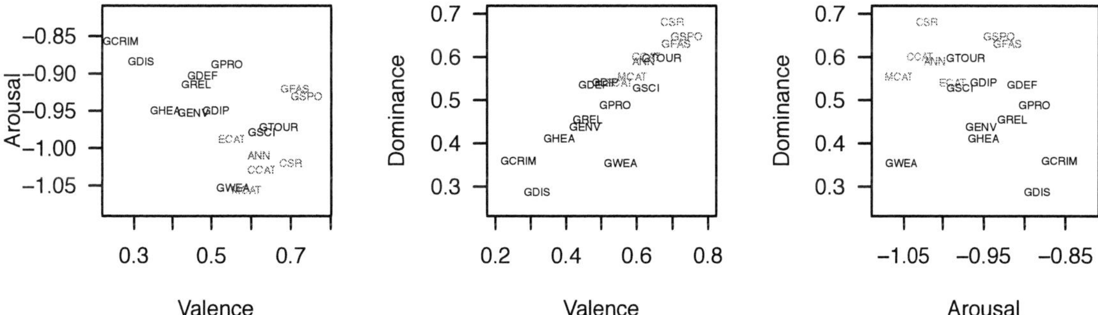

**Figure 2:** Average emotional values for the categories of the RCV1 (business- and economy-related categories (CCAT, ECAT, and MCAT) in green, sports and fashion category (GSPO and GFAS, respectively) in purple) as well as both genres from the enterprise corpus (annual business reports (ANN) in blue, sustainability reports (CSR) in red).

and GSPO, respectively; both in purple). This can be taken as further evidence for the dissimilarity of the two corporation genres mentioned before. The dominance value of sustainability reports is on average greater than that of *all* news categories.

Furthermore, we could show that the reports (in each case with respect to the authoring company) all share a specific tendency in their emotion value which is even relatively constant over time. This is especially true when examining the two subcorpora of annual and sustainability reports separately. In this case, the proportion of explained variance with consideration of the corporation which authored a report reaches values of about 70% (for arousal in annual reports, data are available in Büchel (2016)).

## 5   Conclusion

In summary, our research provides one of the first attempts to study emotional factors in documents representing large corporations—as reflected in the enterprises' annual and sustainability reports—rather than individuals. In comparison with economic newswire material from the RCV1 corpus, we located enterprise documents on three fundamental emotional dimensions, namely valence, arousal and dominance (according to the VAD model), and found strong evidence for particularly high dominance in sustainability reports. Furthermore, the data indicate that organizations exhibit a distinctive and persistent emotional profile. So, indeed, we have reasons to believe that—in the light of their reporting—enterprises have emotions in the sense of an anthropomorphic model and that this profile contributes to a unique organizational identity.

Technically, to the best of our knowledge, the VAD-based emotion lexicon (with $>$10k entries) we employed for our study has never been used for text analytics tasks before. Note that this lexicon exceeds well-known resources with a comparable emotion model (Bradley and Lang, 1999) by an order of magnitude.

## References

Stefano Baccianella, Andrea Esuli, and Fabrizio Sebastiani. 2010. SENTIWORDNET 3.0: An enhanced lexical resource for sentiment analysis and opinion mining. In Nicoletta Calzolari, Khalid Choukri, Bente Maegaard, Joseph Mariani, Jan Odijk, Stelios Piperidis, and Daniel Tapias, editors, *LREC 2010 — Proceedings of the 7th International Conference on Language Resources and Evaluation. La Valletta, Malta, May 17-23, 2010*, pages 2200–2204. European Language Resources Association (ELRA).

Yves Bestgen and Nadja Vincze. 2012. Checking and bootstrapping lexical norms by means of word similarity indexes. *Behavior Research Methods*, 44(4):998–1006.

Johan Bollen, Huina Mao, and Xiaojun Zeng. 2011. Twitter mood predicts the stock market. *Journal of Computational Science*, 2(1):1–8.

Margaret M. Bradley and Peter J. Lang. 1999. Affective Norms for English Words (ANEW): Stimuli, Instruction Manual and Affective Ratings. Technical Report Technical Report C-1, The Center for Research in Psychophysiology, University of Florida, Gainesville, FL.

Sven Eric Büchel. 2016. Automatische Analyse von Emotionen in Geschäfts- und Nachhaltigkeitsberichten. Bachelor thesis, Friedrich-Schiller-Universität Jena, Jena, Germany.

Rafael A Calvo and Sunghwan Mac Kim. 2013. Emotions in text: Dimensional and categorical models. *Computational Intelligence*, 29(3):527–543.

Ann Devitt and Khurshid Ahmad. 2007. Sentiment polarity identification in financial news: A cohesion-based approach. In *ACL 2007 — Proceedings of the 45th Annual Meeting of the Association for Computational Linguistics. Prague, Czech Republic, June 23-30, 2007*, pages 984–991. Association for Computational Linguistics (ACL).

Paul DiMaggio. 2015. Adapting computational text analysis to social science (and vice versa). *Big Data & Society*, 2(2):1–5.

Paul Ekman. 1992. An argument for basic emotions. *Cognition and Emotion*, 6(3-4):169–200.

Andrea Esuli and Fabrizio Sebastiani. 2006. SENTIWORDNET: A publicly available lexical resource for opinion mining. In Nicoletta Calzolari, Aldo Gangemi, Bente Maegaard, Joseph Mariani, Jan Odijk, and Daniel Tapias, editors, *LREC 2006 — Proceedings of the 5th International Conference on Language Resources and Evaluation. Genoa, Italy, 22-28 May, 2006*, pages 417–422. European Language Resources Association (ELRA).

Michel Généreux, Thierry Poibeau, and Moshe Koppel. 2011. Sentiment analysis using automatically labelled financial news. In Khurshid Ahmad, editor, *Affective Computing and Sentiment Analysis. Emotion, Metaphor and Terminology*, number 45 in Text, Speech and Language Technology, pages 111–126. Springer.

Petr Hájek, Vladimír Olej, and Renáta Myšková. 2013. Forecasting stock prices using sentiment information in annual reports: A neural network and support vector regression approach. *WSEAS Transactions on Business and Economics*, 10(4):293–305.

Siavash Kazemian, Shunan Zhao, and Gerald Penn. 2014. Evaluating sentiment analysis evaluation: A case study in securities trading. In *WASSA 2014 — Proceedings of the 5th Workshop on Computational Approaches to Subjectivity, Sentiment and Social Media Analysis @ ACL 2014. Baltimore, Maryland, USA, June 27, 2014*, pages 119–127.

Brayden G. King, Teppo Felin, and David A. Whetten. 2010. Finding the organization in organizational theory. A meta-theory of the organization as a social actor. *Organization Science*, 21(1):290–305.

Antonina Kloptchenko, Tomas Eklund, Barbro Back, Jonas Karlsson, Hannu Vanharanta, and Ari Visa. 2004. Combining data and text mining techniques for analysing financial reports. *Intelligent Systems in Accounting, Finance and Management*, 12(1):29–41.

Shimon Kogan, Dimitry Levin, Bryan R. Routledge, Jacob S. Sagi, and Noah A. Smith. 2009. Predicting risk from financial reports with regression. In *NAACL-HLT 2009 — Proceedings of Human Language Technologies: The 2009 Annual Conference of the North American Chapter of the Association for Computational Linguistics. Boulder, CO, USA, May 31 - June 5, 2009*, volume 1, pages 272–280, Stroudsburg/PA. Association for Computational Linguistics (ACL).

David D. Lewis, Yiming Yang, Tony G. Rose, and Fan Li. 2004. RCV1: A new benchmark collection for text categorization research. *Journal of Machine Learning Research*, 5:361–397, April.

Bing Liu. 2015. *Sentiment Analysis: Mining Opinions, Sentiments and Emotions*. Cambridge University Press, New York, NY.

Tim Loughran and Bill McDonald. 2011. When is a liability not a liability? Textual analysis, dictionaries, and 10-Ks. *The Journal of Finance*, 66(1):35–65.

Dirk Matten and Jeremy Moon. 2008. 'Implicit' and 'explicit' CSR: A conceptual framework for a comparative understanding of Corporate Social Responsibility. *Academy of Management Review*, 33(2):404–424.

Saif M. Mohammad and Peter D. Turney. 2013. Crowdsourcing a word-emotion association lexicon. *Computational Intelligence*, 29(3):436–465.

Myriam D. Munezero, Calkin Suero Montero, Erkki Sutinen, and John Pajunen. 2014. Are they different?

Affect, feeling, emotion, sentiment, and opinion detection in text. *IEEE Transactions on Affective Computing*, 5(2):101–111.

Arman Khadjeh Nassirtoussi, Saeed Aghabozorgi, Teh Ying Wah, and David Chek Ling Ngo. 2014. Text mining for market prediction: A systematic review. *Expert Systems with Applications*, 41(16):7653–7670.

Bo Pang and Lillian Lee. 2008. Opinion mining and sentiment analysis. *Foundation of Trends in Information Retrieval*, 2(1-2):1–135.

James A Russell and Albert Mehrabian. 1977. Evidence for a three-factor theory of emotions. *Journal of Research in Personality*, 11(3):273–294.

Klaus R. Scherer. 2000. Psychological models of emotion. In Joan C. Borod, editor, *The Neuropsychology of Emotion*, pages 137–162. Oxford University Press, Oxford, U.K.; New York, N.Y.

Jacopo Staiano and Marco Guerini. 2014. DEPECHE MOOD: A lexicon for emotion analysis from crowd annotated news. In *ACL 2014 — Proceedings of the 52nd Annual Meeting of the Association for Computational Linguistics. Baltimore, Maryland, USA, June 22-27, 2014*, volume 2: Short Papers, pages 427–433, Stroudsburg/PA. Association for Computational Linguistics (ACL).

Carlo Strapparava and Alessandro Valitutti. 2004. WORDNET-AFFECT: An affective extension of WORDNET. In Maria Teresa Lino, Maria Francisca Xavier, Fátima Ferreira, Rute Costa, and Raquel Silva, editors, *LREC 2004 — Proceedings of the 4th International Conference on Language Resources and Evaluation. In Memory of Antonio Zampolli. Lisbon, Portugal, 24-30 May, 2004*, pages 1083–1086. European Language Resources Association (ELRA).

Carlo Strapparava, Alessandro Valitutti, and Oliviero Stock. 2006. The affective weight of lexicon. In Nicoletta Calzolari, Aldo Gangemi, Bente Maegaard, Joseph Mariani, Jan Odijk, and Daniel Tapias, editors, *LREC 2006 — Proceedings of the 5th International Conference on Language Resources and Evaluation. Genoa, Italy, 22-28 May, 2006*, pages 423–426. European Language Resources Association (ELRA).

Paul C. Tetlock, Maytal Saar-Tsechansky, and Sofus Macskassy. 2008. More than words: Quantifying language to measure firms' fundamentals. *The Journal of Finance*, 63(3):1437–1467.

Matthias W. Uhl. 2014. Reuters sentiment and stock returns. *Journal of Behavioral Finance*, 15(4):287–298.

Chuan-Ju Wang, Ming-Feng Tsai, Tse Liu, and Chin-Ting Chang. 2013. Financial sentiment analysis for risk prediction. In *IJCNLP 2013 — Proceedings of the 6th International Joint Conference on Natural Language Processing. Nagoya, Japan, 14-18 October 2013*, pages 802–808. Asian Federation of Natural Language Processing (AFNLP).

Amy Beth Warriner, Victor Kuperman, and Marc Brysbaert. 2013. Norms of valence, arousal, and dominance for 13,915 English lemmas. *Behavior Research Methods*, 45(4):1191–1207.

David A. Whetten. 2006. Albert and Whetten revisited: Strengthening the concept of organizational identity. *Journal of Management Inquiry*, 15(3):219–234.

# A semantic-affective compositional approach for the affective labelling of adjective-noun and noun-noun pairs

**Elisavet Palogiannidi**[2,3]**, Elias Iosif** [1,3]**, Polychronis Koutsakis**[4]**, Alexandros Potamianos**[1,3]

[1] School of ECE, National Technical University of Athens, Zografou 15780, Athens, Greece
[2] School of ECE, Technical University of Crete, Chania 73100, Crete, Greece
[3] "Athena" Research and Innovation Center, Maroussi 15125, Athens, Greece
[4] School of Engineering and Information Technology, Murdoch University, Australia
`epalogiannidi@isc.tuc.gr, p.koutsakis@murdoch.edu.au, {iosife,potam}@central.ntua.gr`



## Abstract

Motivated by recent advances in the area of Compositional Distributional Semantic Models (CDSMs), we propose a compositional approach for estimating continuous affective ratings for adjective-noun (AN) and noun-noun (NN) pairs. The ratings are computed for the three basic dimensions of continuous affective spaces, namely, valence, arousal and dominance. We propose that similarly to the semantic modification that underlies CDSMs, affective modification may occur within the framework of affective spaces, especially when the constituent words of the linguistic structures under investigation form modifier-head pairs (e.g., AN and NN). The affective content of the entire structure is determined from the interaction between the respective constituents, i.e., the affect conveyed by the head is altered by the modifier. In addition, we investigate the fusion of the proposed model with the semantic-affective model proposed in (Malandrakis et al., 2013) applied both at word- and phrase-level. The automatically computed affective ratings were evaluated against human ratings in terms of correlation. The most accurate estimates are achieved via fusion and absolute performance improvement up to 5% and 4% is reported for NN and AN, respectively.


## 1  Introduction

Affective analysis of text aims at eliciting emotion from linguistic information and it can be relevant for a wide range of applications such as sentiment analysis (Pang and Lee, 2008; Rosenthal et al., 2014; Rosenthal et al., 2015), news headlines analysis (Strapparava and Mihalcea, 2007) or affective analysis of social media (Quercia et al., 2011; Celli, 2012; Rosenthal et al., 2014; Rosenthal et al., 2015).

Word-level affective lexica can be created automatically with high accuracy (Turney and Littman, 2002; Strapparava and Valitutti, 2004; Esuli and Sebastiani,

2006; Malandrakis et al., 2013; Palogiannidi et al., 2015). Affective lexica are required in hierarchical models that combine words' affective ratings for estimating affective ratings of larger lexical units, e.g., phrases (Turney and Littman, 2002; Wilson et al., 2005), sentences (Malandrakis et al., 2013; Rosenthal et al., 2014; Rosenthal et al., 2015) and whole documents (Pang et al., 2002; Pang and Lee, 2008). A sentiment classification approach on movies review documents was proposed in (Pang et al., 2002). Word-level semantic representations constitute the core aspect of DSMs typically constructed from co-occurrence statistics of word tuples. Such representations are the building block for models of larger lexical units, e.g., phrases and sentences, following the principle of semantic compositionality (Pelletier, 1994). They are meant to address a number of properties that are relevant to the compositional aspects of meaning, namely, "linguistic creativity", "order sensitivity", "adaptive capacity", and "information scalability" (Turney, 2012). Compositional approaches have been reported for the estimation of compositional structures semantic similarity (Mitchell and Lapata., 2008; Mitchell and Lapata, 2010; Baroni and Zamparelli., 2010; Georgiladakis et al., 2015). A combination of a symbolic and a distributional compositionality approach was investigated by (Clark and Pulman, 2007), while an approach for compositional neural networks was presented in (Hammer, 2003). A recursive neural network model that learns compositional vector representations for phrases and sentences at any length and syntactic type was proposed by (Socher et al., 2012) and showed that it can be used for the prediction of sentiment as well.

In this work, we propose a compositional semantic-affective model, that is applicable to continuous affective spaces with one or more dimensions. This model is applied for the affective estimation of AN and NN pairs. The semantic-affective models are motivated by the assumption that "*semantic similarity implies affective sim-*

154


*Proceedings of NAACL-HLT 2016*, pages 154–160,
San Diego, California, June 12-17, 2016. ©2016 Association for Computational Linguistics

*ilarity*", while the proposed compositional model is motivated by the CDSM proposed by (Baroni and Zamparelli., 2010), that focuses on adjective-noun composition and represents adjectives as functions and nouns as vectors. The affective ratings estimated by the compositional model are compared and combined with the ones obtained by the non-compositional semantic-affective models. Similar fusion schemes to (Georgiladakis et al., 2015) that aim to capture the compositionality degree of each word pair are investigated.

## 2 Semantic-Affective model

Semantic-affective models are employed in order to estimate affective ratings of AN and NN pairs. We focus on three continuous affective dimensions: *valence* (positive vs. negative), *arousal* (calm vs. activated) and *dominance* (controlled vs. controller). Affective ratings of each dimension are estimated by the semantic-affective model which was proposed in (Malandrakis et al., 2013). This model, that is an expansion of (Turney and Littman, 2002), is defined in (1) and it is applicable both to words as well as n-gram tokens. The assumption of (1) is that the affective rating of a lexical token can be estimated by the linear combination of its semantic similarities to a set of seeds weighted with the seeds' affective ratings and trainable weights:

$$\hat{v}(t_j) = a_0 + \sum_{i=1}^{N} \alpha_i v(w_i) S(t_j, w_i), \qquad (1)$$

where $t_j$ is the unknown lexical token, $w_{1..N}$ are the seed words, $v(w_i)$, $\alpha_i$ are the affective rating and the weight corresponding to the word $w_i$ and $S(\cdot)$ is the semantic similarity between two tokens. $S(\cdot)$ is implemented within the distributional semantic models framework, following the assumption that tokens that occur in similar context tend to be semantically related (Harris, 1954). In this framework, each token is represented by a contextual feature vector that is formulated by the words that occur in a given distance from the current token in a corpus. The elements of the vectors are set according to a mutual information scheme as shown in (Palogiannidi et al., 2015). Then, the semantic similarity between two tokens is computed as the cosine of their feature vectors. The Affective Norms for English Words (Bradley and Lang, 1999) manually annotated affective lexicon was used for the selection of the seed words and Least Squares Estimation (LSE) was used for learning the weights $\alpha_i$.

### 2.1 Unigram and Bigram Affective Models

The unigram affective model ($U$) is based on the assumption that the two words that constitute the word pair contribute equally to its affective content and it is defined as

follows:

$$\hat{v}_U(p) = \frac{\hat{v}(w_1) + \hat{v}(w_2)}{2}, \qquad (2)$$

where $p$ is the word pair, and $\hat{v}(w_1)$ and $\hat{v}(w_2)$ are the affective ratings that are estimated using (1). The bigram semantic-affective model ($B$) handles each word pair as a single token, i.e., $\hat{v}_B(p) = \hat{v}(w_1 w_2)$, where $p$ is the word pair and $\hat{v}_B(p)$ is the affective rating of the word pair that it has been estimated using (1) for the bigram lexical token $t = w_1 w_2$.

## 3 Compositional Affective Models

Word semantics have been represented efficiently with vector space models, as shown in (Androutsopoulos and Malakasiotis, 2010; Malandrakis et al., 2013), however representing the semantics of lexical structures larger than words is not trivial (Baroni and Zamparelli., 2010). The reason is that the meaning of complex structures derives from various compositional phenomena (Pelletier, 1994).

Semantic compositionality allows the construction of complex meanings from simpler elements based on the principle that the meaning of a whole is a function of the meaning of the parts (Partee, 1995). The key characteristic of compositionality is that the meanings of the constituent parts are combined into a single token (Mitchell and Lapata., 2008; Mitchell and Lapata, 2010). Compositional approaches in vector-based semantics can be modelled by applying a function $f$ that acts on two constituents **a**, **b** in order to produce the compositional meaning **p**. Functions that were investigated by (Mitchell and Lapata., 2008; Mitchell and Lapata, 2010) are addition and multiplication. The additive compositional model takes the sum of the two vectors weighted with the appropriate weight matrices **A** and **B** respectively ($\mathbf{p} = \mathbf{Aa} + \mathbf{Bb}$) and the multiplicative model is the projection of the **ab** tensor product using a weight tensor **C** ($\mathbf{p} = \mathbf{Cab}$). These composition forms can be also simplified using the additive model with scalars instead of matrices. Similarly the multiplicative approach can be reduced to component-wise multiplication. Motivated by compositionality modeling (Baroni and Zamparelli., 2010) proposed an approach that focuses on adjective-noun composition according to which nouns are represented as vectors and adjective as functions.

In this work we assume that composition occurs in the affective rather than the semantic space and thus, we combine the affective ratings instead of the semantic representation of a phrase's constituent words. A compositional model that is applicable on continuous affective spaces with one or three dimensions is proposed. Results are shown for valence, however the proposed models are

$$
\begin{bmatrix} 1 & \hat{v}(h_1) & \hat{a}(h_1) & \hat{d}(h_1) \\ \vdots & \vdots & \vdots & \vdots \\ 1 & \hat{v}(h_K) & \hat{a}(h_K) & \hat{d}(h_K) \end{bmatrix} \begin{bmatrix} w_{10} & w_{20} & w_{30} \\ w_{11} & w_{21} & w_{31} \\ w_{12} & w_{22} & w_{32} \\ w_{13} & w_{23} & w_{33} \end{bmatrix} = \begin{bmatrix} \hat{v}(m.h_1) & \hat{a}(m.h_1) & \hat{d}(m.h_1) \\ \vdots & \vdots & \vdots \\ \hat{v}(m.h_K) & \hat{a}(m.h_K) & \hat{d}(m.h_K) \end{bmatrix} \tag{3}
$$

applicable to the rest affective dimensions as well[1].

## 3.1 Proposed compositional approach

In this paper, we focus on word pairs, i.e., the *modifier* (first word) and the *head* (second word). A word pair (also referred as test pair) $p$ is defined as: $p = m.h$, where $m$ is the modifier and $h$ is the head. The assumption of our affective compositional model is that the *modifier* modifies the *head*'s affective rating in order to estimate the word pair's affective rating. Modifier's impact is defined by a weight coefficients matrix or weight scalars depending on the dimensions of the compositional model. The weight coefficients are learned in a distributional approach, according to which $K$ pairs are extracted from a large corpus and serve as the training set of each modifier. The training pairs contain the same modifier with the current test pair and different head, i.e., $p' = m.*$, where $p'$ is the training word pair, $m$ is the modifier and $*$ indicates any head except from the test pair's $p$ head. For each test pair $p$, $K$ training pairs $p'$ are extracted.

The semantic-affective model of (1) is then employed to estimate the affective ratings of the training heads and the training pairs. The estimated affective ratings are incorporated in an LSE formulation where the ratings of the training pairs formulate the dependent variable and the ratings of the training heads formulate the independent variable. The proposed compositional approach is depicted in Figure 1. Training is performed separately

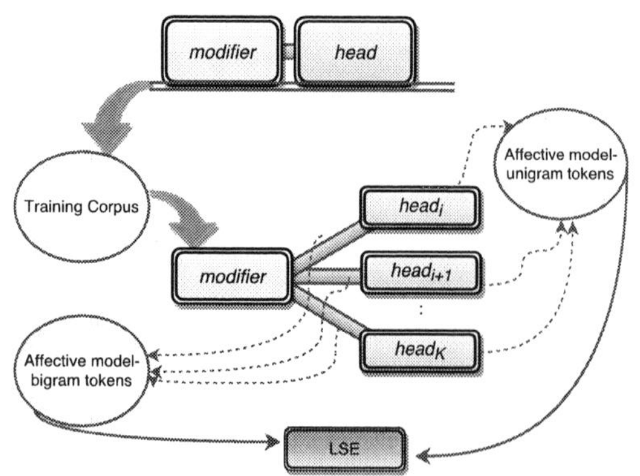


**Figure 1:** Compositional system overview.

for each modifier and the impact of each modifier is estimated through supervised learning, e.g., LSE. Finally,

the continuous affective ratings of the word pair are estimated via an additive model. This model takes directly into consideration only the head, while the modifier's impact is captured by the weight matrix. The general compositional model is shown below:

$$
\hat{v}_c(p) = \vec{\beta} + W\hat{v}(h), \tag{4}
$$

where $\hat{v}_c(p)$ is the compositional affective rating of the word pair $p$, $\vec{\beta}$ is the bias vector, $W$ is the coefficients matrix and $\hat{v}(h)$ is the affective rating of the head, estimated via (1). The compositional model may not always be the most appropriate for the estimation of a word pair's affective ratings. Thus, in order to measure the compositionality degree of each word pair the Mean Squared Error (MSE) of the model is measured. Specifically, the distance between the compositional affective ratings and the affective ratings is estimated via (1) and averaged over all training pairs:

$$
MSE(p) = \frac{1}{K} \sum_{j=1}^{K} (\hat{v}(p_j') - \hat{v}_c(p_j'))^2, \tag{5}
$$

where $MSE(p)$ is the MSE estimated for each pair $p$, $K$ is the number of the training pairs $p'$, $\hat{v}(p_j')$ is the affective rating of the training word pair $p_j'$ estimated using (1) for bigram tokens and $\hat{v}_c(p_j')$ is the corresponding affective rating estimated using the compositional model described in (4).

**3D compositional model (com3D):** Here we assume that three affective dimensions (valence, arousal, dominance) contribute to the affective content of the word pairs. The 3D compositional model is a special case of the general compositional model of (4), where $W \in \mathbb{R}^{3\times3}$ and contains the weight coefficients for the three affective dimensions and the bias vector $\vec{\beta} \in \mathbb{R}^{3\times1}$ and contains the bias of each affective dimension. The coefficient matrix $W$ and the bias vector $\vec{\beta}$ are estimated using LSE. Specifically, for each test pair $p$ with $K$ training pairs $p'$ $K$ linear equations with 4 unknown variables (3 for the affective dimensions and 1 for the bias) have to be solved. The linear system is shown in (3). The columns of the weight matrix correspond to valence ($w_{1*}$), arousal ($w_{2*}$) and dominance ($w_{3*}$), while the first row is the bias. With $\hat{v}(\cdot)$, $\hat{a}(\cdot)$, $\hat{d}(\cdot)$ we denote the valence, arousal and dominance affective ratings respectively.

**1D compositional model (com1D):** The 1D compositional model is a special case of the 3D compositional

---


[1]Evaluation results are not reported for the rest affective dimensions due to lack of groundtruth labels.

model and follows the assumption that each affective dimension is independent of the other affective dimensions. The dimensionality of the model is reduced and thus the behaviour of the modifier, i.e., the coefficient matrix $W$ and the bias vector $\vec{\beta}$ are substituted by two scalars. The general compositional model of (4) is transformed to the 1D compositional model using scalar variables. These two scalar coefficients are estimated similarly to the 3D model.

## 4 Fusion of affective models

The same word may have different contribution to the affective content of a phrase depending on the context. For example, when the word "dog" appears in the word pair "happy dog" the conveyed affect is positive, which it is reversed when it appears in the word pair "dead dog". The accuracy of the proposed affective models depend on the compositionality degree that characterize the pairs of interest. By combining different models we aim to achieve more accurate affective scores.

The first fusion scheme combines the affective ratings estimated by the compositional and semantic-affective models. The underlying assumption is that all models contribute equally to the affective meaning of a word pair, that is a word pair exhibits both compositional and non-compositional aspects. This scheme is based on the averaging of affective ratings defined as follows:

$$\Phi_{avg}(p) = \frac{1}{M} \sum_{i=1}^{M} \hat{v}_i(p), \tag{6}$$

where $\Phi_{avg}(p)$ is the fused affective rating of the word pair $p$, $M$ denotes the number of fused models and $\hat{v}_i(p)$ stands for the estimated affective rating of word pair $p$, i.e., $\hat{v}_1(p) = \hat{v}_U(p)$, $\hat{v}_2(p) = \hat{v}_B(p)$, $\hat{v}_3(p) = \hat{v}_{c1}(p)$, $\hat{v}_4(p) = \hat{v}_{c3}(p)$. A weighted variant of (6) was also investigated, as follows:

$$\Phi_{avg}^{w}(p) = \frac{1}{\sum_{i=1}^{M} w_i} \sum_{i=1}^{M} w_i \hat{v}_i(p), \tag{7}$$

where $\Phi_{avg}^{w}(p)$ is the fused affective rating of the word pair $p$, $\hat{v}_{(}p)$ stands for the affective rating of word pair $p$ estimated by the affective models, as explained in (6) and $w_i$ are weights estimated via linear regression. Motivated by the fusion scheme proposed in (Georgiladakis et al., 2015), we propose the use of MSE weight appropriately the compositional and the semantic-affective models. MSE is estimated during training phase as shown in (5) and the weight parameter is defined as $\lambda'(p) = \frac{0.5}{1+e^{-MSE(p)}}$, where $MSE(p)$ is the MSE measured for each word pair $p$ and $\lambda'(p)$ is estimated for each word pair $p$ based on the compositional model. (4) is applied both on 1D and 3D compositional models and the derived

$\lambda'(p)$ are averaged in order to formulate the parameter $\lambda(p)$ that is used in the fusion scheme as follows:

$$\Phi_{avg}^{\text{MSE}}(p) = \lambda(p)(w_1 \hat{v}_B(p) + w_2 \hat{v}_U(p)) + (1 - \lambda(p))(w_3 \hat{v}_{c1}(p) + w_4 \hat{v}_{c3}(p)), \tag{8}$$

where $w_1, ... w_4$ are the weights that correspond to each affective model and estimated through LSE and $\sum_{i=1}^{4} w_i = 1$, $\hat{v}_*(p)$ is the affective rating of each word pair derived from each affective model, and $\lambda(p)$ is meant for weighting the contribution of compositional and non-compositional models.

## 5 Experimental Procedure and Results

### 5.1 Dataset

For evaluating the proposed semantic-affective models we use two word pairs datasets, one consisting of AN and one consisting of NN. The word pairs of the evaluation datasets were extracted from movie reviews by (Socher et al., 2013) as follows. Each movie review was first split into the constituent sentences and then into the constituent phrases. The derived sentences and phrases were annotated with respect to their polarity using crowdsourcing. We kept only the word pairs that have an adjective or noun as their first word, and their second word is a noun. The created dataset consists of 1009 AN and 357 NN pairs.

### 5.2 Semantic-affective models

The proposed models estimate the affective ratings for each affective dimension in a continuous scale in [-1,1], however we only report results for valence. The semantic-affective model shown in (1) was applied for the unigram (U) and bigram (B) models as defined in Section 2.1. The parameters of the semantic-affective model are set as follows: $N = 600$ seeds, for $S(\cdot)$ a context-based metric of semantic similarity was applied with window size equal to one, while the extracted features were weighted according to positive pointwise mutual information (Church and Hanks, 1990). LSE was applied for estimating the weights $\alpha$ of (1). The parameters of the model are detailed in (Palogiannidi et al., 2015). The compositional model requires a large corpus[2] for extracting the training pairs of each modifier (Iosif et al., 2016). For each modifier all word pairs with the same modifier are extracted creating hundreds of training pairs.

### 5.3 Fusion

We investigate both weighted and unweighted average schemes while a compositionality criterion based on the

---

[2]We use a web harvested corpus that was created posing one query that was formulated for each vocabulary word on search engines and downloading and aggregating the snippets of 1K top-ranked document.

compositional models' MSE is also incorporated. In (6) the average of all affective models is estimated, while a weighted version of this scheme is shown in (7). LSE was adopted in order to estimate the weights that capture each model's contribution. $\Phi_{avg}^{\mathrm{MSE}}$ was implemented in a two-fold cross validation scenario. Moreover, we introduce a compositionality criterion based on the MSE that was measured during the compositional training process. Then the weighted average of the compositional and the non-compositional semantic-affective models were estimated as shown in (8). The weights $w_i$ were estimated through LSE and two-fold cross validation. The parameter $\lambda(p)$ used in (14) was computed as the average of the corresponding parameters that are estimated for the 1D and the 3D compositional models.

### 5.4 Results

We compare the valence ratings that were automatically estimated against the human valence ratings that were collected via crowdsoursing. We report evaluation results based on three evaluation metrics, namely, Pearson correlation coefficient between the estimated and the human valence ratings, binary classification accuracy (positive vs. negative valence ratings) and F-measure.

| Aff. | Correlation | | Acc. (%) | | F-measure | |
|---|---|---|---|---|---|---|
| Model | NN | AN | NN | AN | NN | AN |
| Chance | - | - | 76.4 | 74.1 | - | - |
| $U$ | 0.581 | 0.573 | 84.3 | 80.0 | 0.903 | 0.874 |
| $B$ | 0.507 | 0.451 | 76.8 | 74.6 | 0.841 | 0.824 |
| $com$1D | 0.523 | 0.552 | 79.2 | 77.2 | 0.880 | 0.866 |
| $com$3D | 0.538 | 0.552 | 79.8 | 78.1 | 0.883 | 0.870 |
| $\Phi_{avg}$ | 0.624 | 0.609 | **86.2** | 80.9 | **0.916** | **0.882** |
| $\Phi_{avg}^{w}$ | **0.630** | 0.608 | 85.7 | **81.3** | **0.911** | **0.882** |
| $\Phi_{avg}^{\mathrm{MSE}}$ | 0.624 | **0.613** | 85.5 | 80.9 | **0.912** | **0.883** |

**Table 1:** Performance of affective models for valence estimation.

The evaluation results are reported in Table 1 for several semantic-affective models. Regarding individual models, the highest performance is achieved by the unigram model for both AN and NN. This may be attributed to the very good performance at the unigram model as reported in (Malandrakis et al., 2013; Palogiannidi et al., 2015). However the fact that when moving from words to word pairs the performance drops by about 11% is a strong indicator of the need a compositional modeling. As expected, the accuracy of compositional models is between the accuracy of two semantic-affective models. Similar results have been also obtained for compositional models in the semantic space (Georgiladakis et al., 2015). Using fusion schemes that combine the compositional with the semantic-affective models we can achieve the best performance exceeding the performance of all individual models. Simple fusion schemes such as average of

the affective ratings derived from the individual models can increase the performance of the best model up to 5% in terms of correlation. Similar performance increase is observed for the rest of the evaluation metrics as well.

## 6 Conclusions and Future Work

We proposed a compositional model for estimating continuous affective ratings of AN and NN structures consisting of words that formulate modifier-head pairs. The composition was motivated by the affective interaction of modifier and head words, while it was implemented as a affine operation in the continuous affective space. The compositional models were compared and fused with two semantic-affective models defined at the unigram and bigram level. The best performance overall was achieved by the fusion-based approach suggesting that there is not a single model that works for all word pairs, i.e., the degree and type of compositionality is different for each word pair.

Currently, we are working on the improvement of the fusion schemes with focus on the identifying the parameters that control the degree of compositionality , i.e., the $\lambda(p)$ parameter. Also, we are investigating the generalization of the proposed model across semantically/affectively more complex structures. Our long-term goal is to formulate a generic framework for integrating the compositional and non-compositional aspects of semantic and affective spaces bringing together theories from the areas of cognitive science psycholinguistics and data-driven computational models.

**Acknowledgements:** The authors were partially funded by the SpeDial project supported by the EU Seventh Framework Programme (FP7), grant number 611396 and the BabyRobot project supported by the EU Horizon 2020 Programme, grant number: 687831. Many thanks to Spiros Georgiladakis for the useful discusions on compositional models.

## References

Ion Androutsopoulos and P. Malakasiotis. 2010. A survey of paraphrasing and textual entailment methods. *Journal of Artificial Intelligence Research*, pages 135–187.

M. Baroni and R. Zamparelli. 2010. Nouns are vectors, adjectives are matrices: Representing adjective-noun constructions in semantic space. In *Proc. of Empirical Methods in Natural Language Processing (EMNLP)*.

M. Bradley and P. Lang. 1999. Affective norms for English words (ANEW): Stimuli, instruction manual and affective ratings, technical report c-1. Technical report, The Center for Research in Psychophysiology, University of Florida.

F. Celli. 2012. Unsupervised personality recognition for social network sites. In *Proc. of International Conference on Digital Society (ICDS)*, pages 59–62.

K. W. Church and P. Hanks. 1990. Word association norms, mutual information, and lexicography. *Computational Linguistics*, 16(1):22–29.

S. Clark and S. Pulman. 2007. Combining symbolic and distributional models of meaning. In *AAAI Spring Symposium: Quantum Interaction*, pages 52–55.

A. Esuli and F. Sebastiani. 2006. SentiWordNet: A publicly available lexical resource for opinion mining. In *Proc. of LREC*, pages 417–422.

S. Georgiladakis, Iosif E., and Potamianos A. 2015. Fusion of compositional network-based and lexical function distributional semantic models. In *Proceedings of CMCL*, pages 39–47.

B. Hammer. 2003. Compositionality in neural systems. *The handbook of brain theory and neural networks*, pages 244–248.

Z. Harris. 1954. Distributional structure. *Word*, 10(23):146–162.

E. Iosif, S. Georgiladakis, and A. Potamianos. 2016. Cognitively Motivated Distributional Representations of Meaning. In *Proc. of 10th Language Resources and Evaluation Conference (LREC)*.

N. Malandrakis, A. Potamianos, E. Iosif, and S. S. Narayanan. 2013. Distributional semantic models for affective text analysis. *IEEE Transactions on Audio, Speech, and Language Processing*, 21(11):2379–2392.

J. Mitchell and M. Lapata. 2008. Vector-based models of semantic composition. In *Proc. of (ACL)*, pages 236–244.

J. Mitchell and M. Lapata. 2010. Composition in distributional models of semantics. *Cognitive Science*, 34(8):1388–1429.

E. Palogiannidi, E. Iosif, P. Koutsakis, and A. Potamianos. 2015. Valence, Arousal and Dominance Estimation for English, German, Greek, Portuguese and Spanish Lexica using Semantic Models. In *Proc. of Interspeech*, pages 1527–1531.

B. Pang and L. Lee. 2008. Opinion mining and sentiment analysis. *Foundations and trends in information retrieval*, 2(1-2):1–135.

B. Pang, L. Lee, and S. Vaithyanathan. 2002. Thumbs up?: sentiment classification using machine learning techniques. In *Proc. of the ACL-02 conference on Empirical methods in natural language processing*, pages 79–86. Association for Computational Linguistics.

B. Partee. 1995. Lexical semantics and compositionality. *An invitation to cognitive science: Language*, 1:311–360.

Francis J. Pelletier. 1994. The principle of semantic compositionality. *Journal of Topoi*, 13(1):11–24.

D. Quercia, J. Ellis, L. Capra, and J. Crowcroft. 2011. In the mood for being influential on twitter. In *Proc. of Privacy, Security, Risk and Trust (PASSAT) and IEEE Conference on Social Computing (SocialCom)*, pages 307–314.

S. Rosenthal, A. Ritter, P. Nakov, and V. Stoyanov. 2014. Semeval-2014 Task 9: Sentiment Analysis in Twitter. In *Proc. of the 8th International Workshop on Semantic Evaluation (SemEval 2014)*, pages 73–80. Association for Computational Linguistics and Dublin City University.

S. Rosenthal, P. Nakov, S. Kiritchenko, S. M. Mohammad, A. Ritter, and V. Stoyanov. 2015. Semeval-2015 Task 10: Sentiment Analysis in Twitter. In *Proc. of the 9th International Workshop on Semantic Evaluation (SemEval 2015)*, pages 451–463. Association for Computational Linguistics.

R. Socher, B. Huval, C. D Manning, and A.Y Ng. 2012. Semantic compositionality through recursive matrix-vector spaces. In *Proceedings of the 2012 Joint Conference on Empirical Methods in Natural Language Processing and Computational Natural Language Learning*, pages 1201–1211. AC:.

R. Socher, A. Perelygin, J.W., J. Chuang, C. Manning, A.N., and C. Potts. 2013. Parsing With Compositional Vector Grammars. In *EMNLP*.

C. Strapparava and R. Mihalcea. 2007. SemEval-2007 Task 14: Affective text. In *Proc. of SemEval*, pages 70–74.

C. Strapparava and A. Valitutti. 2004. WordNetAffect: an affective extension of WordNet. In *Proc. of LREC*, pages 1083–1086.

P. Turney and M. Littman. 2002. Unsupervised learning of semantic orientation from a hundred-billion-word corpus, technical report ERC-1094 (NRC 44929). Technical report, National Research Council of Canada.

P. D. Turney. 2012. Domain and function: A dual-space model of semantic relations and compositions. *Journal of Artificial Intelligence Research*, 44:533–585.

T. Wilson, J. Wiebe, and P. Hoffmann. 2005. Recognizing contextual polarity in phrase-level sentiment analysis. In *Proc. of Human Languages Technologies and Empirical Methods in Natural Language Processing*, pages 347–354.

# Fracking Sarcasm using Neural Network

**Aniruddha Ghosh**
University College Dublin
aniruddha.ghosh@ucdconnect.ie

**Tony Veale**
University College Dublin
tony.veale@ucd.ie

## Abstract

Precise semantic representation of a sentence and definitive information extraction are key steps in the accurate processing of sentence meaning, especially for figurative phenomena such as sarcasm, Irony, and metaphor cause literal meanings to be discounted and secondary or extended meanings to be intentionally profiled. Semantic modelling faces a new challenge in social media, because grammatical inaccuracy is commonplace yet many previous state-of-the-art methods exploit grammatical structure. For sarcasm detection over social media content, researchers so far have counted on Bag-of-Words(BOW), N-grams etc. In this paper, we propose a neural network semantic model for the task of sarcasm detection. We also review semantic modelling using Support Vector Machine (SVM) that employs constituency parse-trees fed and labeled with syntactic and semantic information. The proposed neural network model composed of Convolution Neural Network(CNN) and followed by a Long short term memory (LSTM) network and finally a Deep neural network(DNN). The proposed model outperforms state-of-the-art text-based methods for sarcasm detection, yielding an F-score of .92.

## 1 Introduction

Figurative language, such as metaphor, irony and sarcasm, is a ubiquitous aspect of human communication from ancient religious texts to modern micro-texts. Sarcasm detection, despite being a well-studied phenomenon in cognitive science and linguistics (Gibbs and Clark, 1992; gib, 2007; Kreuz and Glucksberg, 1989; Utsumi, 2000), is still at its infancy as a computational task. Detection is difficult because literal meaning is discounted and secondary or extended meanings are instead intentionally profiled. In social contexts, one's ability to detect sarcasm relies heavily on social cues such as sentiment, belief, and speaker's intention. Sarcasm is mocking and often involves harsh delivery to achieve savage putdowns, even though it can be also crafted more gently as the accretion of politeness and the abatement of hostility around a criticism (Brown and Levinson, 1978; Dews and Winner, 1995). Moreover, sarcasm often couches criticism within a humorous atmosphere (Dews and Winner, 1999). (Riloff et al., 2013) addressed one common form of sarcasm as the juxtaposition of a positive sentiment attached to a negative situation, or vice versa. (Tsur et al., 2010) modeled sarcasm via a composition of linguistic elements, such as specific surface features about a product, frequent words, and punctuation marks. (González-Ibánez et al., 2011) views sarcasm as a conformation of lexical and pragmatic factors such as emoticons and profile references in social media. Most research approaches toward the automatic detection of sarcasm are text-based and consider sarcasm to be as a function of contrasting conditions or lexical clues. Such approaches extract definitive lexical cues as features, where the linguistic scale of features is stretched from words to phrases to provide richer contexts for analysis. Lexical feature cues may yield good results, yet without a precise semantic representation of a sentence, which is key for determining the intended gist of a sentence, robust automatic sarcasm



*Proceedings of NAACL-HLT 2016*, pages 161–169,
San Diego, California, June 12-17, 2016. ©2016 Association for Computational Linguistics

detection will remain a difficult challenge to realize. Accurate semantic modelling of context becomes obligatory for automatic sarcasm detection if social cues and extended meaning are to be grasped.

Encouraging an immediate and very social use of language, social media platforms such as Twitter[1] are rich sources of texts for Natural Language Processing (NLP). Social micro-texts are dense in figurative language, and are useful for figurative analysis because of their topicality, ease of access, and the use of self-annotation via hashtag. In Twitter, language is distorted, often plumbing the depths of bad language (Eisenstein, 2013). Yet due to the presence of grammatical errors liberally mixed with social media markers (hashtags, emoticons, profiles), abbreviations, and code switching, these micro-texts are harder to parse, and parsing is the most commonly used method to obtain a semantic representation of a sentence. The accuracy of state-of-the-art constituency parsers over tweets can be significantly lower than that for normal texts, so social media researchers still largely rely on surface level features. With the recent move to artificial neural networks in NLP, ANNs provide an alternative basis for semantic modelling. In this paper, we perform semantic modelling of sentences using neural networks for the task of sarcasm detection. The paper is organized as follows. Section 2 surveys related works, section 3 outlines methods of data collection and data processing, section 4 describes the recursive SVM model, section 5 describes the neural network model, section 6 & 7 outline our experimental setup and experimental analysis respectively, while section 8 presents a simple sarcastic Twitter bot. Finally, section 9 concludes with a short discussion of future work.

## 2 Related work

Semantic modelling of sentence meaning is a well-researched topic in NLP. Due to 'bad language' in Twitter and a noticeable drop of accuracy for start-of-the-art constituency parsers on tweets, the semantic modelling of tweets has captured the attention of researchers. To build a semantic representation of a sentence in various NLP tasks such as sentiment analysis, researchers have used syntactic structure to compose a total representation as a function of the word-vector representation of a sentence's parts. (Nakagawa et al., 2010) describes a Tree-CRF classifier which uses a data-driven dependency parser, maltparser[2], to obtain a parse tree for a sentence, and whose composition function uses the head-modifier relations of the parse tree. (Mitchell and Lapata, 2010) and (Mitchell and Lapata, 2008) defined the composition function of a sentence by algebraic operations over word meaning vectors to obtain sentence meaning vectors. (Guevara, 2010) and (Malakasiotis, 2011) formulated their composition function using a set of specific syntactic relations or specific word categories (Baroni and Zamparelli, 2010). (Socher et al., 2011) proposed a structured recursive neural network based on the convolutional operation, while (Kalchbrenner et al., 2014) proposed a convolution neural network (CNN) with dynamic k-max pooling, considering max pooling as function of input length. For sarcasm detection, due to the complexity of the task and the somewhat poorer accuracy of start-of-the-art constituency parsers on tweets, researchers have considered surface level lexical and syntactic cues as legitimate features. Kreuz and Caucci (Kreuz and Caucci, 2007) explored the role of lexical indicators, such as interjections (e.g., "gee" or "gosh"), punctuation symbols (e.g., '?'), intensifiers, and other linguistic markers for e.g. non-veridicality and hyperbole, in recognizing sarcasm in narratives. Tsur (Tsur et al., 2010) noted the occurrence of "yay!" or "great!" as a recurring aspect of sarcastic patterns in Amazon product reviews. Davidov (Davidov et al., 2010) examined the effectiveness of social media indicators such as hashtags to identify sarcasm. Lukin (Lukin and Walker, 2013) proposed a potential bootstrapping method for sarcasm classification in social dialogue to expand lexical N-gram cues related to sarcasm (e.g. "oh really", "no way", etc.) as well as lexico-syntactic patterns. Riloff (Riloff et al., 2013) and Liebrecht (Liebrecht et al., 2013) applied N-grams features to a classifier for English and Dutch tweets and observed that some topics recur frequently in sarcastic tweets, such as schools, dentists, church life, public transport, the weather and so on.

---

[1] https://twitter.com

[2] http://www.maltparser.org/

In this paper, we investigate the usefulness of neural-network-based semantic modelling for sarcasm detection. We propose a neural network model for semantic modelling in tweets that combines Deep Neural Networks (DNNs) with time-convolution and Long Short-Term Memory (LSTM). The proposed model is compared to a recursive Support Vector Machine (SVM) model based on constituency parse trees.

## 3 Dataset

Twitter provides functionality to users to summarize their intention via hashtags. Using a user's self-declaration of sarcasm as a retrieval cue, #sarcasm, we have crawled the Twittersphere. Since this simple heuristic misses those uses of sarcasm that lack an explicit mention of #sarcasm, we used LSA-based approach to extend the list of indicative hashtags (e.g.to include #sarcastic, #yeahright etc.). We also harvested tweets from user profiles with a strong bias toward sincerity or (for professional wits) sarcasm. To build our sarcastic data set we aggregated all tweets containing one or more positive markers of sarcasm, but removed such markers from the tweets, while tweets which did not contain any positive markers of sarcasm were considered non-sarcastic. The training dataset of 39K tweets is evenly balanced containing 18k sarcastic data and 21K non-sarcastic data. As a test set, we have created a dataset of 2000 tweets annotated by an internal team of researchers. For purposes of comparison, we also used two different publicly available sarcasm datasets.

Social media contains many interesting elements such as hashtags, profile references and emoticons. Due to the size limitation of tweets, users exploit these elements to provide contextual information. To tightly focus our research question, we did not include sarcasm from the larger conversational context and thus dropped all profile information from the input text. As users often use multi-worded hashtags to add an additional sarcastic dimension to a tweet. we used a hashtag splitter to split these phrasal tags and appended their words to the text.

For the recursive-SVM, we used the Stanford constituency parser[3] for parsing tweets. In order to ex-

tract maximum information from the parse tree, we used both a pre-processing and a post-processing method which are described below.

### 3.1 Recursive-SVM Data Processing

Constituency parse trees offer a syntactic model of a sentence which can form a strong basis for semantic modelling. In order to use Stanford constituency parser here, the tweets were first pre-processed by removing social media markers such as profile references, retweets and hashtags. As a tweet may contain multiple sentences, each is split into sentences using the Standford sentence splitter, parsed separately and then stitched back together with a sentence tag (S). Hashtags are dense annotations offered by users of their own texts, and their scope generally applies to the entire content of a tweet. Thus we restored back Hashtags into parse tree by attaching them to the root node of the parse tree of the tweet with a tag (HT). Let's consider the following tweet as example,

```
I love when people start rumors about
me.  #not
```

Hashtag #not is attached to root of parse tree using Part-of-speech tag (HT) (Figure 1).

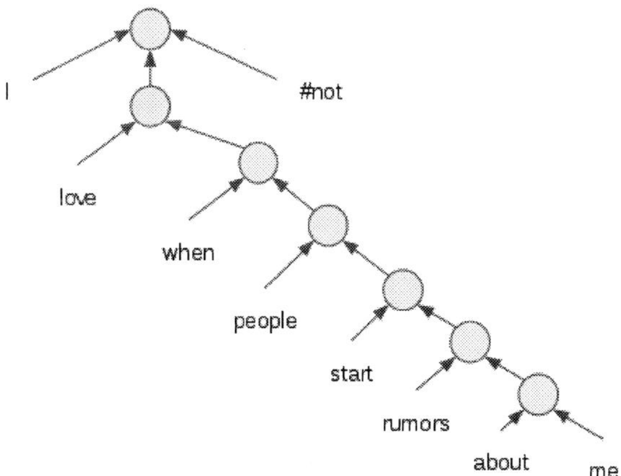



**Figure 1:** parse tree with Hashtag

## 4 Recursive SVM

We now define a recursive-SVM model. Consider a subjective sentence (S) containing n phrases with m words in total. $w_l$, $b_l$ and $pos_l$ denote the surface

---

| Feature Type | Feature |
|---|---|
| Node | $w_i$ |
| Node | $w_i pos_i$ |
| Node | $w_i pos_i b_i$ |
| Node+Edge | $w_i..w_j pos_i..pos_j b_i..pos_j$ |
| Node+Edge | $w_i..w_j pos_i..pos_j b_i..pos_j c_i+1..c_j$ |
| Node+Edge | $w_i..w_j pos_i..pos_j b_i..pos_j c_i \quad + 1..c_j o_i + 1..o_j$ |

Table 1: recursive SVM features

form, root form and part-of-speech respectively of $l^{th}$ word of S, while $n_i$ denotes the $i^{th}$ node and $p_i$, $h_i$, and $o_i$ denote phrase, head node and offensive word-marker of the $i^{th}$ node respectively. The $0^{th}$ node is the root node, while $s_i$ and $sa_i$ denote the predicted values of sentiment polarity and sarcastic polarity of the constituency subtrees whose root is the $i^{th}$ node, ($s_i \in +1, 0, sa_i \in +1, 0$). Table 1 shows training vectors ($x_i \in \Re^n$, i = 0, .. , n) where $y_i$ = 1, 0 is the label for the $i^{th}$ node. As the number of parameters is larger than the number of instances, dual-based solvers offer the best fit for this problem. Through grid-search, the optimum penalty value (C) is determined and set to 1000 and 2000 for sentiment and sarcasm detection respectively. The stopping tolerance value was set to -0.0001. Among the variation of different loss functions, L2-regularized L1-loss and L2-loss function yielded the best results.

## 5 Neural network

Semantic modelling of sentence meaning using neural networks has been a target of attention in the social media community. Neural network architectures, such as CNN, DNN, RNN, and Recursive Neural Networks (RecNN) have shown excellent capabilities for modelling complex word composition in a sentence. A sarcastic text can be considered elementally as a sequence of text signals or word combinations. RNN is a perfect fit for modelling temporal text signals as it includes a temporal memory component, which allows the model to store the temporal contextual information directly in the model. It can aggregate the entire sequence into a temporal context that is free of explicit size constraints. Among the many implementations of RNNs, LSTMs are easy to train and do not suffer from vanishing or exploding gradients while per-

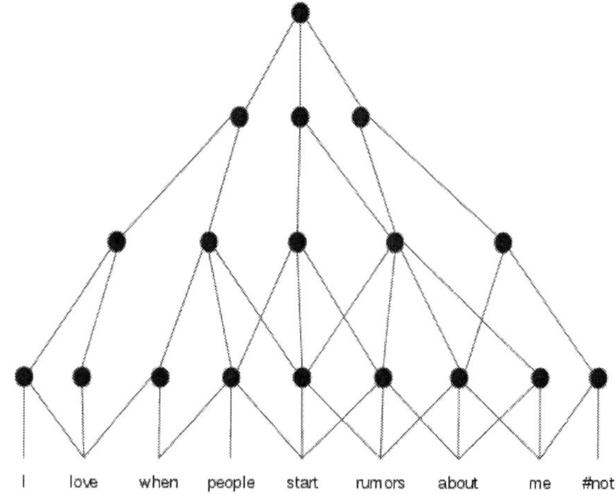


Figure 2: Sentence modelling with CNN

forming back propagation through time. LSTM has the capability to remember long distance temporal dependencies. Moreover, as they performs temporal text modelling over input features, higher level modelling can distinguish factors of linguistic variation within the input. CNNs can also capture temporal text sequence through convolutional filters. CNNs reduce frequency variation and convolutional filters connect a subset of the feature space that is shared across the entire input (Chan and Lane, 2015). (Dos Santos et al., 2015) have shown that CNNs can directly capture temporal text patterns for shorter texts, yet in longer texts, where temporal text patterns may span across 15 to 20 words, CNNs must rely on higher-level fully connected layers to model long distance dependencies as the maximum convolutional filter width for a text is 5 (Figure 2).

Another major limitation of CNNs is the fixed convolutional filter width, which is not suitable for different lengths of temporal text patterns and cannot always resolve dependencies properly. Obtaining the optimal filter size is expensive and corpus-dependent, while LSTM operates without a fixed context window size. LSTM's performance can be improved by providing better features. Following the proposal of (Vincent et al., 2008), it can be beneficial to exploit a CNN's ability to reduce frequency variation and map input features into composite robust features and using it as an input to a LSTM network. DNNs are appropriate for mapping features into a more separable space. A fully connected

DNN, added on top of an LSTM network, can provide better classification by mapping between output and hidden variables by transforming features into an output space. In the following section we define our proposed network in detail.

## 5.1   Input layer

Consider a tweet as input containing n words. The tweet is converted into a vector by replacing each word with its dictionary index $s \in \Re^{1 \times n}$. To resolve different lengths of input, the tweet vector is padded and the tweet is converted into matrix $s \in \Re^{1 \times l}$, where $l$ is the maximum length of tweets in the input corpus. The input vector is fed to the embedding layer which converts each word into a distributional vector of dimension D. Thus the input tweet matrix is converted to $s \in \Re^{l \times D}$.

## 5.2   Convolutional network

The aim of a convolution network is to reduce frequency variation through convolutional filters and extracting discriminating word sequences as a composite feature map for the LSTM layer. The convolution operation maps the input matrix $s \in \Re^{l \times D}$ into $c \in \Re^{|s|+m-1}$ using a convolutional filter $k \in \Re^{D \times m}$. Each component is computed as follows:

$$c_i = (s * k)_i = \sum_{k,j} (S_{:,i-m+1:i} \otimes F)_{kj} \quad (1)$$

Convolution filter, which has the same dimension D of the input matrix, which slides along the column dimension of the input matrix, performing an element wise product between a column slice $s$ and a filter matrix $k$ producing a vector component $c_i$ and summed to create a feature map $c \in R^{1(|s|m+1)}$. f filters create a feature map $C \in R^{f(|s|m+1)}$. We chose *Sigmoid* for non-linearity. Initially we passed the output of the convolutional network through a *pooling* layer and *max-pooling* is used with size 2 and 3. Later, we discarded the *max-pooling* layer and fed the LSTM network with all of the composite features to judge sarcasm, which improved the performance of the model.

## 5.3   LSTM

RNN has demonstrated the power of semantic modelling quite efficiently by incorporating feedback cycles in the network architecture. RNN networks include a temporal memory component, which allows the model to store the temporal contextual information directly in the model. At each time step, it considers the current input $x_t$ and hidden state $h_{t-1}$. Thus the RNN is unable to plot long term dependencies if the gap between two time steps becomes too large. (Hochreiter and Schmidhuber, 1997) introduced LSTM, which is able to plot long term dependencies by defining each memory cell with a set of gates $\Re^d$, where $d$ is the memory dimension of hidden state of LSTM, and it does not suffer from vanishing or exploding gradient while performing back propagation through time. LSTM contains three gates, which are functions of $x_t$ and $h_{t-1}$: input gate $i_t$, forget gate $f_t$, and output gate $o_t$. The gates jointly decide on the memory update mechanism. Equation (3) and (2) denote the amount of information to be discarded or to be stored from and to store in memory. Equation (5) denotes the output of the cell $c_t$.

$$i_t = \sigma(W_i[h_{t-1}, x_t] + b_i) \quad (2)$$

$$f_t = \sigma(W_f[h_{t-1}, x_t] + b_f) \quad (3)$$

$$q_t = tanh(W_q[h_{t-1}, x_t] + b_q) \quad (4)$$

$$o_t = \sigma(W_o[h_{t-1}, x_t] + b_o) \quad (5)$$

$$c_t = f_t \odot c_{t-1} + i_t \odot q_t \quad (6)$$

$$h_t = o_t \odot tanh(c_t) \quad (7)$$

## 5.4   Deep Neural Network Layer

The output of LSTM layer is passed to a fully connected DNN layer, which produces a higher order feature set based on the LSTM output, which is easily separable for the desired number of classes. Finally a softmax layer is added on top of the DNN layer. Training of network is performed by minimizing the binary cross-entropy error. For parameter optimization, we have used ADAM (Kingma and Ba, 2014) with the learning rate set to 0.001.

## 6   Experiment

To evaluate both models, we have tested rigorously with different experimental setups. For the recursive SVM, we employed different sets of feature combinations mentioned in table 1. In the neural network model, we opted for a word embedding dimension

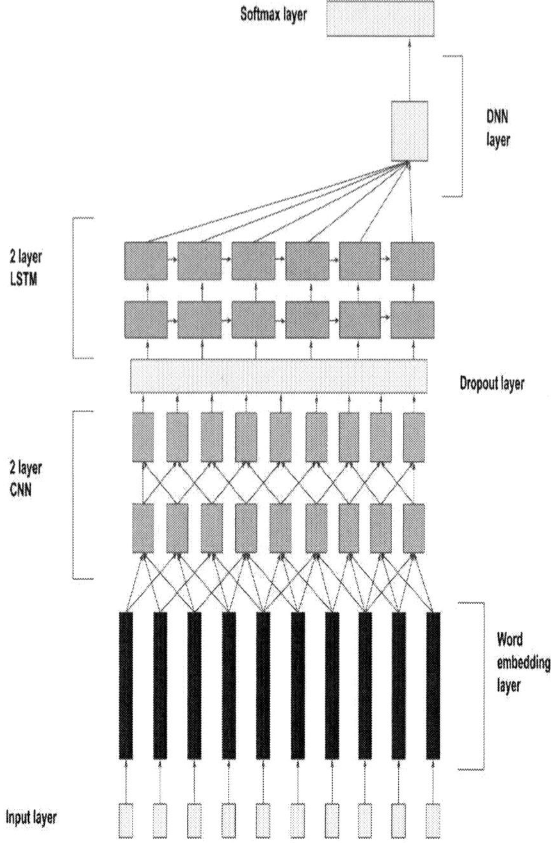



**Figure 3:** Neural network

set to 256. We tested our model with different settings of the hyperparameters for CNN (number of filter, filter size), LSTM (hidden memory dimension, dropout ratio), and DNN (number of hidden memory units (HMU)). Initially we passed the output of CNN via a *maxdropout* layer, with *maxpooling* size 2 and 3, to the LSTM, but later we dropped the maxpooling layer, which improved the performance by 2%.

In our experiment, apart from the combination of CNN, LSTM, and DNN, we observed the performance for each of the neural networks individually. The CNN network is investigated by varying the number of filters and the filter widths, set to 64, 128, 256 and 2, 3 respectively. For the LSTM network, the number of memory units is varied from 64 to 256. *Sigmoid* is chosen as activation function for both networks. We used Gaussian initialization scaled by the fan-in and the fan-out for the embed-

ding layer and Gaussian initialization scaled by the fan-in for the CNN, the LSTM, and the DNN layer as initial probability distribution. The code was implemented using *keras*[4] library.

## 7 Experimental Analysis

In the neural network, success depends on the apt input and the selection of hyperparameters. As we observed that the inclusion of hashtag information in the recursive-SVM method gained a better F-score, we pertained the same input structure for the neural network. Apart from difficulties in training a neural network, enormous training time is another passive obstacle. We observed that compared to stacked LSTM network, the CNN-LSTM network converges faster as CNN reduces frequency variation and produces better composite representation of the input to the LSTM network. Sarcasm detection is considered a complex task, as very subtle contextual information often triggers the sarcastic notion. Thus we noticed that the inclusion of a dropout layer on top of the CNN layer, our model suffered a decrease in performance. In the testing dataset, we observed an interesting example.

```
I don't know about you man but I love
the history homework.
```

With the dropout layer, model identified above mentioned example as non-sarcastic, yet without the dropout layer, our model labeled it as sarcastic. This indicates that the word "man", which functions as an intensifier of sarcasm in this context, was dropped out from the output of the CNN layer. Also we observed that incrementing the filter width of the CNN layer boosted the performance of our model by a small margin. To obtain the apt network size, we have also trained with bigger network sizes and larger filter widths, but no improvement has been observed. Table 2 contains the experimental results over our dataset.

Sarcasm is a very subjective phenomenon. Even for the human annotators, it was quite hard to decide if the speaker was sarcastic or not. It was interesting to observe the performance of our model when human annotators interpreted differently. Since our

---

[4]http://keras.io/

166

| Model | Feature/Hyper parameter | Precision | Recall | F-score |
|---|---|---|---|---|
| recursive SVM | BOW + POS | .719 | .613 | .663 |
| recursive SVM | BOW + POS + Sentiment | .722 | .661 | .691 |
| recursive SVM | BOW + POS + Sentiment + HT-splitter | .743 | .721 | .732 |
| CNN + CNN | filter size = 64 + filter width = 2 | .838 | .857 | .847 |
| CNN + CNN | filter size = 128 + filter width = 2 | .842 | .86 | .854 |
| CNN + CNN | filter size = 256 + filter width = 2 | .855 | .879 | .868 |
| CNN + CNN | filter size = 64 + filter width = 3 | .839 | .854 | .847 |
| CNN + CNN | filter size = 128 + filter width = 3 | .856 | .879 | .868 |
| CNN + CNN | filter size = 256 + filter width = 3 | .861 | .882 | .872 |
| LSTM + LSTM | hidden memory unit = 64 | .849 | .816 | .832 |
| LSTM + LSTM | hidden memory unit = 128 | .854 | .871 | .862 |
| LSTM + LSTM | hidden memory unit = 256 | .868 | .89 | .879 |
| CNN + LSTM + DNN (with dropout) | filter size = 256 + filter width = 2 + HMU = 256 | .899 | .91 | .904 |
| CNN + LSTM + DNN (without dropout) | filter size = 256 + filter width = 2 + HMU = 256 | .912 | .911 | .912 |
| CNN + LSTM + DNN (without dropout) | filter size = 256 + filter width = 3 + HMU = 256 | .919 | .923 | .921 |

**Table 2:** Experimental Results

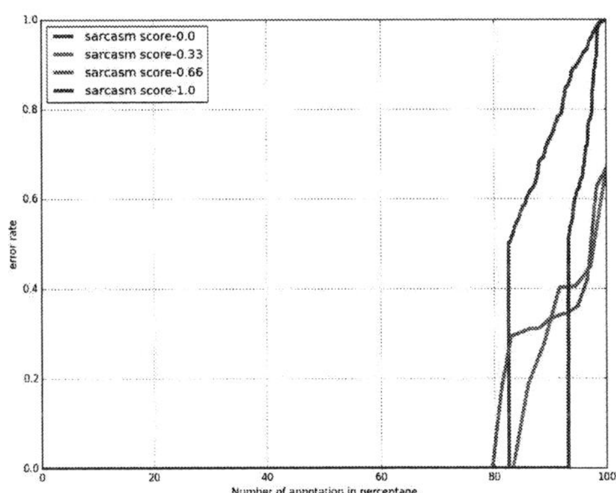

**Figure 4:** Performance evaluation of model

dataset contains 3 annotations per tweet, we obtained 4 different values for an average sarcasm score from the annotations. We divided the dataset based on the average sarcasm score and observed the performance of the model in each section. From figure 4, we observed that our model performed better for distinct sarcastic data than distinct non-sarcastic data. For dicey examples of sarcasm, where the average sarcasm score is between .7 and .3, our model performed better with non-sarcastic data than sarcastic data.

| dataset | Model | P | R | F1 |
|---|---|---|---|---|
| riloff | riloff method | .44 | .62 | .51 |
| riloff | CNN + LSTM + DNN + filter size = 256 + filter width = 2 | .882 | .861 | .872 |
| riloff | CNN + LSTM + DNN + filter size = 256 + filter width = 3 | .883 | .879 | .881 |
| tsur | SASI | .912 | .756 | .827 |
| tsur | CNN + LSTM + DNN + filter size = 256 + filter width = 2 | .878 | .901 | .889 |
| tsur | CNN + LSTM + DNN + filter size = 256 + filter width = 3 | .894 | .912 | .901 |

**Table 3:** Comparison with other datasets

We evaluated our system with two publicly available datasets (Tsur et al., 2010; Riloff et al., 2013). The results are mentioned in table 3. We observed that our model has performed with a better f-score than both of the systems, but it has a lower precision value than SASI (Davidov et al., 2010).

## 8  Twitter Bot

In NLP research, building a carefully crafted corpus has always played a crucial role. In recent research, Twitter has been used as an excellent source for various NLP tasks due to its topicality and availability. While sharing previous datasets, due to copyright and privacy concerns, researchers are forced to share only tweet identifiers along with annotations instead of the actual text of each tweet. As a tweet is a perishable commodity and may be deleted, archived or otherwise made inaccessible over time by their original creators, resources are lost in the course of time. Following our idea of retweeting via a dedicated account (@onlinesarcasm) to refrain tweets from perishing without copyright infringement, we have retweeted only detected sarcastic tweets. Regarding the quality assurance of the automated retweets, we observed that a conflict between human annotation and the output of the model is negligible for those tweets predicted with a softmax class probability higher than 0.75.

## 9  Conclusion & Future work

Sarcasm is a complex phenomenon and it is linguistically and semantically rich. By exploiting the semantic modelling power of the neural network, our model has outperformed existing sarcasm detection systems with a f-score of .92. Even though our model performs very well in sarcasm detection, it still lacks an ability to differentiate sarcasm with similar concepts. As an example, our model classified *"I Just Love Mondays!"* correctly as sarcasm, but it failed to classify *"Thank God It's Monday!"* as sarcasm, even though both are similar at the conceptual level. Feeding the model with word2vec[5] to find similar concepts may not be beneficial, as not every similar concept employs sarcasm. For example, *"Thank God It's Friday!"* is non-sarcastic in nature. For future works, selective use of word2vec can be exploited to improve the model. Also performing a trend analysis from the our twitter bot

---

[5]https://code.google.com/archive/p/word2vec/

can also benefit the system to separate the semantic space of sarcasm and non-sarcasm more efficiently.

## Acknowledgments

This research is supported by Science Foundation Ireland (SFI) as a part of the CNGL Centre for Global Intelligent Content at UCD (Grant No: CNGLII, R13645).

## References

Marco Baroni and Roberto Zamparelli. 2010. Nouns are vectors, adjectives are matrices: Representing adjective-noun constructions in semantic space. In *Proceedings of the 2010 Conference on Empirical Methods in Natural Language Processing*, pages 1183–1193. Association for Computational Linguistics.

Penelope Brown and Stephen C Levinson. 1978. Universals in language usage: Politeness phenomena. In *Questions and politeness: Strategies in social interaction*.

William Chan and Ian Lane. 2015. Deep convolutional neural networks for acoustic modeling in low resource languages. In *IEEE International Conference on Acoustics, Speech and Signal Processing*.

Dmitry Davidov, Oren Tsur, and Ari Rappoport. 2010. Semi-supervised recognition of sarcastic sentences in twitter and amazon. In *Proceedings of the Fourteenth Conference on Computational Natural Language Learning*, pages 107–116. Association for Computational Linguistics.

Shelly Dews and Ellen Winner. 1995. Muting the meaning a social function of irony. *Metaphor and Symbol*, 10(1):3–19.

Shelly Dews and Ellen Winner. 1999. Obligatory processing of literal and nonliteral meanings in verbal irony. *Journal of pragmatics*, 31(12):1579–1599.

Cicero Nogueira Dos Santos, Bing Xiang, and Bowen Zhou. 2015. Classifying relations by ranking with convolutional neural networks. In *Proceedings of the 53rd Annual Meeting of the Association for Computational Linguistics and the 7th International Joint Conference on Natural Language Processing*, volume 1, pages 626–634.

Jacob Eisenstein. 2013. What to do about bad language on the internet. In *HLT-NAACL*, pages 359–369.

2007. *Irony in language and thought: A cognitive science reader*. Psychology Press.

Deanna W. Gibbs and Herbert H. Clark. 1992. Coordinating beliefs in conversation. *Journal of Memory and Language*.

Roberto González-Ibánez, Smaranda Muresan, and Nina Wacholder. 2011. Identifying sarcasm in twitter: a closer look. In *Proceedings of the 49th Annual Meeting of the Association for Computational Linguistics: Human Language Technologies: short papers-Volume 2*, pages 581–586. Association for Computational Linguistics.

Emiliano Guevara. 2010. A regression model of adjective-noun compositionality in distributional semantics. In *Proceedings of the 2010 Workshop on GEometrical Models of Natural Language Semantics*, pages 33–37. Association for Computational Linguistics.

Sepp Hochreiter and Jürgen Schmidhuber. 1997. Long short-term memory. *Neural computation*, 9(8):1735–1780.

Nal Kalchbrenner, Edward Grefenstette, and Phil Blunsom. 2014. A convolutional neural network for modelling sentences. *arXiv preprint arXiv:1404.2188*.

Diederik Kingma and Jimmy Ba. 2014. Adam: A method for stochastic optimization. *arXiv preprint arXiv:1412.6980*.

Roger J. Kreuz and Gina M. Caucci. 2007. Lexical influences on the perception of sarcasm. In *Proceedings of the Workshop on Computational Approaches to Figurative Language*.

Roger J Kreuz and Sam Glucksberg. 1989. How to be sarcastic: The echoic reminder theory of verbal irony. *Journal of Experimental Psychology: General*.

CC Liebrecht, FA Kunneman, and APJ van den Bosch. 2013. The perfect solution for detecting sarcasm in tweets #not.

Stephanie Lukin and Marilyn Walker. 2013. Really? well. apparently bootstrapping improves the performance of sarcasm and nastiness classifiers for online dialogue. In *Proceedings of the Workshop on Language Analysis in Social Media*, pages 30–40.

Prodromos Malakasiotis. 2011. *Paraphrase and Textual Entailment Recognition and Generation*. Ph.D. thesis, Ph. D. thesis, Department of Informatics, Athens University of Economics and Business, Greece.

Jeff Mitchell and Mirella Lapata. 2008. Vector-based models of semantic composition. In *ACL*, pages 236–244.

Jeff Mitchell and Mirella Lapata. 2010. Composition in distributional models of semantics. *Cognitive science*, 34(8):1388–1429.

Tetsuji Nakagawa, Kentaro Inui, and Sadao Kurohashi. 2010. Dependency tree-based sentiment classification using crfs with hidden variables. In *Human Language Technologies: The 2010 Annual Conference of the North American Chapter of the Association for Computational Linguistics*, pages 786–794. Association for Computational Linguistics.

Ellen Riloff, Ashequl Qadir, Prafulla Surve, Lalindra De Silva, Nathan Gilbert, and Ruihong Huang. 2013. Sarcasm as contrast between a positive sentiment and negative situation. In *EMNLP*, pages 704–714.

Richard Socher, Jeffrey Pennington, Eric H Huang, Andrew Y Ng, and Christopher D Manning. 2011. Semi-supervised recursive autoencoders for predicting sentiment distributions. In *Proceedings of the Conference on Empirical Methods in Natural Language Processing*, pages 151–161. Association for Computational Linguistics.

Oren Tsur, Dmitry Davidov, and Ari Rappoport. 2010. Icwsm-a great catchy name: Semi-supervised recognition of sarcastic sentences in online product reviews. In *ICWSM*.

A. Utsumi. 2000. Verbal irony as implicit display of ironic environment: Distinguishing ironic utterances from nonirony. *Journal of Pragmatics*.

Pascal Vincent, Hugo Larochelle, Yoshua Bengio, and Pierre-Antoine Manzagol. 2008. Extracting and composing robust features with denoising autoencoders. In *Proceedings of the 25th international conference on Machine learning*, pages 1096–1103. ACM.

Manfred Klenner
Computational Linguistics
University of Zurich\\
Switzerland
klenner@cl.uzh.ch


**An Hymn of an even Deeper Sentiment Analysis**

A deeper understanding of what is going on in a given text is still one of the most interesting and challenging goals in NLP. Sentiment analysis has recently started to contribute to this area. We no longer just try to predict the polarity of whole product reviews but to distinguish various perspectives inherent to a text, namely, what the author is telling us, how he implicitly or explictely evaluates it and what his text tells us about the attitudes the entities in the text hold towards each other (or towards the mentioned objects, situations, or opinions of others). Other perspectives not yet taken by our systems include the common-sense perspective (what follows from the behaviour of an agent for his perception by the public) or the reader perspective: given that I have  specified the pros and cons of my world view - which are the opponents and proponents of mine given the text at hand. Progress has been made in this direction. Sentiment inferences based on verb-specific polar lexicons and general inference rules have been proposed (see the work of Deng and Wiebe, for instance). Our preprocessing tools for the extraction of predicate argument structures or for semantic role labeling seem to be mature enough to support this kind of deep understanding reasonably well.

This is most exciting, like any attempt to reap the benefits of a bit more semantics compared to attemps that just scratch the surface with crude and brute-force means. Sentiment analysis certainly is a field that takes advantage of lexical resources. For instance, verbs have proved to provide a lot of crucial information for fine-grained sentiment analysis taking the various perspectives into account that I mentioned.

Clearly, all the other problems need to be solved as well: aspect detection/induction, sentiment composition, sense disambiguation and so on. New techniques (deep learning), new theoretical stances (distributional semantics) might prove successful. If not, a shift towards a new playgroud is to be expected, e.g. the focus on emotions. Well, I am quite sure that all this will turn out to be very entertaining and - step by step - sucessful.



*Proceedings of NAACL-HLT 2016*, page 170,
San Diego, California, June 12-17, 2016. ©2016 Association for Computational Linguistics

# Sentiment Analysis in Twitter: A SemEval Perspective

**Preslav Nakov**
Qatar Computing Research Institute, HBKU
Tornado Tower, floor 10
P.O. box 5825
Doha, Qatar
pnakov@qf.org.qa

The recent rise of social media has greatly democratized content creation. Facebook, Twitter, Skype, Whatsapp and LiveJournal are now commonly used to share thoughts and opinions about anything in the surrounding world. This proliferation of social media content has created new opportunities to study public opinion, with Twitter being especially popular for research due to its scale, representativeness, variety of topics discussed, as well as ease of public access to its messages.

Unfortunately, research in that direction was hindered by the unavailability of suitable datasets and lexicons for system training, development and testing. While some Twitter-specific resources were developed, initially they were either small and proprietary, such as the i-sieve corpus (Kouloumpis et al., 2011), were created only for Spanish like the TASS corpus (Villena-Román et al., 2013), or relied on noisy labels obtained automatically (Mohammad, 2012; Pang et al., 2002).

This situation changed with the shared task on *Sentiment Analysis on Twitter*, which was organized at SemEval, the International Workshop on Semantic Evaluation, a semantic evaluation forum previously known as SensEval. The task ran in 2013, 2014, 2015 and 2016, attracting over 40+ of participating teams in all four editions. While the focus was on general tweets, the task also featured out-of-domain testing on SMS messages, LiveJournal messages, as well as on sarcastic tweets.

SemEval-2013 task 2 (Nakov et al., 2013) and SemEval-2014 Task 9 (Rosenthal et al., 2014) had an expression-level and a message-level polarity subtasks.

SemEval-2015 Task 10 (Rosenthal et al., 2015; Nakov et al., 2016b) further added subtasks on topic-based message polarity classification, on detecting trends towards a topic, and on determining the out-of-context (a priori) strength of association of Twitter terms with positive sentiment.

SemEval-2016 Task 4 (Nakov et al., 2016a) dropped the phrase-level subtask, and focused on sentiment with respect to a topic. It further introduced a 5-point scale, which is used for human review ratings on popular websites such as Amazon, TripAdvisor, Yelp, etc.; from a research perspective, this meant moving from classification to *ordinal regression*. Moreover, it focused on *quantification*, i.e., determining what proportion of a set of tweets on a given topic are positive/negative about it. It also featured a 5-point scale *ordinal quantification* subtask (Gao and Sebastiani, 2015).

Other related (mostly non-Twitter) tasks have explored aspect-based sentiment analysis (Pontiki et al., 2014; Pontiki et al., 2015; Pontiki et al., 2016), sentiment analysis of figurative language on Twitter (Ghosh et al., 2015), implicit event polarity (Russo et al., 2015), stance in tweets (Mohammad et al., 2016), out-of-context sentiment intensity of phrases (Kiritchenko et al., 2016), and emotion detection (Strapparava and Mihalcea, 2007). Some of these tasks featured languages other than English.

We expect the quest for more interesting formulations of the general sentiment analysis task to continue. We see SemEval as the engine of this innovation, as it not only does head-to-head comparisons, but also creates databases and tools that enable follow-up research for many years afterwards.

171

*Proceedings of NAACL-HLT 2016*, pages 171–172,
San Diego, California, June 12-17, 2016. ©2016 Association for Computational Linguistics

# References

Wei Gao and Fabrizio Sebastiani. 2015. Tweet sentiment: From classification to quantification. In *Proceedings of the 7th International Conference on Advances in Social Network Analysis and Mining*, ASONAM '15, pages 97–104, Paris, FR.

Aniruddha Ghosh, Guofu Li, Tony Veale, Paolo Rosso, Ekaterina Shutova, John Barnden, and Antonio Reyes. 2015. ScemEval-2015 task 11: Sentiment analysis of figurative language in Twitter. In *Proceedings of the 9th International Workshop on Semantic Evaluation*, SemEval '15, pages 470–478, Denver, Colorado.

Svetlana Kiritchenko, Saif M Mohammad, and Mohammad Salameh. 2016. SemEval-2016 task 7: Determining sentiment intensity of English and Arabic phrases. In *Proceedings of the 10th International Workshop on Semantic Evaluation*, SemEval '16, San Diego, California.

Efthymios Kouloumpis, Theresa Wilson, and Johanna Moore. 2011. Twitter sentiment analysis: The good the bad and the OMG! In *Proceedings of the Fifth International Conference on Weblogs and Social Media*, ICWSM '11, pages 538–541, Barcelona, Catalonia, Spain.

Saif M Mohammad, Svetlana Kiritchenko, Parinaz Sobhani, Xiaodan Zhu, and Colin Cherry. 2016. SemEval-2016 task 6: Detecting stance in tweets. In *Proceedings of the 10th International Workshop on Semantic Evaluation*, SemEval '16, San Diego, California.

Saif Mohammad. 2012. #Emotional tweets. In *Proceedings of *SEM 2012: The First Joint Conference on Lexical and Computational Semantics – Volume 1: Proceedings of the main conference and the shared task*, *SEM '12, pages 246–255, Montreal, Canada.

Preslav Nakov, Sara Rosenthal, Zornitsa Kozareva, Veselin Stoyanov, Alan Ritter, and Theresa Wilson. 2013. SemEval-2013 task 2: Sentiment analysis in Twitter. In *Proceedings of the Second Joint Conference on Lexical and Computational Semantics (*SEM), Volume 2: Proceedings of the Seventh International Workshop on Semantic Evaluation*, SemEval '13, pages 312–320, Atlanta, Georgia.

Preslav Nakov, Alan Ritter, Sara Rosenthal, Veselin Stoyanov, and Fabrizio Sebastiani. 2016a. SemEval-2016 task 4: Sentiment analysis in Twitter. In *Proceedings of the 10th International Workshop on Semantic Evaluation*, SemEval '16, San Diego, California.

Preslav Nakov, Sara Rosenthal, Svetlana Kiritchenko, Saif M. Mohammad, Zornitsa Kozareva, Alan Ritter, Veselin Stoyanov, and Xiaodan Zhu. 2016b. Developing a successful SemEval task in sentiment analysis of Twitter and other social media texts. *Language Resources and Evaluation*, 50(1):35–65.

Bo Pang, Lillian Lee, and Shivakumar Vaithyanathan. 2002. Thumbs up?: Sentiment classification using machine learning techniques. In *Proceedings of the Conference on Empirical Methods in Natural Language Processing*, EMNLP '02, pages 79–86, Philadelphia, Pennsylvania.

Maria Pontiki, Harris Papageorgiou, Dimitrios Galanis, Ion Androutsopoulos, John Pavlopoulos, and Suresh Manandhar. 2014. SemEval-2014 task 4: Aspect based sentiment analysis. In *Proceedings of the 8th International Workshop on Semantic Evaluation*, SemEval '14, pages 27–35, Dublin, Ireland.

Maria Pontiki, Dimitris Galanis, Haris Papageorgiou, Suresh Manandhar, and Ion Androutsopoulos. 2015. SemEval-2015 task 12: Aspect based sentiment analysis. In *Proceedings of the 9th International Workshop on Semantic Evaluation*, SemEval '15, pages 486–495, Denver, Colorado.

Maria Pontiki, Dimitris Galanis, Haris Papageorgiou, Suresh Manandhar, and Ion Androutsopoulos. 2016. SemEval-2016 task 5: Aspect based sentiment analysis. In *Proceedings of the 10th International Workshop on Semantic Evaluation*, SemEval '16, San Diego, California.

Sara Rosenthal, Alan Ritter, Preslav Nakov, and Veselin Stoyanov. 2014. SemEval-2014 Task 9: Sentiment analysis in Twitter. In *Proceedings of the 8th International Workshop on Semantic Evaluation*, SemEval '14, pages 73–80, Dublin, Ireland.

Sara Rosenthal, Preslav Nakov, Svetlana Kiritchenko, Saif Mohammad, Alan Ritter, and Veselin Stoyanov. 2015. SemEval-2015 task 10: Sentiment analysis in Twitter. In *Proceedings of the 9th International Workshop on Semantic Evaluation*, SemEval '15, pages 450–462, Denver, Colorado.

Irene Russo, Tommaso Caselli, and Carlo Strapparava. 2015. SemEval-2015 task 9: CLIPEval implicit polarity of events. In *Proceedings of the 9th International Workshop on Semantic Evaluation*, SemEval '15, pages 442–449, Denver, Colorado.

Carlo Strapparava and Rada Mihalcea. 2007. SemEval-2007 task 14: Affective text. In *Proceedings of the International Workshop on Semantic Evaluation*, SemEval '07, pages 70–74, Prague, Czech Republic.

Julio Villena-Román, Sara Lana-Serrano, Eugenio Martínez-Cámara, and José Carlos González Cristóbal. 2013. TASS - Workshop on Sentiment Analysis at SEPLN. *Procesamiento del Lenguaje Natural*, 50:37–44.

# The Challenge of Sentiment Quantification[*]

**Fabrizio Sebastiani**
Qatar Computing Research Institute
Hamad bin Khalifa University
PO Box 5825 Doha, Qatar
`fsebastiani@qf.org.qa`

Among the many challenges that sentiment analysis (SA) faces, I want to concentrate on one which has not received much attention within the SA community, but that is going to play a major role in future applications: *Sentiment Quantification* (SQ) (Esuli and Sebastiani, 2010). *Quantification* is defined as the task of estimating the prevalence (i.e., relative frequency) of the classes of interest in a set of unlabelled data via supervised learning (Forman, 2008); examples of SQ are (i) determining the prevalence of endorsements in a set of tweets about a political candidate, or (ii) determining the prevalence of rebuttals in a set of reviews of a given book. A naïve way to tackle quantification is by classifying each unlabelled item independently and computing the fraction of such items that have been attributed the class. However, a good classifier is not necessarily a good quantifier: assuming the binary case, even if $(FP + FN)$ is comparatively small, bad quantification accuracy results if $FP$ and $FN$ are significantly different (since perfect quantification coincides with the case $FP = FN$). This has led researchers to study quantification as a task on its own right, rather than as a byproduct of classification.

Within SA, quantification plays a major role, since in many applications we are interested in estimating sentiment not at the individual level, but at the aggregate level. For instance, when SA is applied to tweets, it is rarely (if at all) the case that we are interested in the sentiment conveyed by an individual tweet (Gao and Sebastiani, 2015): it is the sentiment of the crowd, and how it is distributed, that

we are instead interested in, and monitoring this distribution over time is a holy grail within fields such as the social sciences, market research, and online reputation management.

Quantification is still an under-researched area, due to the fact that for years it has not been identified as a task on its own. Challenges that are still in need of satisfactory solutions are:

- Can we devise quantifiers that deliver high accuracy irrespectively of the level of *distribution drift* (i.e., the difference between class prevalence in the labelled and in the unlabelled sets)?

- Can we devise accurate quantifiers that do not use the classification of individual items as an intermediate step? And is this the best way to tackle quantification?

- Aside from the binary case, can we devise accurate quantifiers also for the multiclass case (i.e., when the mutually exclusive classes are $> 2$) and for the ordinal case (i.e., when there is a total order defined on the set of classes)?

## References

Andrea Esuli and Fabrizio Sebastiani. 2010. Sentiment quantification. *IEEE Intelligent Systems*, 25(4):72–75.

George Forman. 2008. Quantifying counts and costs via classification. *Data Mining and Knowledge Discovery*, 17(2):164–206.

Wei Gao and Fabrizio Sebastiani. 2015. Tweet sentiment: From classification to quantification. In *Proceedings of the 7th International Conference on Advances in Social Network Analysis and Mining (ASONAM 2015)*, pages 97–104, Paris, FR.

---

[*]The author is on leave from Consiglio Nazionale delle Ricerche, Italy



*Proceedings of NAACL-HLT 2016*, page 173,
San Diego, California, June 12-17, 2016. ©2016 Association for Computational Linguistics

# A Practical Guide to Sentiment Annotation:
# Challenges and Solutions


**Saif M. Mohammad**
National Research Council Canada
saif.mohammad@nrc-cnrc.gc.ca



## Abstract

Sentences and tweets are often annotated for sentiment simply by asking respondents to label them as positive, negative, or neutral. This works well for simple expressions of sentiment; however, for many other types of sentences, respondents are unsure of how to annotate, and produce inconsistent labels. In this paper, we outline several types of sentences that are particularly challenging for manual sentiment annotation. Next we propose two annotation schemes that address these challenges, and list benefits and limitations for both.


## 1 Introduction

Clear and simple instructions are crucial for obtaining high-quality annotations. This is true even for seemingly simple annotation tasks, such as sentiment annotation, where one is to label instances as positive, negative, or neutral. For word annotations, researchers have often framed the task as 'is this word positive, negative, or neutral?' (Hu and Liu, 2004), 'does this word have associations with positive, negative, or neutral sentiment?' (Mohammad and Turney, 2013), or 'which word is more positive?'/'which word has a greater association with positive sentiment' (Kiritchenko et al., 2016; Kiritchenko and Mohammad, 2016b). Similar instructions are also widely used for sentence-level sentiment annotations—'is this sentence positive, negative, or neutral?' (Rosenthal et al., 2015; Rosenthal et al., 2014; Mohammad et al., 2016a; Mohammad et al., 2015). We will refer to such annotation schemes as *the simple sentiment questionnaires*.

On the one hand, this characterization of the task is simple, terse, and reliant on the intuitions of native speakers of a language (rather than biasing the annotators by providing definitions of what it means to be positive, negative, and neutral). On the other hand, the lack of specification leaves the annotator in doubt over how to label certain kinds of instances—for example, sentences where one side wins against another, sarcastic sentences, or retweets.

A different approach to sentiment annotation is to ask respondents to identify the target of opinion, and the sentiment towards this target of opinion (Pontiki et al., 2014; Mohammad et al., 2015; Deng and Wiebe, 2014). We will refer to such annotation schemes as *the semantic-role based sentiment questionnaires*. This approach of sentiment annotation is more specific, and more involved, than the simple sentiment questionnaire approach; however, it too is insufficient for handling several scenarios. Most notably, the emotional state of the speaker is not under the purview of this scheme. Many applications require that statements expressing positive or negative emotional state of the speaker should be marked as 'positive' or 'negative', respectively. Similarly, many applications require statements that describe positive or negative events or situations to be marked as 'positive' or 'negative', respectively. Instructions for annotating opinion towards targets do not specify how such instances are to be annotated, and worse still, possibly imply that such instances are to be labeled as neutral.

In this paper, we present a list of sentence types that are especially challenging for sentiment annotation. Next, we propose two annotation schemes that

174


*Proceedings of NAACL-HLT 2016*, pages 174–179,
San Diego, California, June 12-17, 2016. ©2016 Association for Computational Linguistics

address these challenges: (1) a simple sentiment annotation questionnaire with more precise annotation directions and some additional label categories; and (2) a semantic-role based questionnaire with additional questions to account for the speaker's emotional state and descriptions of valenced events.

Aspects of annotation that are not specific to sentiment, such as good practices in crowdsourcing, how to aggregate information from multiple annotators, and how to automatically detect and discard poor annotations are beyond the scope of this paper; we refer the readers to Lease (2011), Hsueh et al. (2009), and Mohammad and Turney (2013) for that. Methods for obtaining real-valued sentiment scores are also not covered in this paper; we refer the reader to Kiritchenko and Mohammad (2016a) and Kiritchenko et al. (2014) for the use of best–worst scaling to obtain reliable real-valued sentiment associations. See Mohammad (2016) for a survey on sentiment and emotion datasets.

## 2   Types of Instances that are Difficult to Annotate for Sentiment

There exist several types of sentences that are particularly challenging to annotate for sentiment. Some of the more notable ones are listed below:

- *Speaker's emotional state:* The speaker's emotional state may or may not have the same polarity as the opinion expressed by the speaker. For example, a politician's tweet can imply both a negative opinion about a rival's past indiscretion, and a joyous mental state as the news will impact the rival adversely.

- *Success or failure of one side w.r.t. another:* Often sentences describe the success or failure of one side w.r.t. another side—for example, *'Yay! France beat Germany 3–1'*, *'Supreme court judges in favor of gay marriage'*, and *'the coalition captured the rebels'*. If one supports France, gay marriage, and the coalition, then these events are positive, but if one supports Germany, marriage as a union only between man and woman, and the rebels, then these events can be seen as negative.

  Also note that the framing of an event as the success of one party (or as the failure of another party) does not automatically imply that the speaker is expressing positive (or negative) opinion towards the mentioned party. For example, when Finland beat Russia in ice hockey in the 2014 Sochi Winter Olympics, the event was tweeted around the world predominantly as "Russia lost to Finland" as opposed to "Finland beat Russia". This is not because the speakers were expressing negative opinion towards the Russian team, but rather simply because Russia, being the host nation, was the focus of attention and traditionally Russian hockey teams have been strong.

- *Neutral reporting of valenced information:* If the speaker does not give any indication of her own emotional state but describes valenced events or situations, then it is unclear whether to consider these statements as neutral unemotional reporting of developments or whether to assume that the speaker is in a negative emotional state (sad, angry, etc.). Example:

    *The war has created millions of refugees.*

- *Sarcasm and ridicule:* Sarcasm and ridicule are tricky from the perspective of assigning a single label of sentiment because they can often indicate positive emotional state of the speaker (pleasure from mocking someone or something) even though they have a negative attitude towards someone or something.

- *Different sentiment towards different targets of opinion:* The speaker may express opinion about multiple targets, and sentiment towards the different targets might be different. The targets may be different people or objects (for example, an iPhone vs. an android phone), or they may be different aspects of the same entity (for example, quality of service vs. quality of food at a restaurant).

- *Precisely determining the target of opinion:* Sometimes it is difficult to precisely identify the target of opinion. For example, consider:

    *Glad to see Hillary's lies being exposed.*

  It is unclear whether the target of opinion is 'Hillary', 'Hillary's lies', or 'Hillary's lies being exposed'. One reasonable interpretation is that positive sentiment is expressed about 'Hillary's lies being exposed'. However, one can also infer that the speaker has a negative attitude towards 'Hillary's lies' and probably 'Hillary' in general. It is unclear whether annotators should be asked to provide all three opinion–target pairs or only one (in which case, which one?).

- *Supplications and requests*: Many tweets convey positive supplications to God or positive requests to people in the context of a (usually) negative situation. Examples include:

  *May god help those displaced by war.*
  *Let us all come together and say no to*
  *fear mongering and divisive politics.*

- *Rhetorical questions*: Rhetorical questions can be treated simply as queries (and thus neutral) or as utterances that give away the emotional state of the speaker. For example, consider:

  *Why do we have to quibble every time?*

  On the one hand, this tweet can be treated as a neutral question, but on the other hand, it can be seen as negative because the utterance betrays a sense of frustration on the part of the speaker.

- *Quoting somebody else or re-tweeting*: Quotes and retweets are difficult to annotate for sentiment because it is often unclear and not explicitly evident whether the one who quotes (or retweets) holds the same opinions as that expressed by the quotee.

The challenges listed above can be addressed to varying degrees by providing instructions to the annotators on how such instances are to be labeled. However, detailed and complicated instructions can be counter-productive as the annotators may not understand or may not have the inclination to understand the subtleties involved.

## 3 Proposed Annotation Schemes

Two annotation schemes that address many of the challenges laid out above are presented below. The benefits and limitations of both are outlined. The goal here is not to suggest that these are the only ways to annotate for sentiment, but rather to encourage further thought and improved proposals for sentiment annotation (that may or may not be inspired by the questionnaires shown below). Note also that the precise formulation of the sentiment questionnaire should be guided by the specific needs of the application at hand.

### 3.1 A Simple Sentiment Questionnaire

A simple sentiment questionnaire that addresses many of the challenges listed in Section 2 is presented below:

---

PROPOSED SIMPLE SENTIMENT QUESTIONNAIRE

What kind of language is the speaker using?

1. the speaker is using positive language, for example, expressions of support, admiration, positive attitude, forgiveness, fostering, success, positive emotional state

2. the speaker is using negative language, for example, expressions of criticism, judgment, negative attitude, questioning validity/competence, failure, negative emotion

3. the speaker is using expressions of sarcasm, ridicule, or mockery

4. the speaker is using positive language in part and negative language in part

5. the speaker is neither using positive language nor using negative language

Notes:

- A good response to this question is one that most people will agree with. For example, even if you think that sometimes the language can be considered negative, if you think most people will consider the language to be positive, then select the positive language option.

- Agreeing or disagreeing with the speaker's views should not have a bearing on your response. You are to assess the language being used (not the views). For example, given the tweet, 'Evolution makes no sense', the correct answer is 'the speaker is using negative language' since the speaker's words are criticizing or judging negatively something (in this case the theory of evolution). Note that the answer is not contingent on whether you believe in evolution or not.

---

*Benefits and Limitations.* This questionnaire groups the speaker's emotional state, speaker's opinion, and description of valenced events all into one category and aims simply to determine the dominant sentiment inferable from the sentence. The phrases 'positive language' and 'negative language' encourage respondents to focus on the language itself as opposed to assigning sentiment based on event outcomes that are beneficial to them. For example, 'Yay! France beat Germany 3–1' will be marked as positive because the speaker is using the positive expression 'Yay!'. The 'Russia lost to Finland' example (described earlier in Section 2), may be difficult to annotate with respect to the opinion of the speaker towards the Russian team, but the framing of the event as a loss is easily identified as negative language. Other instances where one side benefits over another, but the text itself does not use positive or negative language can be labeled as option 5. Sarcasm, ridicule, and mockery are included as a separate option (in addition to option 2) so that respondents do not have to struggle with the decision of whether to mark such instances as positive or negative. Downstream applications can make use of all of these annotations as is appropriate for them: for example, by treating tweets labeled sarcasm and ridicule differently from the other positive and negative sentences, or by marking them as negative.

Instances with different sentiment towards different targets of opinion can be marked with option 4. Supplications and requests that convey a sense of fostering and support can be marked as positive. On the other hand, rhetorical questions that betray a sense of frustration and disappointment can be marked as negative. Thus this simple questionnaire addresses many of the issues raised in the earlier section. However, a limitation of this approach is that it does not produce as nuanced a set of annotations as those that can be obtained from the questionnaire shown ahead. Note, however, that the simplcity of the questionnaire entails low annotation costs and no special educational requirements. Mohammad et al. (2016b) used this questionnaire to annotate a set of tweets for sentiment via crowdsourcing. The dataset, which is also annotated for stance, is made freely available.[1]

---

[1]www.saifmohammad.com/WebPages/StanceDataset.htm

## 3.2 A Semantic-Role Based Sentiment Questionnaire

A sentiment questionnaire that includes questions about the target of opinion, as well as additional questions such as those that address the speaker's emotional state, is presented below:

---

PROPOSED SEMANTIC-ROLE BASED SENTIMENT QUESTIONNAIRE

Q1. From reading the text, the speaker's emotional state can best be described as:

- *positive state*: there is an explicit or implicit clue in the text suggesting that the speaker is in a positive state, i.e., happy, admiring, relaxed, forgiving, etc.

- *negative state*: there is an explicit or implicit clue in the text suggesting that the speaker is in a negative state, i.e., sad, angry, anxious, violent, etc.

- *both positive and negative, or mixed, feelings*: there is an explicit or implicit clue in the text suggesting that the speaker is experiencing both positive and negative feelings

- *unknown state*: there is no explicit or implicit indicator of the speaker's emotional state

Q2. From reading the text, identify the entity towards which opinion is being expressed or the entity towards which the speaker's attitude can be determined.

This entity is usually a person, object, company, group of people, or some such entity. We will call this the PRIMARY TARGET OF OPINION (PTO). For example, if the text criticizes certain actions or beliefs of a person (or group of persons), then that person or group is the PTO. If the text mocks people who do not believe in evolution, then the PTO is 'people who do not believe in evolution'. If the text questions or mocks evolution, then the PTO is 'evolution'. If you cannot determine sentiment/attitude of the speaker towards a person, group, or object, but you can identify sentiment/attitude towards an action or event, then consider that action or event as the PTO. If there are more than one targets of opinion, then select that target towards which sentiment is stronger.

NOTE: Where possible, copy and paste the primary target of opinion from the text. If the target can be referred to in different ways, for example, Barack Obama, Obama, Obamaaa, #obama, @obama, President, he, etc., copy and paste the snippet from the text showing how the speaker has referred to the target.

Q3. What best describes the speaker's attitude, evaluation, or judgment towards the primary target of opinion (PTO)? If the whole text is a quote from somebody else (original author) and there is no indication of speaker's attitude, then answer below considering the original author as the speaker.

- *positive*: there is an explicit or implicit clue in the text suggesting that the speaker's attitude or judgment of the PTO is positive (speaker is appreciative, thankful, excited, optimistic, or inspired by the primary entity)

- *negative*: there is an explicit or implicit clue in the text suggesting that the speaker's attitude or judgment of the PTO is negative (speaker is critical, angry, disappointed in, pessimistic, expressing sarcasm about, or mocking the primary entity)

- *mixed*: there is an explicit or implicit clue in the text suggesting that the speaker's attitude or judgment of the PTO is both positive and negative

- *unknown*: there is no explicit or implicit clue indicating that the speaker feels positively or negatively

Q4. What best describes the sentimental impact of the primary target of opinion (PTO) on most people?

- *positive*: the PTO is considered predominantly positive

- *negative*: the PTO is considered predominantly negative

- *mixed (both positive and negative)*: some aspects of the PTO are positive and some are negative

- *mixed (opposing sides)*: the PTO is considered positive by a large group of people AND is considered negative by another large group of people

- *no sentiment*: there is no clear sentiment associated with the PTO

---



*Examples:*

- For Q1:
  - Text: *Mugabe killed millions during his rule*
    Answer: unknown state (since there is no clue about the emotional state of the speaker)
  - Text: *Arggh! When will politicians learn to govern?*
    Answer: negative state (since there is sufficient indication that the speaker is frustrated)

- For Q2:
  - Text: *Sorry to see Mugabe kill so many civilians.*
    Answer: Mugabe
  - Text: *When will they stop killing babies in the womb?'*
    Answer: 'they'

- For Q3:
  - Text: *Sorry to see Mugabe kill so many civilians.*
    Answer: negative (We can infer that the speaker has negative sentiment toward Mugabe.)
  - Text: *We need a diplomat like Kissinger*
    Answer: positive (We can infer that the speaker has a positive attitude towards Kissinger.)

- For Q4:
  - Text: *Hillary has to answer for Benghazi.*
    Answer: mixed (opposing sides) (The speaker is expressing negative sentiment towards Hillary, but there are many who view Hillary favorably.)
  - Text: *The war has displaced millions*
    Answer: negative (this event is predominantly negative)

*Benefits and Limitations:* This detailed questionnaire with questions for the speaker's emotional state, the target of opinion, opinion towards the target, and general opinion (not the speaker's opinion) towards the target provides a rich cross-section of information that can be used by many downstream applications. However, a limitation of this questionnaire is its complexity—annotators (especially on crowdsourcing platforms) might find it difficult to distinguish the subtle difference between Q1, Q3, and Q4. Additionally, even though Q2 is framed with an eye on challenges regarding the identification of the target of opinion, it is difficult to completely address the associated issues. The target may not be explicitly mentioned in the text, it may be mentioned multiple times and in different ways, or it may be referred to via hypernyms, hyponyms, meronyms, and holonyms. It is advisable to first train the annotators on a small set of instances before proceeding to annotate large amounts of data.

## 4  Summary

We outlined several types of sentences that are particularly challenging for manual sentiment annotation. They include sentences describing success (or failure) of one side over another, sentences expressing sarcasm or ridicule, sentences expressing differing sentiment towards multiple entities, supplications, requests, and rhetorical questions. We then presented two different questionnaires that provide clear instructions on how such instances are to be annotated. The first questionnaire, is simple and terse, and thus it is easy and inexpensive to answer. The second questionnaire is markedly more involved, and thus requires more training; however, it provides a plethora of sentiment-related information that can be used in many downstream applications. Apsects of the proposed questionnaires may not be appropriate for all applications. Practitioners are encouraged to tweak the questionnaires as per the needs of the application at hand.

## Acknowledgments

Many thanks to Svetlana Kiritchenko for helpful discussions.

## References

Lingjia Deng and Janyce Wiebe. 2014. Sentiment propagation via implicature constraints. In *EACL*, pages 377–385.

Pei-Yun Hsueh, Prem Melville, and Vikas Sindhwani. 2009. Data quality from crowdsourcing: a study of annotation selection criteria. In *Proceedings of the NAACL HLT 2009 workshop on active learning for natural language processing*, pages 27–35. Association for Computational Linguistics.

Minqing Hu and Bing Liu. 2004. Mining and summarizing customer reviews. In *Proceedings of the 10th ACM SIGKDD International Conference on Knowledge Discovery and Data Mining*, KDD '04, pages 168–177, New York, NY, USA. ACM.

Svetlana Kiritchenko and Saif M. Mohammad. 2016a. Capturing reliable fine-grained sentiment associations by crowdsourcing and best–worst scaling. In *Proceedings of The 15th Annual Conference of the North American Chapter of the Association for Computational Linguistics (NAACL)*, San Diego, California.

Svetlana Kiritchenko and Saif M. Mohammad. 2016b. Sentiment composition of words with opposing polarities. In *Proceedings of The 15th Annual Conference of the North American Chapter of the Association for Computational Linguistics (NAACL)*, San Diego, California.

Svetlana Kiritchenko, Xiaodan Zhu, and Saif M. Mohammad. 2014. Sentiment analysis of short informal texts. *Journal of Artificial Intelligence Research*, 50:723–762.

Svetlana Kiritchenko, Saif M. Mohammad, and Mohammad Salameh. 2016. Semeval-2016 task 7: Determining sentiment intensity of english and arabic phrases. In *Proceedings of the International Workshop on Semantic Evaluation*, SemEval-2016, San Diego, California.

Matthew Lease. 2011. On quality control and machine learning in crowdsourcing. *Human Computation*, 11:11.

Saif M. Mohammad and Peter D. Turney. 2013. Crowdsourcing a word-emotion association lexicon. 29(3):436–465.

Saif M. Mohammad, Xiaodan Zhu, Svetlana Kiritchenko, and Joel Martin. 2015. Sentiment, emotion, purpose, and style in electoral tweets. *Information Processing and Management*, 51(4):480–499.

Saif M. Mohammad, Svetlana Kiritchenko, Parinaz Sobhani, Xiaodan Zhu, and Colin Cherry. 2016a. Semeval-2016 Task 6: Detecting stance in tweets. In *Proceedings of the International Workshop on Semantic Evaluation*, SemEval '16, San Diego, California.

Saif M. Mohammad, Parinaz Sobhani, and Svetlana Kiritchenko. 2016b. Stance and sentiment in tweets. *Special Section of the ACM Transactions on Internet Technology on Argumentation in Social Media*, Submitted.

Saif M. Mohammad. 2016. Sentiment analysis: Detecting valence, emotions, and other affectual states from text. In Herb Meiselman, editor, *Emotion Measurement*. Elsevier.

Maria Pontiki, Harris Papageorgiou, Dimitrios Galanis, Ion Androutsopoulos, John Pavlopoulos, and Suresh Manandhar. 2014. SemEval-2014 task 4: Aspect based sentiment analysis. In *Proceedings of the 8th International Workshop on Semantic Evaluation*, SemEval '14, Dublin, Ireland.

Sara Rosenthal, Alan Ritter, Preslav Nakov, and Veselin Stoyanov. 2014. SemEval-2014 Task 9: Sentiment analysis in Twitter. In *Proceedings of the 8th International Workshop on Semantic Evaluation (SemEval 2014)*, pages 73–80, Dublin, Ireland.

Sara Rosenthal, Preslav Nakov, Svetlana Kiritchenko, Saif Mohammad, Alan Ritter, and Veselin Stoyanov. 2015. SemEval-2015 task 10: Sentiment analysis in Twitter. In *Proceedings of the 9th International Workshop on Semantic Evaluation*, SemEval '15, pages 450–462, Denver, Colorado.

# Emotions and NLP: Future Directions

**Carlo Strapparava**
FBK-irst, Trento, Italy,
`strappa@fbk.eu`

Emotions are not linguistic entities but they are conveniently expressed through the language. Feelings influence actions, thoughts and of course our way of communicate.

It was more than twelve years ago that we developed WordNet-Affect (Strapparava and Valitutti, 2004), and I remember that at that time several people questioned about the utility and even the possibility of studying emotions using computational linguistics techniques. In the recent years, nonetheless there has been a flourishing interest in automatically detecting and generating emotions in texts, with many valuable research contributions by the community. The space here is too short to think to even shortly mention and review them. Anyway I would like to indicate which directions are more promising in my opinion.

**Finer grained emotions.** It seems that in the modern life only the high intensity of few emotions is addressed and matters. The successful use of traditional sentiment analysis, where the focus is on classifying just along positive/negative dimension, slants people toward this attitude. However it is valuable the acquaintance with fine-grained emotions: nuances here are important, with a completely different effect. People should be well-educated to the nuances of emotions and benefit from them, and NLP should help about this issue.

**Event based emotions.** Emotions are elicited by significant and specific events, and events are significant when they touch on one or more of the concerns of the people. Even considering the traditional sentiment analysis, it is a good idea to investigate a more holistic approach, combining the detection of implicit polarity with the expression of opinions on events. For example we proposed CLIPEval, a task based on a dataset of events annotated as instantiations of pleasant and unpleasant events (Russo et al., 2015). Research efforts along this direction will be fruitful. This holds even more when we consider emotion classification. I think that psychological research and cognitive science can help substantially.

**Cultural differences from corpora.** Even an excellent human translator has problems in carrying over the target language all the culture-related aspects that go with words. If the focus is on emotion-related aspects, the matter is even subtler. The relation of a word to emotion concepts may depend on ideology and in general on cultural aspects that can be inferred from extensive word usage rather than from what can be found in dictionaries. Of course it also depends on genres, different periods of text production, sociolinguistic characteristics of the text originators and so on. Thus I think that cross-language computational studies are challenging, compelling, and they can also have an important applicative value, for example when addressing topics such as emotions, negotiation and conflict.

## References

I. Russo, T. Caselli, and C. Strapparava. 2015. Semeval-2015, task 9: Clipeval implicit polarity of events. In *Proceedings of SemEval 2015*.

C. Strapparava and R. Mihalcea. 2014. Affect detection in texts. In R.A. Calvo et al., editor, *The Oxford Handbook of Affective Computing*. Oxford University Press.

C. Strapparava and A. Valitutti. 2004. WordNet-Affect: an affective extension of WordNet. In *Proc. of 4$^{th}$ International Conference on Language Resources and Evaluation (LREC 2004)*.



*Proceedings of NAACL-HLT 2016*, page 180,
San Diego, California, June 12-17, 2016. ©2016 Association for Computational Linguistics